51st Annual Meeting of the Association for Computational Linguistics (ACL 2013)

Student Research Workshop

Sofia, Bulgaria
5-7 August 2013

ISBN: 978-1-62748-976-8

Printed from e-media with permission by:

Curran Associates, Inc.
57 Morehouse Lane
Red Hook, NY 12571

Some format issues inherent in the e-media version may also appear in this print version.

Printed by Curran Associates, Inc. (2013)

For permission requests, please contact the Association for Computational Linguistics
at the address below.

Association for Computational Linguistics
209 N. Eighth Street
Stroudsburg, Pennsylvania 18360

Phone: 1-570-476-8006
Fax: 1-570-476-0860

acl@aclweb.org

Additional copies of this publication are available from:

Curran Associates, Inc.
57 Morehouse Lane
Red Hook, NY 12571 USA
Phone: 845-758-0400
Fax: 845-758-2634
Email: curran@proceedings.com
Web: www.proceedings.com

Introduction

Welcome to the ACL 2013 Student Research Workshop. This workshop provides a venue for student researchers investigating topics in Computational Linguistics and Natural Language Processing to present their research, to meet potential advisors, and to receive feedback from the international research community. The workshop's goal is to aid students at multiple stages of their education: from those in the final stages of undergraduate training to those who are preparing their graduate thesis proposal.

As was the case last year, this year we solicited and accepted two categories of papers:

1. Thesis/Research Proposals: This category is appropriate for experienced students who wish to get feedback on their proposal and broader ideas for the field in order to strengthen their final research.
2. Research Papers: Most appropriate for students who are new to academic conferences. Papers in this category can describe completed work or work in progress with preliminary results.

We asked for original research by students related but not limited to the following topics:

- Cognitive modeling of language processing and psycholinguistics
- Dialogue and interactive systems
- Discourse, coreference and pragmatics
- Evaluation methods
- Information retrieval
- Language resources
- Lexical semantics and ontologies
- Low resource language processing
- Machine translation: methods, applications and evaluation
- Multilinguality in NLP
- NLP applications
- NLP and creativity
- NLP for the languages of Central and Eastern Europe and the Balkans
- NLP for the Web and social media
- Question answering
- Semantics
- Sentiment analysis, opinion mining and text classification
- Spoken language processing
- Statistical and Machine Learning methods in NLP
- Summarization and generation
- Syntax and parsing
- Tagging and chunking
- Text mining and information extraction
- Word segmentation

We selected 25 papers for publishing out of the 52 submissions (an acceptance rate of 48%) that we received from students from a wide variety of countries. Three papers were presented orally in one of the parallel sessions of the main conference. The other 22 papers were shown as posters as part of the poster session of the main conference.

We were able to provide most students with conference registration and travel stipends thanks to generous support from the U.S. National Science Foundation, the ACL Walker Student Fund, the Qatar Computing Research Institute, Google, and the EU projects META-NET and Multilingual Web LT.

The overall quality of the submissions was high and we thank our program committee for their excellent feedback and reviews. In particular, we are grateful to the members of the program committee who agreed to provide pre-submission feedback to students. We also thank our faculty advisors Steven Bethard, Preslav I. Nakov, and Feiyu Xu for their guidance and valuable feedback throughout the whole organization process of the workshop. Finally, thank you and congratulations to all of our Student Research Workshop presenters.

Student Co-Chairs

Anik Dey, *Hong Kong University of Science and Technology*
Sebastian Krause, *German Research Center for Artificial Intelligence*
Ivelina Nikolova, *Bulgarian Academy of Sciences*
Eva Maria Vecchi, *University of Trento*

Faculty Advisors

Steven Bethard, *University of Colorado at Boulder & KU Leuven*
Preslav I. Nakov, *Qatar Computing Research Institute*
Feiyu Xu, *German Research Center for Artificial Intelligence*

Program Committee Members

Eleftherios Avramidis, *German Research Center for Artificial Intelligence*
Mohit Bansal, *University of California, Berkeley*
Marco Baroni, *University of Trento*
Lee Becker, *University of Colorado Boulder*
Gemma Boleda, *University of Texas at Austin*
Benjamin Börschinger, *Macquarie University*
Svetla Boytcheva, *American University in Bulgaria*
Tommaso Caselli, *Hong Kong Polytechnic University*
Marcela Charfuelan, *German Research Center for Artificial Intelligence*
Kevin B. Cohen, *University of Colorado Denver*
Georgiana Dinu, *University of Trento*
Myroslava Dzikovsk, *University of Edinburgh*
Kuzman Ganchev, *Google*
Wei Gao, *Qatar Computing Research Institute*
Georgi Georgiev, *Ontotext AD*
Edward Grefenstette, *University of Oxford*
Kai Hong, *University of Pennsylvania*
Amjad abu Jbara, *University of Michigan*
Sandra Kübler, *Indiana University Bloomington*
Gianluca Lebani, *University of Trento & Fondazione Bruno Kessler*
Junyi Li, *University of Pennsylvania*
Hong Li, *German Research Center for Artificial Intelligence*
Wolfgang Maier, *Department for Computational Linguistics, University of Düsseldorf*
Marco Marelli, *University of Trento*
Petar Mitankin, *Sofia University*
Verginica Barbu Mititelu, *Romanian Academy Research Institute for Artificial Intelligence*
Brian Murphy, *Carnegie Mellon University*
Petya Osenova, *Bulgarian Academy of Sciences*
Alexis Palmer, *Saarland University*
Gabriella Pasi, *University of Milan Bicocca*
Vahed Qazvinian, *University of Michigan*
Markus Saers, *Hong Kong University of Science and Technology*
Ansaf Salleb-Aouissi, *Columbia University*
Lane Schwartz, *Air Force Research Laboratory*
Ang Sun, *Intelius*
John Tait, *Information Retrieval Facility*
Irina Temnikova, *Bulgarian Academy of Sciences*
Marco Turchi, *Fondazione Bruno Kessler*
Tony Veale, *University College Dublin*
Cristina Vertan, *University of Hamburg*
Alexander Volokh, *German Research Center for Artificial Intelligence*
Rui Wang, *German Research Center for Artificial Intelligence*
Michael Zock, *LIF-CNRS*

Table of Contents

Conference Program

Monday August 5, 2013

(18:30 -19:45) Poster Session A

Categorization of Turkish News Documents with Morphological Analysis
Burak Kerim Akkuş and Ruket Cakici

Crawling microblogging services to gather language-classified URLs. Workflow and case study
Adrien Barbaresi

Patient Experience in Online Support Forums: Modeling Interpersonal Interactions and Medication Use
Annie Chen

Detecting Metaphor by Contextual Analogy
Eirini Florou

Survey on parsing three dependency representations for English
Angelina Ivanova, Stephan Oepen and Lilja Øvrelid

What causes a causal relation? Detecting Causal Triggers in Biomedical Scientific Discourse
Claudiu Mihăilă and Sophia Ananiadou

Text Classification based on the Latent Topics of Important Sentences extracted by the PageRank Algorithm
Yukari Ogura and Ichiro Kobayashi

Automated Collocation Suggestion for Japanese Second Language Learners
Lis Pereira, Erlyn Manguilimotan and Yuji Matsumoto

Understanding Verbs based on Overlapping Verbs Senses
Kavitha Rajan

Topic Modeling Based Classification of Clinical Reports
Efsun Sarioglu, Kabir Yadav and Hyeong-Ah Choi

Annotating named entities in clinical text by combining pre-annotation and active learning
Maria Skeppstedt

Monday August 5, 2013 (continued)

(19:45 – 21:00) Poster Session B

Multigraph Clustering for Unsupervised Coreference Resolution
Sebastian Martschat

Computational considerations of comparisons and similes
Vlad Niculae and Victoria Yaneva

Question Analysis for Polish Question Answering
Piotr Przybyła

A Comparison of Techniques to Automatically Identify Complex Words.
Matthew Shardlow

Detecting Chronic Critics Based on Sentiment Polarity and User's Behavior in Social Media
Sho Takase, Akiko Murakami, Miki Enoki, Naoaki Okazaki and Kentaro Inui

Addressing Ambiguity in Unsupervised Part-of-Speech Induction with Substitute Vectors
Volkan Cirik

Psycholinguistically Motivated Computational Models on the Organization and Processing of Morphologically Complex Words
Tirthankar Dasgupta

A New Syntactic Metric for Evaluation of Machine Translation
Melania Duma, Cristina Vertan and Wolfgang Menzel

High-quality Training Data Selection using Latent Topics for Graph-based Semi-supervised Learning
Akiko Eriguchi and Ichiro Kobayashi

Simple, readable sub-sentences
Sigrid Klerke and Anders Søgaard

Exploring Word Order Universals: a Probabilistic Graphical Model Approach
Xia Lu

Tuesday August 6, 2013

Oral Presentation

16:45 *Robust multilingual statistical morphological generation models*
Ondřej Dušek and Filip Jurčíček

17:05 *A corpus-based evaluation method for Distributional Semantic Models*
Abdellah Fourtassi and Emmanuel Dupoux

17:25 *Deepfix: Statistical Post-editing of Statistical Machine Translation Using Deep Syntactic Analysis*
Rudolf Rosa, David Mareček and Aleš Tamchyna

Categorization of Turkish News Documents with Morphological Analysis

Burak Kerim Akkuş
Computer Engineering Department
Middle East Technical University
Ankara, Turkey
burakkerim@ceng.metu.edu.tr

Ruket Çakıcı
Computer Engineering Department
Middle East Technical University
Ankara, Turkey
ruken@ceng.metu.edu.tr

Abstract

Morphologically rich languages such as Turkish may benefit from morphological analysis in natural language tasks. In this study, we examine the effects of morphological analysis on text categorization task in Turkish. We use stems and word categories that are extracted with morphological analysis as main features and compare them with fixed length stemmers in a bag of words approach with several learning algorithms. We aim to show the effects of using varying degrees of morphological information.

1 Introduction

The goal of text classification is to find the category or the topic of a text. Text categorization has popular applications in daily life such as email routing, spam detection, language identification, audience detection or genre detection and has major part in information retrieval tasks.

The aim of this study is to explain the impact of morphological analysis and POS tagging on Turkish text classification task. We train various classifiers such as k-Nearest Neighbours (kNN), Naive Bayes (NB) and Support Vector Machines (SVM) for this task. Turkish NLP tasks have been proven to benefit from morphological analysis or segmentation of some sort (Eryiğit et al., 2008; Çetinoğlu and Oflazer, 2006; Çakıcı and Baldridge, 2006). Two different settings are used throughout the paper to represent different degrees of stemming and involvement of morphological information. The first one uses the first n-characters (prefixes) of each word in a bag of words approach. A variety of number of characters are compared from 4 to 7 to find the optimal length for data representation. This acts as the baseline for word segmentation in order to make the limited amount of data less sparse. The second setting involves word stems that are extracted with a morphological analysis followed by disambiguation. The effects of part of speech tagging are also explored. Disambiguated morphological data are used along with the part of speech tags as informative features about the word category.

Extracting an n-character prefix is simple and considerably cheap compared to complex state-of-the-art morphological analysis and disambiguation process. There is a trade-off between quality and expense. Therefore, we may choose to use a cheap approximation instead of a more accurate representation if there is no significant sacrifice in the success of the system. Turkish is an agglutinative language that mostly uses suffixes[1]. Therefore, approximate stems that are extracted with fixed size stemming rarely contain any affixes.

The training data used in this study consist of news articles taken from Milliyet Corpus that contains 80293 news articles published in the newspaper Milliyet (Hakkani-Tür et al., 2000) [2]. The articles we use for training contain a subset of documents indexed from 1000-5000 and have at least 500 characters. The test set is not included in the original corpus, but it has also been downloaded form Milliyet's public website [3].

The data used in this study have been analyzed with the morphological analyser described in Oflazer (1993) and disambiguated with Sak et al. (2007)'s morphological disambiguator. The data have been manually labelled for training and test. The annotated data is made available for pub-

[1] It has only one prefix for intensifying adjectives and adverbs (**sım**sıcak: very hot). It is just a modified version of the first syllable of the original word and also it is not common. There are other prefixes adopted from foreign languages such as **a**normal (abnormal), **anti**sosyal (antisocial) or **na**mert (not brave).

[2] Thanks to Kemal Oflazer for letting us use the corpus

[3] http://www.milliyet.com.tr

lic use [4]. By making our manually annotated data available, we hope to contribute to future work in this area.

The rest of the paper is organized as follows. Section 2 briefly describes the classification methods used, section 3 explains how these methods are used in implementation and finally the paper is concluded with experimental results.

2 Background

Supervised and unsupervised methods have been used for text classification in different languages (Amasyalı and Diri, 2006; Beil et al., 2002). Among these are Naive Bayes classification (McCallum and Nigam, 1998; Schneider, 2005), decision trees (Johnson et al., 2002) , neural networks (Ng et al., 1997), k-nearest neighbour classifiers (Lim, 2004) and support-vector machines (Shanahan and Roma, 2003).

Bag-of-words model is one of the more intuitive ways to represent text files in text classification. It is simple, it ignores syntax, grammar and the relative positions of the words in the text (Harris, 1970). Each document is represented with an unordered list of words and each of the word frequencies in the collection becomes a feature representing the document. Bag-of-words approach is an intuitive way and popular among document classification tasks (Scott and Matwin, 1998; Joachims, 1997).

Another way of representing documents with term weights is to use term frequency - inverse document frequency (Sparck Jones, 1988). TFIDF is another way of saying that a term is valuable for a document if it occurs frequently in that document but it is not common in the rest of the collection. TFIDF score of a term **t** in a document **d** in a collection **D** is calculated as below:

$$tfidf_{t,d,D} = tf_{t,d} \times idf_{t,D}$$

$tf_{t,d}$ is the number of times **t** occurs in **d** and $idf_{t,D}$ is the number of documents in **D** over the number of document that contain **t**.

The idea behind bag of words and TFIDF is to find a mapping from words to numbers which can also be described as finding a mathematical representation for text files. The output is a matrix representation of the collection. This is also called vector space model representation of the collection in which we can define similarity and distance metrics for documents. One way is to use dot product since each document is represented as a vector (Manning et al., 2008). A number of different dimensions in vector spaces are compared in this study to find the optimal performance.

[4] http://www.ceng.metu.edu.tr/ burakkerim/text_cat

2.1 Morphology

Languages such as Turkish, Czech and Finnish have more complex morphology and cause additional difficulties which requires special handling on linguistic studies compared to languages such as English (Sak et al., 2007). Morphemes may carry semantic or syntactic information, but morphological ambiguity make it hard to pass this information on to other level in a trivial manner especially for languages with productive morphology such as Turkish. An example of possible morphological analyses of a single word in Turkish is presented in Table 1.

alın+Noun+A3sg+Pnon+Nom (forehead)
al+Adj^DB+Noun+Zero+A3sg+P2sg+Nom (your red)
al+Adj^DB+Noun+Zero+A3sg+Pnon+Gen (of red)
al+Verb+Pos+Imp+A2pl ((you) take)
al+Verb^DB+Verb+Pass+Pos+Imp+A2sg ((you) be taken)
alın+Verb+Pos+Imp+A2sg ((you) be offended)

Table 1: Morphological analysis of the word "alın" in Turkish with the corresponding meanings.

We aim to examine the effects of morphological information in a bag-of-words model in the context of text classification. A relevant study explores the prefixing versus morphological analysis/stemming effect on information retrieval in Can et al. (2008). Several stemmers for Turkish are presented for the indexing problem for information retrieval. They use Oflazer's morphological analyzer (Oflazer, 1993), however, they do not use a disambiguator. Instead they choose the most common analysis among the candidates. Their results show that among the fixed length stemmers 5-character prefix is the the best and the lemmatizer based stemmer is slightly better than the fixed length stemmer with five characters. However, they also note that the difference is statistically insignificant. We use Sak et al. (2007)'s disambiguator which is reported with a 96.45% accuracy in their study and with a 87.67% accuracy by Eryiğit (2012)

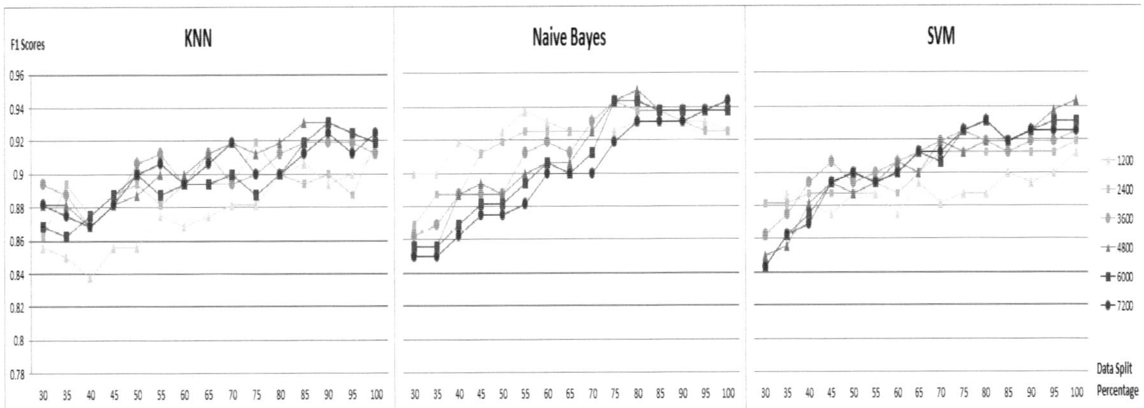

Figure 1: Learning curves with first five characters

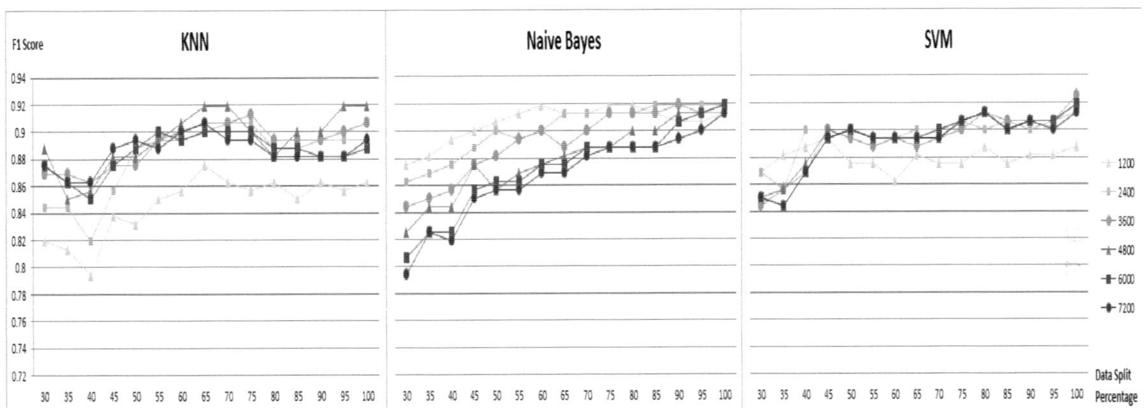

Figure 2: Learning curves with stems

3 Implementation

In the first setting, up to first N characters of each word is extracted as the feature set. A comparison between 4, 5, 6 and 7 characters is performed to choose the best N. In the second setting we use morphological analysis. Each word in documents is analysed morphologically with morphological analyser from Oflazer (1993) and word stems are extracted for each term. Sak's morphological disambiguator for Turkish is used at this step to choose the correct analysis (Sak et al., 2007). Stems are the primary features used for classification. Finally, we add word categories from this analysis as features as POS tags.

We compare these settings in order to see how well morphological analysis with disambiguation performs against a simple baseline of fixed length stemming with a bag-of-words approach. Both stem bags and the first N-character bags are transformed into vector space with TFIDF scoring. Then, different sizes of feature space dimensions are used with ranking by the highest term frequency scores. A range of different dimension sizes from 1200 to 7200 were experimented on to find the optimal dimension size for this study (Table 2). After the collection is mapped into vector space, several learning algorithms are applied for classification. K-Nearest neighbours was implemented with weighted voting of 25 nearest neighbours based on distance and Support Vector Machine is implemented with linear kernel and default parameters. These methods are used with Python, NLTK (Loper and Bird, 2002) and Sci-Kit (Loper and Bird, 2002; Pedregosa et al., 2011).

Training data contains 872 articles labelled and divided into four categories as follows: 235 articles on politics, 258 articles about social news such as culture, education or health, 177 articles on economics and 202 about sports. This data are generated using bootstrapping. Documents are hand annotated with an initial classifier that is trained on a smaller set of hand labelled data. Classifier is used on unknown samples, then the predictions are manually checked to gather enough data for each class. Test data consists of 160 articles with 40 in each class. These are also manually labelled.

4 Experiments

Experiments begin with searching the optimal prefix length for words with different classifiers. After that, stems are used as features and evaluated with the same classifiers. Section 4.3 contains the comparison of these two features. Finally, morphological information is added to these features and the effects of the extra information is inspected in Section 4.4 .

4.1 Optimal Number of Characters

This experiment aims to find out the optimal prefix length for the first N-character feature to represent text documents in Turkish. We conjecture that we can simulate stemming by taking a fixed length prefix of each word. This experiment was performed with all of the 872 training files and 160 test files. Table 2 shows the results of the experiments where columns represent the number of characters used and rows represent the number of features used for classification.

The best performance is acquired using the first five characters of each word for TFIDF transformation for all classifiers. Can et al. (2008) also reported that the five character prefix in the fixed length stemmer performed the best in their experiments. Learning curves for 5-character prefixes are presented in Figure 1. Although, SVM performs poorer on average compared to Naive Bayes, their best performances show no significant statistical difference according to McNemar's Test. On the other hand, kNN falls behind these two on most of the configurations.

4.2 Stems

Another experiment was conducted with the word stems extracted with a morphological analyser and a disambiguator (Sak et al., 2007). kNN, Naive Bayes and SVM were trained with different feature sizes with increasing training data sizes. The learning curves are presented in Figure 2.

Naive Bayes performs best in this setting even with a small feature set with few training samples. When the corpus size is small, using less features gives better results in SVM and Naive Bayes. As the number of features used in classification increases, the number of samples needed for an adequate classification also increases for Naive Bayes. The performance of SVM also increases with the number of data used in training. More documents leave space for repetitions for stop words and common less informative words an their TFIDF scores decrease and the get less impact on the classification while informative words in each category get relatively higher scores, therefore an increase in data size also increases performance. As the training size increases feature space dimension becomes irrelevant and the results converge to a similar point for Naive Bayes. On the other hand, 1200 features are not enough for kNN and SVM. With larger feature sets kNN and SVM also give similar results to Naive Bayes although kNN is left behind especially with less number of features since it directly relies on the similarity based on these features in vector space and most of them are same in each document since we choose them with term frequency.

4.3 5-Character Prefixes vs Stems

This section provides a comparison between two main features used in this study with three different classifiers. F1 scores for the best and worst configurations with each of the three classifiers are presented in Table 3. Using five character prefixes gives better results than using stems. Naive Bayes with stems and five character prefixes disagree only on six instances out of 160 test instances with F1 scores of 0.92 and 0.94 respectively in the best configurations. There is no statistically significant difference.

Similarly, results for SVM with stems for the best and the worst configurations is considered to be not statistically significant. McNemar's Test (McNemar, 1947) is shown to have low error in detecting a significant difference when there is none (Dietterich, 1998).

	Worst		**Best**	
	First 5	**Stems**	**First 5**	**Stems**
KNN	91.250	86.875	92.500	91.875
NB	92.500	91.250	94.375	91.875
SVM	91.250	88.750	93.175	92.500

Table 3: Comparison of F1-scores for best and worst results in each classifier with each feature.

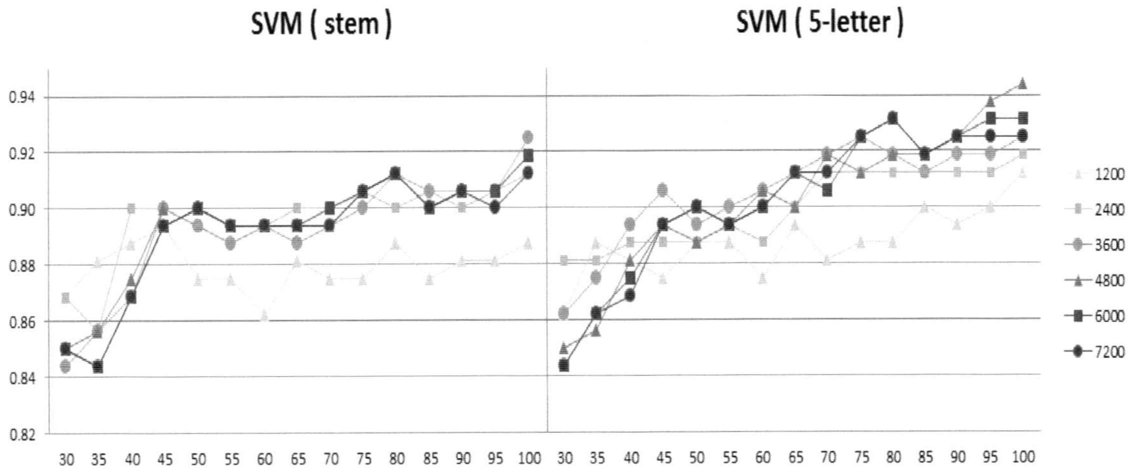

(a) Learning curves without tags

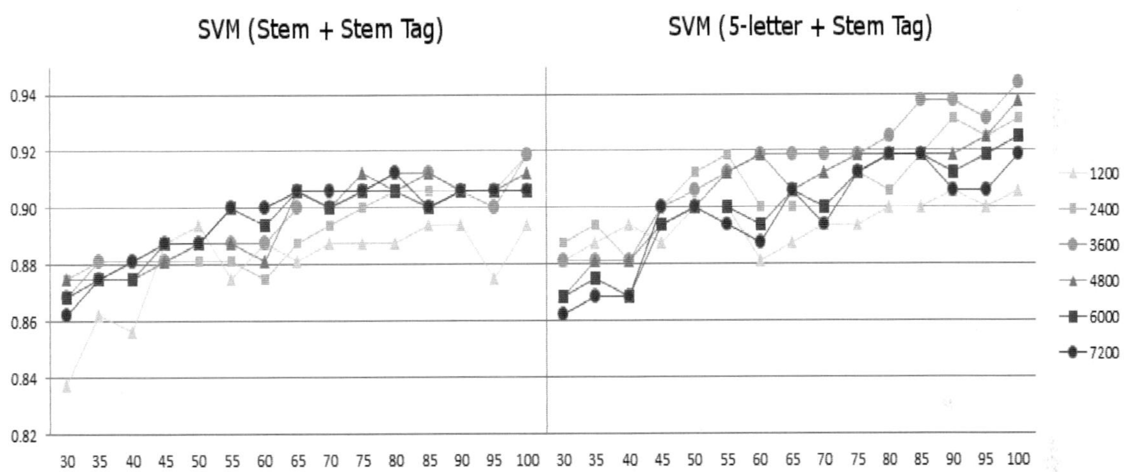

(b) Learning curves with stem tags

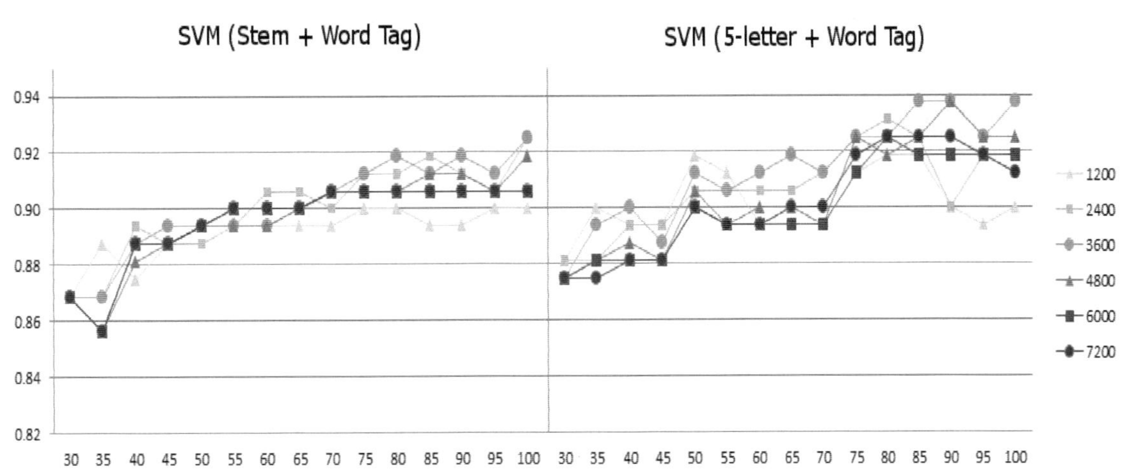

(c) Learning curves with word tags

Figure 3: Learning curves for SVM

	KNN				NB				SVM			
	4	**5**	**6**	**7**	**4**	**5**	**6**	**7**	**4**	**5**	**6**	**7**
1200	90.00	91.25	86.87	84.37	93.12	92.50	93.12	90.00	89.37	91.250	90.62	88.75
2400	89.37	91.25	87.50	86.62	89.37	91.25	87.50	86.62	90.62	91.87	90.00	88.12
3600	86.87	91.25	90.00	88.17	93.75	93.75	92.50	91.87	90.62	91.87	90.00	88.12
4800	90.00	91.87	91.25	88.17	93.12	93.75	91.87	91.25	90.62	91.87	90.00	88.12
6000	88.75	91.87	91.87	90.62	92.50	93.75	92.50	90.62	90.62	**93.12**	**93.12**	90.00
7200	89.37	**92.50**	91.25	89.37	90.62	**94.37**	91.87	91.25	90.62	92.50	91.25	90.62

Table 2: F1-scores with different prefix lengths and dimensions.

4.4 SVM with POS Tags

The final experiment examines the effects of POS tags that are extracted via morphological analysis. Two different features are extracted and compared with the base lines of classifiers with stems and first five characters without tags. Stem tag is the first tag of the first derivation and the word tag is the tag of the last derivation and example features are given in Table 4. Since derivational morphemes are also present in the morphological analyses word tags may differ from stem tags. In addition, words that are spelled in the same way may belong to different categories or have different meanings that can be expressed with POS tags. Al+Verb (take) and Al+Adj (red) are different even though their surface forms are the same.

Analysis	al+Adj^DB+Noun+Zero+ A3sg+Pnon+Gen (of red)
First 5 characters.	alın (of red, forehead, (you) be taken, (you) be offended ...)
Stem	al (red, take)
Stem + Stem Tag	al+Adj (red)
Stem + Word Tag	al+Noun (red)

Table 4: Example features for word "alın".

Using POS tags with stems increases the success rate especially when the number of features is low. However, using tags of the stems does not make significant changes on average. The best and the worst results differ with baseline with less than 0.01 points in F1 scores as seen in Figure 3. This may be due to the fact that the same stem has a higher chance of being in the same category even though the derived final form is different. Even though, this may add extra information to the stems, results show no significant difference. Adding stem or word tags to the first five characters increases the success when the number of training instances are low, however, it has no significant effect on the highest score. Using tags with five characters has positive effects when the number of features are low and negative effects when the number of features are high.

5 Conclusion

In this study, we use K-Nearest Neighbours, Naive Bayes and Support Vector Machine classifiers for examining the effects of morphological information on the task of classifying Turkish news articles. We have compared their performances on different sizes of training data, different number of features and different feature sets. Results suggest that the first five characters of each word can be used for TFIDF transformation to represent text documents in classification tasks. Another feature used in the study is word stems. Stems are extracted with a morphological analyser which is computationally expensive and takes a lot of time compared to extracting first characters of a word. Although different test sets and training data may change the final results, using a simple approximation with first five characters to represent documents instead of results of an expensive morphological analysis process gives similar or better results with much less cost. Experiments also indicate that there is more place for growth if more training data is available as most of the learning curves presented in the experiments point. We particularly expect better results with POS tag experiments with more data. Actual word categories and meanings may differ and using POS tags may solve this problem but sparsity of the data is more prominent at the moment. The future work includes repeating these experiments with larger data sets to explore the effects of the data size.

References

Charu C. Aggarwal and Philip S. Yu. 2000. Finding generalized projected clusters in high dimensional spaces. *SIGMOD Rec.*, 29(2):70–81.

M. Fatih Amasyalı and Banu Diri. 2006. Automatic Turkish text categorization in terms of author, genre and gender. In *Proceedings of the 11th international conference on Applications of Natural Language to Information Systems*, NLDB'06, pages 221–226, Berlin, Heidelberg. Springer-Verlag.

Florian Beil, Martin Ester, and Xiaowei Xu. 2002. Frequent term-based text clustering. In *Proceedings of the eighth ACM SIGKDD international conference on Knowledge discovery and data mining*, KDD '02, pages 436–442, New York, NY, USA. ACM.

Fazlı Can, Seyit Koçberber, Erman Balçık, Cihan Kaynak, H. Çağdaş Öcalan, and Onur M. Vursavaş. 2008. Information retrieval on turkish texts. *JASIST*, 59(3):407–421.

Ruket Çakıcı and Jason Baldridge. 2006. Projective and non-projective Turkish parsing. In *Proceedings of the 5th International Treebanks and Linguistic Theories Conference*, pages 43–54.

Özlem Çetinoğlu and Kemal Oflazer. 2006. Morphology-syntax interface for Turkish LFG. In *Proceedings of the 21st International Conference on Computational Linguistics and the 44th annual meeting of the Association for Computational Linguistics*, ACL-44, pages 153–160, Stroudsburg, PA, USA. Association for Computational Linguistics.

Thomas G. Dietterich. 1998. Approximate statistical tests for comparing supervised classification learning algorithms. *Neural Computation*, 10:1895–1923.

Gülşen Eryiğit. 2012. The impact of automatic morphological analysis & disambiguation on dependency parsing of turkish. In *Proceedings of the Eighth International Conference on Language Resources and Evaluation (LREC)*, Istanbul, Turkey, 23-25 May.

Gülşen Eryiğit, Joakim Nivre, and Kemal Oflazer. 2008. Dependency parsing of Turkish. *Comput. Linguist.*, 34(3):357–389, September.

George Forman. 2003. An extensive empirical study of feature selection metrics for text classification. *J. Mach. Learn. Res.*, 3:1289–1305, March.

Dilek Z. Hakkani-Tür, Kemal Oflazer, and Gökhan Tür. 2000. Statistical morphological disambiguation for agglutinative languages. In *Proceedings of the 18th conference on Computational linguistics - Volume 1*, COLING '00, pages 285–291, Stroudsburg, PA, USA. Association for Computational Linguistics.

Zelig Harris. 1970. Distributional structure. In *Papers in Structural and Transformational Linguistics*, pages 775–794. D. Reidel Publishing Company, Dordrecht, Holland.

M. Ikonomakis, S. Kotsiantis, and V. Tampakas. 2005. Text classification: a recent overview. In *Proceedings of the 9th WSEAS International Conference on Computers*, ICCOMP'05, pages 1–6, Stevens Point, Wisconsin, USA. World Scientific and Engineering Academy and Society (WSEAS).

Thorsten Joachims. 1997. A probabilistic analysis of the rocchio algorithm with tfidf for text categorization. In *Proceedings of the Fourteenth International Conference on Machine Learning*, ICML '97, pages 143–151, San Francisco, CA, USA. Morgan Kaufmann Publishers Inc.

D. E. Johnson, F. J. Oles, T. Zhang, and T. Goetz. 2002. A decision-tree-based symbolic rule induction system for text categorization. *IBM Syst. J.*, 41(3):428–437, July.

Heui-Seok Lim. 2004. Improving kNN based text classification with well estimated parameters. In Nikhil R. Pal, Nikola Kasabov, Rajani K. Mudi, Srimanta Pal, and Swapan K. Parui, editors, *Neural Information Processing, 11th International Conference, ICONIP 2004, Calcutta, India, November 22-25, 2004, Proceedings*, volume 3316 of *Lecture Notes in Computer Science*, pages 516–523. Springer.

Tao Liu, Shengping Liu, and Zheng Chen. 2003. An evaluation on feature selection for text clustering. In *In ICML*, pages 488–495.

Edward Loper and Steven Bird. 2002. Nltk: the natural language toolkit. In *Proceedings of the ACL-02 Workshop on Effective tools and methodologies for teaching natural language processing and computational linguistics - Volume 1*, ETMTNLP '02, pages 63–70, Stroudsburg, PA, USA. Association for Computational Linguistics.

Christopher D. Manning and Hinrich Schütze. 1999. *Foundations of statistical natural language processing*. MIT Press, Cambridge, MA, USA.

Christopher D. Manning, Prabhakar Raghavan, and Hinrich Schütze. 2008. *Introduction to Information Retrieval*. Cambridge University Press, New York, NY, USA.

Andrew McCallum and Kamal Nigam. 1998. A comparison of event models for naive bayes text classification. In *Proceesings of the Workshop on learning for text categorization, AAAI'98*, pages 41–48.

Quinn McNemar. 1947. Note on the Sampling Error of the Difference Between Correlated Proportions or Percentages. *Psychometrika*, 12(2):153–157.

Hwee Tou Ng, Wei Boon Goh, and Kok Leong Low. 1997. Feature selection, perceptron learning, and a usability case study for text categorization. In *Proceedings of the 20th annual international ACM SIGIR conference on Research and development in information retrieval*, SIGIR '97, pages 67–73, New York, NY, USA. ACM.

Kemal Oflazer. 1993. Two-level description of Turkish morphology. In *Proceedings of the sixth conference on European chapter of the Association for Computational Linguistics*, EACL '93, pages 472–472, Stroudsburg, PA, USA. Association for Computational Linguistics.

F. Pedregosa, G. Varoquaux, A. Gramfort, V. Michel, B. Thirion, O. Grisel, M. Blondel, P. Prettenhofer, R. Weiss, V. Dubourg, J. Vanderplas, A. Passos, D. Cournapeau, M. Brucher, M. Perrot, and E. Duchesnay. 2011. Scikit-learn: Machine learning in Python. *Journal of Machine Learning Research*, 12:2825–2830.

Haşim Sak, Tunga Güngör, and Murat Saraçlar. 2007. Morphological disambiguation of Turkish text with perceptron algorithm. In *Proceedings of the 8th International Conference on Computational Linguistics and Intelligent Text Processing*, CICLing '07, pages 107–118, Berlin, Heidelberg. Springer-Verlag.

Karl-Michael Schneider. 2005. Techniques for improving the performance of naive bayes for text classification. In *In Proceedings of CICLing 2005*, pages 682–693.

Sam Scott and Stan Matwin. 1998. Text classification using WordNet hypernyms. In *Workshop: Usage of WordNet in Natural Language Processing Systems, ACL'98*, pages 45–52.

James G. Shanahan and Norbert Roma. 2003. Boosting support vector machines for text classification through parameter-free threshold relaxation. In *Proceedings of the twelfth international conference on Information and knowledge management*, CIKM '03, pages 247–254, New York, NY, USA. ACM.

Karen Sparck Jones. 1988. A statistical interpretation of term specificity and its application in retrieval. In Peter Willett, editor, *Document retrieval systems*, pages 132–142. Taylor Graham Publishing, London, UK, UK.

Yiming Yang and Xin Liu. 1999. A re-examination of text categorization methods. In *Proceedings of the 22nd annual international ACM SIGIR conference on Research and development in information retrieval*, SIGIR '99, pages 42–49, New York, NY, USA. ACM.

Yiming Yang and Jan O. Pedersen. 1997. A comparative study on feature selection in text categorization. In *Proceedings of the Fourteenth International Conference on Machine Learning*, ICML '97, pages 412–420, San Francisco, CA, USA. Morgan Kaufmann Publishers Inc.

Crawling microblogging services to gather language-classified URLs
Workflow and case study

Adrien Barbaresi
ICAR Lab
ENS Lyon & University of Lyon
15 parvis René Descartes, 69007 Lyon, France
adrien.barbaresi@ens-lyon.fr

Abstract

We present a way to extract links from messages published on microblogging platforms and we classify them according to the language and possible relevance of their target in order to build a text corpus. Three platforms are taken into consideration: FriendFeed, identi.ca and Reddit, as they account for a relative diversity of user profiles and more importantly user languages. In order to explore them, we introduce a traversal algorithm based on user pages. As we target lesser-known languages, we try to focus on non-English posts by filtering out English text. Using mature open-source software from the NLP research field, a spell checker (aspell) and a language identification system (`langid.py`), our case study and our benchmarks give an insight into the linguistic structure of the considered services.

1 Introduction

1.1 The 'Web as Corpus' paradigm

The state of the art tools of the 'Web as Corpus' framework rely heavily on URLs obtained from search engines. As a matter of fact, the approach followed by the most researchers of this field consists in querying search engines (e.g. by tuples) to gather links that are crawled in order to build a corpus (Baroni et al., 2009).

This method could be used in free corpus building approach until recently, when it was made impossible because of increasing limitations on the search engines' APIs, which make the gathering process on a low budget very slow or impossible. All in all, the APIs may be too expensive and/or too unstable in time to support large-scale corpus building projects.

Moreover, the question whether the method used so far, i.e. randomizing keywords, provides a good overview of a language is still open. Other technical difficulties include diverse and partly unknown search biases due, in part, to search engine optimization tricks as well as undocumented PageRank adjustments. Using diverse sources of seed URLs could at least ensure that there is not a single bias, but several ones.

The crawling method using these seeds for corpus building may then yield better results, e.g. ensure better randomness in a population of web documents as described by (Henzinger et al., 2000).

1.2 User-based URL gathering

Our hypothesis is that microblogging services are a good alternative to overcome the limitations of seed URL collections and the biases implied by search engine optimization techniques, PageRank and link classification.

It is a user-based language approach. Its obvious limits are the amount of spam and advertisement. Its obvious bias consists in the technology-prone users who are familiar with these platforms and account for numerous short messages which in turn over-represent their own interests and hobbies.

However, user-related biases also have advantages, most notably the fact that documents that are most likely to be important are being shared, which has benefits when it comes to gather links in lesser-known languages, below the English-speaking spammer's radar.

1.3 Interest

The main goal is to provide well-documented, feature-rich software and databases relevant for linguistic studies. More specifically, we would like to be able to cover languages which are more rarely seen on the Internet, which implies the gathering of higher proportions of URLs leading to lesser-known languages. We think that social networks and microblogging services may be of great help when it comes to focus on them.

In fact, the most engaged social networking nations do arguably not use English as a first communicating language[1]. In addition, crawling these services gives an opportunity to perform a case study of existing tools and platforms.

Finally, the method presented here could be used in other contexts : microtext collections, user lists and relations could prove useful for microtext corpus building, network visualization or social network sampling purposes (Gjoka et al., 2011).

2 Data Sources

FriendFeed, identi.ca and Reddit are taken into consideration for this study. These services provide a good overview of the peculiarities of social networks. At least by the last two of them a crawl appears to be manageable in terms of both API accessibility and corpus size, which is not the case concerning Twitter for example.

2.1 identi.ca

identi.ca is a social microblogging service built on open source tools and open standards, which is the reason why we chose to crawl it at first.

The advantages compared to Twitter include the Creative Commons license of the content, the absence of limitations on the total number of pages seen (to our knowledge) and the relatively small amount of messages, which can also be a problem. A full coverage of the network is theoretically possible, where all the information may be publicly available. Thus, all interesting information is collected and no language filtering is used concerning this website.

2.2 FriendFeed

To our knowledge, FriendFeed is the most active of the three microblogging services considered here. It is also the one which seems to have been studied the most by the research community. The service works as an aggregator (Gupta et al., 2009) that offers a broader spectrum of retrieved information. Technically, FriendFeed and identi.ca can overlap, as the latter is integrated in the former. But the size difference between the two platforms makes this hypothesis unlikely.

The API of FriendFeed is somewhat liberal, as no explicit limits are enforced. Nonetheless, our tests showed that after a certain number of successful requests with little or no sleep, the servers start dropping most of the inbound connections. All in all, the relative tolerance of this website makes it a good candidate to gather a lot of text in a short period of time.

2.3 Reddit

Reddit is a social bookmarking and a microblogging platform, which ranks to the 7th place worldwide in the news category according to Alexa.[2] The entries are organized into areas of interest called 'reddits' or 'subreddits'. The users account for the linguistic relevance of their channel, the moderation processes are mature, and since the channels (or subreddits) have to be hand-picked, they ensure a certain stability.

There are 16 target languages so far, which can be accessed via so-called 'multi-reddit expressions', i.e. compilations of subreddits: Croatian, Czech, Danish, Finnish, French, German, Hindi, Italian, Norwegian, Polish, Portuguese, Romanian, Russian, Spanish, Swedish and Turkish[3].

Sadly, it is currently not possible to go back in time further than the 500th oldest post due to API limitations, which severely restricts the number of links one may crawl.

3 Methodology

The following workflow describes how the results below are obtained:

1. URL harvesting: social network traversal, obvious spam and non-text documents filtering, optional spell check of the short message to see if it could be English text, optional record of user IDs for later crawls.

2. Operations on the URL queue: redirection checks, sampling by domain name.

3. Download of the web documents and analysis: HTML code stripping, document validity check, language identification.

[1] http://www.comscore.com/Press_Events/Press_Releases/2011/12/Social_Networking_Leads_as_Top_Online_Activity_Globally

[2] http://www.alexa.com/topsites/category/Top/News

[3] Here is a possible expression to target Norwegian users: http://www.reddit.com/r/norge+oslo+norskenyheter

The only difference between FriendFeed and Reddit on one hand and identi.ca on the other hand is the spell check performed on the short messages in order to target non-English ones. Indeed, all new messages can be taken into consideration on the latter, making a selection unnecessary.

Links pointing to media documents, which represent a high volume of links shared on microblogging services, are excluded from this study, as its final purpose is to be able to build a text corpus. As a page is downloaded or a query is executed, links are filtered on the fly using a series of heuristics described below, and finally the rest of the links is stored.

3.1 TRUC: an algorithm for TRaversal and User-based Crawls

Starting from a publicly available homepage, the crawl engine selects users according to their linguistic relevance based on a language filter (see below), and then retrieves their messages, eventually discovering friends of friends and expanding its scope and the size of the network it traverses. As this is a breadth-first approach its applicability depends greatly on the size of the network.

In this study, the goal is to concentrate on non-English speaking messages in the hope of finding non-English links. The main 'timeline' fosters a users discovery approach, which then becomes user-centered as the spider focuses on a list of users who are expected not to post messages in English and/or spam. The messages are filtered at each step to ensure relevant URLs are collected. This implies that a lot of subtrees are pruned, so that the chances of completing the traversal increase. In fact, experience shows that a relatively small fraction of users and URLs is selected.

This approach is 'static', as it does not rely on any long poll requests (which are for instance used to capture a fraction of Twitter's messages as they are made public), it actively fetches the required pages.

3.2 Check for redirection and sampling

Further work on the URL queue before the language identification task ensures an even smaller fraction of URLs really goes through the resource-expensive process of fetching and analyzing web documents.

The first step of preprocessing consists in finding those URLs that lead to a redirect, which is done using a list comprising all the major URL shortening services and adding all intriguingly short URLs, i.e. less than 26 characters in length, which according to our FriendFeed data occurs at a frequency of about 3%. To deal with shortened URLs, one can perform HTTP HEAD requests for each member of the list in order to determine and store the final URL.

The second step is a sampling that reduces both the size of the list and the probable impact of an overrepresented domain names in the result set. If several URLs contain the same domain name, the group is reduced to a randomly chosen URL.

Due to the overlaps of domain names and the amount of spam and advertisement on social networks such an approach is very useful when it comes to analyze a large list of URLs.

3.3 Language identification

Microtext has characteristics that make it hard for 'classical' NLP approaches like web page language identification based on URLs (Baykan et al., 2008) to predict with certainty the languages of the links. That is why mature NLP tools have to be used to filter the incoming messages.

A similar work on language identification and FriendFeed is described in (Celli, 2009), who uses a dictionary-based approach: the software tries to guess the language of microtext by identifying very frequent words.

However, the fast-paced evolution of the vocabulary used on social networks makes it hard to rely only on lists of frequent terms, so that our approach seems more complete.

A first dictionary-based filter First, a quick test is used in order to guess whether a microtext is English or not. Indeed, this operation cuts the amount of microtexts in half and enables to select the users or the friends which feature the desired response, thus directing the traversal in a more fruitful direction.

The library used, enchant[4], allows the use of a variety of spell-checking backends, like aspell, hunspell or ispell, with one or several locales[5]. Basically, this approach can be used with other languages as well, even if they are not used as discriminating factors in this study. We consider this option to be a well-balanced solution between processing speed on one hand and coverage on

[4] http://www.abisource.com/projects/enchant/

[5] All software mentioned here is open-source.

the other. Spell checking algorithms benefit from years of optimization in both areas.

This first filter uses a threshold to discriminate between short messages, expressed as a percentage of tokens which do not pass the spell check. The filter also relies on software biases, like Unicode errors, which make it nearly certain that the given input microtext is not English.

langid.py A language identification tool is used to classify the web documents and to benchmark the efficiency of the test mentioned above. `langid.py` (Lui and Baldwin, 2011; Lui and Baldwin, 2012) is open-source, it incorporates a pre-trained model and it covers 97 languages, which is ideal to tackle the diversity of the web. Its use as a web service makes it a fast solution enabling distant or distributed work.

The server version of `langid.py` was used, the texts were downloaded, all the HTML markup was stripped and the resulting text was discarded if it was less than 1,000 characters long. According to its authors, `langid.py` could be used directly on microtexts. However, this feature was discarded because it did not prove as efficient as the approach used here when it comes to a substantial amounts of short messages.

4 Results

The surface crawl dealing with the main timeline and one level of depth has been performed on the three platforms[6]. In the case of identi.ca, a deep miner was launched to explore the network. FriendFeed proved too large to start such a breadth-first crawler so that other strategies ought to be used (Gjoka et al., 2011), whereas the multi-reddit expressions used did not yield enough users.

FriendFeed is the biggest link provider on a regular basis (about 10,000 or 15,000 messages per hour can easily be collected), whereas Reddit is the weakest, as the total figures show.

The total number of English websites may be a relevant indication when it comes to establish a baseline for finding possibly non-English documents. Accordingly, English accounts for about 55 % of the websites[7], with the second most-used content-language, German, only representing about 6 % of the web pages. So, there is a gap between English and the other languages, and there is also a discrepancy between the number of Internet users and the content languages.

4.1 FriendFeed

To test whether the first language filter was efficient, a testing sample of URLs and users was collected randomly. The first filter was emulated by selecting about 8% of messages (based on a random function) in the spam and media-filtered posts of the public timeline. Indeed, the messages selected by the algorithm approximately amount to this fraction of the total. At the same time, the corresponding users were retrieved, exactly as described above, and then the user-based step was run, keeping one half of the user's messages, which is also realistic according to real-world data.

The datasets compared here were both of an order of magnitude of at least 10^5 unique URLs before the redirection checks. At the end of the toolchain, the randomly selected benchmark set comprises 7,047 URLs and the regular set 19,573 URLs[8]. The first was collected in about 30 hours and the second one in several weeks. According to the methodology used, this phenomenon may be explained by the fact that the domain names in the URLs tend to be mentioned repeatedly.

Language	URLs	%
English	4,978	70.6
German	491	7.0
Japanese	297	4.2
Spanish	258	3.7
French	247	3.5

Table 1: 5 most frequent languages of URLs taken at random on FriendFeed

According to the language identification system (`langid.py`), the first language filter beats the random function by nearly 30 points (see Table 2). The other top languages are accordingly better represented. Other noteworthy languages are to be found in the top 20, e.g. Indonesian and Persian (Farsi).

[6]Several techniques are used to keep the number of requests as low as possible, most notably user profiling according to the tweeting frequency. In the case of identi.ca this results into approximately 300 page views every hour.

[7]http://w3techs.com/technologies/overview/content_language/all

[8]The figures given describe the situation at the end, after the sampling by domain name and after the selection of documents based on a minimum length. The word URL is used as a shortcut for the web documents they link to.

Language	URLs	%
English	8,031	41.0
Russian	2,475	12.6
Japanese	1,757	9.0
Turkish	1,415	7.2
German	1,289	6.6
Spanish	954	4.9
French	703	3.6
Italian	658	3.4
Portuguese	357	1.8
Arabic	263	1.3

Table 2: 10 most frequent languages of spell-check-filtered URLs gathered on FriendFeed

4.2 identi.ca

The results of the two strategies followed on identi.ca led to a total of 1,113,783 URLs checked for redirection, which were collected in about a week (the deep crawler reached 37,485 user IDs). A large majority of the 192,327 total URLs apparently lead to English texts (64.9 %), since no language filter was used but only a spam filter.

Language	URLs	%
English	124,740	64.9
German	15,484	8.1
Spanish	15,295	8.0
French	12,550	6.5
Portuguese	5,485	2.9
Italian	3,384	1.8
Japanese	1,758	0.9
Dutch	1,610	0.8
Indonesian	1,229	0.6
Polish	1,151	0.6

Table 3: 10 most frequent languages of URLs gathered on identi.ca

4.3 Reddit

The figures presented here are the results of a single crawl of all available languages altogether, but regular crawls are needed to compensate for the 500 posts limit. English accounted for 18.1 % of the links found on channel pages (for a total of 4,769 URLs) and 55.9 % of the sum of the links found on channel and on user pages (for a total of 20,173 URLs).

The results in Table 5 show that the first filter was nearly sufficient to discriminate between the links. Indeed, the microtexts that were under the threshold led to a total of 204,170 URLs. 28,605 URLs remained at the end of the toolchain and English accounted for 76.7 % of the documents they linked to.

Language	URLs	%	Comb. %
English	863	18.1	55.9
Spanish	798	16.7	9.7
German	519	10.9	6.3
French	512	10.7	7.2
Swedish	306	6.4	2.9
Romanian	265	5.6	2.5
Portuguese	225	4.7	2.1
Finnish	213	4.5	1.6
Czech	199	4.2	1.4
Norwegian	194	4.1	2.1

Table 4: 10 most frequent languages of filtered URLs gathered on Reddit channels and on a combination of channels and user pages

Language	URLs	% of total
English	21,926	76.7
Spanish	1,402	4.9
French	1,141	4.0
German	997	3.5
Swedish	445	1.6

Table 5: 5 most frequent languages of links seen on Reddit and rejected by the primary language filter

The threshold was set at 90 % of the words for FriendFeed and 33% for Reddit, each time after a special punctuation strip to avoid the influence of special uses of punctuation on social networks. Yet, the lower filter achieved better results, which may be explained by the moderation system of the subreddits as well as by the greater regularity in the posts of this platform.

5 Discussion

Three main technical challenges had to be addressed, which resulted in a separate workflow: the shortened URLs are numerous, yet they ought to be resolved in order to enable the use of heuristics based on the nature of the URLs or a proper sampling of the URLs themselves. The confrontation with the constantly increasing number of URLs to analyze and the necessarily limited resources make a website sampling by domain name useful. Finally, the diversity of the web documents put the language recognition tools to a test, so that a few tweaks are necessary to correct the results.

The relatively low number of results for Russian may be explained by weaknesses of `langid.py` with deviations of encoding standards. Indeed, a few tweaks are necessary to correct the biases of the software in its pre-trained version, in particular regarding texts falsely considered as being written in Chinese, although URL-based heuristics indicate that the website is most probably hosted in Russia or in Japan. A few charset encodings found in Asian countries are also a source of classification problems. The low-confidence responses as well as a few well-delimited cases were discarded in this study, they account for no more than 2 % of the results. Ideally, a full-fledged comparison with other language identification software may be necessary to identify its areas of expertise.

A common practice known as cloaking has not been addressed so far: a substantial fraction of web pages show a different content to crawler engines and to browsers. This Janus-faced behavior tends to alter the language characteristics of the web page in favor of English results.

Regarding topics, a major user bias was not addressed either: among the most frequently shared links on identi.ca for example, many are related to technology, IT or software and are mostly written in English. The social media analyzed here tend to be dominated by English-speaking users, either native speakers or second-language learners.

In general, there is room for improvement concerning the first filter, the threshold could be tested and adapted to several scenarios. This may involve larger datasets for testing purposes and machine learning techniques relying on feature extraction.

The contrasted results on Reddit shed a different light on the exploration of user pages: in all likelihood, users mainly share links in English when they are not posting them on a language-relevant channel. The results on FriendFeed are better from this point of view, which may suggest that English is not used equally on all platforms by users who speak other languages than English. Nonetheless, the fact that the microblogging services studied here are mainly English-speaking seems to be a strong tendency.

Last but not least, the adequateness of the web documents shared on social networks has yet to be thoroughly assessed. From the output of this toolchain to a full-fledged web corpus, other fine-grained instruments (Schäfer and Bildhauer, 2012) as well as further decisions processes (Schäfer et al., 2013) are needed along the way.

6 Conclusion

We presented a methodology to gather multilingual URLs on three microblogging platforms. In order to do so, we perform traversals of the platforms and use already available tools to filter the URLs accordingly and identify their language.

We provide open source software to access the APIs (FriendFeed and Reddit) and the HTML version of identi.ca, as an authentication is mandatory for the API. The TRUC algorithm is fully implemented. All the operations described in this paper can be reproduced using the same tools, which are part of repositories currently hosted on the GitHub platform[9].

The main goal is achieved, as hundreds if not thousands of URLs for lesser-known languages such as Romanian or Indonesian can be gathered on social networks and microblogging services. When it comes to filter out English posts, a first step using an English spell checker gives better results than the baseline established using microtexts selected at random. However, the discrepancy between the languages one would expect to find based on demographic indicators and the results of the study is remarkable. English websites stay numerous even when one tries to filter them out.

This proof of concept is usable, but a better filtering process and longer crawls may be necessary to unlock the full potential of this approach. Last, a random-walk crawl using these seeds and a state of the art text categorization may provide more information on what is really shared on microblogging platforms.

Future work perspectives include dealing with live tweets (as Twitter and FriendFeed can be queried continuously), exploring the depths of identi.ca and FriendFeed and making the directory of language-classified URLs collected during this study publicly available.

[9] https://github.com/adbar/microblog-explorer

7 Acknowledgments

This work has been partially funded by an internal grant of the FU Berlin (COW project at the German Grammar Dept.). Many thanks to Roland Schäfer and two anonymous reviewers for their useful comments.

References

Marco Baroni, Silvia Bernardini, Adriano Ferraresi, and Eros Zanchetta. 2009. The WaCky Wide Web: A collection of very large linguistically processed web-crawled corpora. *Language Resources and Evaluation*, 43(3):209–226.

Eda Baykan, Monika Henzinger, and Ingmar Weber. 2008. Web Page Language Identification Based on URLs. *Proceedings of the VLDB Endowment*, 1(1):176–187.

Fabio Celli. 2009. Improving Language identification performance with FriendFeed data. Technical report, CLIC, University of Trento.

Minas Gjoka, Maciej Kurant, Carter T. Butts, and Athina Markopoulou. 2011. Practical recommendations on crawling online social networks. *IEEE Journal on Selected Areas in Communications*, 29(9):1872–1892.

Trinabh Gupta, Sanchit Garg, Niklas Carlsson, Anirban Mahanti, and Martin Arlitt. 2009. Characterization of FriendFeed – A Web-based Social Aggregation Service. In *Proceedings of the AAAI ICWSM*, volume 9.

Monika R. Henzinger, Allan Heydon, Michael Mitzenmacher, and Marc Najork. 2000. On near-uniform URL sampling. In *Proceedings of the 9th International World Wide Web conference on Computer Networks: The International Journal of Computer and Telecommunications Networking*, pages 295–308. North-Holland Publishing Co.

Marco Lui and Timothy Baldwin. 2011. Cross-domain Feature Selection for Language Identification. In *Proceedings of the Fifth International Joint Conference on Natural Language Processing (IJCNLP 2011)*, pages 553–561, Chiang Mai, Thailand.

Marco Lui and Timothy Baldwin. 2012. langid.py: An Off-the-shelf Language Identification Tool. In *Proceedings of the 50th Annual Meeting of the Association for Computational Linguistics (ACL 2012)*, Jeju, Republic of Korea.

Roland Schäfer and Felix Bildhauer. 2012. Building large corpora from the web using a new efficient tool chain. In *Proceedings of the Eight International Conference on Language Resources and Evaluation (LREC'12)*, pages 486–493.

Roland Schäfer, Adrien Barbaresi, and Felix Bildhauer. 2013. The Good, the Bad, and the Hazy: Design Decisions in Web Corpus Construction. In *Proceedings of the 8th Web as Corpus Workshop (WAC8)*. To appear.

Patient Experience in Online Support Forums: Modeling Interpersonal Interactions and Medication Use

Annie T. Chen
University of North Carolina, Chapel Hill
School of Information and Library Science
atchen@email.unc.edu

Abstract

Though there has been substantial research concerning the extraction of information from clinical notes, to date there has been less work concerning the extraction of useful information from patient-generated content. Using a dataset comprised of online support group discussion content, this paper investigates two dimensions that may be important in the extraction of patient-generated experiences from text; significant individuals/groups and medication use. With regard to the former, the paper describes an approach involving the pairing of important figures (e.g. family, husbands, doctors, etc.) and affect, and suggests possible applications of such techniques to research concerning online social support, as well as integration into search interfaces for patients. Additionally, the paper demonstrates the extraction of side effects and sentiment at different phases in patient medication use, e.g. adoption, current use, discontinuation and switching, and demonstrates the utility of such an application for drug safety monitoring in online discussion forums.

1 Introduction

Online support groups are a rich source of information concerning patient experiences, but they are far different from clinical content. Instead of "The patient presents with..." and "denies vomiting," patients may speak of their "doc" and "rheumy." There may be utterances like "LOL" (laugh out loud) and "Hugs." Patients may raise issues that they may be reticent to speak with health care practitioners about, day-to-day condition management issues, or personal strategies that they have for taking medicine.

In recent years, it has been observed that patients may be a valuable source of expertise to other patients, and that they provide information that is different from the expertise of clinicians (Civan & Pratt, 2007; Hartzler & Pratt, 2011). This may include: action strategies, recommended knowledge, suggested approaches, and information resources for dealing with problems. This content can be extremely valuable to clinicians and patients alike; however, to date most interfaces for patient-generated content offer few features tailored to the unique nature of the content in these support forums.

Thus, the objective of the current paper was to explore techniques for extracting and visualizing dimensions of patient experience. For this preliminary work, two specific dimensions were selected: interpersonal interactions and medication use.

Interpersonal interactions are an important dimension to consider because others have such a profound impact on patient experience. For example, social support from family, friends and even practitioners can be invaluable to patients; and understanding, (or the lack of it), from practitioners and other people in one's life can be enormously difficult for people, especially those dealing with a stigmatized condition such as fibromyalgia (Barker, 2008). Thus, automatic identification of patient experiences with others, e.g. family, husband, wife, son, daughter, doctor, etc., and ways of highlighting similar types of experiences across patients, might serve various uses. Scientists could use this to study social support, physician-patient communication and other types of interpersonal interactions. Integrated into a search interface, patients could search for others with similar experiences, and see if there are strategies that they could use to address their own problem.

Medication use is another important dimension of patient experience. There has also been an increased interest in the use of online discussion content to predict adverse events and monitor off-label prescription practices (e.g. Wang et al., 2011; Leaman et al., 2010; Chee et al., 2011). This work differs from previous literature in that the method identifies and visually contextualizes patient medication experiences, particularly in terms of stages of use and affect.

2 Background

This work draws primarily upon two streams of literature: automated analyses of health-related discussion content, and extraction of medication-related information from text. With regard to the former, a large number of studies have employed the software, Linguistic Inquiry and Word Count (LIWC), to compare emotional expression in communities or associations between emotional expression and health outcomes (e.g. Siriaraya et al., 2011; Han et al., 2008).

Other studies of online support groups have focused on social support. Wang, Kraut and Levine (2012) used machine learning with features generated using LIWC and Latent Dirichlet Allocation to investigate whether different types and amounts of social support are associated with length of membership. Namkoong et al. (2010) examined the effects of exchanging treatment information within computer-mediated breast cancer support groups on emotional well-being. Treatment information exchange was assessed using InfoTrend, a software program that employs a rule-based system for computer-aided coding of key ideas.

The task of extraction of medication-related information has often been explored in past literature. For example, the 2009 i2b2 medication challenge focused on the extraction of medication-related information from discharge summaries including: medication name, dosage, mode, frequency, duration and reason (Spasic et al., 2010). This study differs from previous work in that, the focus is not on the time of day or the frequency of medication use, but rather, the stage in the adoption/discontinuation of a medication an individual is at.

3 Method

Discussion content was downloaded through a series of focused crawls of a health-related social networking site (SNS), DailyStrength (`http://www.dailystrength.org`). The content from the corpus encompasses a span of time of approximately 3.5 years, from the site's inception in 2006, to early 2010.

Text pre-processing was done to strip code and extract post metadata. The text was parsed and tagged using the Stanford Parts-of-Speech Tagger (Toutanova et al., 2003). An affective lexicon, WordNet-Affect was used to identify words with emotional content in the text (Strapparava & Valitutti, 2004). There are many specialized resources that could be used to extract medical terminology. However, forum participants wrote in ways that often departed from medical terminology; thus, it was decided that manually constructed lexicons of medication names, side effects and people would be more effective.

4 Results

The results are reported in three parts: descriptive statistics for the corpus, interaction with others and medication information.

4.1 Corpus

The corpus is comprised of discussion posts for three conditions. Since the first part of this study examines interpersonal interactions, three conditions were selected in which key support interactions and level of affect were expected to differ.

Unit/Condition	Breast cancer	Type 1 diabetes	Fibromyalgia
Threads	614	514	763
Posts	2,847	3,259	6,095
Tokens	366,121	389,392	541,233
Types	18,181	18,755	25,942

Table 1: Corpus Statistics

4.2 Modeling Interpersonal Interactions

This work first addresses the challenge of modeling interpersonal interactions. There are two methods of visualization that are explored: the coupling of people and affect, and that of people and actions.

The first step in the pairing of people and affect, was to identify and estimate rates of occurrence of important figures appearing in the text such as: family, husband, wife, mother, friend, and doctor. In order to extract these relations, the researcher manually compiled a list of terms indicating such relations through review of social support literature pertaining to the focal conditions and manual analysis of the text. Alternative names such as "hubby" for husband, "doc" and "dr" for doctor, and "rheumy" for rheumatologist, were included. Many of the instances of the word "family" appeared were references to family doctors or family history; these references were excluded from the estimates (Table 2).

These results show that certain types of individuals tend to appear in forum conversations for certain conditions over others: mothers, family and friends in breast cancer; sons, daughters, and "people" in Type 1 diabetes; and doctors in fibromyalgia. As can be seen, many posts do not include references to other people, but rather, focus on other areas such as patients' own experiences.

Term	Breast cancer	Diabetes	Fibromyalgia
Family	5.09	3.95	1.75
Husband	4.03	3.4	3.02
Wife	0.57	0.92	0.41
Mother	8.62	3.86	1.54
Son	1	3.86	0.61
Daughter	2.23	4.8	1
Friend	3.13	2.23	1.85
Doctor	13.28	13.49	16.42
People	8.42	13.37	8.96

Table 2: Percent of Posts Mentioning Important Roles

Next, the degree of affect expressed in proximity with these roles was investigated. Various sentiment lexicons are available, e.g. SentiWordNet, WordNet-Affect and the LIWC lexicon. Many lexicons classify words as positive or negative or by a limited set of emotions; however, with complex issues like health and interpersonal interactions, there may be multiple dimensions. WordNet-Affect was selected for its diverse set of emotion categories. Following a review of emotion research and preliminary content analysis of the corpus, seven emotions were selected on the basis of frequency and relevance to the conditions (Table 3).

Emotion	Example
Anger	I'm happy but also **mad** cuz I've been suffering and no doctor bothered to tell me about this.
Fear	I have the prescription right here and **afraid** to try it.
Frustration	It is extremely **discouraging** to hear that repeatedly...
Sadness	It's **sad** that I am so excited about getting some sleep.
Anxiety	You may be **worrying** over nothing.
Happiness	I'm so **happy** Lyrica is working for you.
Hope	I really **hope** this works for you.

Table 3: Examples of Emotional Expression

The percentage of posts expressing various affect types was calculated (Table 4). Across all conditions, fear and hope were most common. The highest proportion of fear, happiness and hope were seen in the breast cancer forum. Though anger and frustration were not as common as other emotions, higher levels of these emotions in diabetes are perhaps worthy of note.

Emotion	Breast cancer	Diabetes	Fibromyalgia
Hope	15.55	12.2	13.36
Anger	1.5	2.82	1.38
Frustration	0.78	3.49	1.75
Fear	16.05	11.11	6.32
Happiness	10.31	6.41	5.98
Sadness	10.26	9.91	8.21
Anxiety	9.85	8.29	4.81

Table 4: Percentage of Posts Expressing Emotions

Radar graphs illustrating the extent of emotional expression for the various roles were generated to facilitate comparison (Fig. 1). The light blue line, representing "doctor," is the innermost ring in all cases, demonstrating that emotional expression occurs least often in posts that mention doctors. Posts mentioning family (dark blue lines) were generally associated with higher degrees of emotional expression. Moreover, it is interesting that the patterns of emotional expression are quite different across conditions.

This paper also explores the visualization of discussion content by combining important figures and their actions. For this preliminary work, this action was undertaken with the fibromyalgia forum. The approach taken here was to extract high frequency verbs co-occurring in the same sentence with the target role. High frequency verbs that co-occurred with "doctor" included: "said," "told," "gave," "prescribed," "started," and "diagnosed." The verb "asked" also occurred frequently because forum participants often discussed or suggested questions to ask of doctors. Arranging person-verb pairings together in an interface could be a convenient way to acquire a sense of what patients are being told, and what medications doctors are prescribing. One might even add additional search constraints. For example, with regard to patient experiences with doctors prescribing Lyrica, the system might retrieve: "Recently my doctor put me on Lyrica which did help but had me…," "My doctor gave me a 'taper down' schedule," "My doctor prescribed Lyrica which I refused to take." Patients could use such a system to acquire a sense of the range of experiences that others have had with the drug.

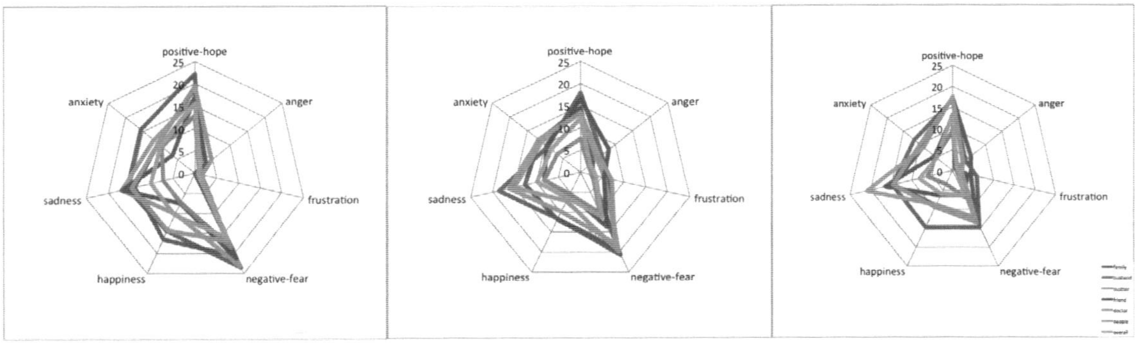

Figure 1: Percent of Posts Containing Affect for Breast Cancer (left), Diabetes (center), and Fibromyalgia (right)

4.3 Modeling Medication Use

Extant literature has found that though some categories of discussion content, e.g. self-introductions, research results and study invites, are common across conditions, other types of discussion content differ, e.g., breast cancer discussion more commonly focuses on treatments, and fibromyalgia discussions tend to focus more on medications (Chen, 2012). Thus, in this study, the researcher selected fibromyalgia as a case study for modeling discussion or comments about medication use.

The researcher created a lexicon of drug names for use in this study, drawn from a review of fibromyalgia literature and information resources, as well as manual review of corpus content. The most common medications are listed in Table 3.

Medication Name	# Posts	% Posts
Lyrica	670	11.36
Cymbalta	329	5.58
Savella	215	3.65
Neurontin	175	2.97
Tramadol	137	2.32
Ultram	79	1.34

Table 5: Common Medications

In order to model temporal differences in patient experience with medications, this study implemented a rule-based system for extraction at five phases in the adoption and use of a medication: adoption, current use, transition, switching, and discontinuation (Table 4). Adoption referred to when an individual began taking a medication. Current use referred to the period in which a person is taking a medication, and has no plans (that he or she reveals at least) to discontinue it. If an individual said that they first had a certain kind of experience with a medication, but that later on it changed, this was referred to as "transition." Discontinuation referred to when an individual stopped using one medication, and switching to when an individual changed from using one medication to another. Information such as whether side effects were temporary, withdrawal symptoms and interactions/contraindications was also extracted. These rules were implemented at the sentence level to prevent misattributions of side effects when multiple medications are mentioned in the same post.

Phase	Rule
Start	"start", "began"
Current Use	"I take", "is working", "currently", "been on" etc.
Transition (A & B)	A: "initially", "at first", "in the beginning" B: "after", "but", "then"
Switching	Fulfills both start and stop criterion or contains "switch".
Discontinuation	"stop", "off" or "quit"

Table 6: Medication Phase Extraction Rules

Using an interface designed for this study, the researcher investigated the reporting of side effects during each phase. Though the most common side effects for a drug were generally reported in multiple phases, certain side effects were reported in a given phase but not another. The last column, "no stage," depicts posts that did not contain explicit references to a specific phase of medication use.

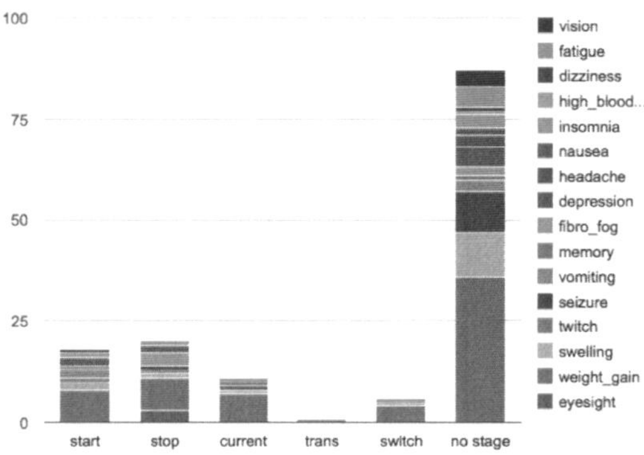

Figure 2: Mentions of Side Effects for Lyrica, Distinguished by Phase

Figure 2 shows that, for Lyrica, the predominant symptom that was reported by patients was weight gain, which appeared in almost all phases. Those who took Savella reported symptoms such as nausea, high blood pressure and dizziness, but there were also a number of reports that these disappear over time (Fig. 3).

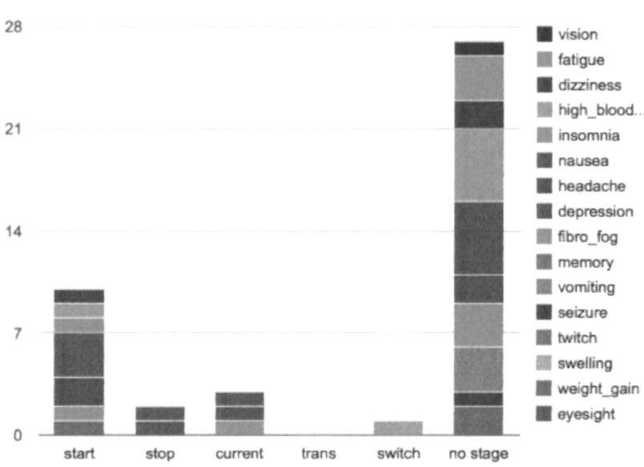

Figure 3: Mentions of Side Effects for Savella, Distinguished by Phase

Another important aspect of patients' experience with certain medications is their attitude towards it. In the previous section, the focus was on emotions because they are important for understanding interpersonal interaction. In the case of medications, rather than tracking the appearance of emotion, it may be useful to consider positive/negative polarity, whether the medication works or not, and side effects.

Thus, in addition to side effects, sentences with positive and negative sentiment were extracted using WordNet-Affect. Words from the "happiness" and "hope" categories of Word-Net Affect were used for positive sentiment, and the "fear," "anger" and "sadness" categories of WordNet-Affect were used for negative sentiment. A lexicon constructed by examining the corpus supplemented the words from WordNet-Affect.

A rule-based system was implemented to identify instances in which participants mentioned whether a medication worked or not. This was implemented using keywords such as "effective," "work" or "help," and recognizing negation. Table 7 lists the number of sentiment and perceptions of efficacy mentions. These do not add up to the number of medication mentions, as many times when medications appear, sentiment is neutral or ambiguous, and perception of efficacy is not the topic of the post. For example, the text might say, "The doctor started me on Savella yesterday."

These results illustrate the utility of extracting multiple facets of patient medication experience, e.g. positive/negative valence, efficacy and side effects, in order to better understand these experiences. Of particular note in these findings are that the estimates of one dimension may appear to conflict with another. For example, overall sentiment towards many medications is negative, but they are reported as working more often than not. The side effects tell yet another story; in many cases, the side effects are different in different phases. Reading the content, one comes to understand that, in an overwhelming number of cases, it is not that patients have found medications that solve all their problems, but that they are selecting ones that work and weighing the costs of the side effects. Thus, an interface that enables users to view all these nuances could be an invaluable asset.

Medication (# mentions)	**Polarity**		**Works**	
	Pos	**Neg**	**Yes**	**No**
Lyrica (934)	42	96	72	21
Cymbalta (413)	11	49	43	20
Savella (338)	21	23	23	2
Neurontin (235)	6	15	13	3
Tramadol (178)	6	3	16	4

Table 7: Sentiment and Efficacy of Medications

The last facet of medication use that was modeled was suggestions and/or recommendations from forum participants. One rule for doing this was by extracting sentences that began with verbs such as: "try," "take," "ask," "tell," and "go." Another was to extract sentences with "suggest" or "recommend." Doing so would retrieve advice such as: "Ask ur doctor about Elavil and Lyrica combination," "She suggested staying on the Lyrica.... while... doing the Vitamin D treatment," and "Word of advice: stop taking SSRI 's at least one week prior to start of Savella."

Forum posts are valuable because they are rich troves of patient experience; however, their richness means that it is also possible to get lost in the story. An interface that organizes the advice, but also allows one to link to the full text, can help users to orient themselves.

5 Discussion and Implications

This study employed NLP techniques in order to model two dimensions of patient experience in online support forums: interpersonal interactions and medication use. With regard to interactions with others, the prominence of different individuals and associated affect differed depending on condition. With regard to medication use, patients' experiences of medication use differed along phase of adoption.

These results may have important implications for the design of support forums. For example, in posts about family that contained fear and anxiety, certain topics tended to occur often: family history, families being supportive or non-supportive, and concerns of worrying the family. Forum participants presented various perspectives and suggestions concerning these issues. Thus, one recommendation is that systems could be designed to organize these various perspectives and suggestions in a form that is easier for the viewer to understand.

The results of this study also yielded various insights concerning fibromyalgia. In particular, the prominence of doctors, and relatively infrequent mention of family and friends was worthy of note. Previous research has found that fibromyalgia patients report a lack of understanding from medical practitioners and others around them (e.g. Madden & Sim, 2006; Sim & Madden, 2008). These reports of interactions with medical practitioners could help researchers to understand where gaps in knowledge and communication exist in both parties, and attempt to rectify them. The content from online support forums may also be helpful for researchers seeking to understand patients' patterns of interpersonal interaction.

The framework presented here for modeling medication use could be useful in many settings. Visualizing side effects at various points in the adoption, use and perhaps discontinuation of a medication could avert potential misunderstandings. For example, sentiment analysis on a medication X might be favorable overall; however, decomposing the posts by phase might show that users initially react favorably, but develop problems with it over time. Of course, the converse, that individuals experience certain side effects initially, but that these disappear over time, could also be true. Such information could be useful to a wide audience, including patients, clinicians, researchers and the pharmaceutical industry.

5.1 Limitations and Future Directions

There are many directions in which the current work could be improved. First, in the case of interpersonal interactions, affect was modeled as dichotomous variable indicating presence or absence. However, the level of emotional expression in a post could vary substantially. Thus, it may be useful to employ a lexicon that provides word rankings, such as SentiWordNet (Esuli & Sebastiani, 2006).

In the case of medication use, extraction of relevant sentences was based on presence of the medication name; thus, the system would not have identified sentences in which pronouns were used. A system that performed coreference resolution might identify significantly more references to medications.

Because previous research has indicated that medications are a common topic in fibromyalgia-related discussion, medication use was a natural target for modeling discussion content. However, it would also be useful to extend the modeling to include treatment experiences. Treatments such as massage and aqua therapy are often used in fibromyalgia, and treatments are the foci for many other conditions, such as breast cancer. Rather than considering phases of medication use, one might consider psychological state and expectations prior to, during and after treatment. Lastly, the interface that was developed for exploring medication use was specific to fibromyalgia; moving forward, it would be useful to expand the interface to other conditions.

Acknowledgments

The author would like to thank Dr. Stephanie W. Haas at the University of North Carolina, Chapel Hill, and the anonymous reviewers for their helpful suggestions in the preparation of this manuscript.

References

Kristin K. Barker. 2008. Electronic support groups, patient-consumers, and medicalization: The case of contested illness. *Journal of Health and Social Behavior, 49*(1):20-36.

Brant W. Chee, Richard Berlin, and Bruce Schatz. 2011. Predicting adverse drug events from personal health messages. In *AMIA Annu Symp Proc. 2011*: 217–226.

Annie T. Chen. 2012. Exploring online support spaces: Using cluster analysis to examine breast cancer, diabetes and fibromyalgia support groups. *Patient Education and Counseling, 87*(2): 250-257.

Andrea Civan and Wanda Pratt. 2007. Threading together patient expertise. In *AMIA Annu Symp Proc. 2007:* 140–144.

Andrea Esuli and Fabrizio Sebastiani. 2006. SENTI-WORDNET: A publicly available lexical resource for opinion mining. In *Proceedings of LREC-06, 5th Conference on Language Resources and Evaluation*: 417–422.

Jeong Yeob Han, Bret R. Shaw, Robert P. Hawkins, Suzanne Pingree, Fiona McTavish, and David H. Gustafson. 2008. Expressing positive emotions within online support groups by women with breast cancer. *Journal of Health Psychology, 13*(8):1002-1007.

Andrea Hartzler and Wanda Pratt. 2011. Managing the personal side of health: How patient expertise differs from the expertise of clinicians. *J Med Internet Res, 13(3):*e62.

Robert Leaman, Laura Wojtulewicz, Ryan Sullivan, Annie Skariah, Jian Yang, and Graciela Gonzalez. 2010. Towards internet-age pharmacovigilance: extracting adverse drug reactions from user posts to health-related social networks. In *Proceedings of the 2010 Workshop on Biomedical Natural Language Processing*: 117–125.

Kang Namkoong, Dhavan V. Shah, Jeong Yeob Han, Sojung C. Kim, Woohyun Yoo, David Fan, . . . David H. Gustafson. 2010. Expression and reception of treatment information in breast cancer support groups: How health self-efficacy moderates effects on emotional well-being. *Patient Education and Counseling, 81*(Suppl):S41-S47.

Sue Madden and Julius Sim. 2006. Creating meaning in fibromyalgia syndrome. *Social Science & Medicine, 63*: 2962–73.

Panote Siriaraya, Caleb Tang, Chee Siang Ang, Ulrike Pfeil, and Panayiotis Zaphiris. 2011. A comparison of empathic communication pattern for teenagers and older people in online support communities. *Behaviour & Information Technology, 30*(5): 617-628.

Irena Spasic, Farzaneh Sarafraz, John A Keane, and Goran Nenadic. 2010. Medication information extraction with linguistic pattern matching and semantic rules. *J Am Med Inform Assoc*;17:532-535.

Carlo Strapparava and Alessandro Valitutti. 2004. WordNet-Affect: an Affective Extension of WordNet. In *Proceedings of the 4th International Conference on Language Resources and Evaluation (LREC 2004)*:1083-1086.

Julius Sim and Sue Madden. 2008. Illness experience in fibromyalgia syndrome: A metasynthesis of qualitative studies. *Social Science & Medicine, 67*: 57–67.

Kristina Toutanova, Dan Klein, Christopher Manning, and Yoram Singer. 2003. Feature-Rich Part-of-Speech Tagging with a Cyclic Dependency Network. In *Proceedings of HLT-NAACL 2003*: 252-259.

Wei Wang, Krystl Haerian, Hojjat Salmasian, Rave Harpaz, Herbert Chase, and Carol Friedman. 2011. A Drug-Adverse Event Extraction Algorithm to Support Pharmacovigilance Knowledge Mining from PubMed Citations. In *AMIA Annu Symp Proc. 2011:* 1464–1470.

Yi-Chia Wang, Robert Kraut, John M. Levine. 2012. To stay or leave? The relationship of emotional and informational support to commitment in online health support groups. Presented at *CSCW 2012*. Seattle, WA.

Detecting Metaphor by Contextual Analogy

Eirini Florou
Dept of Linguistics, Faculty of Philosophy
University of Athens, Greece
eirini.florou@gmail.com

Abstract

As one of the most challenging issues in NLP, metaphor identification and its interpretation have seen many models and methods proposed. This paper presents a study on metaphor identification based on the semantic similarity between literal and non literal meanings of words that can appear at the same context.

1 Introduction

A *metaphor* is a literary figure of speech that describes a subject by asserting that it is, on some point of comparison, the same as another otherwise unrelated object. Metaphor is a type of analogy and is closely related to other rhetorical figures of speech that achieve their effects via association, comparison or resemblance including allegory, hyperbole, and simile. Rhetorical theorists and other scholars of language have discussed numerous dimensions of metaphors, though these nomenclatures are by no means universal nor necessarily mutually exclusive.

A very challenging task in linguistics is the metaphor identification and the its interpretation. *Metaphor identification procedure (MIP)* is a method for identifying metaphorically used words in discourse. It can be used to recognize metaphors in spoken and written language. The procedure aims to determine the relationship of a particular lexical unit in the discourse and recognize its use in a particular context as possibly metaphorical. Since many words can be considered metaphorical in different contexts, MIP requires a clear distinction between words that convey metaphorical meaning and those that do not, despite the fact that language generally differs in the degrees of metaphoricity.

In this paper we propose a method for identifying metaphorical usage in verbs. Our method is looking for semantic analogies in the context of a verb by comparing it against prior known instances of literal and non-literal usage of the same verb in different contexts. After discussing the metaphor identication literature (Section 2), we proceed to present our research proposal (Section 3) and to present and discuss our first experiments based on WordNet similarity measures (Section 4). Experiment results help us to draw conclusions and insights about analogical reasoning and memory-based learning for this task and to outline promising research paths (Section 5).

2 Background

According to Lakoff and Johnson (1980), metaphor is a productive phenomenon that operates at the level of mental processes. Metaphor is thus not merely a property of language, but rather a property of thought. This view was subsequently acquired and extended by a multitude of approaches (Grady, 1997; Narayanan, 1997; Fauconnier and Tuner, 2002; Feldman, 2006; Pinker, 2007) and the term *conceptual metaphor* was adopted to describe it.

In cognitive linguistics, conceptual metaphor, or cognitive metaphor, refers to the understanding of an idea, or conceptual domain, in terms of another, for example, understanding quantity in terms of directionality as in, for example, 'prices are rising'. A conceptual metaphor uses an idea and links it to another in order to better understand something. It is generaly accepted that the conceptual metaphor of viewing communication as a conduit is a large theory explained with a metaphor. These metaphors are prevalent in communication and everyone actually perceives and acts in accordance with the metaphors.

2.1 Metaphor Identification

Automatic processing of metaphor can be clearly divided into two subtasks: metaphor identification (distinguishing between literal and metaphorical language in text) and metaphor interpretation (identifying the intended literal meaning of a metaphorical expression). Both of them have been repeatedly attempted in NLP.

The most influential account of metaphor identification is that of Wilks (1978). According to Wilks, metaphors represent a violation of selectional restrictions in a given context. Consider an example such as *My car drinks gasoline*; the verb *drink* normally takes an *animate* subject and a *liquid* object.

This approach was automated by Fass (1991) in his MET* system. However, Fass himself indicated a problem with the method: it detects any kind of non-literalness or anomaly in language (metaphors, metonymies and others), i.e., it overgenerates with respect to metaphor. The techniques MET* uses to differentiate between those are mainly based on hand-coded knowledge, which implies a number of limitations. First, literalness is distinguished from non-literalness using selectional preference violation as an indicator. In the case that non-literalness is detected, the respective phrase is tested for being a metonymic relation using hand-coded patterns. If the system fails to recognize metonymy, it proceeds to search the knowledge base for a relevant analogy in order to discriminate metaphorical relations from anomalous ones.

Berber Sardinha (2002) describes a collocation-based method for spotting metaphors in corpora. His procedure is based on the notion that two words sharing collocations in a corpus may have been used metaphorically. The first step was to pick out a reasonable number of words that had an initial likelihood of being part of metaphorical expressions. First, words with marked frequency (in relation to a large general corpus of Portuguese) were selected. Then, their collocations were scored for closeness in meaning using a program called 'distance' (Padwardhan et al., 2003), under the assumption that words involved in metaphorical expressions tend to be denotationally unrelated. This program accesses WordNet in order to set the scores for each word pair. The scores had to be adapted in order for them to be useful for metaphor analysis. Finally, those words that had an acceptable semantic distance score were evaluated for their metaphoric potential. The results indicated that the procedure did pick up some major metaphors in the corpus, but it also captured metonyms.

Another approach to finding metaphor in corpora is CorMet, presented by Mason (2004). It works by searching corpora of different domains for verbs that are used in similar patterns. When the system spots different verbs with similar selectional preferences (i.e., with similar words in subject, object and complement positions), it considers them potential metaphors.

CorMet requires specific domain corpora and a list of verbs for each domain. The specific domain corpora are compiled by searching the web for domain-specific words. These words are selected by the author, based on his previous knowledge of subject areas and are stemmed. The most typical verbs for each specific corpus are identified through frequency markedness, by comparing the frequencies of word stems in the domain corpus with those of the BNC. The resulting words have a frequency that is statistically higher in the domain corpus than in the reference corpus. These stems are then classified according to part of speech by consulting WordNet.

Alternative approaches search for metaphors of a specific domain defined a priori in a specific type of discourse. The method by Gedigian et al. (2006) discriminates between literal and metaphorical use. They trained a maximum entropy classifier for this purpose. They obtained their data by extracting the lexical items whose frames are related to MOTION and CURE from FrameNet (Fillmore et al., 2003). Then, they searched the PropBank Wall Street Journal corpus (Kingsbury and Palmer, 2002) for sentences containing such lexical items and annotated them with respect to metaphoricity.

Birke and Sarkar (2006) present a sentence clustering approach for non-literal language recognition implemented in the TroFi system (Trope Finder). This idea originates from a similarity-based word sense disambiguation method developed by Karov and Edelman (1998). The method employs a set of seed sentences, where the senses are annotated, computes similarity between the sentence containing the word to be disambiguated and all of the seed sentences and selects the sense corresponding to the annotation in the most similar seed sentences. Birke and Sarkar (2006) adapt this algorithm to perform a two-way classification: literal vs. non-literal, and they do not clearly define the kinds of tropes they aim to discover. They attain a performance of 53.8% in terms of f-score.

Both Birke and Sarkar (2006) and Gedigian et al. (2006) focus only on metaphors expressed by a verb. As opposed to that the approach of Krishnakumaran and Zhu (2007) deals with verbs, nouns and adjectives as parts of speech. They use hyponymy relation in WordNet and word bigram counts to predict metaphors at the sentence level. Given an IS-A metaphor (e.g. The world is a stage) they verify if the two nouns involved are in hyponymy relation in WordNet, and if this is not the case then this sentence is tagged as containing a metaphor. Along with this they consider expressions containing a verb or an adjective used metaphorically. Hereby they calculate bigram probabilities of verb-noun and adjective-noun pairs (including the hyponyms/hypernyms of the noun in question). If the combination is not observed in the data with sufficient frequency, the system tags the sentence containing it as metaphorical. This idea is a modification of the selectional preference view of Wilks (1978).

Berber Sardinha (2010) presents a computer program for identifying metaphor candidates, which is intended as a tool that can help researchers find words that are more likely to be metaphor vehicles in a corpus. As such, it may be used as a device for signalling those words that the researcher might want to focus on first, because these have a higher probability of being metaphors in their corpus, or conversely, it may indicate those words that are worth looking at because of their apparent low probability of being metaphors. The program is restricted to finding one component of linguistic metaphors and has been trained on business texts in Portuguese, and so it is restricted to that kind of text.

Shutova et al. (2012) present an approach to automatic metaphor identification in unrestricted text. Starting from a small seed set of manually annotated metaphorical expressions, the system is capable of harvesting a large number of metaphors of similar syntactic structure from a corpus. Their method captures metaphoricity by means of verb and noun clustering. Their system starts from a seed set of metaphorical expressions exemplifying a range of source-target domain mappings; performs unsupervised noun clustering in order to harvest various target concepts associated with the same source domain; by means of unsupervised verb clustering creates a source domain verb lexicon; searches the BNC for metaphorical expressions describing the target domain concepts using the verbs from the source domain lexicon. According to Shutova et al. (2012), abstract concepts that are associated with the same source domain are often related to each other on an intuitive and rather structural level, but their meanings, however, are not necessarily synonymous or even semantically close. The consensus is that the lexical items exposing similar behavior in a large body of text most likely have the same meaning. They tested their system starting with a collection of metaphorical expressions representing verb-subject and verb-object constructions, where the verb is used metaphorically. They evaluated the precision of metaphor identification with the help of human judges. Shutova's system employing unsupervised methods for metaphor identification operates with precision of 0.79.

For verb and noun clustering, they used the *subcategorization frame acquisition* system by Preiss et al. (2007) and *spectral clustering* for both verbs and nouns. They acquired selectional preference distributions for Verb-Subject and Verb-Object relations from the BNC parsed by RASP; adopted Resnik's selectional preference measure; and applied to a number of tasks in NLP including word sense disambiguation (Resnik, 1997).

3 Detecting the metaphor use of a word by contextual analogy

The first task for metaphor processing is its identification in a text. We have seen above how previous approaches either utilize hand-coded knowledge (Fass, 1991), (Krishnakumaran and Zhu, 2007) or reduce the task to searching for metaphors of a specific domain defined a priori in a specific type of discourse (Gedigian et al., 2006).

By contrast, our research proposal is a method that relies on distributional similarity; the assumption is that the lexical items showing similar behaviour in a large body of text most likely have related meanings. Noun clustering, specifically, is central to our approach. It is traditionally assumed that noun clusters produced using distributional clustering contain concepts that are similar to each other.

3.1 Word Sense Disambiguation and Metaphor

One of the major developments in metaphor research in the last several years has been the focus on identifying and explicating metaphoric language in real discourse. Most research in Word Sense Disambiguation has concentrated on using contextual features, typically neighboring words, to help infer the correct sense of a target word. In contrast, we are going to discover the predominant sense of a word from raw text because the first sense heuristic is so powerful and because manually sense-tagged data is not always available.

In word sense disambiguation, the first or predominant sense heuristic is used when information from the context is not sufficient to make a more informed choice. We will need to use parsed data to find distributionally similar words (nearest neighbors) to the target word which will reflect the different senses of the word and have associated distributional similarity scores which could be used for ranking the senses according to prevalence.

The predominant sense for a target word is determined from a prevalence ranking of the possible senses for that word. The senses will come from a predefined inventory which might be a dictionary or WordNet-like resource. The ranking will be derived using a distributional thesaurus automatically produced from a large corpus, and a semantic similarity measure will be defined over the sense inventory. The distributional thesaurus will contain a set of words that will be 'nearest neighbors' Lin (1998) to the target word with respect to similarity of the way in which they will be distributed. The thesaurus will assign a distributional similarity score to each neighbor word, indicating its closeness to the target word.

We assume that the number and distributional similarity scores of neighbors pertaining to a given sense of a target word will reflect the prevalence of that sense in the corpus from which the thesaurus was derived. This is because the more prevalent senses of the word will appear more frequently and in more contexts than other, less prevalent senses. The neighbors of the target word relate to its senses, but are themselves word forms rather than senses. The senses of the target word have to be predefined in a sense inventory and we will need to use a semantic similarity score which will be defined over the sense inventory to relate the neighbors to the various senses of the target word.

The measure for ranking the senses will use the sum total of the distributional similarity scores of the k nearest neighbors. This total will be divided between the senses of the target word by apportioning the distributional similarity of each neighbor to the senses. The contribution of each neighbor will be measured in terms of its distributional similarity score so that 'nearer' neighbors count for more. The distributional similarity score of each neighbor will be divided between the various senses rather than attributing the neighbor to only one sense. This is done because neighbors can relate to more than one sense due to relationships such as systematic polysemy. To sum up, we will rank the senses of the target word by apportioning the distributional similarity scores of the top k neighbors between the senses. Each distributional similarity score (dss) will be weighted by a normalized semantic similarity score (sss) between the sense and the neighbor.

We chose to use the distributional similarity score described by Lin (1998) because it is an unparameterized measure which uses pointwise mutual information to weight features and which has been shown Weeds et al. (2004) to be highly competitive in making predictions of semantic similarity. This measure is based on Lin's information-theoretic similarity theorem (Lin, 1997) : The similarity between A and B is measured by the ratio between the amount of information needed to state the commonality of A and B and the information needed to fully describe what A and B are.

3.2 Similarity-based metaphorical usage estimation

After the noun clustering and finding the predominant sense of an ambiguous word, as the local context of this word can give important clues to which of its senses was intended, the metaphor identification system will start from a small set of seed metaphors (the seed metaphors are a model extracted from metaphor-annotated and dependency-parsed sentences), to point out if a word is used literaly or non literaly at the certain context. For the purposes of this work as context should be considered the verb of the seed metaphors. We are going to take as seed metaphors the examples of Lakoff's Master Metaphor List (Lakoff et al., 1991).

Then, as we will have already find the k nearest neighbors for each noun and we will have created clusters for nouns which can appear at the same context, we will be able to calculate their semantic similarity. We then will use the WordNet similarity package Padwardhan et al. (2003) in order to measure the semantic similarity between each member of the cluster and the noun of the annotated metaphor. The WordNet similarity package supports a range of WordNet similarity scores. We will experiment using a lot of these in order to find those which perform the best. Each time, we want to estimate if the similarity between the target noun and the seed metaphor will be higher than the similarity between the target noun and another literal word which could appear at the certain context. Calculating the target word's semantic similarity with the seed words (literal or non literal) we will be able to find out if the certain word has a literal or metaphorical meaning at the concrete context.

By this way, starting from an already known metaphor, we will be able to identify other non literal uses of words which may appear at the same context, estimating the similarity measure of the target word between the seed metaphor and another literal meaning of a word at the same context. If the semantic similarity's rate of the target word (for instance the word 'assistance' at the context of the verb 'give') and the annotated metaphor (like 'quidance' at the certaincontext) is higher that the rate of the target word and the seed word with the literal meaning (for example the word 'apple' at the same context) , then we will be able to assume that the tartget word is used metaphorically, at the concrete context.

4 First Experiments and Results

In order to evaluate our method we search for common English verbs which can take either literal or non literal predicates. As the most common verbs (be, have and do) can function as verbs and auxiliary verbs, we didn't use them for our experiments. As a consequence, we chose common function verbs which can take a direct object as predicate. More specifically, at our experiments we concentrated on literal and non literal predicates of the verbs: *break, catch, cut, draw, drop, find, get, hate, hear, hold, keep, kill, leave, listen, lose, love, make, pay, put, save, see, take, want.*

We used the *VU Amsterdam Metaphor Corpus*[1] in order to extract data for our experiments. We used shallow heuristics to match verbs and direct objects, with manually checking and correcting the result. We have also used the *British National Corpus (BNC)*, in order to take more samples, mostly literal. In the case of he BNC, we were able to extract the direct object from the depency parses, but had manually controlled metaphorical vs. literal usage. In all, we collected 124 instances of literal usage and 275 instances of non-literal usage involving 311 unique nouns.

With this body of literal and non-literal contexts, we tried every possible combination of one literal and one non-literal object for each verb as seed, and tested with the remaining words. The mean results are collected in Table 1, where we see how the LCS-based measures by Resnik (1997) and Wu and Palmer (1994) performed the best.

One observation is that the differences between the different measures although significant, they are not as dramatic as to effect reversals in the decision. This is apparent in the *simple voting* results (right-most column in Table 1) where all measures yield identical results. Only when differences in the similarities accumulate before the comparison between literal and non-literal context is made (three left-most columns in Table 1), does the choice of similarity measure make a difference.

Another observation pertains to relaxing the dependency on WordNet so that method can be based on similarities defined over more widely available lexical resources. In this respect, the low F-score by the adapted Lesk measure is not very encouraging, as variations of the Lesk measure could be defined over the glosses in digital dictionaries without explicit WordNet-style relations. Combined with the high valuation of methods using the LCS, this leads us to conclude that the relative taxonomic position is a very important factor.

Finally, and happily counter to our prior intuition, we would like to note the robustness of the method to the number of different senses test words have: plotting the F-score against the number of senses did not result in consistently deteriorating results as the senses multiply (Figure 1).[2] If this had happened, we would have con-

[1]Please see `http://www.metaphorlab.vu.nl/en/research/funded_research/VU-Amsterdam-Metaphor-Corpus`

[2]Although some of the nouns in our collection have as many as 33 senses, we have only plotted the data for up to 15 senses; the data is too sparse to be reasonably usuable beyond that point.

Table 1: Fβ=1 scores for all combinations of seven different similarity measures and five ways of deriving a single judgement on literal usage by testing all senses of a word against all senses of the seed words.

Measure	Maximum		Average		Sum		Simple Voting	
	Mean	Std dev	Mean	Std dev	Mean	Std dev	Mean	Std dev
Adapted Lesk	63.87	6.96	63.39	9.41	64.77	6.47	68.64	10.69
Jiang *et al.* (1997)	70.92	9.19	64.31	8.41	65.14	6.45	68.64	10.69
Lin (1998)	71.35	10.70	70.39	10.02	70.07	9.47	68.64	10.69
Path length	67.63	9.83	**72.60**	8.83	65.33	6.91	68.64	10.69
Resnik (1993)	66.14	9.13	**72.92**	9.08	70.54	8.24	68.64	10.69
Wu and Palmer (1994)	70.84	9.38	**72.97**	9.05	66.02	6.82	68.64	10.69

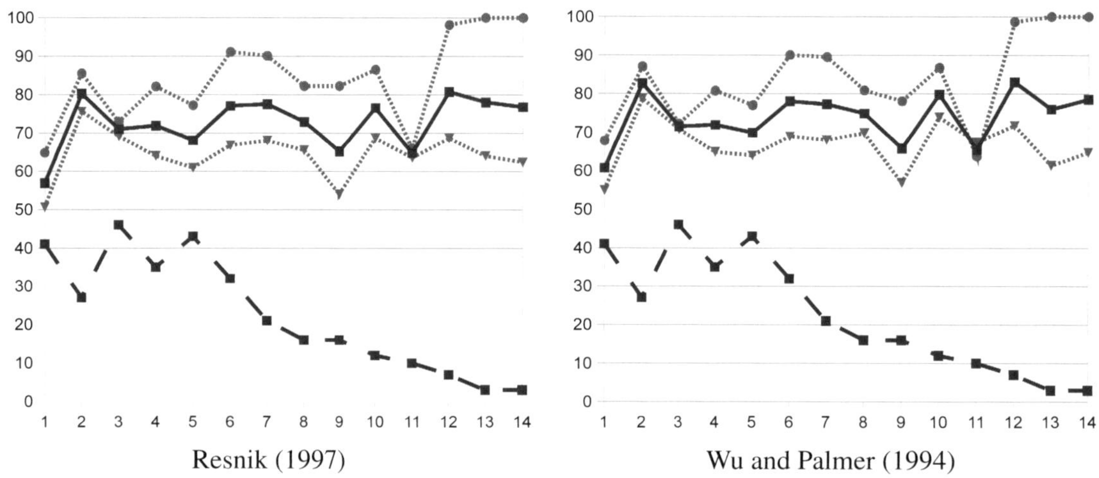

Figure 1: Plot of precision (dotted line, circles), recall (dotted line, triangles), and $F_{\beta=1}$ score (solid line) versus the number of different senses for a word. Also includes the frequency of each sense count (dashed line, squares). For both measures, final judgement is made on average similarity of all senses.

fronted a Catch-22 situation where disambiguation is needed in order to carry out metaphora identification, a disambiguation task itself. The way things stand, our method can be successfully applied to shallow NLP tasks or as a pre-processing and optimization step for WSD and parsing.

5 Conclusions

In this paper, we presented a mildly supervised method for identifying metaphorical verb usage by taking the local context into account. This procedure is different from the majority of the previous works in that it does not rely on any metaphor-specic hand-coded knowledge, but rather on previous observed unambiguous usages of the verb. The method can operates on open domain texts and the memory needed for the seeds can be relatively easily collected by mining unannotated corpora. Furthermore, our method differs as compares the meaning of nouns which appear at the same context without associating them with concepts and then comparing the concepts. We selected this procedure as words of the same abstract concept maybe not appear at the same context while words from different concepts could appear at the same context, especially when the certain context is metaphorical. Although the system has been tested only on verb-direct object metaphors, the described identi- cation method should be immediately applicable to a wider range of word classes, which is one of the future research directions we will pursue. Another promising research direction relates to our observation regarding the importance of measuring similarities by considering the relative taxonomic position of the two concepts; more specifically, we will experiment with clustering methods over unannotated corpora as a way of producing the taxonomy over which we will dene some Resnik-esque similarity measure.

References

Tony Berber Sardinha. 2002. Metaphor in early applied linguistics writing: A corpus-based analysis of lexis in dissertations. In *I Conference on Metaphor in Language and Thought*.

Tony Berber Sardinha. 2010. Creating and using the Corpus do Portugues and the frequency dictionary of portuguese. *Working with Portuguese Corpora*.

Julia Birke and Anoop Sarkar. 2006. A clustering approach for the nearly unsupervised recognition of nonliteral language. In *Proceedings of EACL-06*, pages 329–336. Trento, Italy.

Dan Fass. 1991. met*: a method for discriminating metonymy and metaphor by computer. *Computational Linguistics*, 17(1).

Gilles Fauconnier and Mark Tuner. 2002. *The Way We Think: Conceptual Blending and the Mind's Hidden Complexities*. Basic Books.

Jerome Feldman. 2006. *From Molecule to Metaphor: A Neutral Theory of Language*. The MIT Press.

Charles Fillmore, Christopher Johnson and Miriam Petruck. 2003. Background to framenet. *International Journal of Lexicography*, 16(3):235–250.

Matt Gedigian, John Bryant, Srini Narayanan, and Branimir Ciric. 2006. Catching metaphors. In *Proceedings of the 3rd Workshop on Scalable Natural Language Understanding*, pages 41–48. New York.

Joseph Edward Grady. 1997. *Foundations of meaning: primary metaphors and primary scenes*. University Microfilms International.

Yael Karov and Shimon Edelman. 1998. Similarity-based word sense disambiguation. *Computational Linguistics*, 24(1):41–59.

Paul Kingsbury and Martha Palmer. 2002. From treebank to propbank. In *Proceedings of LREC-2002*, pages 1989–1993. Gran Canaria, Canary Islands, Spain.

Saisuresh Krishnakumaran and Xiaojin Zhu. 2007. Hunting elusive metaphors using lexical resources. In *Proceedings of the Workshop on Computational Approaches to Figurative Language, April, 2007, Rochester, New York*, pages 13–20. Association for Computational Linguistics, Rochester, New York. URL http://www.aclweb.org/anthology/W/W07/W07-0103.

George Lakoff, Jane Espenson, and Alan Schwartz. 1991. *The master metaphor list*. University of California at Berkeley.

George Lakoff and Mark Johnson. 1980. *Metaphors We Live By*. University of Chicago Press.

Dekang Lin. 1997. Using syntactic dependency as local context to resolve word sense ambiguity. In *Proceedings of ACL-97*, pages 64–71. Madrid, Spain.

Dekang Lin. 1998. An information-theoretic definition of similarity. In *Proceedings of the 15th International Conference on Machine Learning (ICML-98). Madison, WI, USA, July 1998.*, page 296304.

Zachary Mason. 2004. Cormet: a computational, corpus-based conventional metaphor extraction system. *Computational Linguistics*, 30(1):23–44.

Srini Narayanan. 1997. *Knowledge-based Action Representations for Metaphor and Aspect (KARMA)*. University of Californial.

Siddharth Padwardhan, Satanjeev Banerjee, and Ted Pedersen. 2003. Using measures of semantic relatedness for word sense disambiguation. In *Proceedings of the 4th International Conference on Intelligent Text Processing and Computational Linguistics (CICLing-03), Mexico City*, pages 241–257.

Stephen Pinker. 2007. *The Stuff of Thought: Language as a Window into Human Nature*. Viking Adult.

Judita Preiss, Ted Briscoe, and Anna Korhonen. 2007. A system for large-scale acquisition of verbal, nominal and adjectival subcategorization frames from corpora. In *Proceedings of ACL-07*, volume 45, page 912.

Philip Resnik. 1997. Selectional preference and sense disambiguation. In *ACL SIGLEX Workshop on Tagging Text with Lexical Semantics*. Washington, D.C.

Ekaterina Shutova, Simone Teufel and Anna Korhonen. 2012. Statistical metaphor processing. *Computational Linguistics*, 39(2).

Julie Weeds, David Weir, and Diana McCarthy. 2004. Characterising measures of lexical distributional similarity. In *Proceedings of Coling 2004*, pages 1015–1021. COLING, Geneva, Switzerland.

Yorick Wilks. 1978. Making preferences more active. *Artificial Intelligence*, 11(3).

Zhibiao Wu and Martha Palmer. 1994. Verb semantics and lexical selection. In *Proceedings of the 32nd Annual Meeting of the ACL (ACL-04)*, pages 133–138.

Survey on parsing three dependency representations for English

Angelina Ivanova **Stephan Oepen** **Lilja Øvrelid**

University of Oslo, Department of Informatics
{angelii|oe|liljao}@ifi.uio.no

Abstract

In this paper we focus on practical issues of data representation for dependency parsing. We carry out an experimental comparison of (a) three syntactic dependency schemes; (b) three data-driven dependency parsers; and (c) the influence of two different approaches to lexical category disambiguation (aka tagging) prior to parsing. Comparing parsing accuracies in various setups, we study the interactions of these three aspects and analyze which configurations are easier to learn for a dependency parser.

1 Introduction

Dependency parsing is one of the mainstream research areas in natural language processing. Dependency representations are useful for a number of NLP applications, for example, machine translation (Ding and Palmer, 2005), information extraction (Yakushiji et al., 2006), analysis of typologically diverse languages (Bunt et al., 2010) and parser stacking (Øvrelid et al., 2009). There were several shared tasks organized on dependency parsing (CoNLL 2006–2007) and labeled dependencies (CoNLL 2008–2009) and there were a number of attempts to compare various dependencies intrinsically, e.g. (Miyao et al., 2007), and extrinsically, e.g. (Wu et al., 2012).

In this paper we focus on practical issues of data representation for dependency parsing. The central aspects of our discussion are (a) three dependency formats: two 'classic' representations for dependency parsing, namely, *Stanford Basic* (SB) and *CoNLL Syntactic Dependencies* (CD), and bilexical dependencies from the HPSG English Resource Grammar (ERG), so-called *DELPH-IN Syntactic Derivation Tree* (DT), proposed recently by Ivanova et al. (2012); (b) three state-of-the art statistical parsers: Malt (Nivre et al., 2007), MST (McDonald et al., 2005) and the parser of Bohnet and Nivre (2012); (c) two approaches to word-category disambiguation, e.g. exploiting common PTB tags and using supertags (i.e. specialized ERG lexical types).

We parse the formats and compare accuracies in all configurations in order to determine how parsers, dependency representations and grammatical tagging methods interact with each other in application to automatic syntactic analysis.

SB and CD are derived automatically from phrase structures of Penn Treebank to accommodate the needs of fast and accurate dependency parsing, whereas DT is rooted in the formal grammar theory HPSG and is independent from any specific treebank. For DT we gain more expressivity from the underlying linguistic theory, which challenges parsing with statistical tools. The structural analysis of the schemes in Ivanova et al. (2012) leads to the hypothesis that CD and DT are more similar to each other than SB to DT. We recompute similarities on a larger treebank and check whether parsing results reflect them.

The paper has the following structure: an overview of related work is presented in Section 2; treebanks, tagsets, dependency schemes and parsers used in the experiments are introduced in Section 3; analysis of parsing results is discussed in Section 4; conclusions and future work are outlined in Section 5.

2 Related work

Schwartz et al. (2012) investigate which dependency representations of several syntactic structures are easier to parse with supervised versions of the Klein and Manning (2004) parser, ClearParser (Choi and Nicolov, 2009), MST Parser, Malt and the Easy First Non-directional parser (Goldberg and Elhadad, 2010). The results imply that all parsers consistently perform better when (a) coordination has one of the conjuncts as the head rather than the coordinating conjunction;

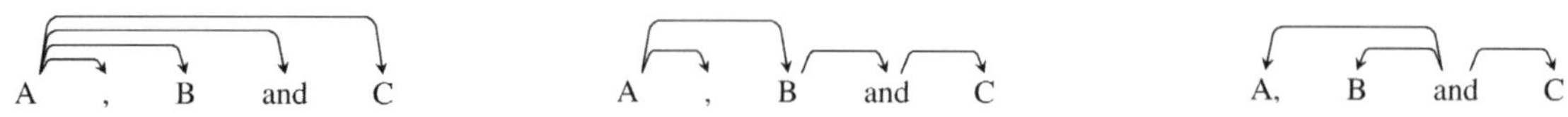

Figure 1: Annotation of coordination structure in SB, CD and DT (left to right) dependency formats

(b) the noun phrase is headed by the noun rather than by determiner; (c) prepositions or subordinating conjunctions, rather than their NP or clause arguments, serve as the head in prepositional phrase or subordinated clauses. Therefore we can expect (a) Malt and MST to have fewer errors on coordination structures parsing SB and CD than parsing DT, because SB and CD choose the first conjunct as the head and DT chooses the coordinating conjunction as the head; (b,c) no significant differences for the errors on noun and prepositional phrases, because all three schemes have the noun as the head of the noun phrase and the preposition as the head of the prepositional phrase.

Miwa et al. (2010) present intristic and extristic (event-extraction task) evaluation of six parsers (GDep, Bikel, Stanford, Charniak-Johnson, C&C and Enju parser) on three dependency formats (Stanford Dependencies, CoNLL-X, and Enju PAS). Intristic evaluation results show that all parsers have the highest accuracies with the CoNLL-X format.

3 Data and software

3.1 Treebanks

For the experiments in this paper we used the **Penn Treebank** (Marcus et al., 1993) and the **DeepBank** (Flickinger et al., 2012). The latter is comprised of roughly 82% of the sentences of the first 16 sections of the Penn Treebank annotated with full HPSG analyses from the English Resource Grammar (ERG). The DeepBank annotations are created on top of the raw text of the PTB. Due to imperfections of the automatic tokenization, there are some token mismatches between DeepBank and PTB. We had to filter out such sentences to have consistent number of tokens in the DT, SB and CD formats. For our experiments we had available a training set of 22209 sentences and a test set of 1759 sentences (from Section 15).

3.2 Parsers

In the experiments described in Section 4 we used parsers that adopt different approaches and implement various algorithms.

Malt (Nivre et al., 2007): transition-based dependency parser with local learning and greedy search.

MST (McDonald et al., 2005): graph-based dependency parser with global near-exhaustive search.

Bohnet and Nivre (2012) parser: transition-based dependency parser with joint tagger that implements global learning and beam search.

3.3 Dependency schemes

In this work we extract DeepBank data in the form of bilexical syntactic dependencies, **DELPH-IN Syntactic Derivation Tree (DT)** format. We obtain the exact same sentences in **Stanford Basic (SB)** format from the automatic conversion of the PTB with the Stanford parser (de Marneffe et al., 2006) and in the **CoNLL Syntactic Dependencies (CD)** representation using the LTH Constituent-to-Dependency Conversion Tool for Penn-style Treebanks (Johansson and Nugues, 2007).

SB and CD represent the way to convert PTB to bilexical dependencies; in contrast, DT is grounded in linguistic theory and captures decisions taken in the grammar. Figure 1 demonstrates the differences between the formats on the coordination structure. According to Schwartz et al. (2012), analysis of coordination in SB and CD is easier for a statistical parser to learn; however, as we will see in section 4.3, DT has more expressive power distinguishing structural ambiguities illustrated by the classic example *old men and women*.

3.4 Part-of-speech tags

We experimented with two tag sets: **PTB tags** and lexical types of the ERG grammar - **supertags**.

PTB tags determine the *part of speech* (PoS) and some *morphological features*, such as number for nouns, degree of comparison for adjectives and adverbs, tense and agreement with person and number of subject for verbs, etc.

Supertags are composed of *part-of-speech*, *valency* in the form of an ordered sequence of complements, and *annotations* that encompass category-internal subdivisions, e.g. mass vs. count vs. proper nouns, intersective vs. scopal adverbs, or referential vs. expletive pronouns. Example of a supertag: *v_np_is_le* (verb "is" that takes noun phrase as a complement).

There are 48 tags in the PTB tagset and 1091 supertags in the set of lexical types of the ERG.

The state of the-art accuracy of PoS-tagging on in-domain test data using gold-standard tokenization is roughly 97% for the PTB tagset and approximately 95% for the ERG supertags (Ytrestøl, 2011). Supertagging for the ERG grammar is an ongoing research effort and an off-the-shelf supertagger for the ERG is not currently available.

4 Experiments

In this section we give a detailed analysis of parsing into SB, CD and DT dependencies with Malt, MST and the Bohnet and Nivre (2012) parser.

4.1 Setup

For Malt and MST we perform the experiments on gold PoS tags, whereas the Bohnet and Nivre (2012) parser predicts PoS tags during testing.

Prior to each experiment with Malt, we used MaltOptimizer to obtain settings and a feature model; for MST we exploited default configuration; for the Bohnet and Nivre (2012) parser we set the beam parameter to 80 and otherwise employed the default setup.

With regards to evaluation metrics we use labelled attachment score (LAS), unlabeled attachment score (UAS) and label accuracy (LACC) excluding punctuation. Our results cannot be directly compared to the state-of-the-art scores on the Penn Treebank because we train on sections 0-13 and test on section 15 of WSJ. Also our results are not strictly inter-comparable because the setups we are using are different.

4.2 Discussion

The results that we are going to analyze are presented in Tables 1 and 2. Statistical significance was assessed using Dan Bikel's parsing evaluation comparator[1] at the 0.001 significance level. We inspect three different aspects in the interpretation of these results: parser, dependency format and tagset. Below we will look at these three angles in detail.

From the **parser** perspective Malt and MST are not very different in the traditional setup with gold PTB tags (Table 1, *Gold PTB tags*). The Bohnet and Nivre (2012) parser outperforms Malt on CD and DT and MST on SB, CD and DT with PTB tags even though it does not receive gold PTB tags during test phase but predicts them (Table 2, *Predicted PTB tags*). This is explained by the fact that the Bohnet and Nivre (2012) parser implements a novel approach to parsing: beam-search algorithm with global structure learning.

MST "loses" more than Malt when parsing SB with gold supertags (Table 1, *Gold supertags*). This parser exploits context features *"POS tag of each intervening word between head and dependent"* (McDonald et al., 2006). Due to the far larger size of the supertag set compared to the PTB tagset, such features are sparse and have low frequencies. This leads to the lower scores of parsing accuracy for MST. For the Bohnet and Nivre (2012) parser the complexity of supertag prediction has significant negative influence on the attachment and labeling accuracies (Table 2, *Predicted supertags*). The addition of gold PTB tags as a feature lifts the performance of the Bohnet and Nivre (2012) parser to the level of performance of Malt and MST on CD with gold supertags and Malt on SB with gold supertags (compare Table 2, *Predicted supertags + gold PTB*, and Table 1, *Gold supertags*).

Both Malt and MST benefit slightly from the combination of gold PTB tags and gold supertags (Table 1, *Gold PTB tags + gold supertags*). For the Bohnet and Nivre (2012) parser we also observe small rise of accuracy when gold supertags are provided as a feature for prediction of PTB tags (compare *Predicted PTB tags* and *Predicted PTB tags + gold supertags* sections of Table 2).

The parsers have different running times: it takes minutes to run an experiment with Malt, about 2 hours with MST and up to a day with the Bohnet and Nivre (2012) parser.

From the point of view of the **dependency format**, SB has the highest LACC and CD is first-rate on UAS for all three parsers in most of the configurations (Tables 1 and 2). This means that SB is easier to label and CD is easier to parse structurally. DT appears to be a more difficult target format because it is both hard to label and attach in most configurations. It is not an unexpected result, since SB and CD are both derived from PTB phrase-structure trees and are oriented to ease dependency parsing task. DT is not custom-designed

[1] `http://nextens.uvt.nl/depparse-wiki/SoftwarePage#scoring`

Gold PTB tags

	LAS		UAS		LACC	
	Malt	MST	Malt	MST	Malt	MST
SB	**89.21**	88.59	90.95	90.88	**93.58**	**92.79**
CD	88.74	**88.72**	**91.89**	**92.01**	91.29	91.34
DT	85.97	86.36	89.22	90.01	88.73	89.22

Gold supertags

	LAS		UAS		LACC	
	Malt	MST	Malt	MST	Malt	MST
SB	87.76	85.25	90.63	88.56	92.38	90.29
CD	88.22	87.27	**91.17**	90.41	91.30	90.74
DT	**89.92**	**89.58**	90.96	**90.56**	**92.50**	**92.64**

Gold PTB tags + gold supertags

	LAS		UAS		LACC	
	Malt	MST	Malt	MST	Malt	MST
SB	90.32[1]	89.43[1]	91.90[1]	91.84[2]	**94.48**[1]	93.26[1]
CD	89.59[1]	89.37[2]	**92.43**[1]	**92.77**[2]	92.32[1]	92.07[2]
DT	**90.69**[1]	**91.19**[2]	91.83[1]	92.33[2]	93.10[1]	**93.69**[2]

Table 1: Parsing results of Malt and MST on Stanford Basic (SB), CoNLL Syntactic Dependencies (CD) and DELPH-IN Syntactic Derivation Tree (DT) formats. Punctuation is excluded from the scoring. *Gold PTB tags:* Malt and MST are trained and tested on gold PTB tags. *Gold supertags:* Malt and MST are trained and tested on gold supertags. *Gold PTB tags + gold supertags:* Malt and MST are trained on gold PTB tags and gold supertags. [1] denotes a feature model in which gold PTB tags function as PoS and gold supertags act as additional features (in CPOSTAG field); [2] stands for the feature model which exploits gold supertags as PoS and uses gold PTB tags as extra features (in CPOSTAG field).

Predicted PTB tags

	LAS	UAS	LACC
	Bohnet and Nivre (2012)		
SB	89.56	92.36	**93.30**
CD	**89.77**	**93.01**	92.10
DT	88.26	91.63	90.72

Predicted supertags

	LAS	UAS	LACC
	Bohnet and Nivre (2012)		
SB	85.41	89.38	**90.17**
CD	**86.73**	**90.73**	89.72
DT	85.76	89.50	88.56

Pred. PTB tags + gold supertags

	LAS	UAS	LACC
	Bohnet and Nivre (2012)		
SB	90.32	93.01	**93.85**
CD	90.55	**93.56**	92.79
DT	**91.51**	92.99	**93.88**

Pred. supertags + gold PTB

	LAS	UAS	LACC
	Bohnet and Nivre (2012)		
SB	87.20	90.07	**91.81**
CD	**87.79**	**91.47**	90.62
DT	86.31	89.80	89.17

Table 2: Parsing results of the Bohnet and Nivre (2012) parser on Stanford Basic (SB), CoNLL Syntactic Dependencies (CD) and DELPH-IN Syntactic Derivation Tree (DT) formats. Parser is trained on gold-standard data. Punctuation is excluded from the scoring. *Predicted PTB:* parser predicts PTB tags during the test phase. *Predicted supertags:* parser predicts supertags during the test phase. *Predicted PTB + gold supertags:* parser receives gold supertags as feature and predicts PTB tags during the test phase. *Predicted supertags + gold PTB:* parser receives PTB tags as feature and predicts supertags during test phase.

to dependency parsing and is independent from parsing questions in this sense. Unlike SB and CD, it is linguistically informed by the underlying, full-fledged HPSG grammar.

The Jaccard similarity on our training set is 0.57 for SB and CD, 0.564 for CD and DT, and 0.388 for SB and DT. These similarity values show that CD and DT are structurally closer to each other than SB and DT. Contrary to our expectations, the accuracy scores of parsers do not suggest that CD and DT are particularly similar to each other in terms of parsing.

Inspecting the aspect of **tagset** we conclude that traditional PTB tags are compatible with SB and CD but do not fit the DT scheme well, while ERG supertags are specific to the ERG framework and do not seem to be appropriate for SB and CD. Neither of these findings seem surprising, as PTB tags were developed as part of the treebank from which CD and SB are derived; whereas ERG supertags are closely related to the HPSG syntactic structures captured in DT. PTB tags were designed to simplify PoS-tagging whereas supertags were developed to capture information that is required to analyze syntax of HPSG.

For each PTB tag we collected corresponding supertags from the gold-standard training set. For open word classes such as nouns, adjectives, adverbs and verbs the relation between PTB tags and supertags is many-to-many. Unique one-to-many correspondence holds only for possessive wh-pronoun and punctuation.

Thus, supertags do not provide extra level of detalization for PTB tags, but PTB tags and supertags are complementary. As discussed in section 3.4, they contain bits of information that are different. For this reason their combination results in slight increase of accuracy for all three parsers on all dependency formats (Table 1, *Gold PTB tags + gold supertags*, and Table 2, *Predicted PTB + gold supertags* and *Predicted supertags + gold PTB*). The Bohnet and Nivre (2012) parser predicts supertags with an average accuracy of 89.73% which is significantly lower than state-of-the-art 95% (Ytrestøl, 2011).

When we consider punctuation in the evaluation, all scores raise significantly for DT and at the same time decrease for SB and CD for all three parsers. This is explained by the fact that punctuation in DT is always attached to the nearest token which is easy to learn for a statistical parser.

4.3 Error analysis

Using the CoNLL-07 evaluation script[2] on our test set, for each parser we obtained the error rate distribution over CPOSTAG on SB, CD and DT.

VBP, VBZ and VBG. VBP (verb, non-3rd person singular present), VBZ (verb, 3rd person singular present) and VBG (verb, gerund or present participle) are the PTB tags that have error rates in 10 highest error rates list for each parser (Malt, MST and the Bohnet and Nivre (2012) parser) with each dependency format (SB, CD and DT) and with each PoS tag set (PTB PoS and supertags) when PTB tags are included as CPOSTAG feature. We automatically collected all sentences that contain 1) attachment errors, 2) label errors, 3) attachment and label errors for VBP, VBZ and VBG made by Malt parser on DT format with PTB PoS. For each of these three lexical categories we manually analyzed a random sample of sentences with errors and their corresponding gold-standard versions.

In many cases such errors are related to the root of the sentence when the verb is either treated as complement or adjunct instead of having a root status or vice versa. Errors with these groups of verbs mostly occur in the complex sentences that contain several verbs. Sentences with coordination are particularly difficult for the correct attachment and labeling of the VBP (see Figure 2 for an example).

Coordination. The error rate of Malt, MST and the Bohnet and Nivre (2012) parser for the coordination is not so high for SB and CD (1% and 2% correspondingly with MaltParser, PTB tags) whereas for DT the error rate on the CPOSTAGS is especially high (26% with MaltParser, PTB tags). It means that there are many errors on incoming dependency arcs for coordinating conjunctions when parsing DT. On outgoing arcs parsers also make more mistakes on DT than on SB and CD. This is related to the difference in choice of annotation principle (see Figure 1). As it was shown in (Schwartz et al., 2012), it is harder to parse coordination headed by coordinating conjunction.

Although the approach used in DT is harder for parser to learn, it has some advantages: using SB and CD annotations, we cannot distinguish the two cases illustrated with the sentences (a) and (b):

[2] http://nextens.uvt.nl/depparse-wiki/SoftwarePage#scoring

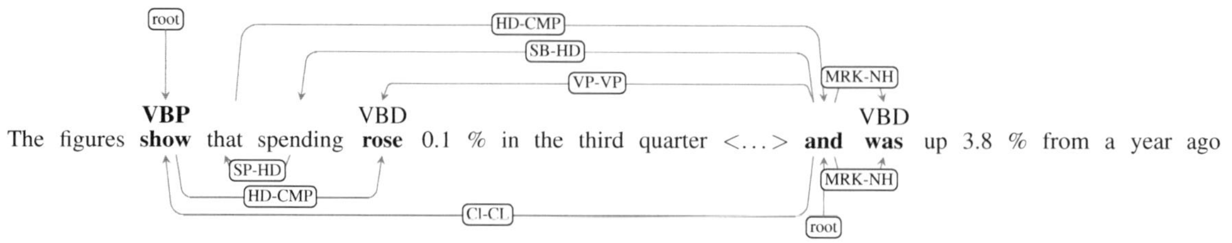

Figure 2: The gold-standard (*in green above the sentence*) and the incorrect Malt's (*in red below the sentence*) analyses of the utterance from the DeepBank in DT format with PTB PoS tags

a) The fight is putting a tight squeeze on profits of many, threatening to drive the smallest ones out of business and straining relations between *the national fast-food chains and their franchisees.*
b) Proceeds from the sale will be used for remodelling and reforbishing projects, as well as for *the planned MGM Grand hotel/casino and theme park.*

In the sentence a) "the national fast-food" refers only to the conjunct "chains", while in the sentence b) "the planned" refers to both conjuncts and "MGM Grand" refers only to the first conjunct.

The Bohnet and Nivre (2012) parser succeeds in finding the correct conjucts (shown in bold font) on DT and makes mistakes on SB and CD in some difficult cases like the following ones:

a) <...> investors **hoard** gold and **help** underpin its price <...>
b) Then **take** the expected return and **subtract** one standard deviation.

CD and SB wrongly suggest "gold" and "help" to be conjoined in the first sentence and "return" and "deviation" in the second.

5 Conclusions and future work

In this survey we gave a comparative experimental overview of (i) parsing three dependency schemes, viz., Stanford Basic (SB), CoNLL Syntactic Dependencies (CD) and DELPH-IN Syntactic Derivation Tree (DT), (ii) with three leading dependency parsers, viz., Malt, MST and the Bohnet and Nivre (2012) parser (iii) exploiting two different tagsets, viz., PTB tags and supertags.

From the *parser* perspective, the Bohnet and Nivre (2012) parser performs better than Malt and MST not only on conventional formats but also on the new representation, although this parser solves a harder task than Malt and MST.

From the dependency *format* perspective, DT appeares to be a more difficult target dependency representation than SB and CD. This suggests that the expressivity that we gain from the grammar theory (e.g. for coordination) is harder to learn with state-of-the-art dependency parsers. CD and DT are structurally closer to each other than SB and DT; however, we did not observe sound evidence of a correlation between structural similarity of CD and DT and their parsing accuracies

Regarding the *tagset* aspect, it is natural that PTB tags are good for SB and CD, whereas the more fine-grained set of supertags fits DT better. PTB tags and supertags are complementary, and for all three parsers we observe slight benefits from being supplied with both types of tags.

As future work we would like to run more experiments with predicted supertags. In the absence of a specialized supertagger, we can follow the pipeline of (Ytrestøl, 2011) who reached the state-of-the-art supertagging accuracy of 95%.

Another area of our interest is an extrinsic evaluation of SB, CD and DT, e.g. applied to semantic role labeling and question-answering in order to find out if the usage of the DT format grounded in the computational grammar theory is beneficial for such tasks.

Acknowledgments

The authors would like to thank Rebecca Dridan, Joakim Nivre, Bernd Bohnet, Gertjan van Noord and Jelke Bloem for interesting discussions and the two anonymous reviewers for comments on the work. Experimentation was made possible through access to the high-performance computing resources at the University of Oslo.

References

Bernd Bohnet and Joakim Nivre. 2012. A transition-based system for joint part-of-speech tagging and labeled non-projective dependency parsing. In *EMNLP-CoNLL*, pages 1455–1465. ACL.

Harry Bunt, Paola Merlo, and Joakim Nivre, editors. 2010. *Trends in Parsing Technology*. Springer Verlag, Stanford.

Jinho D Choi and Nicolas Nicolov. 2009. K-best, locally pruned, transition-based dependency parsing using robust risk minimization. *Recent Advances in Natural Language Processing V*, pages 205–216.

Marie-Catherine de Marneffe, Bill MacCartney, and Christopher D. Manning. 2006. Generating typed dependency parses from phrase structure trees. In *LREC*.

Yuan Ding and Martha Palmer. 2005. Machine translation using probabilistic synchronous dependency insertion grammars. In *Proceedings of the 43rd Annual Meeting of the Association for Computational Linguistics (ACL'05)*, pages 541–548, Ann Arbor, Michigan, June. Association for Computational Linguistics.

Daniel Flickinger, Yi Zhang, and Valia Kordoni. 2012. DeepBank: a Dynamically Annotated Treebank of the Wall Street Journal. In *Proceedings of the Eleventh International Workshop on Treebanks and Linguistic Theories*, pages 85–96. Edies Colibri.

Yoav Goldberg and Michael Elhadad. 2010. An efficient algorithm for easy-first non-directional dependency parsing. In *Human Language Technologies: The 2010 Annual Conference of the North American Chapter of the Association for Computational Linguistics*, HLT '10, pages 742–750, Stroudsburg, PA, USA. Association for Computational Linguistics.

Angelina Ivanova, Stephan Oepen, Lilja Øvrelid, and Dan Flickinger. 2012. Who did what to whom? a contrastive study of syntacto-semantic dependencies. In *Proceedings of the Sixth Linguistic Annotation Workshop*, pages 2–11, Jeju, Republic of Korea, July. Association for Computational Linguistics.

Richard Johansson and Pierre Nugues. 2007. Extended constituent-to-dependency conversion for English. In *Proceedings of NODALIDA 2007*, pages 105–112, Tartu, Estonia, May 25-26.

Dan Klein and Christopher D. Manning. 2004. Corpus-based induction of syntactic structure: models of dependency and constituency. In *Proceedings of the 42nd Annual Meeting on Association for Computational Linguistics*, ACL '04, Stroudsburg, PA, USA. Association for Computational Linguistics.

Mitchell P. Marcus, Mary Ann Marcinkiewicz, and Beatrice Santorini. 1993. Building a large annotated corpus of English: the Penn Treebank. *Computational Linguistics*, 19(2):313–330, June.

Ryan McDonald, Fernando Pereira, Kiril Ribarov, and Jan Hajič. 2005. Non-projective dependency parsing using spanning tree algorithms. In *Proceedings of the conference on Human Language Technology and Empirical Methods in Natural Language Processing*, HLT '05, pages 523–530, Stroudsburg, PA, USA. Association for Computational Linguistics.

Ryan McDonald, Kevin Lerman, and Fernando Pereira. 2006. Multilingual dependency analysis with a two-stage discriminative parser. In *Proceedings of the Tenth Conference on Computational Natural Language Learning*, CoNLL-X '06, pages 216–220, Stroudsburg, PA, USA. Association for Computational Linguistics.

Makoto Miwa, Sampo Pyysalo, Tadayoshi Hara, and Jun ichi Tsujii. 2010. Evaluating dependency representations for event extraction. In Chu-Ren Huang and Dan Jurafsky, editors, *COLING*, pages 779–787. Tsinghua University Press.

Yusuke Miyao, Kenji Sagae, and Jun'ichi Tsujii. 2007. Towards framework-independent evaluation of deep linguistic parsers. In Ann Copestake, editor, *Proceedings of the GEAF 2007 Workshop*, CSLI Studies in Computational Linguistics Online, page 21 pages. CSLI Publications.

Joakim Nivre, Johan Hall, Jens Nilsson, Atanas Chanev, Gülsen Eryigit, Sandra Kübler, Svetoslav Marinov, and Erwin Marsi. 2007. MaltParser: A language-independent system for data-driven dependency parsing. *Natural Language Engineering*, 13(2):95–135.

Lilja Øvrelid, Jonas Kuhn, and Kathrin Spreyer. 2009. Cross-framework parser stacking for data-driven dependency parsing. *TAL*, 50(3):109–138.

Roy Schwartz, Omri Abend, and Ari Rappoport. 2012. Learnability-based syntactic annotation design. In *Proc. of the 24th International Conference on Computational Linguistics (Coling 2012)*, Mumbai, India, December. Coling 2012 Organizing Committee.

Xianchao Wu, Katsuhito Sudoh, Kevin Duh, Hajime Tsukada, and Masaaki Nagata. 2012. A Comparative Study of Target Dependency Structures for Statistical Machine Translation. In *ACL (2)*, pages 100–104. The Association for Computer Linguistics.

Akane Yakushiji, Yusuke Miyao, Tomoko Ohta, Yuka Tateisi, and Jun'ichi Tsujii. 2006. Automatic construction of predicate-argument structure patterns for biomedical information extraction. In *Proceedings of the 2006 Conference on Empirical Methods in Natural Language Processing*, EMNLP '06, pages 284–292, Stroudsburg, PA, USA. Association for Computational Linguistics.

Gisle Ytrestøl. 2011. Cuteforce: deep deterministic HPSG parsing. In *Proceedings of the 12th International Conference on Parsing Technologies*, IWPT '11, pages 186–197, Stroudsburg, PA, USA. Association for Computational Linguistics.

What causes a causal relation?
Detecting Causal Triggers in Biomedical Scientific Discourse

Claudiu Mihăilă and Sophia Ananiadou
The National Centre for Text Mining,
School of Computer Science,
The University of Manchester,
131 Princess Street, Manchester M1 7DN, UK
claudiu.mihaila@manchester.ac.uk
sophia.ananiadou@manchester.ac.uk

Abstract

Current domain-specific information extraction systems represent an important resource for biomedical researchers, who need to process vaster amounts of knowledge in short times. Automatic discourse causality recognition can further improve their workload by suggesting possible causal connections and aiding in the curation of pathway models. We here describe an approach to the automatic identification of discourse causality triggers in the biomedical domain using machine learning. We create several baselines and experiment with various parameter settings for three algorithms, i.e., Conditional Random Fields (CRF), Support Vector Machines (SVM) and Random Forests (RF). Also, we evaluate the impact of lexical, syntactic and semantic features on each of the algorithms and look at errors. The best performance of 79.35% F-score is achieved by CRFs when using all three feature types.

1 Introduction

The need to provide automated, efficient and accurate means of retrieving and extracting user-oriented biomedical knowledge has significantly increased according to the ever-increasing amount of knowledge pusblished daily in the form of research articles (Ananiadou and McNaught, 2006; Cohen and Hunter, 2008). Biomedical text mining has seen significant recent advancements in recent years (Zweigenbaum et al., 2007), including named entity recognition (Fukuda et al., 1998), coreference resolution (Batista-Navarro and Ananiadou, 2011; Savova et al., 2011) and relation (Miwa et al., 2009; Pyysalo et al., 2009) and event extraction (Miwa et al., 2012b; Miwa et al., 2012a). Using biomedical text mining technology, text can now be enriched via the addition of semantic metadata and thus can support tasks such as analysing molecular pathways (Rzhetsky et al., 2004) and semantic searching (Miyao et al., 2006).

However, more complex tasks, such as question answering and automatic summarisation, require the extraction of information that spans across several sentences, together with the recognition of relations that exist across sentence boundaries, in order to achieve high levels of performance.

The notion of *discourse* can be defined as a coherent sequence of clauses and sentences. These are connected in a logical manner by *discourse relations*, such as causal, temporal and conditional, which characterise how facts in text are related. In turn, these help readers infer deeper, more complex knowledge about the facts mentioned in the discourse. These relations can be either explicit or implicit, depending whether or not they are expressed in text using overt *discourse connectives* (also known as *triggers*). Take, for instance, the case in example (1), where the trigger *Therefore* signals a justification between the two sentences: because "a normal response to mild acid pH from PmrB requires both a periplasmic histidine and several glutamic acid residues", the authors believe that the "regulation of PmrB activity could involve protonation of some amino acids".

(1) In the case of PmrB, a normal response to mild acid pH requires not only a periplasmic histidine

but also several glutamic acid residues. *Therefore*, regulation of PmrB activity may involve protonation of one or more of these amino acids.

Thus, by identifying this causal relation, search engines become able to discover relations between biomedical entities and events or between experimental evidence and associated conclusions. However, phrases acting as causal triggers in certain contexts may not denote causality in all cases. Therefore, a dictionary-based approach is likely to produce a very high number of false positives. In this paper, we explore several supervised machine-learning approaches to the automatic identification of triggers that actually denote causality.

2 Related Work

A large amount of work related to discourse parsing and discourse relation identification exists in the general domain, where researchers have not only identified discourse connectives, but also developed end-to-end discourse parsers (Pitler and Nenkova, 2009; Lin et al., 2012). Most work is based on the Penn Discourse Treebank (PDTB) (Prasad et al., 2008), a corpus of lexically-grounded annotations of discourse relations.

Until now, comparatively little work has been carried out on causal discourse relations in the biomedical domain, although causal associations between biological entities, events and processes are central to most claims of interest (Kleinberg and Hripcsak, 2011). The equivalent of the PDTB for the biomedical domain is the BioDRB corpus (Prasad et al., 2011), containing 16 types of discourse relations, e.g., temporal, causal and conditional. The number of purely causal relations annotated in this corpus is 542. There are another 23 relations which are a mixture between causality and one of either background, temporal, conjunction or reinforcement relations. A slightly larger corpus is the BioCause (Mihăilă et al., 2013), containing over 850 manually annotated causal discourse relations in 19 full-text open-access journal articles from the infectious diseases domain.

Using the BioDRB corpus as data, some researchers explored the identification of discourse connectives (Ramesh et al., 2012). However, they do not distinguish between the types of discourse relations. They obtain the best F-score of 75.7% using CRF, with SVM reaching only 65.7%. These results were obtained by using only syntactic features, as sematic features were shown to lower the performance. Also, they prove that there exist differences in discourse triggers between the biomedical and general domains by training a model on the BioDRB and evaluating it against PDTB and vice-versa.

3 Methodology

In this section, we describe our data and the features of causal triggers. We also explain our evaluation methodology.

3.1 Data

The data for the experiments comes from the BioCause corpus. BioCause is a collection of 19 open-access full-text journal articles pertaining to the biomedical subdomain of infectious diseases, manually annotated with causal relationships. Two types of spans of text are marked in the text, namely causal triggers and causal arguments. Each causal relation is composed of three text-bound annotations: a trigger, a cause or evidence argument and an effect argument. Some causal relations have implicit triggers, so these are excluded from the current research.

Figure 1 shows an example of discourse causality from BioCause, marking the causal trigger and the two arguments with their respective relation. Named entities are also marked in this example.

BioCause contains 381 unique explicit triggers in the corpus, each being used, on average, only 2.10 times. The number decreases to 347 unique triggers when they are lemmatised, corresponding to an average usage of 2.30 times per trigger. Both count settings show the diversity of causality-triggering phrases that are used in the biomedical domain.

3.2 Features

Three types of features have been employed in the development of this causality trigger model, i.e., lexical, syntactic and semantic. These features are categorised and described below.

3.2.1 Lexical features

The lexical features are built from the actual tokens present in text. Tokenisation is performed by

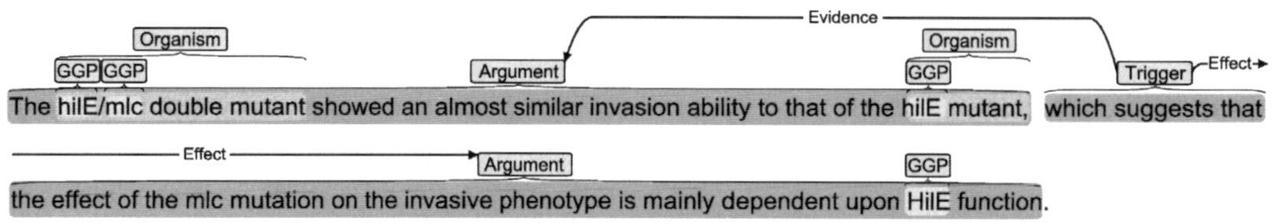

Figure 1: Causal relation in the BioCause.

the GENIA tagger (Tsuruoka et al., 2005) using the biomedical model. The first two features represent the token's surface expression and its base form.

Neighbouring tokens have also been considered. We included the token immediately to the left and the one immediately to the right of the current token. This decision is based on two observations. Firstly, in the case of tokens to the left, most triggers are found either at the beginning of the sentence (311 instances) or are preceded by a comma (238 instances). These two left contexts represent 69% of all triggers. Secondly, for the tokens to the right, almost 45% of triggers are followed by a determiner, such as *the*, *a* or *an*, (281 instances) or a comma (71 instances).

3.2.2 Syntactic features

The syntax, dependency and predicate argument structure are produced by the Enju parser (Miyao and Tsujii, 2008). Figure 2 depicts a partial lexical parse tree of a sentence which starts with a causal trigger, namely *Our results suggest that*. From the lexical parse trees, several types of features have been generated.

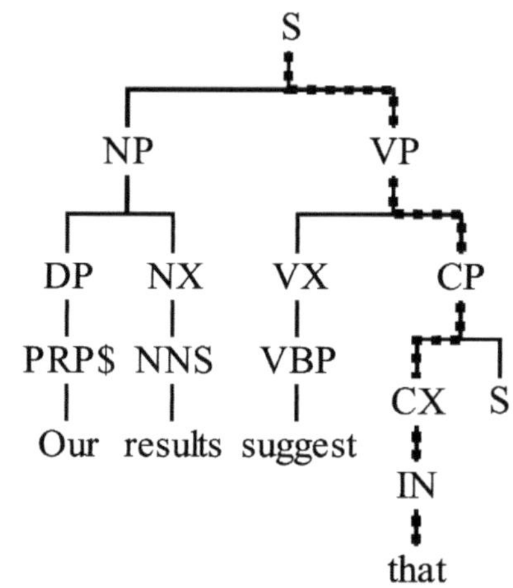

Figure 2: Partial lexical parse tree of a sentence starting with a causal trigger.

The first two features represent the part-of-speech and syntactic category of a token. For instance, the figure shows that the token *that* has the part-of-speech *IN*. These features are included due to the fact that either many triggers are lexicalised as an adverb or conjunction, or are part of a verb phrase. For the same reason, the syntactical category path from the root of the lexical parse tree to the token is also included. The path also encodes, for each parent constituent, the position of the token in its subtree, i.e., beginning (*B*), inside (*I*) or end (*E*); if the token is the only leaf node of the constituent, this is marked differently, using a *C*. Thus, the path of *that*, highlighted in the figure, is *I-S/I-VP/B-CP/C-CX*.

Secondly, for each token, we extracted the predicate argument structure and checked whether a relation exista between the token and the previous and following tokens. The values for this feature represent the argument number as allocated by Enju.

Thirdly, the ancestors of each token to the third degree are instantiated as three different features. In the case that such ancestors do not exist (i.e., the root of the lexical parse tree is less than three nodes away), a "none" value is given. For instance, the token *that* in Figure 2 has as its first three ancestors the constituents marked with *CX*, *CP* and *VP*.

Finally, the lowest common ancestor in the lexical parse tree between the current token and its left neighbour has been included. In the example, the lowest common ancestor for *that* and *suggest* is *VP*.

These last two feature types have been produced on the observation that the lowest common ancestor for all tokens in a causal trigger is S or VP in over 70% of instances. Furthermore, the percentage of cases of triggers with V or ADV as lowest common ancestor is almost 9% in each case. Also, the average distance to the lowest common ancestor is 3.

3.2.3 Semantic features

We have exploited several semantic knowledge sources to identify causal triggers more accurately, as a mapping to concepts and named entities acts as a back-off smoothing, thus increasing performance.

One semantic knowledge source is the BioCause corpus itself. All documents annotated for causality in BioCause had been previously manually annotated with biomedical named entity and event information. This was performed in the context of various shared tasks, such as the BioNLP 2011 Shared Task on Infectious Diseases (Pyysalo et al., 2011). We therefore leverage this existing information to add another semantic layer to the model. Moreover, another advantage of having a gold standard annotation is the fact that it is now possible to separate the task of automatic causal trigger recognition from automatic named entity recognition and event extraction. The named entity and event annotation in the BioCause corpus is used to extract information about whether a token is part of a named entity or event trigger. Furthermore, the type of the named entity or event is included as a separate feature.

The second semantic knowledge source is WordNet (Fellbaum, 1998). Using this resource, the hypernym of every token in the text has been included as a feature. Only the first sense of every token has been considered, as no sense disambiguation technique has been employed.

Finally, tokens have been linked to the Unified Medical Language System (UMLS) (Bodenreider, 2004) semantic types. Thus, we included a feature to say whether a token is part of a UMLS type and another for its semantic type if the previous is true.

3.3 Experimental setup

We explored with various machine learning algorithms and various settings for the task of identifying causal triggers.

On the one hand, we experimented with CRF (Lafferty et al., 2001), a probabilistic modelling framework commonly used for sequence labelling tasks. In this work, we employed the CRFSuite implementation[1].

[1]http://www.chokkan.org/software/crfsuite

On the other hand, we modelled trigger detection as a classification task, using Support Vector Machines and Random Forests. More specifically, we employed the implementation in Weka (Hall et al., 2009; Witten and Frank, 2005) for RFs, and LibSVM (Chang and Lin, 2011) for SVMs.

4 Results and discussion

Several models have been developed and 10-fold cross-evaluated to examine the complexity of the task, the impact of various feature types (lexical, syntactic, semantic). Table 1 shows the performance evaluation of baseline systems and other classifiers. These are described in the following subsections. It should be noted that the dataset is highly skewed, with a ratio of positive examples to negative examples of approximately 1:52.

	Classifier	**P**	**R**	**F_1**
Baseline	*Dict*	8.36	100	15.43
	Dep	7.51	76.66	13.68
	Dict+Dep	14.30	75.33	24.03
2-way	CRF	**89.29**	**73.53**	**79.35**
	SVM	81.62	61.05	69.85
	RandFor	78.16	66.96	72.13
3-way	CRF	**89.13**	**64.04**	**72.87**
	SVM	74.21	56.82	64.36
	RandFor	73.80	60.95	66.76

Table 1: Performance of various classifiers in identifying causal connectives

4.1 Baseline

Several baselines have been devised. The first baseline is a dictionary-based heuristic, named *Dict*. A lexicon is populated with all annotated causal triggers and then this is used to tag all instances of its entries in the text as connectives. The precision of this heuristic is very low, 8.36%, which leads to an F-score of 15.43%, considering the recall is 100%. This is mainly due to triggers which are rarely used as causal triggers, such as *and*, *by* and *that*.

Building on the previously mentioned observation about the lowest common ancestor for all tokens in a causal trigger, we built a baseline system that checks all constituent nodes in the lexical parse tree for the S, V, VP and ADV tags and marks them as causal triggers. The name of this system is *Dep*. Not only does *Dep* obtain a lower precision than *Dict*, but it also performs worse in terms of recall. The F-score is 13.68%, largely due to the high number of intermediate nodes in the lexical parse tree that have VP as their category.

The third baseline is a combination of *Dict* and *Dep*: we consider only constituents that have the necessary category (S, V, VP or ADV) and include a trigger from the dictionary. Although the recall decreases slightly, the precision increases to almost twice that of both *Dict* and *Dep*. This produces a much better F-score of 24.03%.

4.2 Sequence labelling task

As a sequence labelling task, we have modelled causal trigger detection as two separate tasks. Firstly, each trigger is represented in the B-I-O format (further mentioned as the 3-way model). Thus, the first word of every trigger is tagged as B (*begin*), whilst the following words in the trigger are tagged as I (*inside*). Non-trigger words are tagged as O (*outside*).

The second model is a simpler version of the previous one: it does not distinguish between the first and the following words in the trigger. In other words, each word is tagged either as being part of or outside the trigger, further known as the 2-way model. Hence, a sequence of contiguous tokens marked as part of a trigger form one trigger.

CRF performs reasonably well in detecting causal triggers. In the 3-way model, it obtains an F-score of almost 73%, much better than the other algorithms. It also obtains the highest precision (89%) and recall (64%). However, in the 2-way model, CRF's performance is slightly lower than that of Random Forests, achieving only 79.35%. Its precision, on the other hand, is the highest in this model. The results from both models were obtained by combining features from all three feature categories.

Table 2 show the effect of feature types on both models of CRFs. As can be observed, the best performances, in terms of F-score, including the previously mentioned ones, are obtained when combining all three types of features, i.e., lexical, syntactic and semantic. The best precision and recall, however, are not necessarily achieved by using all three feature types. In the two-way model, the best precision is obtained by using the syntactic features only, reaching over 92%, almost 3% higher than when all three feature types are used. In the three-way model, syntactic and semantic features produce the best recall (almost 65%), which is just under 1% higher than the recall when all features are used.

	Features	P	R	F_1
2-way	Lex	88.99	67.09	73.59
	Syn	**92.20**	68.68	75.72
	Sem	87.20	63.30	69.36
	Lex-Syn	87.76	73.29	78.73
	Lex+Sem	89.54	69.10	75.61
	Syn+Sem	87.48	72.62	78.13
	Lex-Syn-Sem	89.29	**73.53**	**79.35**
3-way	Lex	85.87	56.34	65.18
	Syn	87.62	61.44	70.22
	Sem	80.78	51.43	59.39
	Lex+Syn	87.80	63.04	72.59
	Lex+Sem	85.50	58.11	66.80
	Syn+Sem	84.83	**64.94**	72.41
	Lex-Syn-Sem	**89.13**	64.04	**72.87**

Table 2: Effect of feature types on the sequence labelling task, given in percentages.

4.3 Classification task

As a classification task, an algorithm has to decide whether a token is part of a trigger or not, similarly to the previous two-way subtask in the case of CRF.

Firstly, we have used RF for the classification task. Various parameter settings regarding the number of constructed trees and the number of random features have been explored.

The effect of feature types on the performance of RF is shown in Table 3. As can be observed, the best performance is obtained when combining lexical and semantic features. Due to the fact that causal triggers do not have a semantic mapping to concepts in the named entity and UMLS annotations, the trees in the random forest classifier can easily produce rules that distinguish triggers from non-triggers. As such, the use of semantic features alone produce a very good precision of 84.34%. Also, in all cases where semantic features are combined with other feature types, the precision increases by 0.5% in the case of lexical features and 3.5% in the case of syntactic features. However, the recall of semantic features alone is the lowest. The best recall is obtained when using only lexical features.

Features	P	R	F_1
Lex	78.47	**68.30**	73.03
Syn	68.19	62.36	65.15
Sem	**84.34**	56.83	67.91
Lex+Syn	77.11	65.92	71.09
Lex+Sem	79.10	67.91	**73.08**
Syn+Sem	71.83	64.45	67.94
Lex+Syn+Sem	77.98	67.31	72.25

Table 3: Effect of feature types on Random Forests.

Secondly, we explored the performance of SVMs in detecting causal triggers. We have experimented with two kernels, namely polynomial (second degree) and radial basis function (RBF) kernels. For each of these two kernels, we have evaluated various combinations of parameter values for cost and weight. Both these kernels achieved similar results, indicating that the feature space is not linearly separable and that the problem is highly complex.

The effect of feature types on the performance of SVMs is shown in Table 4. As can be observed, the best performance is obtained when combining the lexical and semantic feature types (69.85% F-score). The combination of all features produces the best precision, whilst the best recall is obtained by combining lexical and semantic features.

Features	P	R	F_1
Lex	80.80	60.94	69.47
Syn	82.94	55.60	66.57
Sem	85.07	56.51	67.91
Lex+Syn	86.49	53.63	66.81
Lex+Sem	81.62	**61.05**	**69.85**
Syn+Sem	84.49	55.31	66.85
Lex+Syn+Sem	**87.70**	53.96	66.81

Table 4: Effect of feature types on SVM.

4.4 Error analysis

As we expected, the majority of errors arise from sequences of tokens which are only used infrequently as non-causal triggers. This applies to 107 trigger types, whose number of false positives (FP) is higher than the number of true positives (TP). In fact, 64 trigger types occur only once as a causal instance, whilst the average number of FPs for these types is 14.25. One such example is *and*, for which the number of non-causal instances (2305) is much greater than that of causal instances (1). Other examples of trigger types more commonly used as causal triggers, are *suggesting* (9 TP, 54 FP), *indicating* (8 TP, 41 FP) and *resulting in* (6 TP, 14 FP). For instance, example (2) contains two mentions of *indicating*, but neither of them implies causality.

(2) Buffer treated control cells showed intense green staining with syto9 (*indicating* viability) and a lack of PI staining (*indicating* no dead/dying cells or DNA release).

5 Conclusions and Future Work

We have presented an approach to the automatic identification of triggers of causal discourse relations in biomedical scientific text. The task has proven to be a highly complex one, posing many challenges. Shallow approaches, such as dictionary matching and lexical parse tree matching, perform very poorly, due to the high ambiguity of causal triggers (with F-scores of approximately 15% each and 24% when combined). We have explored various machine learning algorithms that automatically classify tokens into triggers or non-triggers and we have evaluated the impact of multiple lexical, syntactic and semantic features. The performance of SVMs prove that the task of identifying causal triggers is indeed complex. The best performing classifier is CRF-based and combines lexical, syntactical and semantical features in order to obtain an F-score of 79.35%.

As future work, integrating the causal relations in the BioDRB corpus is necessary to check whether a data insufficiency problem exists and, if so, estimate the optimal amount of necessary data. Furthermore, evaluations against the general domain need to be performed, in order to establish any differences in expressing causality in the biomedical domain. One possible source for this is the PDTB corpus. A more difficult task that needs attention is that of identifying implicit triggers. Finally, our system needs to be extended in order to identify the two arguments of causal relations, the cause and effect, thus allowing the creation of a complete discourse causality parser.

Acknowledgements

This work was partially funded by the Engineering and Physical Sciences Research Council [grant number EP/P505631/1].

References

Sophia Ananiadou and John McNaught, editors. 2006. *Text Mining for Biology And Biomedicine*. Artech House, Inc.

Riza Theresa B. Batista-Navarro and Sophia Ananiadou. 2011. Building a coreference-annotated corpus from the domain of biochemistry. In *Proceedings of BioNLP 2011*, pages 83–91.

Olivier Bodenreider. 2004. The unified medical language system (UMLS): integrating biomedical terminology. *Nucleic Acids Research*, 32(suppl 1):D267–D270.

Chih-Chung Chang and Chih-Jen Lin. 2011. LIBSVM: A library for support vector machines. *ACM Transactions on Intelligent Systems and Technology*, 2:27:1–27:27. Software available at `http://www.csie.ntu.edu.tw/~cjlin/libsvm`.

Kevin Bretonnel Cohen and Lawrence Hunter. 2008. Getting started in text mining. *PLoS Computational Biology*, 4(1):e20, 01.

Christiane Fellbaum, editor. 1998. *WordNet: An Electronic Lexical Database*. MIT Press, Cambridge, MA.

Ken-ichiro Fukuda, Tatsuhiko Tsunoda, Ayuchi Tamura, and Toshihisa Takagi. 1998. Toward information extraction: Identifying protein names from biological papers. In *Proceedings of the Pacific Symposium on Biocomputing*, volume 707, pages 707–718.

Mark Hall, Eibe Frank, Geoffrey Holmes, Bernhard Pfahringer, Peter Reutemann, and Ian H. Witten. 2009. The WEKA data mining software: an update. *SIGKDD Explor. Newsl.*, 11:10–18, November.

Samantha Kleinberg and George Hripcsak. 2011. A review of causal inference for biomedical informatics. *Journal of Biomedical Informatics*, 44(6):1102 – 1112.

John D. Lafferty, Andrew McCallum, and Fernando C. N. Pereira. 2001. Conditional random fields: Probabilistic models for segmenting and labeling sequence data. In *Proceedings of the Eighteenth International Conference on Machine Learning*, ICML '01, pages 282–289, San Francisco, CA, USA. Morgan Kaufmann Publishers Inc.

Ziheng Lin, Hwee Tou Ng, and Min-Yen Kan. 2012. A pdtb-styled end-to-end discourse parser. *Natural Language Engineering*, FirstView:1–34, 10.

Claudiu Mihăilă, Tomoko Ohta, Sampo Pyysalo, and Sophia Ananiadou. 2013. BioCause: Annotating and analysing causality in the biomedical domain. *BMC Bioinformatics*, 14(1):2, January.

Makoto Miwa, Rune Sætre, Yusuke Miyao, and Jun'ichi Tsujii. 2009. Protein-protein interaction extraction by leveraging multiple kernels and parsers. *International Journal of Medical Informatics*, 78(12):e39–e46, June.

Makoto Miwa, Paul Thompson, and Sophia Ananiadou. 2012a. Boosting automatic event extraction from the literature using domain adaptation and coreference resolution. *Bioinformatics*, 28(13):1759–1765.

Makoto Miwa, Paul Thompson, John McNaught, Douglas B. Kell, and Sophia Ananiadou. 2012b. Extracting semantically enriched events from biomedical literature. *BMC Bioinformatics*, 13:108.

Yusuke Miyao and Jun'ichi Tsujii. 2008. Feature forest models for probabilistic HPSG parsing. *Computational Linguistics*, 34(1):3580, March.

Yusuke Miyao, Tomoko Ohta, Katsuya Masuda, Yoshimasa Tsuruoka, Kazuhiro Yoshida, Takashi Ninomiya, and Jun'ichi Tsujii. 2006. Semantic retrieval for the accurate identification of relational concepts in massive textbases. In *ACL*.

Emily Pitler and Ani Nenkova. 2009. Using syntax to disambiguate explicit discourse connectives in text. In *ACL/AFNLP (Short Papers)*, pages 13–16.

Rashmi Prasad, Nikhil Dinesh, Alan Lee, Eleni Miltsakaki, Livio Robaldo, Aravind Joshi, and Bonnie Webber. 2008. The Penn Discourse TreeBank 2.0. In Nicoletta Calzolari, Khalid Choukri, Bente Maegaard, Joseph Mariani, Jan Odjik, Stelios Piperidis, and Daniel Tapias, editors, *In Proceedings of the 6th International Conference on language Resources and Evaluation (LREC)*, pages 2961–2968.

Rashmi Prasad, Susan McRoy, Nadya Frid, Aravind Joshi, and Hong Yu. 2011. The biomedical discourse relation bank. *BMC Bioinformatics*, 12(1):188.

Sampo Pyysalo, Tomoko Ohta, Jin-Dong Kim, and Jun'ichi Tsujii. 2009. Static relations: a piece in the biomedical information extraction puzzle. In *Proceedings of the Workshop on Current Trends in Biomedical Natural Language Processing*, BioNLP '09, pages 1–9, Stroudsburg, PA, USA. Association for Computational Linguistics.

Sampo Pyysalo, Tomoko Ohta, Rafal Rak, Dan Sullivan, Chunhong Mao, Chunxia Wang, Bruno Sobral, Jun'ichi Tsujii, and Sophia Ananiadou. 2011. Overview of the infectious diseases (ID) task of BioNLP shared task 2011. In *Proceedings of the BioNLP Shared Task 2011 Workshop*, pages 26–35, Portland, Oregon, USA, June. Association for Computational Linguistics.

Polepalli Balaji Ramesh, Rashmi Prasad, Tim Miller, Brian Harrington, and Hong Yu. 2012. Automatic discourse connective detection in biomedical text. *Journal of the American Medical Informatics Association*.

Andrey Rzhetsky, Ivan Iossifov, Tomohiro Koike, Michael Krauthammer, Pauline Kra, Mitzi Morris, Hong Yu, Ariel Pablo Duboué, Wubin Weng, W.John Wilbur, Vasileios Hatzivassiloglou, and Carol Friedman. 2004. Geneways: a system for extracting, analyzing, visualizing, and integrating molecular pathway data. *Journal of Biomedical Informatics*, 37(1):43 – 53.

Guergana K Savova, Wendy W Chapman, Jiaping Zheng, and Rebecca S Crowley. 2011. Anaphoric relations in the clinical narrative: corpus creation. *Journal of the American Medical Informatics Association*, 18(4):459–465.

Yoshimasa Tsuruoka, Yuka Tateishi, Jin-Dong Kim, Tomoko Ohta, John McNaught, Sophia Ananiadou, and Jun'ichi Tsujii. 2005. Developing a robust part-of-speech tagger for biomedical text. In *Advances in Informatics - 10th Panhellenic Conference on Informatics*, volume 3746 of *LNCS*, pages 382–392. Springer-Verlag, Volos, Greece, November.

Ian Witten and Eibe Frank. 2005. *Data Mining: Practical Machine Learning Tools and Techniques (Second Edition)*. Morgan Kaufmann.

Pierre Zweigenbaum, Dina Demner-Fushman, Hong Yu, and Kevin B. Cohen. 2007. Frontiers of biomedical text mining: current progress. *Briefings in Bioinformatics*, 8(5):358–375.

Text Classification based on the Latent Topics of Important Sentences extracted by the PageRank Algorithm

Yukari Ogura and **Ichiro Kobayashi**
Advanced Sciences, Graduate School of Humanities and Sciences,
Ochanomizu University
2-1-1 Ohtsuka Bunkyo-ku Tokyo, 112-8610 JAPAN
{ogura.yukari, koba}@is.ocha.ac.jp

Abstract

In this paper, we propose a method to raise the accuracy of text classification based on latent topics, reconsidering the techniques necessary for good classification – for example, to decide important sentences in a document, the sentences with important words are usually regarded as important sentences. In this case, *tf.idf* is often used to decide important words. On the other hand, we apply the PageRank algorithm to rank important words in each document. Furthermore, before clustering documents, we refine the target documents by representing them as a collection of important sentences in each document. We then classify the documents based on latent information in the documents. As a clustering method, we employ the k-means algorithm and investigate how our proposed method works for good clustering. We conduct experiments with Reuters-21578 corpus under various conditions of important sentence extraction, using latent and surface information for clustering, and have confirmed that our proposed method provides better result among various conditions for clustering.

1 Introduction

Text classification is an essential issue in the field of natural language processing and many techniques using latent topics have so far been proposed and used under many purposes. In this paper, we aim to raise the accuracy of text classification using latent information by reconsidering elemental techniques necessary for good classification in the following three points: 1) important words extraction — to decide important words in documents is a crucial issue for text classification, *tf.idf* is often used to decide them. Whereas, we apply the PageRank algorithm (Brin et al., 1998) for the issue, because the algorithm scores the centrality of a node in a graph, and important words should be regarded as having the centrality (Hassan et al., 2007). Besides, the algorithm can detect centrality in any kind of graph, so we can find important words for any purposes. In our study, we express the relation of word co-occurrence in the form of a graph. This is because we use latent information to classify documents, and documents with high topic coherence tend to have high PMI of words in the documents (Newman et al., 2010). So, we construct a graph from a viewpoint of text classification based on latent topics. 2) Refinement of the original documents — we recompile the original documents with a collection of the extracted important sentences in order to refine the original documents for more sensitive to be classified. 3) Information used for classification — we use latent information estimated by latent Dirichlet allocation (LDA) (Blei et al., 2003) to classify documents, and compare the results of the cases using both surface and latent information. We experiment text classification with Reuters-21578 corpus; evaluate the result of our method with the results of those which have various other settings for classification; and show the usefulness of our proposed method.

2 Related studies

Many studies have proposed to improve the accuracy of text classification. In particular, in terms of improving a way of weighting terms in a document for text classification, there are many studies which use the PageRank algorithm. In (Hassan et al., 2007), they have applied a random-walk model on a graph constructed based on the words which co-occur within a given window size, e.g., 2,4,6,8 words in their experiments, and confirmed that the windows of size 2 and 4 supplied the most significant results across the multiple data set they used. Zaiane et al. (2002) and Wang et al. (2005) have introduced association rule mining to decide important words for text classification. In particular, Wang et al. have used a PageRank-style algorithm to rank words and shown their method is useful for text classification. Scheible et al. (2012) have proposed a method for bootstrapping a sentiment classifier from a seed lexicon. They apply topic-specific PageRank to a graph of both words and documents, and introduce Polarity PageRank, a new semi-supervised sentiment classifier that integrates lexicon induction with document classification. As a study related to topic detection by important words obtained by the PageRank algorithm, Kubek et al. (2011) has detected topics in a document by constructing a graph of word co-occurrence and applied the PageRank algorithm on it.

To weight words is not the issue for only text classification, but also an important issue for text summarization, Erkan et al. (2004) and Mihlcea et al. (2004b; 2004a) have proposed multi-document summarization methods using the PageRank algorithm, called LexRank and TextRank, respectively. They use PageRank scores to extract sentences which have centrality among other sentences for generating a summary from multi-documents.

On the other hand, since our method is to classify texts based on latent information. The graph used in our method is constructed based on word co-occurrence so that important words which are sensitive to latent information can be extracted by the PageRank algorithm. At this point, our attempt differs from the other approaches.

3 Techniques for text classification

3.1 Extraction of important words

To decide important words, *tf.idf* is often adopted, whereas, another methods expressing various relation among words in a form of a graph have been proposed (2005; Hassan et al., 2007). In particular, (Hassan et al., 2007) shows that the PageRank score is more clear to rank important words rather than *tf.idf*. In this study, we refer to their method and use PageRank algorithm to decide important words.

The PageRank algorithm was developed by (Brin et al., 1998). The algorithm has been used as the basic algorithm of Google search engine, and also used for many application to rank target information based on the centrality of information represented in the form of a graph.

In this study, the important words are selected based on PageRank score of a graph which represents the relation among words. In other words, in order to obtain good important sentences for classification, it is of crucial to have a good graph (Zhu et al., 2005) because the result will be considerably changed depending on what kind of a graph we will have for important words. In this study, since we use latent information for text classification, therefore, we construct a graph representing the relation of words from a viewpoint topic coherence. According to (Newman et al., 2010), topic coherence is related to word co-occurrence. Referring to their idea, we construct a graph over words in the following manner: each word is a node in the graph, and there is an undirected edge between every pair of words that appear within a three-sentence window – to take account of contextual information for words, we set a three-sentence window. We then apply the PageRank algorithm to this graph to obtain a score for every word which is a measurement of its centrality – the centrality of a word corresponds to the importance of a word. A small portion of a graph might look like the graph in Figure 1.

3.2 Refinement of target documents

After selecting important words, the important sentences are extracted until a predefined ratio of whole sentences in each document based on the selected important words, and then we reproduce refined documents with a collection of extracted important sentences. An important sentence is decided by how many important words are included in the sentence. The refined documents are composed of the important sentences extracted from a viewpoint of latent information, i.e., word co-occurrence, so they are proper to be classified based on latent information.

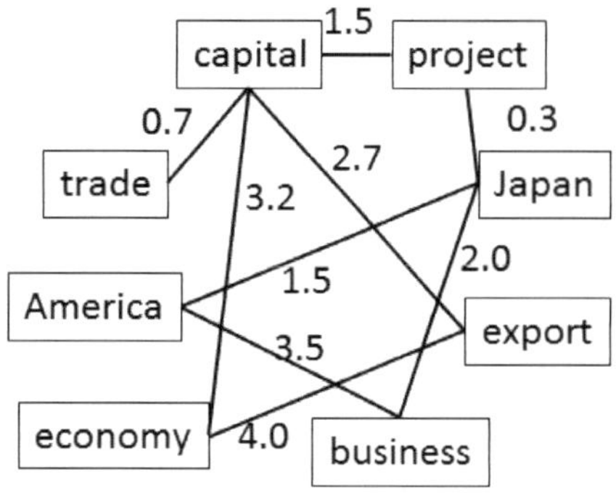

Figure 1: A graph of word cooccurrence

3.3 Clustering based on latent topics

After obtaining a collection of refined documents for classification, we adopt LDA to estimate the latent topic probabilistic distributions over the target documents and use them for clustering. In this study, we use the topic probability distribution over documents to make a topic vector for each document, and then calculate the similarity among documents.

3.4 Clustering algorithm

step.1 *Important words determination*

The important words are decided based on *tf.idf* or PageRank scores. As for the words decided based on PageRank scores, we firstly have to make a graph on which the PargeRank algorithm is applied. In our study, we construct a graph based on word co-occurrence. So, important words are selected based on the words which have centrality in terms of word co-occurrence. In particular, in our study we select co-occurred words in each three sentences in a document, taking account of the influence of contextual information.

step.2 *Refinement of the target documents*

After selecting the important words, we select the sentences with at least one of the words within the top 3 PageRank score as important sentences in each document, and then we reproduce refined documents with a collection of the extracted important sentences.

step.3 *Clustering based on latent topics*

As for the refined document obtained in step 2, the latent topics are estimated by means of LDA. Here, we decide the number of latent topics k in the target documents by measuring the value of perplexity $P(\boldsymbol{w})$ shown in equation (1). The similarity of documents are measured by the Jenshen-Shannon divergence shown in equation (2).

$$P(\boldsymbol{w}) = exp(-\frac{1}{N}\sum_{mn} log(\sum_{z} \theta_{mz}\phi_{zw_{mn}})) \tag{1}$$

Here, N is the number of all words in the target documents, w_{mn} is the n-th word in the m-th document; θ is the topic probabilistic distribution for the documents, and ϕ is the word probabilistic distribution for every topic.

$$\begin{aligned} &D_{JS}(P||Q) \\ &= \frac{1}{2}(\sum_{x} P(x)log\frac{P(x)}{R(x)} + \sum_{x} log\frac{Q(x)}{R(x)}) \\ &\qquad where, R(x) = \frac{P(x)+Q(x)}{2} \end{aligned} \tag{2}$$

4 Experiment

We evaluate our proposed method by comparing the accuracy of document clustering between our method and the method using *tf.idf* for extracting important words.

4.1 Experimental settings

As the documents for experiments, we use Reuters-21578 dataset [1] collected from the Reuters newswire in 1987.In our proposed method, the refined documents consisting of important sentences extracted from the original documents are classified, therefore, if there are not many sentences in a document, we will not be able to verify the usefulness of our proposed method. So, we use the documents which have more than 5 sentences in themselves. Of the 135 potential topic categories in Reuters-21578, referring to other clustering study (Erkan, 2006; 2005; Subramanya et al., 2008), we also use the most frequent 10 categories: i.e., *earn, acq, grain, wheat, money, crude, trade, interest, ship, corn*. In the

[1] http://www.daviddlewis.com/resources/testcollections/reuters21578/

sequel, we use 792 documents whose number of words is 15,835 for experiments – the 792 documents are the all documents which have more than 5 sentences in themselves in the corpus. For each document, stemming and stop-word removal processes are adopted. Furthermore, the hyper-parameters for topic probability distribution and word probability distribution in LDA are α=0.5 and β=0.5, respectively. We use Gibbs sampling and the number of iteration is 200. The number of latent topics is decided by perplexity, and we decide the optimal number of topics by the minimum value of the average of 10 times trial, changing the number of topics ranging from 1 to 30.

As the first step for clustering with our method, in this study we employ the k-means clustering algorithm because it is a representative and a simple clustering algorithm.

4.2 Evaluation method

For evaluation, we use both accuracy and F-value, referring to the methods used in (Erkan, 2006). As for a document d_i, l_i is the label provided to d_i by the clustering algorithm, and α_i is the correct label for d_i. The accuracy is expressed in equation (3).

$$Accuracy = \frac{\sum_{i=1}^{n} \delta\left(map\left(l_i\right), \alpha_i\right)}{n} \tag{3}$$

$\delta(x, y)$ is 1 if $x = y$, otherwise 0. $map(l_i)$ is the label provided to d_i by the k-means clustering algorithm. For evaluation, the F-value of each category is computed and then the average of the F-values of the whole categories, used as an index for evaluation, is computed (see, equation (4)).

$$F = \frac{1}{|C|} \sum_{c_i \in C} F\left(c_i\right) \tag{4}$$

As the initial data for the k-means clustering algorithm, a correct document of each category is randomly selected and provided. By this, the category of classified data can be identified as in (Erkan, 2006).

4.3 Experiment results

To obtain the final result of the experiment, we applied the k-means clustering algorithm for 10 times for the data set and averaged the results. Here, in the case of clustering the documents based on the topic probabilistic distribution by LDA, the topic distribution over documents θ is changed in every estimation. Therefore, we estimated θ for 8 times and then applied the k-means clustering algorithm with each θ for 10 times. We averaged the results of the 10 trials and finally evaluated it. The number of latent topics was estimated as 11 by perplexity. We used it in the experiments. To measure the latent similarity among documents, we construct topic vectors with the topic probabilistic distribution, and then adopt the Jensen-Shannon divergence to measures it, on the other hand, in the case of using document vectors we adopt cosine similarity.

Table 1 and Table 2 show the cases of with and without refining the original documents by recompiling the original documents with the important sentences.

Table 1: Extracting important sentences

Methods	Measure	Accuracy	F-value
PageRank	Jenshen-Shannon	**0.567**	**0.485**
	Cosine similarity	0.287	0.291
tf.idf	Jenshen-Shannon	0.550	0.435
	Cosine similarity	0.275	0.270

Table 2: Without extracting important sentences

Similarity measure	Accuracy	F-value
Jenshen-Shannon	0.518	0.426
Cosine similarity	0.288	0.305

Table 3, 4 show the number of words and sentences after applying each method to decide important words.

Table 3: Change of number of words

Methods	1 word	2 words	3 words	4 words	5 words
PageRank	12,268	13,141	13,589	13,738	13,895
$tf \cdot idf$	13,999	14,573	14,446	14,675	14,688

Furthermore, Table 5 and 6 show the accuracy and F-value of both methods, i.e., PageRank scores and *tf.idf*, in the case that we use the same number of sentences in the experiment to experiment under the same conditions.

Table 4: Change of number of sentences

Methods	1 word	2 words	3 words	4 words	5 words
PageRank	1,244	1,392	1,470	1,512	1,535
$tf \cdot idf$	1,462	1,586	1,621	1,643	1,647

Table 5: Accuracy to the number of topics

Num. of topics	8	9	10	11	12
PageRank	0.525	0.535	**0.566**	0.553	0.524
tf.idf	0.556	0.525	0.557	0.550	0.541

4.4 Discussion

We see from the experiment results that as for the measures based on the Jenshen-Shannon divergence, both accuracy and F-value of the case where refined documents are clustered is better than the case where the original documents are clustered. We have conducted t-test to confirm whether or not there is significant difference between the cases: with and without extracting important sentences. As a result, there is significant difference with 5 % and 1 % level for the accuracy and F-value, respectively.

When extracting important sentences, although the size of the document set to be clustered is smaller than the original set, the accuracy increases. So, it can be said that necessary information for clustering is adequately extracted from the original document set.

From this, we have confirmed that the documents are well refined for better clustering by recompiling the documents with important sentences. We think the reason for this is because only important sentences representing the contents of a document are remained by refining the original documents and then it would become easier to measure the difference between probabilistic distributions of topics in a document. Moreover, as for extracting important sentences, we confirmed that the accuracy of the case of using PageRank scores is better than the case of using *tf.idf*. By this, constructing a graph based on word co-occurrence of each 3 sentences in a document works well to rank important words, taking account of the context of the word.

We see from Table 3 , 4 that the number of words and sentences decreases when applying PageRank scores. In the case of applying *tf.idf*, the *tf.idf* value tends to be higher for the words which often appear in a particular document. Therefore, the extraction of sentences including the words with high *tf.idf* value may naturally lead to the extraction of many sentences.

The reason for low accuracy in the case of using cosine similarity for clustering is that it was observed that the range of similarity between documents is small, therefore, the identification of different categorized documents was not well achieved.

Table 6: F-value to the number of topics

Num. of topics	8	9	10	11	12
PageRank	0.431	0.431	**0.467**	0.460	0.434
tf.idf	0.466	0.430	0.461	0.435	0.445

Table 5 and Table 6 show the accuracy and F-value to the number of latent topics, respectively. We see that both accuracy and F-value of the case of using PageRank scores are better than those of the case of using *tf.idf* in the case of the number of topics is 9,10,and 11. In particular, the highest score is made when the number of topics is 10 for both evaluation measures — we think the reason for this is because we used document sets of 10 categories, therefore, it is natural to make the highest score when the number of topics is 10. So, we had better look at the score of the case where the number of topics is 10 to compare the ability of clustering. By the result, we can say that PageRank is better in refining the documents so as they suit to be classified based on latent information.

5 Conclusions

In this study, we have proposed a method of text clustering based on latent topics of important sentences in a document. The important sentences are extracted through important words decided by the PageRank algorithm. In order to verify the usefulness of our proposed method, we have conducted text clustering experiments with Reuters-21578 corpus under various conditions — we have adopted either PageRank scores or *tf.idf* to decide important words for important sentence extraction, and then adopted the k-means clustering algorithm for the documents recompiled with the extracted important sentences based on either latent or surface information. We see from the results of the experiments that the clustering based on latent information is generally better than that based on surface information in terms of clustering accuracy. Furthermore, deciding important words with PageRank scores is better than that with *tf.idf* in terms of clustering accuracy. Com pared to the number of the extracted words in important sentences between PageRank scores and *tf.idf*, we see that the number of sentences extracted based on PageRank scores is smaller than that based on *tf.idf*, therefore, it can be thought that more context-sensitive sentences are extracted by adopting PageRank scores to decide important words.

As future work, since clustering accuracy will be changed by how many sentences are compiled in a refined document set, therefore, we will consider a more sophisticated way of selecting proper important sentences. Or, to avoid the problem of selecting sentences, we will also directly use the words extracted as important words for clustering. Moreover, at this moment, we use only k-means clustering algorithm, so we will adopt our proposed method to other various clustering methods to confirm the usefulness of our method.

References

David M. Blei and Andrew Y. Ng and Michael I. Jordan and John Lafferty. 2003. *Latent dirichlet allocation*, Journal of Machine Learning Research,

Sergey Brin and Lawrence Page. 1998. The Anatony of a Large-scale Hypertextual Web Search Engine, Computer Networks and ISDN Systems, pages. 107–117.

Gunes Erkan, 2004. *LexRank: Graph-based Lexical Centrality as Salience in Text Summarization* Journal of Artificial Intelligence Research 22, pages.457-479

Gunes Erkan. 2006. *Language Model-Based Document Clustering Using Random Walks*, Association for Computational Linguistics, pages.479–486.

Samer Hassan, Rada Mihalcea and Carmen Banea. 2007. *Random-Walk Term Weighting for Improved Text Classification*, SIGIR '07 Proceedings of the 30th annual international ACM SIGIR conference on Research and development in information retrieval, pages.829-830.

Mario Kubek and Herwig Unger, 2011 *Topic Detection Based on the PageRank's Clustering Property*, IICS'11, pages.139-148,

Rada Mihalcea. 2004. *Graph-based Ranking Algorithms for Sentence Extraction, Applied to Text Summarization*, Proceeding ACLdemo '04 Proceedings of the ACL 2004 on Interactive poster and demonstration sessions Article No. 20.

Rada Mihalcea and Paul Tarau 2004. *TextRank: Bringing Order into Texts*, Conference on Empirical Methods in Natural Language Processing.

David Newman, Jey Han Lau, Karl Grieser, and Timothy Baldwin, 2010. *Automatic evaluation of topic coherence*, Human Language Technologies: The 2010 Annual Conference of the North Ametican Chapter of the Association for Computational Linguistics, pages. 100–108, Los Angeles.

Christian Scheible, Hinrich Shutze. 2012. *Bootstrapping Sentiment Labels For Unannotated Documents With Polarity PageRank*, Proceedings of the Eight International Conference on Language Resources and Evaluation.

Amarnag Subramanya, Jeff Bilmes. 2008. *Soft-Supervised Learning for Text Classification* Proceedings of the 2008 Conference on Empirical Methods in Natural Language Processing, pages.1090–1099, Honolulu.

Wei Wang, Diep Bich Do, and Xuemin Lin. 2005. *Term Graph Model for Text Classification*, Springer-Verlag Berlin Heidelberg 2005, pages.19–30.

Osmar R. Zaiane and Maria-luiza Antonie. 2002. *Classifying Text Documents by Associating Terms with Text Categories*, In Proc. of the Thirteenth Australasian Database Conference (ADC'02), pages.215–222,

X Zhu. 2005. *Semi-supervised learning with Graphs*, Ph.D thesis, Carnegie Mellon University.

Automated Collocation Suggestion for Japanese Second Language Learners

Lis W. Kanashiro Pereira Erlyn Manguilimotan Yuji Matsumoto

Nara Institute of Science and Technology
Department of Information Science
{lis-k, erlyn-m, matsu}@is.naist.jp

Abstract

This study addresses issues of Japanese language learning concerning word combinations (collocations). Japanese learners may be able to construct grammatically correct sentences, however, these may sound "unnatural". In this work, we analyze correct word combinations using different collocation measures and word similarity methods. While other methods use well-formed text, our approach makes use of a large Japanese language learner corpus for generating collocation candidates, in order to build a system that is more sensitive to constructions that are difficult for learners. Our results show that we get better results compared to other methods that use only well-formed text.

1 Introduction

Automated grammatical error correction is emerging as an interesting topic of natural language processing (NLP). However, previous research in second language learning are focused on restricted types of learners' errors, such as article and preposition errors (Gamon, 2010; Rozovskaya and Roth, 2010; Tetreault et al., 2010). For example, research for Japanese language mainly focuses on Japanese case particles (Suzuki and Toutanova, 2006; Oyama and Matsumoto, 2010). It is only recently that NLP research has addressed issues of collocation errors.

Collocations are conventional word combinations in a language. In Japanese, *ocha wo ireru* "お茶を入れる[1] [to make tea]" and *yume wo miru* " 夢を見る[2] [to have a dream]" are examples of collocations. Even though their accurate use is crucial to make communication precise and to sound like a native speaker, learning them is one of the most difficult tasks for second language learners. For instance, the Japanese collocation *yume wo miru* [lit. to see a dream] is unpredictable, at least, for native speakers of English, because its constituents are different from those in the Japanese language. A learner might create the unnatural combination *yume wo suru*, using the verb *suru* (a general light verb meaning "do" in English) instead of *miru* "to see".

In this work, we analyze various Japanese corpora using a number of collocation and word similarity measures to deduce and suggest the best collocations for Japanese second language learners. In order to build a system that is more sensitive to constructions that are difficult for learners, we use word similarity measures that generate collocation candidates using a large Japanese language learner corpus. By employing this approach, we could obtain a better result compared to other methods that use only well-formed text.

The remainder of the paper is organized as follows. In Section 2, we introduce related work on collocation error correction. Section 3 explains our method, based on word similarity and association measures, for suggesting collocations. In Section 4, we describe different word similarity and association measures, as well as the corpora used in our experiments. The experimental setup and the results are described in Sections 5 and 6, respectively. Section 7 points out the future directions for our research.

2 Related Work

Collocation correction currently follows a similar approach used in article and preposition correction. The general strategy compares the learner's word choice to a confusion set generated from well-formed text during the training phase. If one or more alternatives are more appropriate to the context, the learner's word is flagged as an error and the alternatives are suggested as corrections. To constrain the size of the confusion set,

[1] lit. to put in tea
[2] lit. to see a dream

similarity measures are used. To rank the best candidates, the strength of association in the learner's construction and in each of the generated alternative construction are measured.

For example, Futagi et al. (2008) generated synonyms for each candidate string using WordNet and Roget's Thesaurus and used the rank ratio measure to score them by their semantic similarity. Liu et al. (2009) also used WordNet to generate synonyms, but used Pointwise Mutual Information as association measure to rank the candidates. Chang et al. (2008) used bilingual dictionaries to derive collocation candidates and used the log-likelihood measure to rank them. One drawback of these approaches is that they rely on resources of limited coverage, such as dictionaries, thesaurus or manually constructed databases to generate the candidates. Other studies have tried to offer better coverage by automatically deriving paraphrases from parallel corpora (Dahlmeier and Ng, 2011), but similar to Chang et al. (2008), it is essential to identify the learner's first language and to have bilingual dictionaries and parallel corpora for every first language (L1) in order to extend the resulting system. Another problem is that most research does not actually take the learners' tendency of collocation errors into account; instead, their systems are trained only on well-formed text corpora. Our work follows the general approach, that is, uses similarity measures for generating the confusion set and association measures for ranking the best candidates. However, instead of using only well-formed text for generating the confusion set, we use a large learner corpus created by crawling the revision log of a language learning social networking service (SNS), Lang-8[3]. Another work that also uses data from Lang-8 is Mizumoto et al. (2011), which uses Lang-8 in creating a large-scale Japanese learner's corpus. The biggest benefit of using such kind of data is that we can obtain in large scale pairs of learners' sentences and their corrections assigned by native speakers.

3 Combining Word Similarity and Association Measures to Suggest Collocations

In our work, we focus on suggestions for noun and verb collocation errors in "*noun wo verb* (noun-を-verb)" constructions, where *noun* is the direct object of *verb*. Our approach consists of three steps: 1) for each extracted tuple in the second learner's composition, we created a set of candidates by substituting words generated using word similarity algorithms; 2) then, we measured the strength of association in the writer's phrase and in each generated candidate phrase using association measures to compute collocation scores; 3) the highest ranking alternatives are suggested as corrections. In our evaluation, we checked if the correction given in the learner corpus matches one of the suggestions given by the system. Figure 1 illustrates the method used in this study.

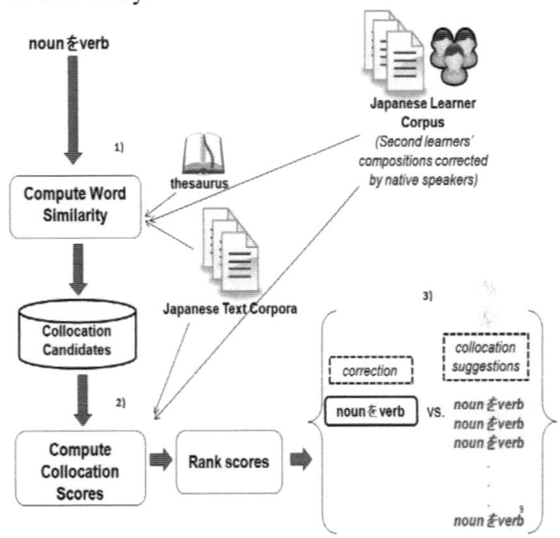

Figure 1 Word Similarity and Association Measures combination method for suggesting col-locations.

We considered only the tuples that contain noun or verb error. A real application, however, should also deal with error detection. For each example of the construction on the writer's text, the system should create the confusion set with alternative phrases, measure the strength of association in the writer's phrase and in each generated alternative phrase and flag as error only if the association score of the writer's phrase is lower than one or more of the alternatives generated and suggest the higher-ranking alternatives as corrections.

4 Approaches to Word Similarity and Word Association Strength

4.1 Word Similarity

Similarity measures are used to generate the collocation candidates that are later ranked using association measures. In our work, we used the following three measures to analyze word simila-

[3] www.lang-8.com

		Confusion Set							
Word	する	受ける	始める	作る	書く	言う	食べる	やる	持つ
Meaning	*do*	*accept*	*begin*	*make*	*write*	*say*	*eat*	*do*	*carry*
Word	ビル	ビール	生ビール	お金	札	金額	景色	料金	建築物
Meaning	*building*	*beer*	*draft beer*	*money*	*bill*	*amount of money*	*scenery*	*fee*	*building*

Table 1 Confusion Set example for the words *suru* (する) and *biru* (ビル)

	書く write	読む read	つける put on
日記を diary	15	11	8

Table 2 Context of a particular noun represented as a co-occurrence vector

	ご飯を rice	ラーメンを ramen noodle soup	カレーを curry
食べる eat	164	53	39

Table 3 Context of a particular noun represented as a co-occurrence vector

rity: 1) thesaurus-based word similarity, 2) distributional similarity and 3) confusion set derived from learner corpus. The first two measures generate the collocation candidates by finding words that are analogous to the writer's choice, a common approach used in the related work on collocation error correction (Liu et al., 2009; Östling and O. Knutsson, 2009; Wu et al., 2010) and the third measure generates the candidates based on the corrections given by native speakers in the learner corpus.

Thesaurus-based word similarity: The intuition of this measure is to check if the given words have similar glosses (definitions). Two words are considered similar if they are near each other in the thesaurus hierarchy (have a path within a pre-defined threshold length).

Distributional Similarity: Thesaurus-based methods produce weak recall since many words, phrases and semantic connections are not covered by hand-built thesauri, especially for verbs and adjectives. As an alternative, distributional similarity models are often used since it gives higher recall. On the other hand, distributional similarity models tend to have lower precision (Jurafsky et al., 2009), because the candidate set is larger. The intuition of this measure is that two words are similar if they have similar word contexts. In our task, context will be defined by some grammatical dependency relation, specifically, 'object-verb' relation. Context is represented as co-occurrence vectors that are based on syntactic dependencies. We are interested in computing similarity of nouns and verbs and hence the context of a particular noun is a vector of verbs that are in an object relation with that noun. The context of a particular verb is a vector of nouns that are in an object relation with that verb. Table 2 and Table 3 show examples of part of co-occurrence vectors for the noun "日記 [*diary*]" and the verb "食べる [*eat*]", respectively. The numbers indicate the co-occurrence frequency in the BCCWJ corpus (Maekawa, 2008). We computed the similarity between co-occurrence vectors using different metrics: Cosine Similarity, Dice coefficient (Curran, 2004), Kullback-Leibler divergence or KL divergence or relative entropy (Kullback and Leibler, 1951) and the Jenson-Shannon divergence (Lee, 1999).

Confusion Set derived from learner corpus: In order to build a module that can "guess" common construction errors, we created a confusion set using Lang-8 corpus. Instead of generating words that have similar meaning to the learner's written construction, we extracted *all* the possible noun and verb corrections for each of the nouns and verbs found in the data. Table 1 shows some examples extracted. For instance, the confusion set of the verb *suru* "する [*to do*]" is composed of verbs such as *ukeru* "受ける [*to accept*]", which does not necessarily have similar meaning with *suru*. The confusion set means that in the corpus, *suru* was corrected to either one of these verbs, i.e., when the learner writes the verb *suru*, he/she might actually mean to write one of the verbs in the confusion set. For the noun *biru*"ビル [*building*]", the learner may have, for example, misspelled the word *bīru* "ビール [*beer*]", or may have got confused with the translation of the English words *bill* ("お金[*money*]", "札 [*bill*]", "金額 [amount of money]", "料金 [*fee*]") or *view* ("景色 [*scenery*]") to Japanese.

4.2 Word Association Strength

After generating the collocation candidates using word similarity, the next step is to identify the "true collocations" among them. Here, the association strength was measured, in such a way that word pairs generated by chance from the sampling process can be excluded. An association measure assigns an association score to each word pair. High scores indicate strong association, and can be used to select the "true collocations". We adopted the Weighted Dice coefficient (Kitamura and Matsumoto, 1997) as our association measurement. We also tested using other association measures (results are omitted): Pointwise Mutual Information (Church and Hanks, 1990), log-likelihood ratio (Dunning, 1993) and Dice coefficient (Smadja et al., 1996), but Weighted Dice performed best.

5 Experiment setup

We divided our experiments into two parts: verb suggestion and noun suggestion. For verb suggestion, given the learners' "*noun wo verb*" construction, our focus is to suggest "*noun wo verb*" collocations with alternative verbs other than the learner's written verb. For noun suggestion, given the learners' "*noun wo verb*" construction, our focus is to suggest "*noun wo verb*" collocations with alternative nouns other than the learner's written noun.

5.1 Data Set

For computing word similarity and association scores for verb suggestion, the following resources were used:

1) Bunrui Goi Hyo Thesaurus (The National Institute for Japanese Language, 1964): a Japanese thesaurus, which has a vocabulary size of around 100,000 words, organized into 32,600 unique semantic classes. This thesaurus was used to compute word similarity, taking the words that are in the same subtree as the candidate word. By subtree, we mean the tree with distance 2 from the leaf node (learner's written word) doing the pre-order tree traversal.

2) Mainichi Shimbun Corpus (Mainichi Newspaper Co., 1991): one of the major newspapers in Japan that provides raw text of newspaper articles used as linguistic resource. One year data (1991) were used to extract the "*noun wo verb*" tuples to compute word similarity (using cosine similarity metric) and collocation scores. We extracted 224,185 tuples composed of 16,781 unique verbs and 37,300 unique nouns.

3) Balanced Corpus of Contemporary Written Japanese, BCCWJ Corpus (Maekawa, 2008): composed of one hundred million words, portions of this corpus used in our experiments include magazine, newspaper, textbooks, and blog data[4]. Incorporating a variety of topics and styles in the training data helps minimize the domain gap problem between the learner's vocabulary and newspaper vocabulary found in the Mainichi Shimbun data. We extracted 194,036 "*noun wo verb*" tuples composed of 43,243 unique nouns and 18,212 unique verbs. These data are necessary to compute the word similarity (using cosine similarity metric) and collocation scores.

4) Lang-8 Corpus: Consisted of two year data (2010 and 2011):

A) Year 2010 data, which contain 1,288,934 pairs of learner's sentence and its correction, was used to: i) Compute word similarity (using cosine similarity metric) and collocation scores: We took out the learners' sentences and used only the corrected sentences. We extracted 163,880 "*noun wo verb*" tuples composed of 38,999 unique nouns and 16,086 unique verbs. ii) Construct the confusion set (explained in Section 4.1): We constructed the confusion set for all the 16,086 verbs and 38,999 nouns that appeared in the data.

B) Year 2011 data were used to construct the test set (described in Section 5.2).

5.2 Test set selection

We used Lang-8 (2011 data) for selecting our test set. For the verb suggestion task, we extracted all the "*noun wo verb*" tuples with incorrect verbs and their correction. From the tuples extracted, we selected the ones where the verbs were corrected to the same verb 5 or more times by the native speakers. Similarly, for the noun suggestion task, we extracted all the "*noun wo verb*" tuples with incorrect nouns and their correction. There are cases where the learner's construction sounds more acceptable than its correction, cases where in the corpus, they were corrected due to some contextual information. For our application, since we are only considering

[4] Although the language used in blog data is usually more informal than the one used in newspaper, maganizes, etc., and might contain errors like spelling and grammar, collocation errors are much less frequent compared to spelling and grammar errors, since combining words appropriately is one the vital competencies of a native speaker of a language.

the noun, particle and verb that the learner wrote, there was a need to filter out such contextually induced corrections. To solve this problem, we used the Weighted Dice coefficient to compute the association strength between the noun and all the verbs, filtering out the pairs where the learner's construction has a higher score than the correction. After applying those conditions, we obtained 185 tuples for the verb suggestion test set and 85 tuples for the noun suggestion test set.

5.3 Evaluation Metrics

We compared the verbs in the confusion set ranked by collocation score suggested by the system with the human correction verb and noun in the Lang-8 data. A match would be counted as a true positive (*tp*). A false negative (*fn*) occurs when the system cannot offer any suggestion.

The metrics we used for the evaluation are: precision, recall and the mean reciprocal rank (MRR). We report precision at rank *k*, *k*=1, 5, computing the rank of the correction when a true positive occurs. The MRR was used to assess whether the suggestion list contains the correction and how far up it is in the list. It is calculated as follows:

$$MRR = \frac{1}{N}\sum_{i=1}^{N}\frac{1}{rank(i)} \tag{1}$$

where N is the size of the test set. If the system did not return the correction for a test instance, we set $\frac{1}{rank(i)}$ to zero. Recall rate is calculated with the formula below:

$$\frac{tp}{tp + fn} \tag{2}$$

6 Results

Table 4 shows the ten models derived from combining different word similarity measures and the Weighted Dice measure as association measure, using different corpora. In this table, for instance, we named *M1* the model that uses thesaurus for computing word similarity and uses Mainichi Shimbun corpus when computing collocation scores using the association measure adopted, Weighted Dice. *M2* uses Mainichi Shimbun corpus for computing both word similarity and collocation scores. *M10* computes word similarity using the confusing set from Lang-8 corpus and uses BCCWJ and Lang-8 corpus when computing collocation scores.

Considering that the size of the candidate set generated by different word similarity measures vary considerably, we limit the size of the confusion set to 270 for verbs and 160 for nouns, which correspond to the maximum values of the confusion set size for nouns and verbs when using Lang-8 for generating the candidate set. Setting up a threshold was necessary since the size of the candidate set generated when using Distributional Similarity methods may be quite large, affecting the system performance. When computing Distributional Similarity, scores are also assigned to each candidate, thus, when we set up a threshold value *n*, we consider the list of *n* candidates with highest scores. Table 4 reports the precision of the k-best suggestions, the recall rate and the MRR for verb and noun suggestion.

6.1 Verb Suggestion

Table 4 shows that the model using thesaurus (M1) achieved the highest precision rate among the other models; however, it had the lowest recall. The model could suggest for cases where the wrong verb written by the learner and the correction suggested in Lang-8 data have similar meaning, as they are near to each other in the thesaurus hierarchy. However, for cases where the wrong verb written by the learner and the correction suggested in Lang-8 data do not have similar meaning, M1 could not suggest the correction.

In order to improve the recall rate, we generated models *M2-M6*, which use distributional similarity (cosine similarity) and also use corpora other than Mainichi Shimbun corpus to minimize the domain gap problem between the learner's vocabulary and the newspaper vocabulary found in the Mainichi Shimbun data. The recall rate improved significantly but the precision rate decreased. In order to compare it with other distributional similarity metrics (Dice, KL-Divergence and Jenson-Shannon Divergence) and with the method that uses Lang-8 for generating the confusion set, we chose the model with the highest recall value as baseline, which is the one that uses BCCWJ and Lang-8 (*M6*) and generated other models (*M7-M10*). The best MRR value obtained among all the Distributional Similarity methods was obtained by Jenson-Shannon divergence. The highest recall and MRR values are achieved when Lang-8 data were used to generate the confusion set (*M10*).

	Similarity used for Confusion Sets	Thesaurus	Cosine Similarity					Dice Coefficient	KL Divergence	Jenson-Shannon Divergence	Confusion Set from Lang-8
	K-Best	Mainichi Shimbun	Mainichi Shimbun	BCCWJ	Lang-8	Mainichi Shimbun + BCCWJ	BCCWJ + Lang-8	BCCWJ + Lang-8	BCCWJ + Lang-8	BCCWJ + Lang-8	BCCWJ + Lang-8
		M1	*M2*	*M3*	*M4*	*M5*	*M6*	*M7*	*M8*	*M9*	*M10*
Verb Suggestion	*1*	**0.94**	0.48	0.42	0.60	0.62	0.56	0.59	0.63	0.60	0.64
	5	**1**	0.91	0.94	0.90	0.90	0.86	0.86	0.84	0.88	0.95
	Recall	0.20	0.40	0.30	0.68	0.49	0.71	0.81	0.35	0.74	**0.97**
	MRR	0.19	0.26	0.19	0.49	0.36	0.50	0.58	0.26	0.53	**0.75**
Noun Suggestion	*1*	0.16	0.20	0.42	0.58	0.50	0.55	0.30	0.63	0.57	**0.73**
	5	**1**	0.66	0.94	0.89	1	0.91	0.83	1	0.84	0.98
	Recall	0.07	0.17	0.22	0.45	0.04	0.42	0.35	0.12	0.38	**0.98**
	MRR	0.03	0.06	0.13	0.33	0.02	0.29	0.18	0.10	0.26	**0.83**

Table 4 The precision and recall rate and MRR of the Models of Word Similarity and Association Strength method combination.

6.2 Noun Suggestion

Similar to the verb suggestion experiments, the best recall and MRR values are achieved when Lang-8 data were used to generate the confusion set (*M10*).

For noun suggestion, our automatically constructed test set includes a number of spelling correction cases, such as cases for the combination *eat ice cream*, where the learner wrote *aisukurimu wo taberu* "アイスクリムを食べる" and the correction is *aisukurīmu wo taberu* "アイスクリームを食べる". Such phenomena did not occur with the test set for verb suggestion. For those cases, the fact that only spelling correction is necessary in order to have the right collocation may also indicate that the learner is more confident regarding the choice of the noun than the verb. This also justifies the even lower recall rate obtained (0.07) when using a thesaurus for generating the candidates

7 Conclusion and Future Work

We analyzed various Japanese corpora using a number of collocation and word similarity measures to deduce and suggest the best collocations for Japanese second language learners. In order to build a system that is more sensitive to constructions that are difficult for learners, we use word similarity measures that generate collocation candidates using a large Japanese language learner corpus, instead of only using well-formed text. By employing this approach, we could obtain better recall and MRR values compared to thesaurus based method and distributional similarity methods.

Although only noun-wo-verb construction is examined, the model is designed to be applicable to other types of constructions, such as adjective-noun and adverb-noun. Another straightforward extension is to pursue constructions with other particles, such as "*noun ga verb* (subject-verb)", "*noun ni verb* (dative-verb)", etc. In our experiments, only a small context information is considered (only the noun, the particle wo (を) and the verb written by the learner). In order to verify our approach and to improve our current results, considering a wider context size and other types of constructions will be the next steps of this research.

Acknowledgments

Special thanks to Yangyang Xi for maintaining Lang-8.

References

Y. C. Chang, J. S. Chang, H. J. Chen, and H. C. Liou. 2008. An automatic collocation writing assistant for Taiwanese EFL learners: A case of corpus-based NLP technology. *Computer Assisted Language Learning*, 21(3):283–299.

K. Church, and P. Hanks. 1990. Word Association Norms, Mutual Information and Lexicography, *Computational Linguistics*, Vol. 16:1, pp. 22-29.

J. R. Curran. 2004. From Distributional to Semantic Similarity. Ph.D. thesis, University of Edinburgh.

D. Dahlmeier, H. T. Ng. 2011. Correcting Semantic Collocation Errors with L1-induced Paraphrases. In *Proceedings of the 2011 Conference on Empirical Methods in Natural Language Processing*, pages 107–117, Edinburgh, Scotland, UK, July. Association for Computational Linguistics

T. Dunning. 1993. Accurate methods for the statistics of surprise and coincidence. *Computational Linguistics* 19.1 (Mar. 1993), 61-74.

Y. Futagi, P. Deane, M. Chodorow, and J. Tetreault. 2008. A computational approach to detecting collocation errors in the writing of non-native speakers of English. *Computer Assisted Language Learning*, 21, 4 (October 2008), 353-367.

M. Gamon. 2010. Using mostly native data to correct errors in learners' writing: A meta-classifier approach. In *Proceedings of Human Language Technologies: The 2010 Annual Conference of the North American Chapter of the ACL*, pages 163–171, Los Angeles, California, June. Association for Computational Linguistics.

D. Jurafsky and J. H. Martin. 2009. *Speech and Language Processing: An Introduction to Natural Language Processing*, Speech Recognition, and Computational Linguistics. 2nd edition. Prentice-Hall.

K. Maekawa. 2008. Balanced corpus of contemporary written japanese. In *Proceedings of the 6th Workshop on Asian Language Resources (ALR)*, pages 101–102.

M. Kitamura, Y. Matsumoto. 1997. Automatic extraction of translation patterns in parallel corpora. In *IPSJ*, Vol. 38(4), pp.108-117, April. In Japanese.

S. Kullback, R.A. Leibler. 1951. On Information and Sufficiency. *Annals of Mathematical Statistics* **22** (1): 79–86.

L. Lee. 1999. Measures of Distributional Similarity. In *Proc of the 37th annual meeting of the ACL*, Stroudsburg, PA, USA, 25.

A. L. Liu, D. Wible, and N. L. Tsao. 2009. Automated suggestions for miscollocations. In *Proceedings of the NAACL HLT Workshop on Innovative Use of NLP for Building Educational Applications*, pages 47–50, Boulder, Colorado, June. Association for Computational Linguistics.

Mainichi Newspaper Co. 1991. Mainichi Shimbun CD-ROM 1991.

T. Mizumoto, K. Mamoru, M. Nagata, Y. Matsumoto. 2011. Mining Revision Log of Language Learning SNS for Automated Japanese Error Correction of Second Language Learners. In *Proceedings of the 5th International Joint Conference on Natural Language Processing*, pp.147-155. Chiang Mai, Thailand, November. AFNLP.

R. Östling and O. Knutsson. 2009. A corpus-based tool for helping writers with Swedish collocations. In *Proceedings of the Workshop on Extracting and Using Constructions in NLP*, Nodalida, Odense, Denmark. 70, 77.

H. Oyama and Y. Matsumoto. 2010. Automatic Error Detection Method for Japanese Case Particles in Japanese Language Learners. *In Corpus, ICT, and Language Education*, pages 235–245.

A. Rozovskaya and D. Roth. 2010. Generating confusion sets for context-sensitive error correction. In *Proceedings of the 2010 Conference on Empirical Methods in Natural Language Processing, pages 961–970, MIT, Massachusetts, USA, October.* Association for Computational Linguistics.

F. Smadja, K. R. Mckeown, V. Hatzivassiloglou. 1996. Translation collocations for bilingual lexicons: a statistical approach. *Computational Linguistics*, 22:1-38.

H. Suzuki and K. Toutanova. 2006. Learning to Predict Case Markers in Japanese. In *Proceedings of the 21st International Conference on Computational Linguistics and 44th Annual Meeting of the ACL, pages 1049–1056 , Sydney, July. Association for Computational Linguistics.*J. Tetreault, J. Foster, and M. Chodorow. 2010. Using parse features for preposition selection and error detection. In *Proceedings of ACL 2010 Conference Short Papers*, pages 353-358, Uppsala, Sweden, July. Association for Computational Linguistics.

The National Institute for Japanese Language, editor. 1964. Bunrui-Goi-Hyo. Shuei shuppan. In Japanese.

J. C. Wu, Y. C. Chang, T. Mitamura, and J. S. Chang. 2010. Automatic collocation suggestion in academic writing. In *Proceedings of the ACL 2010 Conference Short Papers*, pages 115-119, Uppsala, Sweden, July. Association for Computational Linguistics.

Understanding Verbs based on Overlapping Verbs Senses

Kavitha Rajan
Language Technologies Research Centre
International Institute of Information Technology Hyderabad (IIIT-H)
Gachibowli, Hyderabad. 500 032.
AP. India.
kavitha@research.iiit.ac.in

Abstract

Natural language can be easily understood by everyone irrespective of their differences in age or region or qualification. The existence of a conceptual base that underlies all natural languages is an accepted claim as pointed out by Schank in his Conceptual Dependency (CD) theory. Inspired by the CD theory and theories in Indian grammatical tradition, we propose a new set of meaning primitives in this paper. We claim that this new set of primitives captures the meaning inherent in verbs and help in forming an inter-lingual and computable ontological classification of verbs. We have identified seven primitive overlapping verb senses which substantiate our claim. The percentage of coverage of these primitives is 100% for all verbs in Sanskrit and Hindi and 3750 verbs in English.

1 Introduction

Communication in natural language is simple. Looking at the ease to learn and communicate in and across natural languages, the claim of existence of interlingual conceptual base (Schank, 1972) seems plausible .

Conceptual Dependency (CD) theory tried to represent a conceptual base using a small set of meaning primitives. To achieve this goal, they put forward a proposal consisting of a small set of 12 primitive actions, a set of dependencies which connects the primitive actions with each other and with their actors, objects, instruments, etc. Their claim was that this small set of representational elements could be used to produce a canonical form for sentences in English as well as other natural languages. Representational theories like Scripts, Plans, Goals and Understanding(SPGU) representations (Schank and Abelson, 1977) were developed from the CD theory. None of the descendant theories of CD could focus on the notion of 'primitives' and the idea faded in the subsequent works.

Identification of meaning primitives is an area intensely explored and a vast number of theories have been put forward, namely, (PRO: Conceptual semantics (Jackendoff, 1976), Meaning-text theory (Mel'čuk,1981), Semantic Primes (Wierzbicka, 1996), Conceptual dependency theory (Schank, 1972) Preference Semantics (Wilks, 1975) CONTRA: Language of Thought (Fodor, 1975)). Through our work, we put forward a set of seven meaning primitives and claim that the permutation/combination of these seven meaning primitives along with ontological attributes is sufficient to develop a computational model for meaning representation across languages.

This paper looks at the Conceptual Dependency Theory created by Roger Schank (Schank, 1973; Schank, 1975) and compares it with theories in Indian grammatical tradition. We discuss these in section 2 and section 3. We then analyze if we can modify Schank's approach to define a more efficient set of primitives. We conclude by introducing the small set of meaning primitives which we have found to cover all verbs in Indian languages like Sanskrit, Hindi and almost all verbs in English.

2 Conceptual Dependency

According to Schank, linguistic and situational contexts in which a sentence is uttered is important for understanding the meaning of that sentence. The CD theory was developed to create a theory of human natural language understanding. The initial premise of the theory is: basis of natural language is conceptual. According to the theory, during communication, to-and-fro mapping happens between linguistic structures and the conceptual base through concepts. It is due to the existence of this conceptual base and concept based mapping that a person, who is multilingual, is able to switch between languages easily.

The conceptual base consists of concepts and the relations between concepts. Therefore, it is responsible for formally representing the concepts underlying an utterance. There are three types of concepts: a) nominal; b) action and c) modifier. We will concentrate only on 'action' since our work is related to verbs.

CD's basic premise is that the ACTION is the basis of any proposition that is not descriptive of a static piece of the world. Conceptualization consists of action, actors and cases that are dependent on that action. An ACTOR is defined as an animate object and an OBJECT as any concrete physical entity. CD representations use 12 primitive ACTs out of which the meaning of verbs, abstract and complex nouns are constructed.

Primitives are elements that can be used in many varied combinations to express the meaning of what underlies a given word. In CD, primitives were arrived at by noticing structural similarities that existed when sentences were put into an actor-action-object framework. Using these acts, set of states and set of conceptual roles, it is possible to express a large amount of the meanings expressible in a natural language.

3 Indian grammatical tradition

The Nirukta[1](Sarup,1920; Kunjunni et. al., 1990) statement "Verbs have operation as its predominant element" proposes that "process" is the most important element in a verb. As all words can be derived from verbal roots, we can say that words in a natural language are either activities (verbs) or derived from some activity (nouns). For example:

rājā (king) is derived from (the root) rāj (to shine)

vṛkṣa (tree) is derived from (the root) vṛ (to cover) kṣā (the earth)

Verb is called *kriyā* in Sanskrit. kriyā stands for action or activity. Verbs consists of both action and state verbs. Sage Kātyāyana (3rd century BC) put forward the *bhāva*-based definition to define all types of verbs. According to Nirukta verse 1.1 (Sarup, 1920) the characteristic that defines a verb form is its verb having bhāva as its principal meaning. In Sanskrit, bhāva is a morphological form of bhavati and bhavati means 'happening'. So structure of bhāva can be defined as structure of happening which is explained in section 4.1.

According to sage Vārśyāyaṇi, Nirukta verse 1.2 (Sarup, 1920), there are 6 variants of bhāva or verb which, we believe, can be compared to 6 fundamental processes. That is, a process 'verb' consists of six stages. They are:

coming into being	- jāyate 'is born, comes into being'
existing	- asti 'is'
changing	- vipariṇamate 'undergoes modification'
increasing	- vardhate 'grows, increases'
diminishing	- apakśIyate 'diminishes'
ceasing to be	- vinaśyati f'perishes'

4 Our Approach

We are trying to use existing theories in the traditional school of Sanskrit language, namely, Navya-Nyāya for identification and formal representation of primitive actions. We work within the formal framework of Neo- Vaiśesika Formal Ontology (NVFO)[2].

4.1 Form of verb

Happening is formally conceived as punctuation between two discrete states in a context. Since every happening consists of minimally two different states, there is an atomic sense of movement in it. Movement means whenever an action takes place two states come into existence. The initial state, at the beginning of an action and a final state, after the completion of the action. The two states can be same or different. Time is an inseparable part of this structure because between initial and final states there can be *n* number of intermediate states which are sequential.

Happening (Sanskrit, *bhavati*) is the change of state from one to another in a context. According to Bhartṛihari (5th century CE) every verb has

[1] Nirukta (Kunjunni et.al., page-88).

[2] Vaiśesika ontology, due to Kaṇāda (Rensink, 2004), Pras astapāda (Hutton, 2010) and Udayana (Kaṇāda, 1986) has been formalized by Navjyoti (Tavva and Singh, 2010).

'sense of sequence' and 'state' in it. Hence, every verb projects a 'sense of happening', making this sense omnipresent in all verbs. Therefore, *bhavati* is a 'universal verb'. In the nominalization of bhavati, 'bhāva[3]' has a formal structure and has been named '**punct**'[4]. The formal representation of bhāva is shown in Figure1.

The structure of (universal verb) 'punct' is:

< state1 | state2, (Context) Feature Space >

The structure can also be represented in short format as: < s1 / s2 | FS (C)>

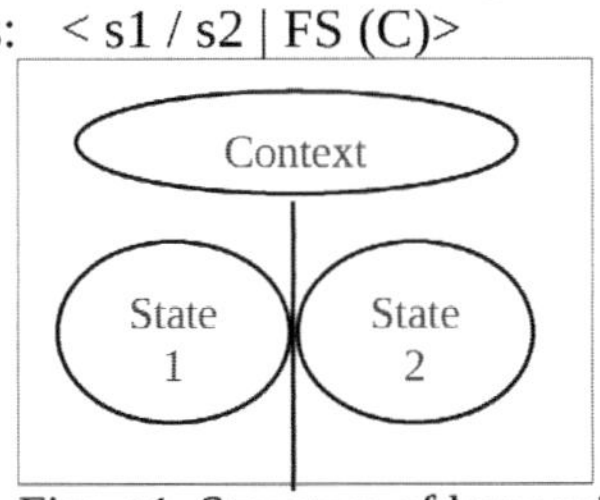

Figure1. Structure of happening

From Sanskritist tradition, we have adopted the concept of universal verb. Our original contribution is that we have defined an ontological structure (see Figure1) to represent 'universal verb' and have used it to represent the seven primary verb senses (primitives) which we have identified. All verbs in a language can be represented formally using this structure.

4.2 Identifying Overlapping Verbal senses

Can we have a few number of primitive meaning senses whose permutation / combination will enable us to explain all meanings in a language? Primitive verb senses in language were identified using an approach similar to Lesk's method (Lesk, 1986) of finding meaning overlaps for solving Word Sense Disambiguation problem.

All verbs and definitions of all senses of each verb in Sanskrit (2500) and 3750 verbs in English were collected. The verb senses were collected from various on-line dictionaries in both the languages. From these definitions, verbs which are used to explicate defined verbs were identified. The procedure followed for identifying frequent verbs is explained using a sample verb 'fall':

Definitions of different verb senses of 'fall' from two different sources are given below:

Source 1 (Dictionary.com):

(to **drop** or **descend** under the force of gravity, as to a lower place through loss or lack of support), (to come or **drop down** suddenly to a lower position, especially to leave a standing or erect position suddenly, whether voluntarily or not), (to **become less** or lower; become of a lower level, degree, amount, quality, value, number, etc.; decline)

Source 2 (WordNet):

(**descend** in free fall under the influence of gravity), (**decrease** in size, extent, or range), (**move downward** and lower, but not necessarily all the way), (move in a specified direction), (**lose** an upright position suddenly), (**drop** oneself to a lower or less erect position) are few senses.

All words in bold represent 'movement' in a negative manner. Since movement is the most common concept, **'move'** is taken as an overlapping primitive verb sense. Other primitives like know, do, is, have, cut, and cover were obtained by similar procedure.

In dictionaries, overlapping verb senses used to explicate meaning of defined verbs, show the relatedness of two verbs. The phenomenon known as 'Dictionary circularity' (Wierzbicka, 1996) confirms the existence of this claim.

In WordNet, the existence of most frequently used verbs is represented through 8 'common verbs' (Miller et. al, 1990): have/ has, be, make, run, set, go, take and get. State is dealt with separately in WordNet. We have modified the 'common verbs' concept of WordNet to include the concept of verbiality – the ability to denote a process developing in time (Lyudmila, 2010).

To analyze the phenomena of overlapping meanings of verbs, we studied verbs from a database of 3750 verbs and two other lexical resources:WordNet, Webster English Dictionary. From the word frequencies of the verbs in these three resources, we calculated the percentages[5] of overlapping verb senses used to explicate meaning of defined verbs. The results are shown in Table 1. Total verbs (unique word forms) in the three resources –

[3] Bhāva is defined by Patañjali as (1)existence, (2)something that comes into being, and (3) something that is brought into being.

[4] The formalization in NVFO is based on the idea of an ontological form which is recursive. This form is called 'punct'. Using punct's categories of Vaiśesika ontology can be derived.

[5] Percentage is calculated taking the frequency of a verb w.r.t the total verbs in the particular source.

Our database	3750
Webster Dictionary (Morehead, 2001)	1928
WordNet (Princeton University)	3400

Percentages of overlapping atomic meanings used to explicate meaning of defined verbs in the three resources are shown in Table 1.

Our Database	**WordNet**	**Webster Dictionary**
'do' 58.96%	'do' 37.40%	'is' 8.60%
'is' 6.36%	'is' 9.88%	'do' 16.18%
'have' 4.12%	'have' 11.7%	'know' 11.98%
'move' 17.69%	'move' 11.6%	'move' 11.93%
'know' 4.96%	'cut' 7.17%	'have' 10.48%
'cover' 4.75%	'cover' 5.3%	'cover' 8.86%
'cut' 3.22%	'know' 4.97%	'cut' 3.68%

Table1. Sample data of percentages of verbs in three resources.

When verbs and their definitions in English language were analyzed it was found that basic verb senses like 'know', 'do', 'have', 'move', 'is', 'cut', and 'cover' have higher frequency. The occurrence of higher frequencies of some verbs indicated that those were the verbs with maximum meaning sense overlap with other verbs.

4.3 The Seven Puncts

In order to handle similarities and overlaps in meaning we have developed the concept of overlapping verbal sense or 'punct'. These primitive verbal senses are intended to be building blocks out of which meaning of verbs can be constructed. We have identified seven 'puncts'. Two works WordNet (8 common verbs) and Nirukta (6 fundamental processes) were influential in restricting the number of overlapping verb senses to 7. We have modified the 8 common verbs in WordNet (have, be, get, set, make, do, run, take) in a way that each primitive meaning sense can be represented as a combination of 'state' and 'change'. Concepts like exist and un-exist, join and un-join, know and un-know, do and un-do, ascribing some actions to some objects and un-ascribe, movement / change and possess and un-possess are the basic meaning senses we have identified. 'un' stand for opposite here. Each primitive meaning sense consists of a sense and its negation. We have seen that verbs across languages can be classified using this seven primitives. Percentage of coverage of these seven primitives in Sanskrit and English are given in Table 2.

Puncts	**Percentage in English Verbs**	**Percentage in Sanskrit Verbs**
Know	4.96	4.27
Move	17.69	12.41
Do	58.90	56.99
Have	4.12	7.79
Is	6.36	7.41
Cut	3.22	7.06
Cover	4.75	4.07

Table2. Percentage[6] of coverage of the seven verb senses (puncts) in English & Sanskrit

Using this set of 7 'puncts' it is possible to express meaning inherent in verbs in a language and also to link the related verbs across languages. We will explain this by a deeper analysis of the seven 'puncts' (see Table 3).

The 'punct' can be used for identifying similarities between verbs like 'fall', 'plummet', 'flow' all of which have 'move' as primary sense and they can be used for finding out different senses of the same verb like 'break'. Thus 'break' can have primary sense of 'cut' and secondary sense of 'do' when the meaning is 'to destroy or stop or interrupt or cause something to separate something'. Similarly, 'break' can also have 'move' as primary sense and 'is' as secondary sense when the meaning is 'voice change of a person or day or dawn break or breaking news '. Though a verb can have two to all seven verbal senses, we are grouping verbs looking at just the primary and secondary verb senses. A verb can be in more than one group. Once they are classified according to their primary and secondary meanings we put verbs in groups, say all verbs having 'move' as primary sense and 'do' as secondary sense will be in a group.

Punct (Elementary Bhāva-s)	**Explanation**
Know: Sense of knowing	Know / Knower Conceptualize, construct or transfer information between or

[6]A verb can be explicated by more than one verb (*overlapping meaning component*) hence the total of the percentages of the verbs, which have been identified as the overlapping components is not 100.

	within an animal.
Move: Sense of Move/ change / process	Before / After Every process has a movement in it. The movement maybe a change of state or location.
Do : Sense of agency	Agent / Action A process which cannot be accomplished without a doer.
Have : Sense of possession or having	Grip / Grasp Possessing, obtaining or transferring a quality or object.
Be : Sense of state of being	Locus / Locatee Continuously having or possessing a quality.
Cut : Sense of part and whole	Part / Whole Separation of a part from whole or joining of parts into a whole. Processes which causes a pain. Processes which disrupt the normal state.
Cover : Sense of ascribe and ascription	Wrap / Wrapped Processes which pertain to a certain specific object or category. It is like a bounding.

Table3. Puncts

We believe that every word is distinct. 'There are no real synonyms and that no two words have exactly the same meaning' (Palmer, 1986 page-89). If all words are distinct how can we show its distinctness? We have observed that there is at least one ontological attribute which makes each word different from the other. They are called ontological attributes as they are concepts like space, time, manner, reason and sub-features like direction-linear, source, destination, effect etc. which can be represented inter-lingually. We have named the set of attributes as 'feature set'. Feature set is a part of the context *C* defined in the structure of 'punct'. Verbs with same feature set across languages can be cross-linked. For example, if we want to represent verb 'breathe' in another language, we just have to map the attributes identified for 'breathe' which are –

breathe1) move, instrument-lungs, object-air, manner-into and out of

breathe2) say, object-something, manner- very quietly

breathe3) open, object-wine bottle, duration-short time, purpose-improve flavor.

5 Comparison of primitives

A comparison of primitives of CD theory and our approach is given in Table 4. Corresponding to each ACT of CD theory the explanation and Puncts in order of priority of meaning senses is given.

ACT	Explanation about ACT	PUNCTS in order of meaning sense
ATRANS	Transfer of an abstract relationship such as possession ownership or control (give)	Do / Have / Cut
PTRANS	Transfer of the physical location of an object (go)	Do / Move / Cut
PROPEL	Application of a physical force to an object (push)	Do / Move / Cut
MOVE	Movement of a body part of an animal by that animal (kick)	Do / Move
GRASP	Grasping of an object by an actor (grasp)	Do / Have / Cut
INGEST	Taking in of an object by an animal to the inside of that animal (eat)	Do / Have / Move / Cut
EXPEL	Expulsion of an object from the object of an animal into the physical world (cry)	Move / Do / Is
MTRANS	Transfer of mental information between animals or within an animal (tell)	Do / Know / Move
MBUILD	Construction by an animal of new information of old information (decide)	Know / Do / Cover / Move
CONC	Conceptualize or think about an idea (think)	Know / Do / Move
SPEAK	Actions of producing sounds	Do / Move

	(say)	
ATTEND	Action of attending or focusing a sense organ towards a stimulus (listen)	Know / Do

Table4. Comparison of ACT and Punct.

6 Issue and Solution

The uniform identification of verb sense means identifying the most general sense attached to a verb, as done by an ordinary person. One can see that more than one verb can be used to explicate the meaning of a verb and there is an order in which the verbs are used. This order helps in finding the primary, secondary and tertiary meaning senses. The order is found by nominalizing verbs in a simple sentence. This method helps in resolving inconsistencies, if any, while identifying meaning senses. For example:
— you confuse me -> you create {confusion in me} →
—You create {{confused (state of Knowledge) about something (object of knowledge)} in me} →
— {You do creation of} {{'Confused (state of Knowledge) about something (object of knowledge)} in me}.
In the last sentence: 'do' is tertiary sense, 'know' is secondary sense and 'is {state of knowledge} 'is the primary sense of verb 'confuse'.

The seven verb senses thus identified are the building blocks out of which meanings of verbs are constructed. The primary and secondary senses of all verbs in English and Sanskrit were identified. For English verbs, the entire verb list (3750) enlisted by Levin (Levin, 1993) including extensions (Dang et. al, 1998; Kipper et. al, 2006; Korhonen and Briscoe, 2004) was classified according to the new classification. For Sanskrit verbs, data (more than 3000 verbs (Sanskrit dhātu[7]) including variations in accentuation) was collected from various resources (Palsule, 1955; Palsule, 1961; Liebich, 1922; Varma, 1953; Kale, 1961; Apte, 1998; Williams, 2008; Capeller, 1891). The meanings of English verbs were obtained from various dictionaries (on-line English dictionaries) and the senses were identified based on intuition.
The annotation process was to identify the primary and secondary meaning senses of all verbs and ontological attributes of verbs in 7 groups (all verbs with the same primary verb senses formed one group). The annotation of verbs was done for four languages: Sanskrit, English, Hindi and Telugu. Verbs in Sanskrit and English were compiled and annotated by one trained annotator and cross-checked by an equally trained second annotator. The differences in annotation, around 10%, were resolved by discussion. Annotation in Hindi and Telugu was done by 9 and 25 annotators respectively. The annotators were humans and native speakers of their languages, having an idea of the new approach. The average ratio of correctness was 64%. The classification was done manually.

Based on this classification the verb groups formed have exhibited similarity in syntactic and semantic behavior. The pattern of Stanford dependency relations formed among verbs of same groups showed a similarity of 60%. This similarity in relations were used to form WSD rules which helped in increasing the accuracy of English to Hindi Anusaaraka[8] Machine Translation system output by 36.04%.

7 Conclusion

Conceptual Dependency theory was based on two assumptions:
1. If two sentences have same meaning they must have similar representation regardless of the words used.
2. Information implicitly stated in the sentence should be stated explicitly.
Our approach is based on two assumptions:
1. There is a conceptual base underlying all natural languages.
2. All content words are derived from verb root.
'Punct' is a mathematical representation of conceptual base in terms of state and change which can be used for computational purpose. Identification of overlapping verbal sense enables a classification based on meaning. Verbal sense identification along with feature space which includes ontological attributes can give a better classification and understanding of verbs and their behavior. Application of the concept of 'punct' in NLP applications like

[7]Patañjali's basic semantic definition of the term dhātu is as follows :- An item which denotes by its intrinsic denotative nature something that is brought into being - such a thing is referred to by the term bhāva or kriyā - is called dhātu

[8] http://anusaaraka.iiit.ac.in

machine translation has shown to increase its performance by 36.04%.

8 References

Anna Korhonen and Ted Briscoe. 2004. *Extended Lexical-Semantic Classification of English Verbs.* Proc. of the 42nd Meeting of the ACL, Workshop on Computational Lexical Semantics.

Anna Wierzbicka. 1996. *Semantics: Primes and universals* .Oxford: Oxford University Press.

Arend Rensink. 2004. *GROOVE.GRaphs for Object-Oriented VErifiction* .http:// groove.cs.utwe nte.nl/.

Beth Levin. 1993. *English Verb Classes and Alternation, A Preliminary Investigation*. The University of Chicago Press.

Bruno Liebich. 1922. *Materialien zum Dhatu patha*, Heidelberg. Carl Winter's University.

Capeller. 1891. *'Sanskrit-English Online Dictionary'*. Retrieved from http://www.sanskrit-lexicon. unikoeln.de/scans/MWScan/tamil/index.html

Frank Robert Palmer. 1976. *Semantics*. Cambridge: CUP.

Hoa Trang *Dang* , Karin *Kipper* , Martha *Palmer,* and Joseph Rosenzweig. 1998. *Investigating regular sense extensions based on intersective Levin classes.* Proc. of the 36th Meeting of the ACL and the 17th COLING.

Gajanan Balkrishna Palsule. 1955. *A Concordance of Sanskrit Dhatupath,* Deccan College Dissertation Series, Bhandarkar Oriental Research Institute, Poona.

Gajanan Balkrishna Palsule. 1961. *The Sanskrit Dhatupathas,* University of Poona.

Graham Hutton. 2010. *'Introduction to Categories'* Lecture notes. University of Birmingham, 23-27 April.

George A. Miller, Richard Beckwith, Christiane Fellbaum,

Derek Gross, and Katherine Miller

. 1990. *'Introduction to WordNet: An On-Line Lexical Database,'* Int'l J. Lexicography, vol. 3, no. 4, pp. 235-244.

Igor A Mel'čuk. (1981). "Meaning-Text Models: A recent trend in Soviet linguistics". *Annual Review of Anthropology* **10**: 27–62.

James R. Hurford. 2007. *The Origins of Meaning: Language in the Light of Evolution,* Oxford University Press

Jerry A Fodor. 1975. *The Language Of Thought.* Crowell Press. pp 214.

John W M Verhaar,1966. *The Verb `Be' and Its Synonyms,* Foundation of Language Supplementary Series. Springer.

Kaṇāda. 1986. *The Vais´esika sutras of Kaṇāda with the commentary of S´amkara Mis´ra and extracts from the gloss of Jayanārāyaṇa.* Translation in English by Nandalal Sinha. Allahabad (1911); Delhi (1986).

Karin Kipper Schuler. 2005. *VerbNet: A Broad-coverage, Comprehensive Verb Lexicon.* PhDdissertation, University of Pennsylvania.

Kunjunni. K. Raja and Harold G. Coward. 1990. *Encyclopedia of Indian Philosophies: The philosophy of the grammarians,* Volume 5. New Delhi, India: Motilal Banarsidass. p. 324.

Lakshman Sarup. 1920. *The Nighantu and Nirukta.* Motilal Banarasidass. Delhi.

Lyudmila Osinovskaya. 2010. *Verb Classification.* Tyumen State University.

Michael E. Lesk. 1986. *Automatic sense disambiguation using machine readable dictionaries: how to tell a pine cone from an ice cream cone.* In SIGDOC '86: Proceedings of the 5th annual international conference on Systems documentation, pages 24-26, New York, NY, USA. ACM.

Monier Williams. 2008. *'Sanskrit English online Dictionary'*,retrieved from http://www.sanskrit lexicon. uni-koeln.de/monier/

Moreshvar Ramchandra Kale 1962. *A higher Sanskrit grammar, for the use of schools and colleges.* Online: Retrieved from http://ia700307.us.archive.org/35/ items/highersanskritgr00kaleuoft/highersanskritgr0 0kaleuoft .pdf.

Philip D. Morehead. 2001. *The New American Webster Handy College Dictionary.* Signet Book. Fourth Edition.

Rajesh Tavva and Navjoti Singh. 2010. *Generative Graph Grammar of Neo-Vai´esika Formal Ontology.* In G.N.Jha, editor, Sanskrit Computational Linguistics, pages 91–105. Springer.

Ray Jackendoff. 1976. Toward an explanatory semantic representation. *Linguistic Inquiry* **7** (1): 89–150.

Roger Schank. 1972 *Conceptual Dependency: A Theory of Natural Language Understanding*. Cognitive Psychology 3, pp. 552-631.

Roger Schank. 1973. *Conceptualizations underlying natural language. In Computer Models of Thought and Language*, R. Schank & K. Colby, eds. San Francisco: W.H. Freeman.

Roger Schank. 1975. *The Primitive ACTs of Conceptual Dependency*. Yale University. New Haven CT. TINLAP'75. Proceedings of the 1975 workshop on Theoretical issues in natural language processing. Pages 34-37.

Roger Schank and Robert Paul *Abelson*. 1977. *Scripts, Plans, Goals, and Understanding*. Lawrence Erlbaum Amociates. Hilldale NJ.

Siddheshwar Varma. 1953. *The Etymologies of Yaska*. Vishveshvaranand Institute Publications.

Vaman Shivram Apte, 1998. *'Apte Sanskrit Dictionary'*, Retrieved from http://www.aa.tufs .ac.jp /~tj un/sktdic/.

Yorick Wilks, 1975 An intelligent analyzer and understander of English. Comm. Assn. Comp. Mach. 18, 264-274.

Topic Modeling Based Classification of Clinical Reports

Efsun Sarioglu
Computer Science Department
The George Washington University
Washington, DC, USA
efsun@gwu.edu

Kabir Yadav
Emergency Medicine Department
The George Washington University
Washington, DC, USA
kyadav@gwu.edu

Hyeong-Ah Choi
Computer Science Department
The George Washington University
Washington, DC, USA
hchoi@gwu.edu

Abstract

Electronic health records (EHRs) contain important clinical information about patients. Some of these data are in the form of free text and require preprocessing to be able to used in automated systems. Efficient and effective use of this data could be vital to the speed and quality of health care. As a case study, we analyzed classification of CT imaging reports into binary categories. In addition to regular text classification, we utilized topic modeling of the entire dataset in various ways. Topic modeling of the corpora provides interpretable themes that exist in these reports. Representing reports according to their topic distributions is more compact than bag-of-words representation and can be processed faster than raw text in subsequent automated processes. A binary topic model was also built as an unsupervised classification approach with the assumption that each topic corresponds to a class. And, finally an aggregate topic classifier was built where reports are classified based on a single discriminative topic that is determined from the training dataset. Our proposed topic based classifier system is shown to be competitive with existing text classification techniques and provides a more efficient and interpretable representation.

1 Introduction

Large amounts of medical data are now stored as electronic health records (EHRs). Some of these data are in the form of free text and they need to be processed and coded for better utilization in automatic or semi-automatic systems. One possible utilization is to support clinical decision-making, such as recommending the need for a certain medical test while avoiding intrusive tests or medical costs. This type of automated analysis of patient reports can help medical professionals make clinical decisions much faster with more confidence by providing predicted outcomes. In this study, we developed several topic modeling based classification systems for clinical reports.

Topic modeling is an unsupervised technique that can automatically identify themes from a given set of documents and find topic distributions of each document. Representing reports according to their topic distributions is more compact and can be processed faster than raw text in subsequent automated processing. It has previously been shown that the biomedical concepts can be well represented as noun phrases (Huang et al., 2005) and nouns, compared to other parts of speech, tend to specialize into topics (Griffiths et al., 2004). Therefore, topic model output of patient reports could contain very useful clinical information.

2 Background

This study utilized prospective patient data previously collected for a traumatic orbital fracture project (Yadav et al., 2012). Staff radiologists dictated each CT report and the outcome of acute orbital fracture was extracted by a trained data abstractor. Among the 3,705 reports, 3,242 had negative outcome while 463 had positive. A random subset of 507 CT reports were double-coded, and inter-rater analysis revealed excellent agreement between the data abstractor and study physician, with Cohen's kappa of 0.97.

2.1 Bag-of-Words (BoW) Representation

Text data need to be converted to a suitable format for automated processing. One way of doing this is bag-of-words (BoW) representation where each document becomes a vector of its words/tokens.

The entries in this matrix could be binary stating the existence or absence of a word in a document or it could be weighted such as number of times a word exists in a document.

2.2 Topic Modeling

Topic modeling is an unsupervised learning algorithm that can automatically discover themes of a document collection. Several techniques can be used for this purpose such as Latent Semantic Analysis (LSA) (Deerwester et al., 1990), Probabilistic Latent Semantic Analysis (PLSA) (Hofmann, 1999), and Latent Dirichlet Allocation (LDA) (Blei et al., 2003). LSA is a way of representing hidden semantic structure of a term-document matrix where rows are documents and columns are words/tokens (Deerwester et al., 1990) based on Singular Value Decomposition (SVD). One of the problems of LSA is that each word is treated as having the same meaning due to the word being represented as a single point; therefore in this representation, polysemes of words cannot be differentiated. Also, the final output of LSA, which consists of axes in Euclidean space, is not interpretable or descriptive (Hofmann, 2001).

PLSA is considered probabilistic version of LSA where an unobserved class variable $z_k \in \{z_1, ..., z_K\}$ is associated with each occurrence of a word in a particular document (Hofmann, 1999). These classes/topics are then inferred from the input text collection. PLSA solves the polysemy problem; however it is not considered a fully generative model of documents and it is known to be overfitting (Blei et al., 2003). The number of parameters grows linearly with the number of documents.

LDA, first defined by (Blei et al., 2003), defines topic as a distribution over a fixed vocabulary, where each document can exhibit them with different proportions. For each document, LDA generates the words in a two-step process:

1. Randomly choose a distribution over topics.

2. For each word in the document:

   (a) Randomly choose a topic from the distribution over topics.

   (b) Randomly choose a word from the corresponding distribution over the vocabulary.

The probability of generating the word w_j from document d_i can be calculated as below:

$$P(w_j|d_i; \theta, \phi) = \sum_{k=1}^{K} P(w_j|z_k; \phi_z)P(z_k|d_i; \theta_d)$$

where θ is sampled from a Dirichlet distribution for each document d_i and ϕ is sampled from a Dirichlet distribution for each topic z_k. Either sampling methods such as Gibbs Sampling (Griffiths and Steyvers, 2004) or optimization methods such as variational Bayes approximation (Asuncion et al., 2009) can be used to train a topic model based on LDA. LDA performs better than PLSA for small datasets since it avoids overfitting and it supports polysemy (Blei et al., 2003). It is also considered a fully generative system for documents in contrast to PLSA.

2.3 Text Classification

Text classification is a supervised learning algorithm where documents' categories are learned from pre-labeled set of documents. Support vector machines (SVM) is a popular classification algorithm that attempts to find a decision boundary between classes that is the farthest from any point in the training dataset. Given labeled training data $(x_t, y_t), t = 1, ..., N$ where $x_t \in R^M$ and $y_t \in \{1, -1\}$, SVM tries to find a separating hyperplane with the maximum margin (Platt, 1998).

2.3.1 Evaluation

Once the classifier is built, its performance is evaluated on training dataset. Its effectiveness is then measured in the remaining unseen documents in the testing set. To evaluate the classification performance, *precision, recall*, and *F-score* measures are typically used (Manning et al., 2008).

3 Related Work

For text classification, topic modeling techniques have been utilized in various ways. In (Zhang et al., 2008), it is used as a keyword selection mechanism by selecting the top words from topics based on their entropy. In our study, we removed the most frequent and infrequent words to have a manageable vocabulary size but we did not utilize topic model output for this purpose. (Sarioglu et al., 2012) and (Sriurai, 2011) compare BoW representation to topic model representation for classification using varying and fixed number of topics respectively. This is similar to our topic vector classification results with SVM, however (Sriurai, 2011) uses a fixed number of topics, whereas we evaluated different number of topics since typically this is not known in advance. In (Banerjee, 2008), topics are used as additional features to BoW features for the purpose of classification. In our approaches, we used topic vector representation as an alternative to BoW and not additional. This way, we can achieve great dimension reduction. Finally, (Chen et al., 2011) developed a resampling approach based on topic modeling when the class distributions are not balanced. In this study, resampling approaches are also utilized to compare skewed dataset results to datasets with equal class distributions; however, we used randomized resampling approaches for this purpose.

4 Experiments

Figure 1 shows the three approaches of using topic model of clinical reports to classify them and they are explained below.

4.1 Preprocessing

During preprocessing, all protected health information were removed to meet Institutional Review Board requirements. Medical record numbers from each report were replaced by observation numbers, which are sequence numbers that are automatically assigned to each report. Frequent words were also removed from the vocabulary to prevent it from getting too big. In addition, these frequent words typically do not add much information; most of them were stop words such as *is, am, are, the, of, at, and.*

4.2 Topic Modeling

LDA was chosen to generate the topic models of clinical reports due to its being a generative probabilistic system for documents and its robustness to overfitting. Stanford Topic Modeling Toolbox (TMT) [1] was used to conduct the experiments which is an open source software that provides ways to train and infer topic models for text data.

4.3 Topic Vectors

Topic modeling of reports produces a topic distribution for each report which can be used to represent them as topic vectors. This is an alternative representation to BoW where terms are replaced with topics and entries for each report show the probability of a specific topic for that report. This representation is more compact than BoW as the vocabulary for a text collection usually has thousands of entries whereas a topic model is typically built with a maximum of hundreds of topics.

4.4 Supervised Classification

SVM was chosen as the classification algorithm as it was shown that it performs well in text classification tasks (Joachims, 1998; Yang and Liu, 1999) and it is robust to overfitting (Sebastiani, 2002). Weka was used to conduct classification which is a collection of machine learning algorithms for data mining tasks written in Java (Hall et al., 2009). It uses attribute relationship file format (ARFF) to store data in which each line represents a document followed by its assigned class. Accordingly, the raw text of the reports and topic vectors are compiled into individual files with their corresponding outcomes in ARFF and then classified with SVM.

4.5 Aggregate Topic Classifier (ATC)

With this approach, a representative topic vector for each class was composed by averaging their corresponding topic distributions in the training dataset. A discriminative topic was then chosen so that the difference between positive and negative representative vectors is maximum. The reports in the test datasets were then classified by analyzing the values of this topic and a threshold was chosen to determine the predicted class. This threshold could be chosen automatically based on class distributions if the dataset is skewed or cross validation methods can be applied to pick a threshold that gives the best classification performance in a validation dataset. This approach is called Aggregate Topic Classifier (ATC) since training labels were utilized in an aggregate fashion using an average function and not individually.

4.6 Binary Topic Classification (BTC)

Topic modeling of the data with two topics was also analyzed as an unsupervised classification technique. In this approach, binary topics were assumed to correspond to the binary classes. After topic model was learned, the topic with the higher probability was assigned as the predicted class for each document. If the dataset is skewed, which topic corresponds to which class was found out by checking predicted class proportions. For datasets

[1] http://nlp.stanford.edu/software/tmt/tmt-0.4/

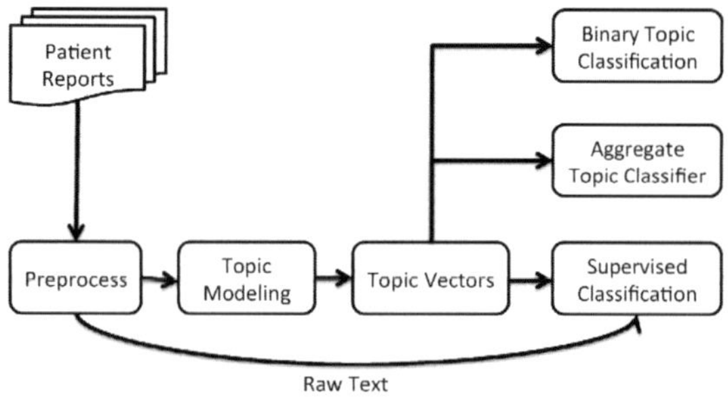

Figure 1: System overview

with equal class distributions, each of the possible assignments were checked and the one with the better classification performance was chosen.

5 Results

Classification results using ATC and SVM are shown in Figures 2, 3, and 4 for precision, recall, and f-score respectively. They are each divided into five sections to show the result of using different training/testing proportions. These training and test datasets were randomized and stratified to make sure each subset is a good representation of the original dataset. For ATC, we evaluated different quantile points: 75, 80, 82, 85, 87 as threshold and picked the one that gives the best classification performance. These were chosen as candidates based on the positive class ratio of original dataset of 12%. Best classification performance was achieved with 15 topics for ATC and 100 topics for SVM. For smaller number of topics, ATC performed better than SVM. As number of topics increased, it got harder to find a very discriminative single topic and therefore ATC's performance got worse whereas SVM's performance got better as it got more information with more number of topics. However, using topic vectors to represent reports still provided great dimension reduction as raw text of the reports had 1,296 terms and made the subsequent classification with SVM faster. Finally, different training and test set proportions did not have much effect on both of ATC's and SVM's performance. This could be considered a good outcome as using only 25% of data for training would be sufficient to build an accurate classifier.

We analyzed the performance of classification using binary topics with three datasets: original, undersampled, and oversampled. In the undersampled dataset, excess amount of negative cases were removed and the resulting dataset consisted of 463 documents for each class. For oversampled dataset, positive cases were oversampled while keeping the total number of documents the same. This approach produced a dataset consisting of 1,895 positive and 1,810 negative cases. With the original dataset, we could see the performance on a highly skewed real dataset and with the resampled datasets, we could see the performance on data with equal class distributions. Classification results using this approach are summarized in Table 2. As a baseline, a trivial rejector/zero rule classifier was used. This classifier simply predicted the majority class. Balanced datasets performed better compared to skewed original dataset using this approach. This is also due to the fact that skewed dataset had a higher baseline compared to the undersampled and oversampled datasets. In Table 3, the best performance of each technique for the original dataset is summarized. Although BTC performed better than baseline for

Figure 2: Precision

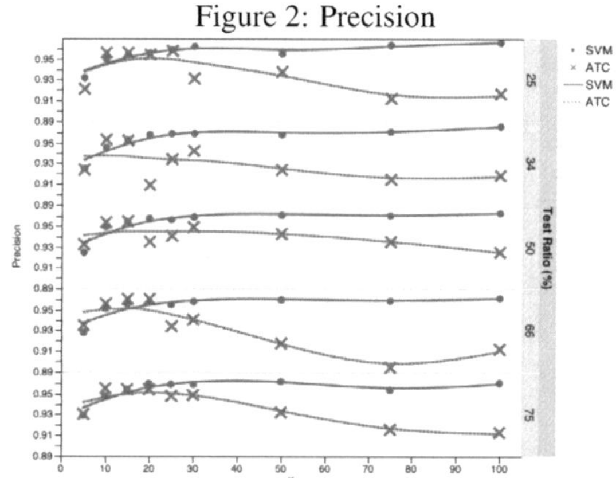

Figure 3: Recall

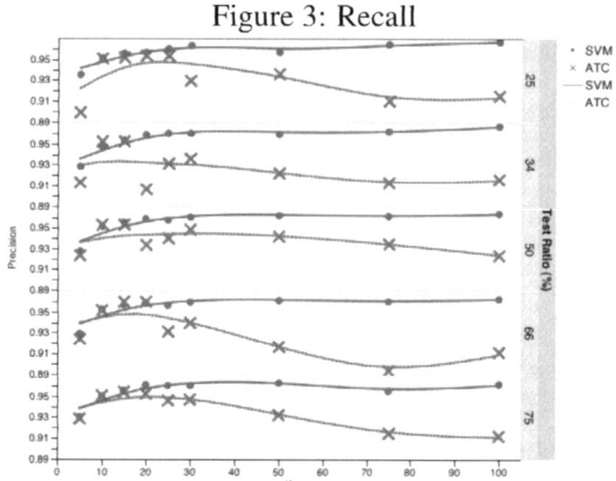

Table 1: Classification performance using ATC and SVM

K	Dimension Reduction (%)	Train-Test (%)	ATC			SVM		
			Precision	Recall	F-score	Precision	Recall	F-score
5	99.61	75 - 25	92.15	89.96	90.11	93.19	93.52	93.28
		66 - 34	92.40	91.26	91.37	92.50	92.85	92.62
		50 - 50	93.24	92.37	92.44	92.48	92.76	92.59
		34 - 66	93.50	92.43	92.50	92.80	92.92	92.86
		25 - 75	93.03	92.84	92.87	92.93	93.06	92.99
10	99.23	75 - 25	95.65	95.03	95.23	95.01	95.14	95.05
		66 - 34	95.38	95.23	95.30	94.58	94.76	94.64
		50 - 50	95.38	95.29	95.33	94.98	95.14	95.03
		34 - 66	95.61	95.13	95.26	95.11	95.26	95.16
		25 - 75	95.53	95.07	95.20	94.81	95.00	94.85
15	98.84	75 - 25	95.61	95.14	95.18	95.48	95.57	95.51
		66 - 34	95.26	95.23	95.24	95.31	95.39	95.34
		50 - 50	95.49	95.35	95.41	95.46	95.57	95.49
		34 - 66	96.07	96.03	96.05	95.58	95.71	95.61
		25 - 75	95.47	95.43	95.45	95.42	95.57	95.45
20	98.46	75 - 25	95.45	95.36	95.40	95.62	95.68	95.65
		66 - 34	90.89	90.62	90.75	95.83	95.87	95.85
		50 - 50	93.59	93.35	93.40	95.79	95.90	95.82
		34 - 66	96.07	95.95	95.97	95.77	95.87	95.80
		25 - 75	95.40	95.28	95.30	96.00	96.11	96.02
25	98.07	75 - 25	95.85	95.36	95.44	95.89	96.00	95.92
		66 - 34	93.37	93.16	93.26	95.92	96.03	95.95
		50 - 50	94.10	94.00	94.05	95.65	95.79	95.68
		34 - 66	93.38	93.17	93.20	95.52	95.66	95.55
		25 - 75	94.79	94.56	94.59	95.92	96.04	95.94
30	97.69	75 - 25	93.12	92.98	93.04	96.23	96.33	96.26
		66 - 34	94.21	93.64	93.73	95.93	96.03	95.96
		50 - 50	94.95	94.86	94.90	95.94	96.06	95.95
		34 - 66	94.05	93.95	94.00	95.85	95.95	95.88
		25 - 75	94.86	94.71	94.73	95.92	96.04	95.94
50	96.14	75 - 25	93.75	93.63	93.69	95.53	95.68	95.54
		66 - 34	92.44	92.21	92.32	95.82	95.95	95.84
		50 - 50	94.32	94.21	94.26	96.12	96.22	96.15
		34 - 66	91.78	91.70	91.74	96.02	96.11	96.04
		25 - 75	93.26	93.20	93.22	96.19	96.29	96.18
75	94.21	75 - 25	91.21	91.04	91.12	96.35	96.44	96.30
		66 - 34	91.51	91.26	91.37	96.10	96.19	96.01
		50 - 50	93.57	93.46	93.51	96.07	96.17	96.00
		34 - 66	89.43	89.33	89.38	95.91	96.03	95.89
		25 - 75	91.54	91.47	91.50	95.38	95.54	95.34
100	92.28	75 - 25	91.63	91.47	91.55	96.59	96.65	96.61
		66 - 34	91.82	91.57	91.69	96.62	96.66	96.64
		50 - 50	92.51	92.37	92.44	96.30	96.38	96.32
		34 - 66	91.21	91.12	91.17	96.16	96.24	96.19
		25 - 75	91.26	91.18	91.22	96.05	96.15	96.08

Figure 4: F-Score

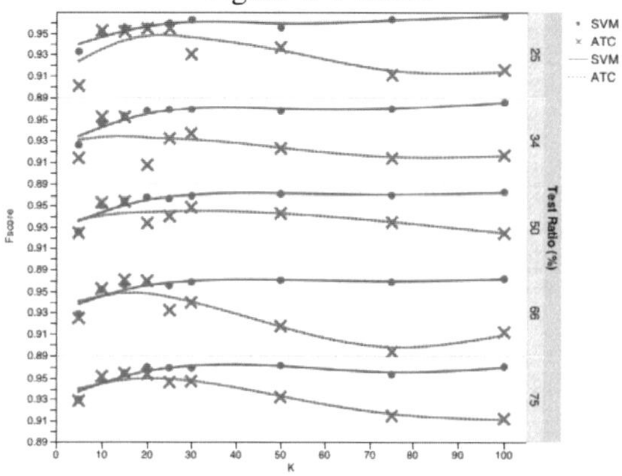

Table 2: Binary Topic Classification Results

Dataset	Algorithm	Precision	Recall	F-score
Original	Baseline	76.6	87.5	81.7
	BTC	88.6	73.4	77.7
Undersampled	Baseline	49.6	49.7	47.6
	BTC	84.4	84.2	84.2
Oversampled	Baseline	26.2	51.1	34.6
	BTC	83.4	82.5	82.5

datasets with equal class distribution, for the original skewed dataset, it got worse results than the baseline. ATC, on the other hand, got comparable results with SVM using both topic vectors and raw text. In addition, ATC used fewer number of topics than SVM for its best performance.

Table 3: Overall classification performance

Algorithm	Precision	Recall	F-score
Baseline	76.6	87.5	81.7
BTC	88.6	73.4	77.7
ATC	96.1	96.0	96.1
Topic vectors	96.6	96.7	96.6
Raw Text	96.4	96.3	96.3

6 Conclusion

In this study, topic modeling of clinical reports are utilized in different ways with the end goal of classification. Firstly, bag-of-words representation is replaced with topic vectors which provide good dimensionality reduction and still get comparable classification performance. In aggregate topic classifier, representative topic vectors for positive and negative classes are composed and used as a guide to classify the reports in the test dataset. This approach was competitive with classification with SVM using raw text and topic vectors. In addition, it required few topics to get the best performance. And finally, in the unsupervised setting, binary topic models are built for each dataset with the assumption that each topic corresponds to a class. For datasets with equal class distribution, this approach showed improvement over baseline approaches.

References

Arthur Asuncion, Max Welling, Padhraic Smyth, and Yee-Whye Teh. 2009. On smoothing and inference for topic models. In *UAI*.

Somnath Banerjee. 2008. Improving text classification accuracy using topic modeling over an additional corpus. In *Proceedings of the 31st annual international ACM SIGIR conference on Research and development in information retrieval*, pages 867–868.

David M. Blei, Andrew Y. Ng, and Michael I. Jordan. 2003. Latent Dirichlet Allocation. *J. Mach. Learn. Res.*, 3:993–1022.

Enhong Chen, Yanggang Lin, Hui Xiong, Qiming Luo, and Haiping Ma. 2011. Exploiting probabilistic topic models to improve text categorization under class imbalance. *Inf. Process. Manage.*, 47(2):202–214.

Scott Deerwester, Susan T. Dumais, George W. Furnas, Thomas K. Landauer, and Richard Harshman. 1990. Indexing by latent semantic analysis. *Journal of the American Society for Information Science*, 41(6):391–407.

Thomas L. Griffiths and Mark Steyvers. 2004. Finding scientific topics. *PNAS*, 101(suppl. 1):5228–5235.

Thomas L. Griffiths, Mark Steyvers, David M. Blei, and Joshua B. Tenenbaum. 2004. Integrating Topics and Syntax. In *NIPS*, pages 537–544.

Mark Hall, Eibe Frank, Geoffrey Holmes, Bernhard Pfahringer, Peter Reutemann, and Ian H. Witten. 2009. The WEKA data mining software: an update. *SIGKDD Explor. Newsl.*, 11(1):10–18.

Thomas Hofmann. 1999. Probabilistic latent semantic analysis. In *UAI*.

Thomas Hofmann. 2001. Unsupervised learning by probabilistic latent semantic analysis. *Mach. Learn.*, 42(1-2):177–196.

Yang Huang, Henry J Lowe, Dan Klein, and Russell J Cucina. 2005. Improved identification of noun phrases in clinical radiology reports using a high-performance statistical natural language parser augmented with the UMLS specialist lexicon. *J Am Med Inform Assoc*, 12(3):275–285.

Thorsten Joachims. 1998. Text Categorization with Support Vector Machines: Learning with Many Relevant Features. In *Proceedings of the 10th European Conference on Machine Learning*, pages 137–142.

Christopher D. Manning, Prabhakar Raghavan, and Hinrich Schütze. 2008. *Introduction to Information Retrieval*. Cambridge University Press, New York, NY, USA.

John C. Platt. 1998. Sequential Minimal Optimization: A Fast Algorithm for Training Support Vector Machines.

Efsun Sarioglu, Kabir Yadav, and Hyeong-Ah Choi. 2012. Clinical Report Classification Using Natural Language Processing and Topic Modeling. *11th International Conference on Machine Learning and Applications (ICMLA)*, pages 204–209.

Fabrizio Sebastiani. 2002. Machine learning in automated text categorization. *ACM Comput. Surv.*, 34(1):1–47.

Wongkot Sriurai. 2011. Improving Text Categorization by Using a Topic Model. *Advanced Computing: An International Journal (ACIJ)*, 2(6).

Kabir Yadav, Ethan Cowan, Jason S Haukoos, Zachary Ashwell, Vincent Nguyen, Paul Gennis, and Stephen P Wall. 2012. Derivation of a clinical risk score for traumatic orbital fracture. *J Trauma Acute Care Surg*, 73(5):1313–1318.

Yiming Yang and Xin Liu. 1999. A re-examination of text categorization methods. In *Proceedings of the 22nd annual international ACM SIGIR conference on Research and development in information retrieval*, pages 42–49.

Zhiwei Zhang, Xuan-Hieu Phan, and Susumu Horiguchi. 2008. An Efficient Feature Selection Using Hidden Topic in Text Categorization. In *Proceedings of the 22nd International Conference on Advanced Information Networking and Applications - Workshops*, AINAW '08, pages 1223–1228.

Annotating named entities in clinical text by combining pre-annotation and active learning

Maria Skeppstedt
Dept. of Computer and Systems Sciences (DSV)
Stockholm University, Forum 100, 164 40 Kista, Sweden
mariask@dsv.su.se

Abstract

For expanding a corpus of clinical text, annotated for named entities, a method that combines pre-tagging with a version of active learning is proposed. In order to facilitate annotation and to avoid bias, two alternative automatic pre-taggings are presented to the annotator, without revealing which of them is given a higher confidence by the pre-tagging system. The task of the annotator is to select the correct version among these two alternatives. To minimise the instances in which none of the presented pre-taggings is correct, the texts presented to the annotator are actively selected from a pool of unlabelled text, with the selection criterion that one of the presented pre-taggings should have a high probability of being correct, while still being useful for improving the result of an automatic classifier.

1 Introduction

One of the key challenges for many NLP applications is to create the annotated corpus needed for development and evaluation of the application. Such a corpus is typically created through manual annotation, which is a time-consuming task. Therefore, there is a need to explore methods for simplifying the annotation task and for reducing the amount of data that must be annotated.

Annotation can be simplified by automatic pre-annotation, in which the task of the annotator is to improve or correct annotations provided by an existing system. The amount of data needed to be annotated can be reduced by active learning, i.e. by actively selecting data to annotate that is useful to a machine learning system. When using pre-tagged data, the annotator might, however, be biased to choose the annotation provided by the pre-tagger. Also, if the produced pre-taggings are not good enough, it is still a time-consuming task to correct them or select the correct tagging among many suggestions.

Consequently, there is a need to further explore how an annotated corpus can be expanded with less effort and using methods that will not bias the annotators.

2 Background

The background discusses basic ideas of pre-annotation and active learning, as well as the particular challenges associated with annotating clinical text.

2.1 Annotating clinical text

A number of text annotation projects have been carried out in the clinical domain, some of them including annotations of clinical named entities, such as mentions of symptoms, diseases and medication. Such studies have for example been described by Ogren et al. (2008), Chapman et al. (2008), Roberts et al. (2009), Wang (2009), Uzuner et al. (2010), Koeling et al. (2011) and Albright et al. (2013).

As in many specialised domains, expert annotators are typically required to create a reliable annotated clinical corpus. These expert annotators are often more expensive than annotators without the required specialised knowledge. It is also difficult to use crowdsourcing approaches, such as using e.g. Amazon's Mechanical Turk to hire online annotators with the required knowledge (Xia and Yetisgen-Yildiz, 2012). A further challenge is posed by the content of the clinical data, which is often sensitive and should therefore only be accessed by a limited number of people. Research community annotation is consequently another option that is not always open to annotation projects in the clinical domain, even if there are examples of such community annotations also for clinical text, e.g. described by Uzuner et al. (2010).

To simplify the annotation process, and to minimise the amount of annotated data is therefore even more important for annotations in the clinical domain than for annotation in general.

2.2 Pre-annotation

A way to simplify annotation is automatic pre-annotation (or pre-tagging), in which a text is automatically annotated by an existing system, before it is given to the annotator. Instead of annotating unlabelled data, the annotator either corrects mistakes made by this existing system (Chou et al., 2006), or chooses between different taggings provided by the system (Brants and Plaehn, 2000). The system providing the pre-annotations could be rule- or terminology based, not requiring annotated data (Mykowiecka and Marciniak, 2011), as well as a machine learning/hybrid system that uses the annotations provided by the annotator to constantly improve the pre-annotation (Tomanek et al., 2012). There exist several annotation tools that facilitate the use of pre-annotation by allowing the user to import pre-annotations or by providing pre-annotation included in the tools (Neves and Leser, 2012).

A condition for pre-annotation to be useful is that the produced annotations are good enough, or the effect can be the opposite, slowing the annotators down (Ogren et al., 2008). Another potential problem with pre-annotation is that it might bias towards the annotations given by the pre-tagging, for instance if a good pre-tagger reduces the attention of the annotators (Fort and Sagot, 2010).

2.3 Active learning

Active learning can be used to reduce the amount of annotated data needed to successfully train a machine learning model. Instead of randomly selecting annotation data, instances in the data that are highly informative, and thereby also highly useful for the machine learning system, are then actively selected. (Olsson, 2008, p. 27).

There are several methods for selecting the most informative instances among the unlabelled ones in the available pool of data. A frequently used method is uncertainty sampling, in which instances that the machine learner is least certain how to classify are selected for annotation. For a model learning to classify into two classes, instances, for which the classifier has no clear preference for one of the two alternatives, are chosen for annotation. If there are more than two classes, the confidence for the most probable class can be used as the measure of uncertainty. Only using the certainty level for the most probable classification means that not all available information is used, i.e. the information of the certainty levels for the less probable classes. (Settles, 2009)

An alternative for a multi-class classifier is therefore to instead use the difference of the certainty levels for the two most probable classes. If c_{p1} is the most probable class and c_{p2} is the second most probable class for the observation $\boldsymbol{x_n}$, the margin used for measuring uncertainty for that instance is:

$$M_n = P(c_{p1}|\boldsymbol{x_n}) - P(c_{p2}|\boldsymbol{x_n}) \quad (1)$$

An instance with a large margin is easy to classify because the classifier is much more certain of the most probable classification than on the second most probable. Instances with a small margin, on the other hand, are difficult to classify, and therefore instances with a small margin are selected for annotation (Schein and Ungar, 2007). A common alternative is to use entropy as an uncertainty measure, which takes the certainty levels of all possible classes into account (Settles, 2009).

There are also a number of other possible methods for selecting informative instances for annotation, for instance to use a committee of learners and select the instances for which the committee disagrees the most, or to search for annotation instances that would result in the largest expected change to the current model (Settles, 2009).

There are also methods to ensure that the selected data correctly reflects the distribution in the pool of unlabelled data, avoiding a selection of outliers that would not lead to a correct model of the available data. Such methods for structured prediction have been described by Symons et al. (2006) and Settles and Craven (2008).

Many different machine learning methods have been used together with active learning for solving various NLP tasks. Support vector machines have been used for text classification (Tong and Koller, 2002), using properties of the support vector machine algorithm for determining what unlabelled data to select for classification. For structured output tasks, such as named entity recognition, hidden markov models have been used by Scheffer et al. (2001) and conditional random fields (CRF) by Settles and Craven (2008) and Symons et al. (2006).

Olsson (2008) suggests combining active learning and pre-annotation for a named entity recognition task, that is providing the annotator with pre-tagged data from an actively learned named entity recogniser. It is proposed not to indiscriminately pre-tagg the data, but to only provide those pre-annotated labels to the human annotator, for which the pre-tagger is relatively certain.

3 Method

Previous research on pre-annotation shows two seemingly incompatible desirable properties in a pre-annotation system. A pre-annotation that is not good enough might slow the human annotator down, whereas a good pre-annotation might make the annotator lose concentration, trusting the pre-annotation too much, resulting in a biased annotation. One possibility suggested in previous research, is to only provide pre-annotations for which the pre-annotation system is certain of its classification. For annotations of named entities in text, this would mean to only provide pre-tagged entities for which the pre-annotations system is certain. Such a high precision pre-tagger might, however, also bias the human annotator towards not correcting the pre-annotation.

Even more incompatible seems a combination between pre-annotation and active learning, that is to provide the human annotator with pre-tagged data that has been selected for active learning. The data selected for annotation when using active learning, is the data for which the pre-annotator is most uncertain and therefore the data which would be least suitable for pre-annotation.

The method proposed here aims at finding a way of combining pre-annotation and active learning while reducing the risk of annotation bias. Thereby decreasing the amount of data that needs to be annotated as well as facilitating the annotation, without introducing bias. A previous version of this idea has been outlined by Skeppstedt and Dalianis (2012).

The method is focused on the annotation of named entities in clinical text, that is marking of spans of text as well as classification of the spans into an entity class.

3.1 Pre-annotation

As in standard pre-annotation, the annotator will be presented with pre-tagged data, and does not have to annotate the data from scratch.

To reduce the bias problem that might be associated with pre-tagging, the mode of presentation will, however, be slightly different in the method proposed here. Instead of presenting the best tagging for the human annotator to correct, or to present the n best taggings, the two best taggings produced by a pre-tagger will be presented, without informing the annotator which of them that the pre-tagger considers most likely.

When being presented with two possible annotations of the same text without knowing which of them that the pre-annotation system considers as most likely, the annotator always has to make an active choice of which annotation to choose. This reduces the bias to one particular pre-annotation, thereby eliminating a drawback associated with standard pre-annotation. Having to consider two alternatives might add cognitive load to the annotator compared to correcting one alternative, but ought to be easier than annotating a text that is not pre-tagged.

The reason for presenting two annotations, as opposed to three or more, is that it is relatively easy to compare two texts, letting your eyes wander from one text to the other, when you have one comparison to make. Having three optional annotations would result in three comparisons, and having four would result in six comparisons, and so on. Therefore, having two optional annotations to choose from, reduces the bias problem while at the same time still offering a method for speeding up the annotation.

A simple Java program for choosing between two alternative pre-annotated sentences has been created (Figure 1). The program randomly chooses in which of the two text boxes to place which pre-annotation. The user can either choose the left or the right annotation, or that none of them is correct.

The data will be split into sentences, and one sentence at time will be presented to the annotator for annotation.

3.2 Active learning

To choose from two presented annotations might also potentially be faster than making corrections to one presented annotation. For this to be the case, however, one of the presented annotations has to be a correct annotation. In order to achieve that, the proposed method is to use a version of active learning.

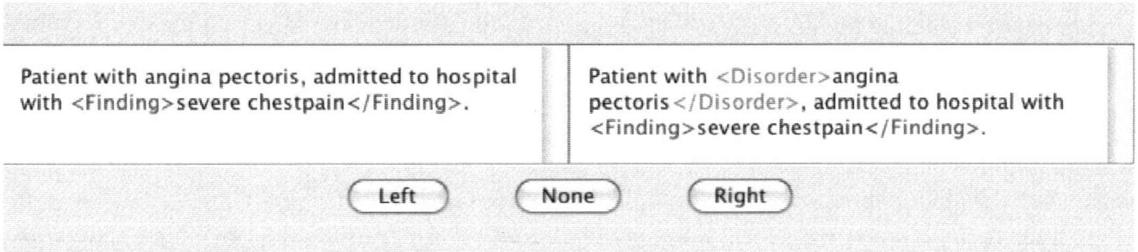

Figure 1: A simple program for choosing between two alternative annotations, showing a constructed example in English.

The standard use of active learning is to actively select instances to annotate that are useful to a machine learner. Instances for which the machine learning model can make a confident classification are not presented to the annotator, as these instances will be of little benefit for improving the machine learning system.

The version of active learning proposed here is retaining this general idea of active learning, but is also adding an additional constraint to what instances that are actively selected for annotation. This constraint is to only select text passages for which it is probable that one of the two best pre-taggings is correct, i.e. the pre-tagger has to be confident that one of the two presented pre-annotations is correct, but it should be uncertain as to which one of them is correct.

For ensuring that the sentences selected for annotation are informative enough, the previously described difference of the certainty level of the two most probable classes will be used. The same standard for expressing margin as used in (1), can be used here, except that in (1), c_{p1} and c_{p2} stand for classification of one instance, whereas in this case the output is a sequence of labels, labelling each token in a sentence. Therefore, c_{p1} and c_{p2} stand for the classification of a sequence of labels.

Let c_{p1} be the most probable labelling sequence, c_{p2} the second most probable labelling sequence and c_{p3} the third most probable labelling sequence. Moreover, let $\boldsymbol{x_n}$ be the observations in sentence n, then the following margins can be defined for that sentence:

$$M_{toSecond\_n} = P(c_{p1}|\boldsymbol{x_n}) - P(c_{p2}|\boldsymbol{x_n}) \quad (2)$$

$$M_{toThird\_n} = P(c_{p1}|\boldsymbol{x_n}) - P(c_{p3}|\boldsymbol{x_n}) \quad (3)$$

To make the probability high that one of the two presented pre-annotations is correct, the same method that is used for determining that an annotation instance is informative enough could be used. However, instead of minimising the margin between two classification instances, it is ensured that the margin in high enough. That is, the difference in certainty level between the two most probable annotations and the third most probable must be high enough to make it probable that one of the two best classification candidates is correct. This can be achieved by forcing $M_{toThird}$ to be above a threshold, t.

The criteria for selecting the next candidate sentence to annotate can then be described as:

$$\boldsymbol{x}^* = \underset{x}{\operatorname{argmin}}\, P(c_{p1}|\boldsymbol{x}) - P(c_{p2}|\boldsymbol{x}) \quad (4)$$

where

$$P(c_{p1}|\boldsymbol{x}) - P(c_{p3}|\boldsymbol{x}) > t$$

As instances with the highest possible $P(c_{p2}|\boldsymbol{x})$ in relation to $P(c_{p1}|\boldsymbol{x})$ are favoured, no threshold for the margin between $P(c_{p2}|\boldsymbol{x})$ and $P(c_{p3}|\boldsymbol{x})$ is needed.

It might be difficult to automatically determine an appropriate value of the threshold t. Therefore, the proposed method for finding a good threshold, is to adapt it to the behaviour of the annotator. If the annotator often rejects the two presented pre-taggings, text passages for which the pre-tagger is more certain ought to be selected, that is the value of t ought to be increased. On the other hand, if one of the presented pre-taggings often is selected by the annotator as the correct annotation, the value of t can be decreased, possibly allowing for annotation instances with a smaller $M_{toSecond}$.

3.3 Machine learning system

As machine learning system, the conditional random fields system CRF++ (Kudo, 2013) will be used. This system uses a combination of forward Viterbi and backward A* search for finding the best classification sequence for an input sentence, given the trained model. It can also produce the n-best classification sequences for each sentence, which is necessary for the proposed pre-tagger that presents the two best pre-taggings to the human annotator.

CRF++ can also give the conditional probably for the output, that is for the entire classification sequence of a sentence, which is needed in the proposed active learning algorithm.

3.4 Materials

There is a corpus of Swedish clinical text, i.e. the text in the narrative part of the health record, that contains clinical text from the Stockholm area, from the years 2006-2008 (Dalianis et al., 2009). A subset of this corpus, containing texts from an emergency unit of internal medicine, has been annotated for four types of named entities: *disorder*, *finding*, *pharmaceutical drug* and *body structure* (Skeppstedt et al., 2012). For approximately one third of this annotated corpus, double annotation has been performed, and the instances, for which there were a disagreement, have been resolved by one of the annotators.

The annotated corpus will form the main source of materials for the study proposed here, and additional data to annotate will be selected from a pool of unlabelled data from internal medicine emergency notes.

The larger subset of the annotated data, only annotated by one annotator, will be referred to as *Single* (containing 45 482 tokens), and the smaller subset, annotated by two annotators, will be referred to as *Double* (containing 25 370 tokens). The *Single* subset will be the main source for developing the pre-annotation/active learning method, whereas the *Double* subset will be used for a final evaluation.

3.5 Step-by-step explanation

The proposed method can be divided into 8 steps:

1. Train a CRF model with a randomly selected subset of the *Single* part of the annotated corpus, the *seed set*. The size of this *seed set*, as well as suitable features for the CRF model will be evaluated using cross validation on the *seed set*. The size should be as small as possible, limiting the amount of initial annotation needed, but large enough to have results in line with a baseline system using terminology matching for named entity recognition (Skeppstedt et al., 2012).

2. Apply the constructed CRF model on unlabelled data from the pool of data from internal medicine emergency notes. Let the model, which operates on a sentence level, provide the three most probable label sequences for each sentence, together with its level of certainty.

3. Calculate the difference in certainty between the most probable and the third most probable suggestion sequence for each sentence, that is $M_{toThird}$. Start with a low threshold t and place all sentences with $M_{toThird}$ above the threshold t in a list of candidates for presenting to the annotator (that is the sentences fulfilling the criterion $P(c_{p1}|\boldsymbol{x}) - P(c_{p3}|\boldsymbol{x}) > t$).

4. Order the sentences in the list of selected candidates in increasing order of $M_{toSecond}$. Present the sentence with the lowest $M_{toSecond}$ to the annotator. This is the sentence, for which the pre-tagger is most uncertain of which one of the two most probable pre-taggings is correct.

   Present the most probable pre-annotation as well as the second most probable pre-annotation, as shown in Figure 1.

5. If the annotator chooses that none of the presented pre-annotations is correct, discard the previous candidate selection and make a new one from the pool with a higher threshold value t. Again, order the sentences in increasing order of $M_{toSecond}$, and present the sentence with the lowest $M_{toSecond}$ to the annotator.

   Repeat step 3., 4. and 5., gradually increasing the threshold until the annotator accepts one of the presented pre-annotations.

6. Continue presenting the annotator with the two most probable pre-annotations for the sentences in the list of selected candidate sentences, and allow the human annotator to choose one of the pre-annotations.

The threshold t could be further adjusted according to how often the option 'None' is chosen.

7. Each selected annotation is added to a set of annotated data. When a sufficiently large amount of new sentences have been added to this set, the model needs to be retrained with the new data. The retraining of the model can be carried out as a background process while the human annotator is annotating. In order to use the annotator time efficiently, there should not be any waiting time while retraining.

8. When the model has been retrained, the process starts over from step 2.

3.6 Evaluation

The text passages chosen in the selection process will, as explained above, be used to re-train the machine learning model, and used when selecting new text passages for annotation. The effect of adding additional annotations will also be constantly measured, using cross validation on the *seed set*. The additional data added by the active learning experiments will, however, not be used in the validation part of the cross validation, but only be used as additional training data, in order to make sure that the results are not improved due to easily classified examples being added to the corpus.

When an actively selected corpus of the same size as the entire *Single* subset of the corpus has been created, this actively selected corpus will be used for training a machine learning model. The performance of this model will then be compared to a model trained on the single subset. Both models will be evaluated on the *Double* subset of the corpus. The hypothesis is that the machine learning model trained on the corpus partly created by pre-tagging and active learning will perform better than the model created on the original *Single* subset.

4 Conclusion

A method that combines pre-annotation and active learning, while reducing annotation bias, is proposed. A program for presenting pre-annotated data to the human annotator for selection has been constructed, and a corpus of annotated data suitable as a seed set and as evaluation data has been constructed. The active learning part of the proposed method remains, however, to be implemented.

Applying the proposed methods aims at creating a corpus suitable for training a machine learning system to recognise the four entities *Disorder*, *Finding*, *Pharmaceutical drug* and *Body structure*. Moreover, methods for facilitating annotated corpus construction will be explored, potentially adding new knowledge to the science of annotation.

Acknowledgements

I am very grateful to the reviewers and the pre-submission mentor for their many valuable comments. I would also like to thank Hercules Dalianis and Magnus Ahltorp as well as the participants of the 'Southern California Workshop on Medical Text Analysis and Visualization' for fruitful discussions on the proposed method.

References

Daniel Albright, Arrick Lanfranchi, Anwen Fredriksen, William F 4th Styler, Colin Warner, Jena D Hwang, Jinho D Choi, Dmitriy Dligach, Rodney D Nielsen, James Martin, Wayne Ward, Martha Palmer, and Guergana K Savova. 2013. Towards comprehensive syntactic and semantic annotations of the clinical narrative. *J Am Med Inform Assoc*, Jan.

Thorsten Brants and Oliver Plaehn. 2000. Interactive corpus annotation. In *LREC*. European Language Resources Association.

Wendy W Chapman, John N Dowling, and George Hripcsak. 2008. Evaluation of training with an annotation schema for manual annotation of clinical conditions from emergency department reports. *Int J Med Inform, Epub 2007 Feb 20*, 77(2):107–113, February.

Wen-chi Chou, Richard Tzong-han Tsai, and Ying-shan Su. 2006. A semi-automatic method for annotating a biomedical proposition bank. In *FLAC'06. ACL.*

Hercules Dalianis, Martin Hassel, and Sumithra Velupillai. 2009. The Stockholm EPR Corpus - Characteristics and Some Initial Findings. In *Proceedings of ISHIMR 2009, Evaluation and implementation of e-health and health information initiatives: international perspectives. 14th International Symposium for Health Information Management Research, Kalmar, Sweden*, pages 243–249.

Karën Fort and Benoît Sagot. 2010. Influence of pre-annotation on pos-tagged corpus development.

In *Proceedings of the Fourth Linguistic Annotation Workshop*, LAW IV '10, pages 56–63, Stroudsburg, PA, USA. Association for Computational Linguistics.

Rob Koeling, John Carroll, Rosemary Tate, and Amanda Nicholson. 2011. Annotating a corpus of clinical text records for learning to recognize symptoms automatically. In *Proceedings of the LOUHI 2011, Third International Workshop on Health Document Text Mining and Information Analysis*.

Taku Kudo. 2013. CRF++: Yet Another CRF toolkit. http://crfpp.sourceforge.net/. Accessed 2013-05-21.

Agnieszka Mykowiecka and Małgorzata Marciniak. 2011. Some remarks on automatic semantic annotation of a medical corpus. In *Proceedings of the LOUHI 2011, Third International Workshop on Health Document Text Mining and Information Analysis*.

Mariana Neves and Ulf Leser. 2012. A survey on annotation tools for the biomedical literature. *Briefings in Bioinformatics*.

Philip Ogren, Guergana Savova, and Christopher Chute. 2008. Constructing evaluation corpora for automated clinical named entity recognition. In *Proceedings of the Sixth International Language Resources and Evaluation (LREC'08)*, pages 3143–3149, Marrakech, Morocco, May. European Language Resources Association (ELRA).

Fredrik Olsson. 2008. *Bootstrapping Named Entity Annotation by Means of Active Machine Learning*. Ph.D. thesis, University of Gothenburg. Faculty of Arts.

Angus Roberts, Robert Gaizauskas, Mark Hepple, George Demetriou, Yikun Guo, Ian Roberts, and Andrea Setzer. 2009. Building a semantically annotated corpus of clinical texts. *J. of Biomedical Informatics*, 42:950–966, October.

Tobias Scheffer, Christian Decomain, and Stefan Wrobel. 2001. Active hidden markov models for information extraction. In *Proceedings of the 4th International Conference on Advances in Intelligent Data Analysis*, IDA '01, pages 309–318, London, UK, UK. Springer-Verlag.

Andrew I. Schein and Lyle H. Ungar. 2007. Active learning for logistic regression: an evaluation. *Mach. Learn.*, 68(3):235–265, October.

Burr Settles and Mark Craven. 2008. An analysis of active learning strategies for sequence labeling tasks. In *Proceedings of the Conference on Empirical Methods in Natural Language Processing*, EMNLP '08, pages 1070–1079, Stroudsburg, PA, USA. Association for Computational Linguistics.

Burr Settles. 2009. Active learning literature survey. Computer Sciences Technical Report 1648, University of Wisconsin–Madison.

Maria Skeppstedt and Hercules Dalianis. 2012. Using active learning and pre-tagging for annotating clinical findings in health record text. In *Proceedings of SMBM 2012 - The 5th International Symposium on Semantic Mining in Biomedicine*, pages 98–99, Zurich, Switzerland, September 3-4.

Maria Skeppstedt, Maria Kvist, and Hercules Dalianis. 2012. Rule-based entity recognition and coverage of SNOMED CT in Swedish clinical text. In *Proceedings of the Eight International Conference on Language Resources and Evaluation (LREC'12)*, pages 1250–1257, Istanbul, Turkey, may. European Language Resources Association (ELRA).

Christopher T. Symons, Nagiza F. Samatova, Ramya Krishnamurthy, Byung H. Park, Tarik Umar, David Buttler, Terence Critchlow, and David Hysom. 2006. Multi-criterion active learning in conditional random fields. In *Proceedings of the 18th IEEE International Conference on Tools with Artificial Intelligence*, ICTAI '06, pages 323–331, Washington, DC, USA. IEEE Computer Society.

Katrin Tomanek, Philipp Daumke, Frank Enders, Jens Huber, Katharina Theres, and Marcel Müller. 2012. An interactive de-identification-system. In *Proceedings of SMBM 2012 - The 5th International Symposium on Semantic Mining in Biomedicine*, pages 82–86, Zurich, Switzerland, September 3-4.

Simon Tong and Daphne Koller. 2002. Support vector machine active learning with applications to text classification. *J. Mach. Learn. Res.*, 2:45–66, March.

Özlem Uzuner, Imre Solti, Fei Xia, and Eithon Cadag. 2010. Community annotation experiment for ground truth generation for the i2b2 medication challenge. *J Am Med Inform Assoc*, 17(5):519–523.

Yefeng Wang. 2009. Annotating and recognising named entities in clinical notes. In *Proceedings of the ACL-IJCNLP Student Research Workshop*, pages 18–26, Singapore.

Fei Xia and Meliha Yetisgen-Yildiz. 2012. Clinical corpus annotation: Challenges and strategies. In *The Third Workshop on Building and Evaluating Resources for Biomedical Text Mining (BioTxtM), an LREC Workshop. Turkey.*

Multigraph Clustering for Unsupervised Coreference Resolution

Sebastian Martschat
Heidelberg Institute for Theoretical Studies gGmbH
Schloss-Wolfsbrunnenweg 35
69118 Heidelberg, Germany
sebastian.martschat@h-its.org

Abstract

We present an unsupervised model for coreference resolution that casts the problem as a clustering task in a directed labeled weighted multigraph. The model outperforms most systems participating in the English track of the CoNLL'12 shared task.

1 Introduction

Coreference resolution is the task of determining which mentions in a text refer to the same entity. With the advent of machine learning and the availability of annotated corpora in the mid 1990s the research focus shifted from rule-based approaches to supervised machine learning techniques. Quite recently, however, rule-based approaches regained popularity due to Stanford's multi-pass sieve approach which exhibits state-of-the-art performance on many standard coreference data sets (Raghunathan et al., 2010) and also won the CoNLL-2011 shared task on coreference resolution (Lee et al., 2011; Pradhan et al., 2011). These results show that carefully crafted rule-based systems which employ suitable inference schemes can achieve competitive performance. Such a system can be considered unsupervised in the sense that it does not employ training data for optimizing parameters.

In this paper we present a graph-based approach for coreference resolution that models a document to be processed as a graph. The nodes are mentions and the edges correspond to relations between mentions. Coreference resolution is performed via graph clustering. Our approach belongs to a class of recently proposed graph models for coreference resolution (Cai and Strube, 2010; Sapena et al., 2010; Martschat et al., 2012) and is designed to be a simplified version of existing approaches. In contrast to previous models belonging to this class we do not learn any edge weights but perform inference on the graph structure only which renders our model unsupervised. On the English data of the CoNLL'12 shared task the model outperforms most systems which participated in the shared task.

2 Related Work

Graph-based coreference resolution. While not developed within a graph-based framework, factor-based approaches for pronoun resolution (Mitkov, 1998) can be regarded as greedy clustering in a multigraph, where edges representing factors for pronoun resolution have negative or positive weight. This yields a model similar to the one presented in this paper though Mitkov's work has only been applied to pronoun resolution. Nicolae and Nicolae (2006) phrase coreference resolution as a graph clustering problem: they first perform pairwise classification and then construct a graph using the derived confidence values as edge weights. In contrast, work by Culotta et al. (2007), Cai and Strube (2010) and Sapena et al. (2010) omits the classification step entirely. Sapena et al. (2010) and Cai and Strube (2010) perform coreference resolution in one step using graph partitioning approaches. These approaches participated in the recent CoNLL'11 shared task (Pradhan et al., 2011; Sapena et al., 2011; Cai et al., 2011b) with excellent results. The approach by Cai et al. (2011b) has been modified by Martschat et al. (2012) and ranked second in the English track at the CoNLL'12 shared task (Pradhan et al., 2012). The top performing system at the CoNLL'12 shared task (Fernandes et al., 2012) also represents the problem as a graph by performing inference on trees constructed using the multi-pass sieve approach by Raghunathan et al. (2010) and Lee et al. (2011), which in turn won the CoNLL'11 shared task.

Unsupervised coreference resolution. Cardie and Wagstaff (1999) present an early approach to unsupervised coreference resolution based on a straightforward clustering approach. Angheluta et al. (2004) build on their approach and devise more sophisticated clustering algorithms. Haghighi and Klein (2007), Ng (2008) and Charniak and Elsner (2009) employ unsupervised generative models. Poon and Domingos (2008) present a Markov Logic Network approach to unsupervised coreference resolution. These approaches reach competitive performance on gold mentions but not on system mentions (Ng, 2008). The multi-pass sieve approach by Raghunathan et al. (2010) can also be viewed as unsupervised.

3 A Multigraph Model

We aim for a model which directly represents the relations between mentions in a graph structure. Clusters in the graph then correspond to entities.

3.1 Motivation

To motivate the choice of our model, let us consider a simple made-up example.

> *Leaders* met in *Paris* to discuss *recent developments*. *They* left the city today.

We want to model that *Paris* is not a likely candidate antecedent for *They* due to number disagreement, but that *Leaders* and *recent developments* are potential antecedents for *They*. We want to express that *Leaders* is the preferred antecedent, since *Leaders* and *They* are in a parallel construction both occupying the subject position in their respective sentences.

In other words, our model should express the following relations for this example:

- number disagreement for (*They*, *Paris*), which indicates that the mentions are not coreferent,
- the anaphor being a pronoun for (*They*, *Leaders*), (*They*, *recent developments*) and (*They*, *Paris*), which is a weak indicator for coreference if the mentions are close to each other,
- syntactic parallelism for (*They*, *Leaders*): both mentions are in a parallel construction in adjacent sentences (both in the subject slot), which is also a weak coreference indicator.

We denote these relations as N_Number, P_AnaPron and P_Subject respectively. The graphical structure depicted in Figure 1 models these relations between the four mentions *Leaders*, *Paris*, *recent developments* and *They*.

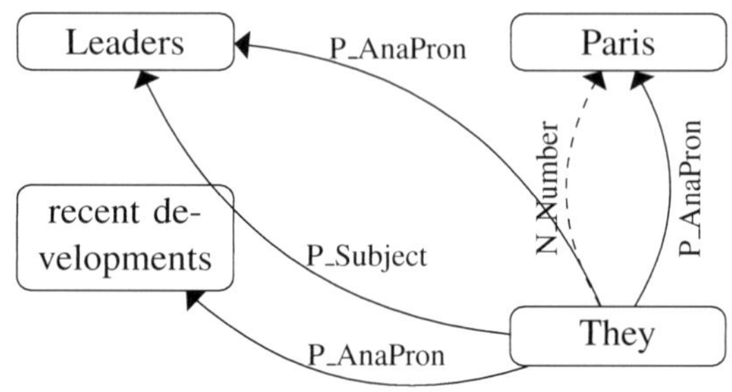

Figure 1: An example graph modeling relations between mentions.

A directed edge from a mention m to n indicates that n precedes m and that there is some relation between m and n that indicates coreference or non-coreference. Labeled edges describe the relations between the mentions, multiple relations can hold between a pair. Edges may be weighted.

3.2 Multigraphs for Coreference Resolution

Formally, the model is a *directed labeled weighted multigraph*. That is a tuple $D = (R, V, A, w)$ where

- R is the set of labels (in our case relations such as P_Subject that hold between mentions),
- V is the set of nodes (the mentions extracted from a document),
- $A \subseteq V \times V \times R$ is the set of edges (relations between two mentions),
- w is a mapping $w\colon\ A \to \mathbb{R} \cup \{\pm\infty\}$ (weights for edges).

Many graph models for coreference resolution operate on $A = V \times V$. Our multigraph model allows us to have multiple edges with different labels between mentions.

To have a notion of *order* we employ a directed graph: We only allow an edge from m to n if m appears later in the text than n.

To perform coreference resolution for a document d, we first construct a directed labeled multigraph (Section 3.3). We then assign a weight to each edge (Section 3.4). The resulting graph is clustered to obtain the mentions that refer to the same entity (Section 3.5).

3.3 Graph Construction

Given a set M of mentions extracted from a document d, we set $V = M$, i.e. the nodes of the graph are the mentions. To construct the edges A, we consider each pair (m, n) of mentions with $n \prec m$. We then check for every relation $r \in R$ if r holds for the pair (m, n). If this is the case we add the edge (m, n, r) to A. For simplicity, we restrict ourselves to binary relations that hold between pairs of mentions (see Section 4).

The graph displayed in Figure 1 is the graph constructed for the mentions *Leaders*, *Paris*, *recent developments* and *They* from the example sentence at the beginning of this Section, where $R = \{$P_AnaPron, P_Subject, N_Number$\}$.

3.4 Assigning Weights

Depending on whether a relation $r \in R$ is indicative for non-coreference (e.g. number disagreement) or for coreference (e.g. string matching) it should be weighted differently. We therefore divide R into a set of *negative relations* R_- and a set of *positive relations* R_+.

Previous work on multigraphs for coreference resolution disallows any edge between mentions for which a negative relations holds (Cai et al., 2011b; Martschat et al., 2012). We take a similar approach and set $w(m, n, r) = -\infty$ for $(m, n, r) \in A$ when $r \in R_-$[1].

Work on graph-based models similar to ours report robustness with regard to the amount of training data used (Cai et al., 2011b; Cai et al., 2011a; Martschat et al., 2012). Motivated by their observations we treat every positive relation equally and set $w(m, n, r) = 1$ for $(m, n, r) \in A$ if $r \in R_+$.

In contrast to previous work on similar graph models we do not learn any edge weights from training data. We compare this unsupervised scheme with supervised variants empirically in Section 5.

3.5 Clustering

To describe the clustering algorithm used in this work we need some additional terminology. If there exists an edge $(m, n, r) \in A$ we say that n is a *child* of m.

In the graph constructed according to the procedure described in Section 3.3, all children of a mention m are candidate antecedents for m. The relations we employ are indicators for coreference (which get a positive weight) and indicators for non-coreference (which get a negative weight). We aim to employ a simple and efficient clustering scheme on this graph and therefore choose 1-nearest-neighbor clustering: for every m, we choose as antecedent m's child n such that the sum of edge weights is maximal and positive. We break ties by choosing the closest mention.

In the unsupervised setting described in Section 3.4 this algorithm reduces to choosing the child that is connected via the highest number of positive relations and via no negative relation.

For the graph depicted in Figure 1 this algorithm computes the clusters $\{$*They*, *Leaders*$\}$, $\{$*Paris*$\}$ and $\{$*recent developments*$\}$.

4 Relations

The graph model described in Section 3 is based on expressing relations between pairs of mentions via edges built from such relations. We now describe the relations currently used by our system. They are well-known indicators and constraints for coreference and are taken from previous work (Cardie and Wagstaff, 1999; Soon et al., 2001; Rahman and Ng, 2009; Lee et al., 2011; Cai et al., 2011b). All relations operate on pairs of mentions (m, n), where m is the anaphor and n is a candidate antecedent. If a relation r holds for (m, n), the edge (m, n, r) is added to the graph. We finalized the set of relations and their distance thresholds on development data.

4.1 Negative Relations

Negative relations receive negative weights. They allow us to introduce well-known constraints such as agreement into our model.

(1) N_Gender, (2) N_Number: Two mentions do not agree in gender or number. We compute number and gender for common nouns using the number and gender data provided by Bergsma and Lin (2006).

(3) N_SemanticClass: Two mentions do not agree in semantic class (we only use the top categories *Object*, *Date* and *Person* from WordNet (Fellbaum, 1998)).

(4) N_ItDist: The anaphor is *it* or *they* and the sentence distance to the antecedent is larger

[1]We experimented with different weighting schemes for negative relations on development data (e.g. setting $w(m, n, r) = -1$) but did not observe a gain in performance.

than one.

(5) N_Speaker12Pron: Two first person pronouns or two second person pronouns with different speakers, or one first person pronoun and one second person pronoun with the same speaker[2].

(6) N_ContraSubObj: Two mentions are in the subject/object positions of the same verb, the anaphor is a non-possessive/reflexive pronoun.

(7) N_Mod: Two mentions have the same syntactic heads, and the anaphor has a nominal modifier which does not occur in the antecedent.

(8) N_Embedding: Two mentions where one embeds the other, which is not a reflexive or possessive pronoun.

(9) N_2PronNonSpeech: Two second person pronouns without speaker information and not in direct speech.

4.2 Positive Relations

Positive relations are coreference indicators which are added as edges with positive weights.

(10) P_NonPron_StrMatch: Applies only if the anaphor is definite or a proper name[3]. This relation holds if after discarding stop words the strings of mentions completely match.

(11) P_HeadMatch: If the syntactic heads of mentions match.

(12) P_Alias: If mentions are aliases of each other (i.e. proper names with partial match, full names and acronyms, etc.).

(13) P_Speaker12Pron: If the speaker of the second person pronoun is talking to the speaker of the first person pronoun (applies only to first/second person pronouns).

(14) P_DSPron: One mention is a *speak verb*'s subject, the other mention is a first person pronoun within the corresponding direct speech.

(15) P_ReflPronSub: If the anaphor is a reflexive pronoun, and the antecedent is the subject of the sentence.

(16) P_PossPronSub: If the anaphor is a possessive pronoun, and the antecedent is the subject of the anaphor's sentence or subclause.

(17) P_PossPronEmb: The anaphor is a possessive pronoun embedded in the antecedent.

(18) P_AnaPron: If the anaphor is a pronoun and none of the mentions is a first or second person pronoun. This relation is restricted to a sentence distance of 3.

(19) P_VerbAgree: If the anaphor is a third person pronoun and has the same predicate as the antecedent. This relation is restricted to a sentence distance of 1.

(20) P_Subject, (21) P_Object: The anaphor is a third person pronoun and both mentions are subjects/objects. These relations are restricted to a sentence distance of 1.

(22) P_Pron_StrMatch: If both mentions are pronouns and their strings match.

(23) P_Pron_Agreement: If both mentions are different pronoun tokens but agree in number, gender and person.

5 Evaluation

5.1 Data and Evaluation Metrics

We use the data provided for the English track of the CoNLL'12 shared task on multilingual coreference resolution (Pradhan et al., 2012) which is a subset of the upcoming OntoNotes 5.0 release and comes with various annotation layers provided by state-of-the-art NLP tools. We used the official dev/test split for development and evaluation. We evaluate the model in a setting that corresponds to the shared task's *closed track*, i.e. we use only WordNet (Fellbaum, 1998), the number and gender data of Bergsma and Lin (2006) and the provided annotation layers. To extract system mentions we employ the mention extractor described in Martschat et al. (2012).

We evaluate our system with the coreference resolution evaluation metrics that were used for the CoNLL shared tasks on coreference, which are MUC (Vilain et al., 1995), B^3 (Bagga and Baldwin, 1998) and $CEAF_e$ (Luo, 2005). We also report the unweighted *average* of the three scores, which was the official evaluation metric in the shared tasks. To compute the scores we employed the official scorer supplied by the shared task organizers.

5.2 Results

Table 1 displays the performance of our model and of the systems that obtained the best (Fernandes et al., 2012) and the median performance in the

[2] Like all relations using speaker information, this relation depends on the gold speaker annotation layer in the corpus.

[3] This condition is necessary to cope with the high-recall output of the mention tagger.

	MUC			B^3			$CEAF_e$			average
	R	P	F1	R	P	F1	R	P	F1	
CoNLL'12 English development data										
best	64.88	74.74	69.46	66.53	78.28	71.93	54.93	43.68	48.66	63.35
median	62.3	62.8	62.0	66.7	71.8	69.1	46.4	44.9	45.6	58.9
this work (weights_fraction)	64.00	68.56	66.20	66.59	75.67	70.84	50.48	45.52	47.87	61.63
this work (weights_MaxEnt)	63.72	65.78	64.73	66.60	73.76	70.00	47.46	45.30	46.36	60.36
this work (unsupervised)	64.01	68.58	66.22	67.00	76.45	71.41	51.10	46.16	48.51	62.05
CoNLL'12 English test data										
best	65.83	75.91	70.51	65.79	77.69	71.24	55.00	43.17	48.37	63.37
median	62.08	63.02	62.55	66.23	70.45	68.27	45.74	44.74	45.23	58.68
this work (weights_fraction)	64.25	68.31	66.22	65.44	74.20	69.54	49.18	44.71	46.84	60.87
this work (weights_MaxEnt)	63.58	64.70	64.14	65.63	72.09	68.71	45.58	44.41	44.99	59.28
this work (unsupervised)	63.95	67.99	65.91	65.47	74.93	69.88	49.83	45.40	47.51	61.10

Table 1: Results of different systems on the CoNLL'12 English data sets.

CoNLL'12 shared task, which are denoted as *best* and *median* respectively. *best* employs a structured prediction model with learned combinations of 70 basic features. We also compare with two supervised variants of our model which use the same relations and the same clustering algorithm as the unsupervised model: *weights_fraction* sets the weight of a relation to the fraction of positive instances in training data (as in Martschat et al. (2012)). *weights_MaxEnt* trains a mention-pair model (Soon et al., 2001) via the maximum entropy classifier implemented in the BART toolkit (Versley et al., 2008) and builds a graph where the weight of an edge connecting two mentions is the classifier's prediction[4]. We use the official CoNLL'12 English training set for training.

Our unsupervised model performs considerably better than the median system from the CoNLL'12 shared task on both data sets according to all metrics. It also seems to be able to accommodate well for the relations described in Section 4 since it outperforms both supervised variants[5]. The model performs worse than *best*, the gap according to B^3 and $CEAF_e$ being considerably smaller than according to MUC. While we observe a decrease of 1 point average score when evaluating on test data the model still would have ranked fourth in the English track of the CoNLL'12 shared task with only 0.2 points difference in average score to the second ranked system.

[4]The classifier's output is a number $p \in [0, 1]$. In order to have negative weights we use the transformation $p' = 2p - 1$.

[5]Compared with the supervised variants all improvements in F1 score are statistically significant according to a paired t-test ($p < 0.05$) except for the difference in MUC F1 to *weights_fraction*.

6 Error Analysis

In order to understand weaknesses of our model we perform an error analysis on the development data. We distinguish between *precision* and *recall* errors. For an initial analysis we split the errors according to the mention type of anaphor and antecedent (name, nominal and pronoun).

6.1 Precision Errors

Our system operates in a pairwise fashion. We therefore count one precision error whenever the clustering algorithm assigns two non-coreferent mentions to the same cluster. Table 2 shows the

	NAM	NOM	PRO
NAM	3413 (21%)	67 (66%)	11 (46%)
NOM	43 (67%)	2148 (49%)	9 (89%)
PRO	868 (32%)	1771 (55%)	5308 (24%)

Table 2: Number of clustering decisions made according to mention type (rows anaphor, columns antecedent) and percentage of wrong decisions.

number of clustering decisions made according to the mention type and in brackets the fraction of decisions that erroneously assign two non-coreferent mentions to the same cluster. We see that two main sources of error are nominal-nominal pairs and the resolution of pronouns. We now focus on gaining further insight into the system's performance for pronoun resolution by investigating the performance per pronoun type. The results are displayed in Table 3. We obtain good performance for *I* and *my* which in the majority of cases can be resolved unambiguously by the speaker relations employed by our system. The relations we use also seem

Anaphor	all	anaphoric
I	1260 (13%)	1239 (11%)
my	192 (14%)	181 (9%)
he	824 (14%)	812 (13%)
...	...	
they	764 (29%)	725 (26%)
...	...	
you	802 (41%)	555 (15%)
it	1114 (64%)	720 (44%)

Table 3: Precision statistics for pronouns. Rows are pronoun surfaces, columns number of clustering decisions and percentage of wrong decisions for all and only anaphoric pronouns respectively.

to work well for *he*. In contrast, the local, shallow approach we currently employ is not able to resolve highly ambiguous pronouns such as *they*, *you* or *it* in many cases. The reduction in error rate when only considering anaphoric pronouns shows that our system could benefit from an improved detection of expletive *it* and *you*.

6.2 Recall Errors

Estimating recall errors by counting all missing pairwise links would consider each entity many times. Therefore, we instead count one recall error for a pair (m, n) of anaphor m and antecedent n if (i) m and n are coreferent, (ii) m and n are not assigned to the same cluster, (iii) m is the first mention in its cluster that is coreferent with n, and (iv) n is the closest mention coreferent with m that is not in m's cluster.

This can be illustrated by an example. Considering mentions $m_1, \ldots, m_5$, assume that m_1, m_3, m_4 and m_5 are coreferent but the system clusters are $\{m_2, m_3\}$ and $\{m_4, m_5\}$. We then count two recall errors: one for the missing link from m_3 to m_1 and one for the missing link from m_4 to m_3.

According to this definition we count 3528 recall errors on the development set. The distribution of errors is displayed in Table 4. We see that

	NAM	NOM	PRO
NAM	321	220	247
NOM	306	797	330
PRO	306	476	525

Table 4: Number of recall errors according to mention type (rows anaphor, columns antecedent).

the main source of recall errors are missing links of nominal-nominal pairs. We randomly extracted 50 of these errors and manually assigned them to different categories.

29 errors: missing semantic knowledge. In these cases lexical or world knowledge is needed to build coreference links between mentions with different heads. For example our system misses the link between *the sauna* and *the hotbox sweatbox*.
14 errors: too restrictive N_Mod. In these cases the heads of the mentions matched but no link was built due to N_Mod. An example is the missing link between *our island's last remaining forest of these giant trees* and *the forest of Chilan*.
4 errors: too cautious string match. We only apply string matching for common nouns when the noun is definite.

Three errors could not be attributed to any of the above categories.

7 Conclusions and Future Work

We presented an unsupervised graph-based model for coreference resolution. Experiments show that our model exhibits competitive performance on the English CoNLL'12 shared task data sets.

An error analysis revealed that two main sources of errors of our model are the inaccurate resolution of highly ambiguous pronouns such as *it* and missing links between nominals with different heads. Future work should investigate how semantic knowledge and more complex relations capturing deeper discourse properties such as coherence or information status can be added to the model. Processing these features efficently may require a more sophisticated clustering algorithm.

We are surprised by the good performance of this unsupervised model in comparison to the state-of-the-art which uses sophisticated machine learning techniques (Fernandes et al., 2012) or well-engineered rules (Lee et al., 2011). We are not sure how to interpret these results and want to leave different interpretations for discussion:

- our unsupervised model is really that good (hopefully),
- the evaluation metrics employed are to be questioned (certainly),
- efficiently making use of annotated training data still remains a challenge for the state-of-the-art (likely).

Acknowledgments

This work has been funded by the Klaus Tschira Foundation, Germany. The author has been supported by a HITS PhD scholarship.

References

Roxana Angheluta, Patrick Jeuniaux, Rudradeb Mitra, and Marie-Francine Moens. 2004. Clustering algorithms for noun phrase coreference resolution. In *Proceedings of the 7èmes Journées Internationales d'Analyse Statistique des Données Textuelles,* Louvain La Neuve, Belgium, 10–12 March 2004, pages 60–70.

Amit Bagga and Breck Baldwin. 1998. Algorithms for scoring coreference chains. In *Proceedings of the 1st International Conference on Language Resources and Evaluation,* Granada, Spain, 28–30 May 1998, pages 563–566.

Shane Bergsma and Dekang Lin. 2006. Bootstrapping path-based pronoun resolution. In *Proceedings of the 21st International Conference on Computational Linguistics and 44th Annual Meeting of the Association for Computational Linguistics,* Sydney, Australia, 17–21 July 2006, pages 33–40.

Jie Cai and Michael Strube. 2010. End-to-end coreference resolution via hypergraph partitioning. In *Proceedings of the 23rd International Conference on Computational Linguistics,* Beijing, China, 23–27 August 2010, pages 143–151.

Jie Cai, Éva Mújdricza-Maydt, Yufang Hou, and Michael Strube. 2011a. Weakly supervised graph-based coreference resolution for clinical data. In *Proceedings of the 5th i2b2 Shared Tasks and Workshop on Challenges in Natural Language Processing for Clinical Data,* Washington, D.C., 20-21 October 2011.

Jie Cai, Éva Mújdricza-Maydt, and Michael Strube. 2011b. Unrestricted coreference resolution via global hypergraph partitioning. In *Proceedings of the Shared Task of the 15th Conference on Computational Natural Language Learning,* Portland, Oreg., 23–24 June 2011, pages 56–60.

Claire Cardie and Kiri Wagstaff. 1999. Noun phrase coreference as clustering. In *Proceedings of the 1999 SIGDAT Conference on Empirical Methods in Natural Language Processing and Very Large Corpora,* College Park, Md., 21–22 June 1999, pages 82–89.

Eugene Charniak and Micha Elsner. 2009. EM works for pronoun anaphora resolution. In *Proceedings of the 12th Conference of the European Chapter of the Association for Computational Linguistics,* Athens, Greece, 30 March – 3 April 2009, pages 148–156.

Aron Culotta, Michael Wick, and Andrew McCallum. 2007. First-order probabilistic models for coreference resolution. In *Proceedings of Human Language Technologies 2007: The Conference of the North American Chapter of the Association for Computational Linguistics,* Rochester, N.Y., 22–27 April 2007, pages 81–88.

Christiane Fellbaum, editor. 1998. *WordNet: An Electronic Lexical Database.* MIT Press, Cambridge, Mass.

Eraldo Fernandes, Cícero dos Santos, and Ruy Milidiú. 2012. Latent structure perceptron with feature induction for unrestricted coreference resolution. In *Proceedings of the Shared Task of the 16th Conference on Computational Natural Language Learning,* Jeju Island, Korea, 12–14 July 2012, pages 41–48.

Aria Haghighi and Dan Klein. 2007. Unsupervised coreference resolution in a nonparametric Bayesian model. In *Proceedings of the 45th Annual Meeting of the Association for Computational Linguistics,* Prague, Czech Republic, 23–30 June 2007, pages 848–855.

Heeyoung Lee, Yves Peirsman, Angel Chang, Nathanael Chambers, Mihai Surdeanu, and Dan Jurafsky. 2011. Stanford's multi-pass sieve coreference resolution system at the CoNLL-2011 shared task. In *Proceedings of the Shared Task of the 15th Conference on Computational Natural Language Learning,* Portland, Oreg., 23–24 June 2011, pages 28–34.

Xiaoqiang Luo. 2005. On coreference resolution performance metrics. In *Proceedings of the Human Language Technology Conference and the 2005 Conference on Empirical Methods in Natural Language Processing,* Vancouver, B.C., Canada, 6–8 October 2005, pages 25–32.

Sebastian Martschat, Jie Cai, Samuel Broscheit, Éva Mújdricza-Maydt, and Michael Strube. 2012. A multigraph model for coreference resolution. In *Proceedings of the Shared Task of the 16th Conference on Computational Natural Language Learning,* Jeju Island, Korea, 12–14 July 2012, pages 100–106.

Ruslan Mitkov. 1998. Robust pronoun resolution with limited knowledge. In *Proceedings of the 17th International Conference on Computational Linguistics and 36th Annual Meeting of the Association for Computational Linguistics,* Montréal, Québec, Canada, 10–14 August 1998, pages 869–875.

Vincent Ng. 2008. Unsupervised models for coreference resolution. In *Proceedings of the 2008 Conference on Empirical Methods in Natural Language Processing,* Waikiki, Honolulu, Hawaii, 25–27 October 2008, pages 640–649.

Cristina Nicolae and Gabriel Nicolae. 2006. BestCut: A graph algorithm for coreference resolution. In *Proceedings of the 2006 Conference on Empirical Methods in Natural Language Processing,* Sydney, Australia, 22–23 July 2006, pages 275–283.

Hoifung Poon and Pedro Domingos. 2008. Joint unsupervised coreference resolution with Markov Logic. In *Proceedings of the 2008 Conference on Empirical Methods in Natural Language Processing,* Waikiki, Honolulu, Hawaii, 25–27 October 2008, pages 650–659.

Sameer Pradhan, Lance Ramshaw, Mitchell Marcus, Martha Palmer, Ralph Weischedel, and Nianwen Xue. 2011. CoNLL-2011 Shared Task: Modeling unrestricted coreference in OntoNotes. In *Proceedings of the Shared Task of the 15th Conference on Computational Natural Language Learning,* Portland, Oreg., 23–24 June 2011, pages 1–27.

Sameer Pradhan, Alessandro Moschitti, and Nianwen Xue. 2012. CoNLL-2012 Shared Task: Modeling multilingual unrestricted coreference in OntoNotes. In *Proceedings of the Shared Task of the 16th Conference on Computational Natural Language Learning,* Jeju Island, Korea, 12–14 July 2012, pages 1–40.

Karthik Raghunathan, Heeyoung Lee, Sudarshan Rangarajan, Nathanael Chambers, Mihai Surdeanu, Dan Jurafsky, and Christopher Manning. 2010. A multipass sieve for coreference resolution. In *Proceedings of the 2010 Conference on Empirical Methods in Natural Language Processing,* Cambridge, Mass., 9–11 October 2010, pages 492–501.

Altaf Rahman and Vincent Ng. 2009. Supervised models for coreference resolution. In *Proceedings of the 2009 Conference on Empirical Methods in Natural Language Processing,* Singapore, 6–7 August 2009, pages 968–977.

Emili Sapena, Lluís Padró, and Jordi Turmo. 2010. A global relaxation labeling approach to coreference resolution. In *Proceedings of Coling 2010: Poster Volume,* Beijing, China, 23–27 August 2010, pages 1086–1094.

Emili Sapena, Lluís Padró, and Jordi Turmo. 2011. RelaxCor participation in CoNLL shared task on coreference resolution. In *Proceedings of the Shared Task of the 15th Conference on Computational Natural Language Learning,* Portland, Oreg., 23–24 June 2011, pages 35–39.

Wee Meng Soon, Hwee Tou Ng, and Daniel Chung Yong Lim. 2001. A machine learning approach to coreference resolution of noun phrases. *Computational Linguistics*, 27(4):521–544.

Yannick Versley, Simone Paolo Ponzetto, Massimo Poesio, Vladimir Eidelman, Alan Jern, Jason Smith, Xiaofeng Yang, and Alessandro Moschitti. 2008. BART: A modular toolkit for coreference resolution. In *Companion Volume to the Proceedings of the 46th Annual Meeting of the Association for Computational Linguistics,* Columbus, Ohio, 15–20 June 2008, pages 9–12.

Marc Vilain, John Burger, John Aberdeen, Dennis Connolly, and Lynette Hirschman. 1995. A model-theoretic coreference scoring scheme. In *Proceedings of the 6th Message Understanding Conference (MUC-6)*, pages 45–52, San Mateo, Cal. Morgan Kaufmann.

Computational considerations of comparisons and similes

Vlad Niculae
University of Wolverhampton
vlad@vene.ro

Victoria Yaneva
University of Wolverhampton
v.yaneva@wlv.ac.uk

Abstract

This paper presents work in progress towards automatic recognition and classification of comparisons and similes.

Among possible applications, we discuss the place of this task in text simplification for readers with Autism Spectrum Disorders (ASD), who are known to have deficits in comprehending figurative language.

We propose an approach to comparison recognition through the use of syntactic patterns. Keeping in mind the requirements of autistic readers, we discuss the properties relevant for distinguishing semantic criteria like figurativeness and abstractness.

1 Introduction

Comparisons are phrases that express the likeness of two entities. They rely on specific patterns that make them recognisable. The most obvious pattern, __ `be` *like* __, is illustrated by the following example, but many subtler ways of building comparisons exist:

> "He was like his father, except he had a crooked nose and his ears were a little lopsided." (In "Black cat" by Alex Krill)

Similes are a subset of comparisons. The simile is a figure of speech that builds on a comparison in order to exploit certain attributes of an entity in a striking manner. According to the Oxford English Dictionary, what sets a simile apart from a comparison is that it compares "one thing with another thing of a different kind"[1].

A popular example by Charles Dickens is:

> "Mrs. Cratchit entered: flushed, but smiling proudly: with the pudding, like a speckled cannon-ball, so hard and firm, (...)" (In "A Christmas Carol" by Charles Dickens)

The comparison between a Christmas pudding and a cannon-ball is so unexpected, as delicious deserts are not conventionally associated with cannon-balls (or any kind of metal objects), that the author needs to clarify the resemblance by adding "so hard and firm" right after the simile. Intuitively, the OED definition is confirmed by these two examples: *a Christmas pudding* and *a cannon-ball* are things of different kinds, whereas *he* and *his father* are things of the same kind (namely, human males). As we shall see, the borderline which divides some similes and fixed expressions is the degree of conventionality. Many other phrases used by Dickens in "A Christmas Carol" also link two notions of different kinds: Old Marley was "as dead as a doornail" and Scrooge was "as hard as flint" and "as solitary as an oyster". In these cases, however, the link between the two entities is a pattern repeated so many times that it has consequently lost its innovativeness and turned into a dead metaphor ("as dead as a doornail") or a conventional simile (sections 4.1, 5.4.2).

The scholarly discussion of the simile has been controversial, especially with respect to its relative, the metaphor. The two were regarded as very close by Aristotle's *Rhetoric*: "The simile, also, is a metaphor, the difference is but slight" (Aristoteles and Cooper, 1932). However, modern research has largely focused on metaphor, while the simile suffered a *defiguration*, described and argued against by Bethlehem (1996): in order to support the idea that the metaphor embodies the essence of figurativeness, the simile was gradually stripped of

[1] "simile, n. a figure of speech involving the comparison of one thing with another thing of a different kind, used to make a description more emphatic or vivid (e.g. as brave as a lion)" OED Online. June 2004. Oxford University Press. 06 February 2013 http://dictionary.oed.com/.

its status as figure of speech.

Metaphor is defined as "a word or phrase applied to an object or action to which it is not literally applicable"[2].

In other words, a metaphor links features of objects or events from two different, often incompatible domains, thus being a "realization of a cross-domain conceptual mapping" (Deignan, 2005). We are interested in the parallel between similes and metaphors insofar as it points to an overlap. There are types of similes that can be transformed into equivalent metaphors, and certain metaphors can be rewritten as similes, but neither set is included in the other. This view is supported by corpus evidence (Hanks, 2012) and contradicts reductionist *defiguration* point of view, in a way that Israel et al. (2004) suggest: some metaphors express things that cannot be expressed by similes, and vice versa.

In computational linguistics, similes have been neglected in favour of metaphor even more than in linguistics[3] , despite the fact that comparisons have a structure that makes them rather amenable to automated processing. In sections 2 we discuss one motivation for studying comparisons and similes: their simplification to language better suited for people with ASD. Section 3 reviews related work on figurative language in NLP. In section 4 we present the structure of comparisons and some associated patterns, emphasising the difficulties posed by the flexibility of language. Section 5 describes computational approaches to the tasks, along with results from preliminary experiments supporting our ideas. The study is wrapped up and future work is presented in section 6.

2 Autism and simile comprehension

2.1 Autism and figurative language

Highly abstract or figurative metaphors and similes may be problematic for certain groups of language users amongst which are people with different types of acquired language disorders (aphasias) or developmental ones like ASD. As a result of impairment in communication, social interaction and behaviour, ASD are characterised by atypical information processing in diverse areas of cognition (Skoyles, 2011). People with autism, especially if they are children, experience disturbing confusion when confronted with figurative language. Happé (1995) describes:

> A request to "Stick your coat down over there" is met by a serious request for glue. Ask if she will "give you a hand", and she will answer that she needs to keep both hands and cannot cut one off to give to you. Tell him that his sister is "crying her eyes out" and he will look anxiously on the floor for her eye-balls...

The decreased ability of autistic people to understand metaphors and figurative language as a whole (Rundblad and Annaz, 2010; MacKay and Shaw, 2004; Happé, 1995), could be seen as an obstacle in communication, given that we all "think in metaphors" and a language system is "figurative in its nature" (Lakoff and Johson, 1980). The growing demand to overcome this barrier has led to the investigation of possible ways in which NLP can detect and simplify non-literal expressions in a text.

2.2 Comprehending similes

People with ASD[4] show almost no impairment in comprehending those similes which have literal meaning (Happé, 1995). This relative ease in processing is probably due to the fact that similes contain explicit markers (e.g. *like* and *as*), which evoke comparison between two things in a certain aspect.

With regard to understanding figurative similes, Hobson (2012) describes in the case of fifteen-year-old L.: "He could neither grasp nor formulate similarities, differences or absurdities, nor could he understand metaphor".

Theoretically, one of the most obvious markers of similes, the word *like*, could be a source of a lot of misinterpretations. For example, *like* could be a verb, a noun, or a preposition, depending on the context. Given that autistic people have problems understanding context (Skoyles, 2011), how would an autistic reader perceive the role of *like* in a more elaborate and ambiguous comparison? Another possible linguistic reason for the impaired understanding of similes might be that *like* is used

[2] "metaphor, n." OED Online. June 2004. Oxford University Press. 06 February 2013 http://dictionary.oed.com/

[3] A Google Scholar search for papers containing the word *linguistic* have the word *metaphor* in the title approximately 5000 times, but *simile* only around 645 times. In the ACL anthology, *metaphor* occurs around 1070 times while *simile* occurs 52 times.

[4] With level of cognitive ability corresponding to at least first level of Theory of Mind (Baron-Cohen et al., 1985)

ambiguously in many expressions which are neither similes nor comparisons, such as *I feel like an ice cream* or *I feel like something is wrong*.

Even if the expression does not include such an ambiguous use of *like*, there are other cases in which a person with autism might be misled. For example, if the simile is highly figurative or abstract, it may be completely incomprehensible for people with ASD (e.g. the conventional *Love is like a flame*). A step forward towards the simplification of such expressions is their identification and filtering of the ones that are not problematic. Through manipulations, the difficult aspects such as abstractness, figurativeness, and ambiguity can be attenuated.

3 Relevant literature

Comprehensive theoretical investigations into the expressive power of similes can be found in (Bethlehem, 1996) and (Israel et al., 2004). Weiner (1984) applies ontologies to discriminate simple literal and figurative comparisons (loosely using the term *metaphor* to refer to what we call the intersection of similes and metaphors).

Most of the recent computational linguistics research involving similes comes from Veale. In (Veale and Hao, 2008), the pattern *as* _ *as* _ is exploited to mine salient and stereotypical properties of entities using the Google search engine. A similar process has been applied to both English and Chinese by Li et al. (2012). The *Metaphor Magnet* system presented in (Veale and Li, 2012) supports queries against a rich ontology of metaphorical meanings and affects using the same simple simile patterns. The *Jigsaw Bard* (Veale and Hao, 2011) is a thesaurus driven by figurative conventional similes extracted from the Google Ngram corpus.

The role played by figurative language in the field of text simplification has not been extensively studied outside of a few recent publications (Temnikova, 2012; Štajner et al., 2012).

4 Anatomy of a comparison

4.1 Conventionality: norms and exploitations

The theory of norms and exploitations (Hanks, 2013) describes language norms as "a pattern of ordinary usage in everyday language with which a particular meaning or implicature is associated" and argues that norms can be exploited in different ways in order to "say new things or to say old things in new and interesting ways". This distinction can be applied to similes: *as slow as a snail* is a conventional simile that evokes strong association between slowness and snails. On the contrary, in *she looked like a cross between a Christmas tree and an American footballer* (example adapted from the British National Corpus, henceforth BNC) a person (the topic) is not conventionally associated with a Christmas tree (the vehicle), let alone if it is crossed with a football player. In this example the vehicle is not merely unexpected, it also does not exist as a common pattern, and can, by itself, create amazement.

Though figures of speech are good ways to exploit norms, figurative language can become conventional, and an exploitation can be literal (e.g. word creation, ellipsis).

The border between conventionality and creativeness is fuzzy and heuristics such as the ones proposed in (Deignan, 2005) can only approximate it. Possible alternative methods are discussed in section 5.4.2.

4.2 Syntactic structure

The breadth of comparisons and similes hasn't been extensively studied, so there is no surprise in the small amount of coverage in computational linguistics research on the subject. In order to develop a solid foundation for working with complex comparisons, we will follow and argue for the terminology from (Hanks, 2012), where the structure of a simile is analysed. The same structure applies to comparisons, since as we have said, all similes are comparisons and they are indistinguishable syntactically. The constituents of a comparison are:

- T: the topic, sometimes called tenor: it is usually a noun phrase and acts as logical subject.
- E: the eventuality (event or state): usually a verb, it sets the frame for the observation of the common property.
- P: the shared property or ground: it expresses what the two entities have in common.
- C: the comparator: commonly a preposition (*like* or part of an adjectival phrase (*better than*), it is the trigger word or phrase that marks the presence of a comparison.

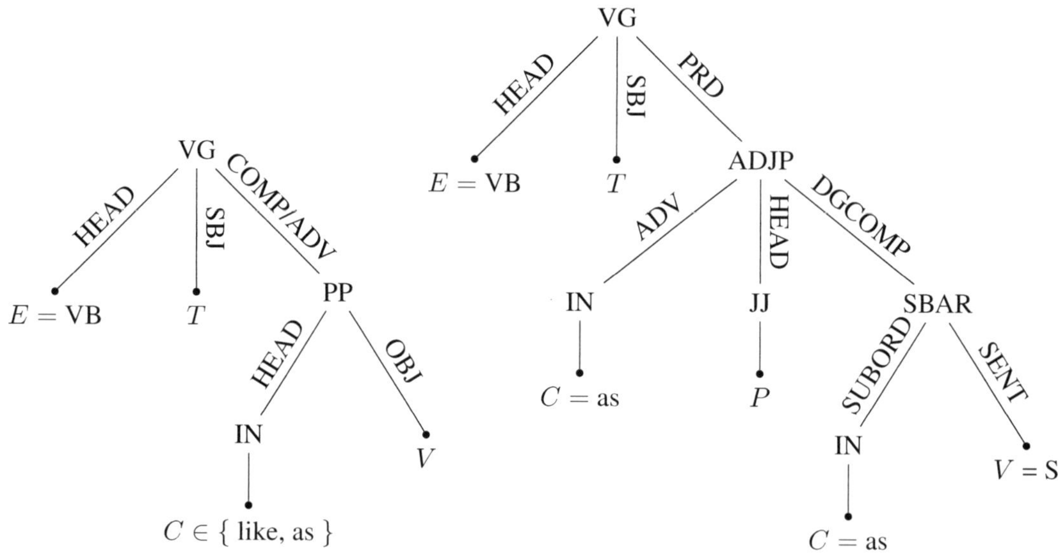

(a) Basic comparison pattern. Matches *he eats like a pig* and *it is seen as a release*.

(b) Explicit comparison with double *as*. Matches expressions like *it's as easy as pie*.

Figure 1: GLARF-style representation of two basic comparison patterns.

- V: the vehicle: it is the object of the comparison and is also usually a noun phrase.

An example (adapted from the BNC) of a simile involving all of the above would be:

> [He ^{T}] [looked ^{E}] [like ^{C}] [a broiled frog ^{V}], [hunched ^{P}] over his desk, grinning and satisfied.

The order of the elements is flexible. Fishelov (1993) attributes this reordering to poetic simile, along with other deviations from the norm that he defines as non-poetic simile. We note, in agreement with Bethlehem (1996), that the distinction is rendered less useful when the focus is on the vague notion of poeticality. Fishelov even suggested that poetic similes can be found outside of poetic text, and vice versa. We will therefore focus on exploitations that change the meaning.

More often than not, the property is left for the reader to deduce:

> [His mouth ^{T}] [tasted ^{E}] [like ^{C}] [the bottom of a parrot's cage ^{V}]

But even when all elements appear, the comparison may be ambiguous, as lexical choice in P and in E lead to various degrees of specificity. For example replacing the word *tasted*, which forms the E in the example above, with the more general predicator *is*, results in a simile that might have the same meaning, but is more difficult to decode. On the other hand, the whole V phrase *the bottom of a parrot's cage*, which is an euphemistic metonymy, could be substituted with its concrete, literal meaning thus transforming the creative simile into what might be a conventional pattern. Nested figures of speech can also occur at this level, for example the insertion of a metaphorical and synesthetic P: *it tasted [dirty ^{P}], like a parrot's cage*.

We consider the eventuality E as the syntactic core of the comparison structure. Despite the apparently superior importance of the comparator, which acts as a trigger word, the event acts as a predicator, attracting to it the entire structure in the form of a set of arguments. This observation is missing from the work of Fishelov (1993) and Bethlehem (1996), who lump the event together with either P or T. In terms of meaning, the two constituents are of course tightly connected, but to computationally identify the components, their separation is important.

Roncero (2006) pointed out that for certain common similes (e.g. *love is like a rose*) found on the Internet, it is likely that an explanation of the shared property follows, whereas for all topic-vehicle pairs studied, the corresponding metaphor is less often explained. However, these simpler similes form a special case, as most similes cannot be made into metaphors (Hanks, 2012).

4.3 Comparisons without *like*

Hanks (2012) observes that there are plenty of other ways to make a simile in addition to using *like* or *as*. Most definitions of similes indeed claim that there are more possible comparators, but examples are elusive.

Israel et al. (2004) point out that any construction that can make a comparison can be used to make a simile. This is a crucial point given the amount of flexibility available for such constructions. An example they give is:

> [The retirement of Yves Saint Laurent ^{T}] [is ^{E}] [the fashion equivalent ^{C}] of [the breakup of the Beatles ^{V}]. (heard on the National Public Radio)

We can see that it is possible for the comparator to be informative and not just an empty marker, in this case marking the domain (fashion) to which the topic refers to.

5 Approaches proposed

5.1 Overview

Simplifying creative language involves understanding. The task of understanding similes may be hard to achieve. We will not just write about the components we have already developed (the pattern matching), but also present a broader plan. At a coarse scale, the process breaks down into a syntactic *recognition* step and a semantic step that could be called *entailment*. The goal is to find out what is being said about the topic. Often similes claim that a property is present or absent, but this is not always the case.

5.2 Dataset

At the moment there is no available dataset for comparison and simile recognition and classification. We have begun our investigation and developed the patterns on a toy dataset consisting of the examples from (Hanks, 2005), which are comparisons, similes and other ambiguous uses of the preposition *like* extracted from the BNC. We also evaluated the system on around 500 sentences containing *like* and *as* from the BNC and the VUAMC[5]. The latter features some marking of trigger words, but we chose to score manually in order to assess the relevance of the annotation.

[5]VU Amsterdam Metaphor Corpus (Steen et al., 2010), available at `www.metaphorlab.vu.nl`

5.3 Recognizing comparisons and similes

5.3.1 Comparison pattern matching

We have seen that similes are a subset of comparisons and follow comparison structures. A good consequence is that they follow syntactic patterns that can be recognised. We have used GLARF (Meyers et al., 2001), an argument representation framework built on the output of the BLLIP parser. It enhances the constituency-based parse tree with additional roles and arguments by applying rules and resources like Propbank. The *like* and *as* comparators form the GLARF-style patterns shown in figure 1. The matching process iterates over all nodes with arguments, principally verbs and nominalisations. If the subtree rooted under it matches certain filters, then we assign to the root the role of E and the arguments can fill the other slots.

We evaluated the process on the small development set as well as on the larger set of lexical matches described above. The results are presented in table 1. The mistakes on the development set, as well as many on the other corpus, are caused by slightly different patterns (e.g. *he didn't look much like a doctor*). This can be addressed by adjustment or through automatic discovery of patterns. Expressions like in *hold your hands like this* are mistaken as comparisons. Ad hoc set constructions are mostly correctly unmatched (e.g. *big earners like doctors and airline pilots* but incorrectly matches semantically ambiguous uses of *feel like*.

On the lexical matches of *as*, the behaviour is different as the word seems much less likely to be a trigger. Most errors are therefore returning spurious matches, as opposed to *like*, where most errors are omissions This suggests that each trigger word behaves differently, and therefore robustness across patterns is important.

Overall, our method handles typical comparisons in short sentences rather well. Complex or long sentences sometimes cause T and V to be incompletely identified, or sometimes the parse to fail. This suggests that deep syntactic parsing is a limitation of the approach.

5.3.2 Discovering new patterns

Using a seed-based semi-supervised iterative process, we plan to identify most of the frequent structures used to build conventional comparisons. We expect that, in addition to idiomatic expressions, some T-V pairs often compared to each

	full	part	none
comparison	24	5	4
not comparison	1	1	5

(a) Counts of 40 examples with *like* from the development set in (Hanks, 2005). Partial match $P = 94\%$, $R = 88\%$.

full	part	none
0.17	0.07	0.33
0.05	0.05	0.33

(b) Proportions of 410 examples with *like* from BNC and VUAMC. Partial match $P = 70.5\%$, $R = 41.7\%$

full	part	none
0.11	0.05	0.09
0.26	0.11	0.39

(c) Proportions of 376 examples with *as* from BNC and VUAMC. Partial match $P = 29.6\%$, $R = 64.8\%$

Table 1: Confusion matrices and precision/recall scores for comparison identification. Full matching is when the heads of T, E, V and C are correctly identified, while partial is if only some of them are.

other with the *like* pattern will occur in other syntactical patterns or lexical collocations.

5.4 Semantic aspects

5.4.1 Classifying comparisons

The phrases that match patterns like the ones described are not necessarily comparisons. Due to ambiguities, sentences such as *I feel like an ice cream* are indistinguishable from comparisons in our model.

Another aspect we would like to distinguish is whether an instance of a pattern is a simile or not. We plan to tackle this using machine learning. Semantic features from an ontology like the one used in PDEV[6], or a more comprehensive work such as WordNet[7], can carry the information whether T and V belong to similar semantic categories. We expect other information, such as distributional and distributed word vector representations, to be of use.

5.4.2 Conventional similes

It may also be of interest to decide whether an instance is conventional or creative. This can be implemented by measuring corpus frequencies. Instead of looking for perfect matches, patterns can be applied to simply count how many times something is compared to a V, regardless of the specific syntax used[8].

5.4.3 Simplification

The goal of text simplification is to generate syntactically well-formed language[9] that is easier to understand than the original phrase.

A comparison can be formalized as predicate $E(T; P)$. We can think of *his mouth tasted like the bottom of a parrot's cage* as a way to express **taste(his mouth; very bad)**. There is more than one way to build such an encoding.

The task reduces to the generation a simple phrase of the form $T'E'P'$, by simplifying the elements of the representation above. Useful resources are corpus occurrence counts of related phrases, word similarity and relatedness, and conventional associations.

6 Conclusions and future work

The problem of automatic identification of similes has its place in the paradigm of text simplification for people with language impairments. In particular, people with ASD have difficulties understanding figurative language.

We applied the idea of comparison patterns to match subtrees of an enhanced parse tree to easily match comparison structures and their constituents. This lead us to investigate corpus-driven mining of new comparison patterns, to go beyond *like* and *as*.

We are working on semi-automatically developing a dataset of comparisons and ambiguous non-comparisons, labelled with the interesting properties and with a focus on pattern variety and ambiguous cases. This will be useful for evaluating our system at a proper scale. We plan to perform extrinsic evaluation with respect to tasks like text simplification, textual entailment and machine translation.

Acknowledgements

The research described in this paper was partially funded by the European Commission through the FIRST project (FP7-287607) and partially by the BCROCE project.

[6] `http://deb.fi.muni.cz/pdev/`

[7] `http://wordnet.princeton.edu/`

[8] Care must be taken to avoid contradictions from exploitations: *The aircraft is like a rock* or *is built like a rock* seems like a conventional simile, but *The aircraft would gently skip like a rock and then settle down on the surface of the ocean* (Example from the BNC) is unconventional.

[9] Especially for ASD readers, who are very sensitive to language mistakes to the point that it completely distracts them from the meaning.

References

Aristoteles and Lane Cooper. 1932. *The rhetoric of Aristotle*. Appleton.

Simon Baron-Cohen, Alan M Leslie, and Uta Frith. 1985. Does the autistic child have a "theory of mind"? *Cognition*, 21(1):37–46.

Louise Shabat Bethlehem. 1996. Simile and figurative language. *Poetics Today*, v17(n2):p203(38). table.

Alice Deignan. 2005. *Metaphor and Corpus Linguistics*. Converging Evidence in Language and Communication Research Series. John Benjamins.

David Fishelov. 1993. Poetic and non-poetic simile: Structure, semantics, rhetoric. *Poetics Today*, pages 1–23.

Patrick Hanks. 2005. Similes and Sets: The English Preposition 'like'. In R. Blatná and V. Petkevic, editors, *Languages and Linguistics: Festschrift for Fr. Cermak*.

Patrick Hanks. 2012. The Roles and Structure of Comparisons, Similes, and Metaphors in Natural Language (An Analogical System). In *Presented at the Stockholm Metaphor Festival*, September 6-8.

Patrick Hanks. 2013. *Lexical Analysis: Norms and Exploitations*. Mit Press.

Francesca G. E. Happé. 1995. Understanding minds and metaphors: Insights from the study of figurative language in autism. *Metaphor and Symbolic Activity*, 10(4):275–295.

R. Peter Hobson. 2012. Autism, literal language and concrete thinking: Some developmental considerations. *Metaphor and Symbol*, 27(1):4–21.

Michael Israel, Jennifer Riddle Harding, and Vera Tobin. 2004. On simile. *Language, Culture, and Mind. CSLI Publications*.

George Lakoff and Mark Johson. 1980. *Metaphors We Live By*. Cátedra.

Bin Li, Jiajun Chen, and Yingjie Zhang. 2012. Web based collection and comparison of cognitive properties in english and chinese. In *Proceedings of the Joint Workshop on Automatic Knowledge Base Construction and Web-scale Knowledge Extraction*, AKBC-WEKEX '12, pages 31–34, Stroudsburg, PA, USA. Association for Computational Linguistics.

Gilbert MacKay and Adrienne Shaw. 2004. A comparative study of figurative language in children with autistic spectrum disorders. *Child Language Teaching and Therapy*, 20(1):13–32.

Adam Meyers, Ralph Grishman, Michiko Kosaka, and Shubin Zhao. 2001. Covering treebanks with glarf. In *Proceedings of the ACL 2001 Workshop on Sharing Tools and Resources - Volume 15*, STAR '01, pages 51–58, Stroudsburg, PA, USA. Association for Computational Linguistics.

Carlos Roncero, John M. Kennedy, and Ron Smyth. 2006. Similes on the internet have explanations. *Psychonomic Bulletin & Review*, 13:74–77.

Gabriella Rundblad and Dagmara Annaz. 2010. The atypical development of metaphor and metonymy comprehension in children with autism. *Autism*, 14(1):29–46.

John R Skoyles. 2011. Autism, context/noncontext information processing, and atypical development. *Autism research and treatment*, 2011.

G.J. Steen, A.G. Dorst, and J.B. Herrmann. 2010. *A Method for Linguistic Metaphor Identification: From Mip to Mipvu*. Converging evidence in language and communication research. Benjamins.

Irina Temnikova. 2012. *Text Complexity and Text Simplification in the Crisis Management domain*. Ph.D. thesis, University of Wolverhampton, Wolverhampton, UK, May.

Tony Veale and Yanfen Hao. 2008. A context-sensitive framework for lexical ontologies. *Knowledge Eng. Review*, 23(1):101–115.

Tony Veale and Yanfen Hao. 2011. Exploiting readymades in linguistic creativity: A system demonstration of the jigsaw bard. In *ACL (System Demonstrations)*, pages 14–19. The Association for Computer Linguistics.

Tony Veale and Guofu Li. 2012. Specifying viewpoint and information need with affective metaphors: A system demonstration of the metaphor-magnet web app/service. In *ACL (System Demonstrations)*, pages 7–12. The Association for Computer Linguistics.

Sanja Štajner, Richard Evans, Constantin Orasan, and Ruslan Mitkov. 2012. What can readability measures really tell us about text complexity? In Luz Rello and Horacio Saggion, editors, *Proceedings of the LREC'12 Workshop: Natural Language Processing for Improving Textual Accessibility (NLP4ITA)*, page 14, Istanbul, Turkey, may. European Language Resources Association (ELRA).

E. Judith Weiner. 1984. A knowledge representation approach to understanding metaphors. *Comput. Linguist.*, 10(1):1–14, January.

Question Analysis for Polish Question Answering

Piotr Przybyła
Institute of Computer Science, Polish Academy of Sciences,
ul. Jana Kazimierza 5, 01-248 Warszawa, Poland,
P.Przybyla@phd.ipipan.waw.pl

Abstract

This study is devoted to the problem of question analysis for a Polish question answering system. The goal of the question analysis is to determine its general structure, type of an expected answer and create a search query for finding relevant documents in a textual knowledge base. The paper contains an overview of available solutions of these problems, description of their implementation and presents an evaluation based on a set of 1137 questions from a Polish quiz TV show. The results help to understand how an environment of a Slavonic language affects the performance of methods created for English.

1 Introduction

The main motivation for building Question Answering (QA) systems is that they relieve a user of a need to translate his problem to a machine-readable form. To make it possible, we need to equip a computer system with an ability to understand requests in a natural language, find answers in a knowledge base and formulate them in the natural language. The aim of this paper is to deal with the first of these steps, i.e. **question analysis** module. It accepts the question as an input and returns a data structure containing relevant information, herein called **question model**. It consists of two elements: a **question type** and a **search query**.

The question type classifies a question to one of the categories based on its structure. A **general question type** takes one of the following values: verification (*Czy Lee Oswald zabił Johna Kennedy'ego?*, Eng. *Did Lee Oswald kill John Kennedy?*), option choosing (*Który z nich zabił Johna Kennedy'ego: Lance Oswald czy Lee Oswald?*, Eng. *Which one killed John Kennedy: Lance Oswald or Lee Oswald?*), named entity (*Kto zabił Johna Kennedy'ego?*, Eng. *Who killed John Kennedy?*), unnamed entity (*Czego użył Lee Oswald, żeby zabić Johna Kennedy'ego?*, Eng. *What did Lee Oswald use to kill John Kennedy?*), other name for a given named entity (*Jakiego pseudonimu używał John Kennedy w trakcie służby wojskowej?*, Eng. *What nickname did John Kennedy use during his military service?*) and multiple entities (*Którzy prezydenci Stanów Zjednoczonych zostali zabici w trakcie kadencji?*, Eng. *Which U.S. presidents were assassinated in office?*). There are many others possible, such as definition or explanation questions, but they require specific techniques for answer finding and remain beyond the scope of this work. For example, the *Question Answering for Machine Reading Evaluation* (QA4MRE) competition (Peñas et al., 2012) included these complex questions (e.g. *What caused X?*, *How did X happen?*, *Why did X happen?*). In case of named entity questions, it is also useful to find its **named entity type**, corresponding to a type of an entity which could be provided as an answer. A list of possible options, suited to questions about general knowledge, is given in Table 1. As some of the categories include others (e.g. CITY is a PLACE), the goal of a classifier is to find the narrowest available.

The need for a **search query** is motivated by performance reasons. A linguistic analysis applied to a source text to find the expected answer is usually resource-consuming, so it cannot be performed on the whole corpus (in case of this experiment 839,269 articles). To avoid it, we transform the question into the search query, which is subsequently used in a search engine, incorporating a full-text index of the corpus. As a result we get a list of documents, possibly related to the question. Although the query generation plays an auxiliary role, failure at this stage may lead both to too long processing times (in case of excessive number of returned documents) and lack of a final answer (in

Question type	Occurrences
NAMED_ENTITY	657
OPTION	28
VERIFICATION	25
MULTIPLE	28
UNNAMED_ENTITY	377
OTHER_NAME	22
PLACE	33
CONTINENT	4
RIVER	11
LAKE	9
MOUNTAIN	4
RANGE	2
ISLAND	5
ARCHIPELAGO	2
SEA	2
CELESTIAL_BODY	8
COUNTRY	52
STATE	7
CITY	52
NATIONALITY	12
PERSON	260
NAME	11
SURNAME	10
BAND	6
DYNASTY	6
ORGANISATION	20
COMPANY	2
EVENT	7
TIME	2
CENTURY	9
YEAR	34
PERIOD	1
COUNT	31
QUANTITY	6
VEHICLE	10
ANIMAL	1
TITLE	38

Table 1: The 6 general question types and the 31 named entity types and numbers of their occurrences in the test set.

case of not returning a relevant document).

2 Related work

The problem of determination of the general question type is not frequent in existing QA solutions, as most of the public evaluation tasks, such as the *TREC question answering track* (Dang et al., 2007) either provide it explicitly or focus on one selected type. However, when it comes to named entity type determination, a proper classification is indispensable for finding an answer of a desired type. Some of the interrogative pronouns, such as *gdzie* (Eng. *where*) or *kiedy* (Eng. *when*) uniquely define this type, so the most obvious approach uses a list of manually defined patterns. For example, Lee et al. (2005) base solely on such rules, but need to have 1273 of them. Unfortunately, some pronouns (i.e. *jaki*, Eng. *what*, and *który*, Eng. *which*) may refer to different types of entities. In questions created with them, such as *Który znany malarz twierdził, że obciął sobie ucho?* (Eng. *Which famous painter claimed to have cut his ear?*) the **question focus** (*znany malarz*, Eng. *famous painter*), following the pronoun, should be analysed, as its type corresponds to a named entity type (a PERSON in this case). Such approach is applied in a paper by Harabagiu et al. (2001), where the *Princeton WordNet* (Fellbaum, 1998) serves as an ontology to determine foci types. Finally, one could use a machine learning (ML) approach, treating the task as a classification problem. To do that, a set of features (such as occurrences of words, beginning pronouns, etc.) should be defined and extracted from every question. Li and Roth (2002) implemented this solution, using as much as 200,000 features, and also evaluated an influence of taking into account hierarchy of class labels. Čeh and Ojsteršek (2009) used this approach in a Slovene QA system for closed domain (students' faculty-related questions) with a SVM (support vector machines) classifier.

The presented problem of question classification for Polish question answering is studied in a paper by Przybyła (2013). The type determination part presented here bases on that solution, but includes several improvements.

To find relevant documents, existing QA solutions usually employ one of the widely available general-purpose search engines, such as *Lucene*. Words of the question are interpreted as keywords and form a boolean query, where all the constituents are considered required. This procedure suffices only in case of a web-based QA, where we can rely on a high redundancy of the WWW, which makes finding a similar expression probable enough. Such an approach, using the *Google* search engine is presented by Brill et al. (2002). When working with smaller corpora, one needs to take into account different formulations of the desired information. Therefore, an initial query is subject to some modifications. First, some of the keywords may be dropped from the query; Moldovan et al. (2000) present 8 different heuristics of selecting them, based on quotation marks, parts of speech, detected named entities and other features, whereas Katz et al. (2003) drop terms in order of increasing IDF. Čeh and Ojsteršek (2009) start term removal from the end of the sentence. Apart from simplifying the query, its expansion is also possible. For example, Hovy et al. (2000) add synonyms for each keyword, extracted from *WordNet* while Katz et al. (2003) introduce their inflectional and derivational morphological forms.

3 Question analysis

For the purpose of building an open-domain corpus-based Polish question answering system, a question analysis module, based on some of the solutions presented above, has been implemented. The module accepts a single question in Polish and outputs a data structure, called a **question model**. It includes a general question type, a set of named entity types (if the general type equals NAMED_ENTITY) and a *Lucene* search query. A set of named entity types, instead of a single one, is possible as some of the question constructions are ambiguous, e.g. a *Kto?* (Eng. *Who?*) question may be answered by a PERSON, COUNTRY, BAND, etc.

3.1 Question type classification

For the question type classification all the techniques presented above are implemented. Pattern matching stage bases on a list of 176 regular expressions and sets of corresponding question types. If any of the expressions matches the question, its corresponding set of types may be immediately returned at this stage. These expressions cover only the most obvious cases and have been created using general linguistic knowledge. The length of the list arises from some of the features of Polish, typical for Slavonic languages, i.e. relatively free word order and rich nominal inflection (Przepiórkowski, 2007). For example one English pattern *Whose ... ?* corresponds to 11 Polish patterns (*Czyj ... ?*, *Czyjego ... ?*, *Czyjemu ... ?*, *Czyim ... ?*, *Czyja ... ?*,*Czyjej ... ?*, *Czyją ... ?*, *Czyje ... ?*, *Czyi ... ?*, *Czyich ... ?*, *Czyimi ... ?*).

However, in case of ambiguous interrogative pronouns, such as *jaki* (Eng. *what*) or *który* (Eng. *which*), a further analysis gets necessary to determine a question focus type. The question is annotated using the morphological analyser *Morfeusz* (Woliński, 2006), the tagger *PANTERA* (Acedański, 2010) and the shallow parser *Spejd* (Przepiórkowski, 2008). The first nominal group after the pronoun is assumed to be a question focus. The Polish WordNet database *plWordNet* (Maziarz et al., 2012) is used to find its corresponding lexeme. If nothing is found, the procedure repeats with the current group's semantic head until a single segment remains. Failure at that stage results in returning an UNNAMED_ENTITY label, whereas success leads us to a synset in WordNet. Then, we check whether its direct and indirect parents (i.e. synsets connected via hypernymy relations) include one of the predefined synsets, corresponding to the available named entity types. The whole procedure is outlined in Figure 1. The error analysis of this procedure performed in (Przybyła, 2013) shows a high number of errors caused by a lack of a word sense disambiguation. A lexeme may be connected to many synsets, each corresponding to a specific word sense and having a different parent list. Among the possible ways to combine them are: intersection (corresponding to using only the parents common for all word senses), union (the parents of any word sense), voting (the parents common for the majority of word senses) and selecting only the first word sense (which usually is the most common in the language). The experiments have shown a better precision of classification using the first word sense (84.35%) than other techniques (intersection - 72.00%, union - 80.95%, voting - 79.07%). Experimental details are provided in the next section.

As an alternative, a machine learning approach has been implemented. After annotation using the same tools, we extract the features as a set of root forms appearing in the question. Only the lemmas appearing in at least 3 sentences are used for further processing. In this way, each sentence is described with a set of boolean features (420 for the evaluation set described in next section), denoting the appearance of a particular root form. Additionally, morphological interpretations of the first five words in the question are also extracted as features. Two classifiers, implemented in the *R* statistical environment, were used: a decision tree (for human-readable results) and a random forest (for high accuracy).

3.2 Query formation

The basic procedure for creating a query treats each segment from the question (apart from the words included in a matched regular expression) as a keyword of an OR boolean query. No term weighting or stop-words removal is implemented as *Lucene* uses TF/IDF statistic, which penalizes omnipresent tokens. However, several other im-

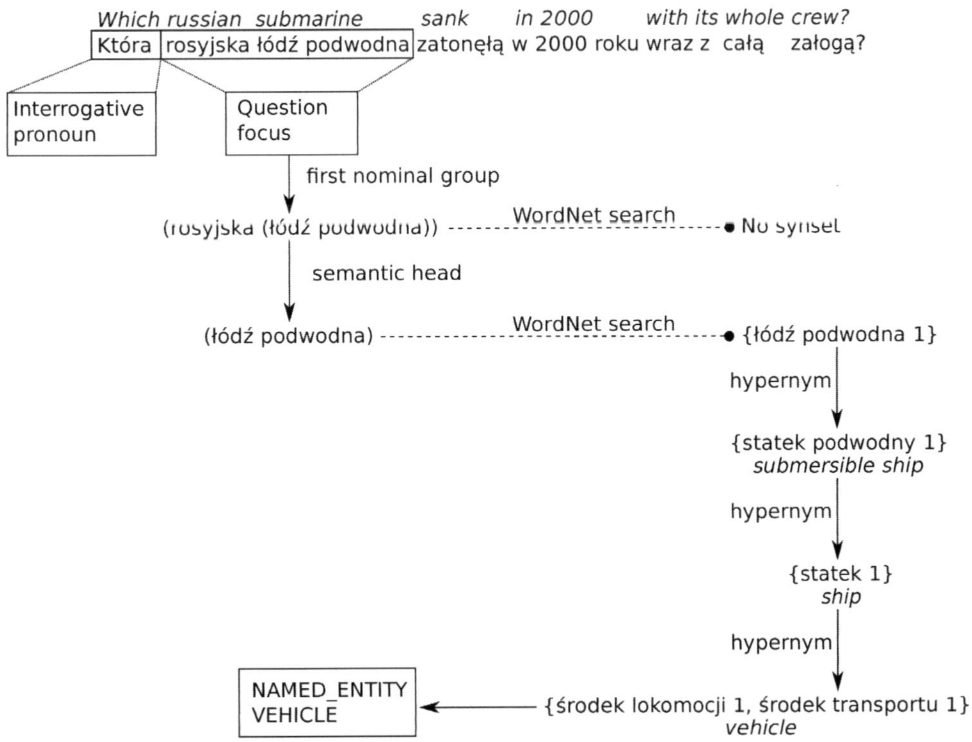

Figure 1: Outline of the disambiguation procedure, used to determine named entity type in case of ambiguous interrogative pronouns (see explanation in text).

provements are used. First, we start with a restrictive AND query and fall back into OR only in case it provides no results. A question focus removal (applied by Moldovan et al. (2000)) requires special attention. For example, let us consider again the question *Który znany malarz twierdził, że obciął sobie ucho?*. The words of the question focus *znany malarz* are not absolutely necessary in a source document, but their appearance may be a helpful clue. The query could also be expanded by replacing each keyword by a nested OR query, containing synonyms of the keyword, extracted from *plWordNet*. Both the focus removal and synonym expansion have been implemented as options of the presented query formation mechanism.

Finally, one needs to remember about an important feature of Polish, typical for a Slavonic language, namely rich nominal inflection (Przepiórkowski, 2007). It means that the orthographic forms of nouns change as they appear in different roles in a sentence. We could either ignore this fact and look for exact matches between words in the question and a document or allow some modifications. These could be done by stemming (available for Polish in *Lucene*, see the description in (Galambos, 2001)), fuzzy queries (allowing a difference between the keyword and a document word restricted by a specified Levenshtein distance) or a full morphological analysis and tagging of the source corpus and the query. All the enumerated possibilities are evaluated in this study, apart from the last one, requiring a sizeable amount of computing resources. This problem is less acute in case of English; most authors (e.g. Hovy et al. (2000)) use simple (such as Porter's) stemmers or do not address the problem at all.

4 Evaluation

For the purpose of evaluation, a set of 1137 questions from a Polish quiz TV show *"Jeden z dziesięciu"*, published in (Karzewski, 1997), has been manually reviewed and updated. A general question type and a named entity type has been assigned to each of the questions. Table 1 presents the number of question types occurrences in the test set. As a source corpus, a textual version of the Polish Wikipedia has been used. To evaluate query generation an article name has been assigned to those questions (1057), for which a single article in Wikipedia containing an answer exists.

Outputs of type classifiers have been gathered

Classifier	Classified	Precision	Overall
pattern matching	36.15%	95.37%	34.48%
WordNet-aided	98.33%	84.35%	**82.94%**
decision tree	100%	67.02%	67.02%
random forest	100%	72.91%	72.91%

Table 2: Accuracy of the four question type classifiers: numbers of questions classified, percentages of correct answers and products of these two.

and compared to the expected ones. The machine learning classifiers have been evaluated using 100-fold cross-validation[1].

Four of the presented improvements of query generation tested here include: basic OR query, AND query with fallback to OR, focus segments removal and expansion with synonyms. For each of those, three types of segment matching strategies have been applied: exact, stemming-based and fuzzy. The recorded results include recall (percentage of result lists including the desired article among the first 100) and average position of the article in the list.

5 Results

The result of evaluation of classifiers is presented in Table 2. The pattern matching stage behaves as expected: accepts only a small part of questions, but yields a high precision. The WordNet-aided focus analysis is able to handle almost all questions with an acceptable precision. Unfortunately, the accuracy of ML classifiers is not satisfactory, which could be easily explained using Table 1: there are many categories represented by very few cases. An expansion of training set or dropping the least frequent categories (depending on a particular application) is necessary for better classification.

Results of considered query generation techniques are shown in Table 3. It turns out that the basic technique generally yields the best result. Starting with an AND query and using OR only in case of a failure leads to an improvement of the expected article ranking position but the recall ratio drops significantly, which means that quite often the results of a restrictive query do not include the relevant article. The removal of the question focus from the list of keywords also has a negative impact on performance. The most surprising

[1]I.e. the whole test set has been divided into 100 nearly equal subsets and each of them has been classified using the classifier trained on the remaining 99 subsets.

Query \ Match	Exact	Stemming	Fuzzy
basic OR query	69.97% 14.32	80.08% 12.90	**82.19%** **12.36**
priority for AND query	57.94% 11.36	57.07% 8.80	34.84% 7.07
with focus segments removed	62.75% 14.65	71.99% 14.00	73.34% 12.84
with synonyms	47.06% 21.42	65.64% 15.47	58.71% 16.00

Table 3: Results of the four considered query generation techniques, each with the three types of matching strategy. For each combination a recall (measured by the presence of a given source document in the first 100 returned) and an average position on the ranked list is given.

results are those of expanding a query with synonyms - the number of matching articles grows abruptly and *Lucene* ranking mechanism does not lead to satisfying selection of the best 100. One needs to remember that only one article has been selected for each test question, whereas probably there are many relevant Wikipedia entries in most cases. Unfortunately, finding all of them manually would require a massive amount of time.

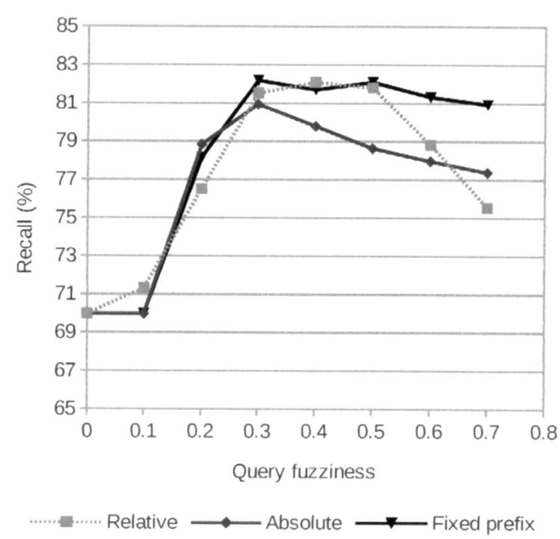

Figure 2: Impact of the fuzziness of queries on the recall using three types of fuzzy queries. To show the relative and absolute fuzziness on one plot, a word-length of 10 letters is assumed. See a description in text.

We can also notice a questionable impact of the stemming. As expected, taking into account inflection is necessary (cf. results of exact matching), but fuzzy queries provide more accurate results, although they use no linguistic knowledge.

As the fuzzy queries yield the best results, an additional experiment becomes necessary to find an optimal fuzziness, i.e. a maximal Levenshtein distance between the matched words. This parameter needs tuning for particular language of implementation (in this case Polish) as it reflects a mutability of its words, caused by inflection and derivation. Three strategies for specifying the distance have been used: relative (with distance being a fraction of a keyword's length), absolute (the same distance for all keywords) and with prefix (same as absolute, but with changes limited to the end of a keyword; with fixed prefix). In Figure 2 the results are shown - it seems that allowing 3 changes at the end of the keyword is enough. This option reflects the Polish inflection schemes and is also very fast thanks to the fixedness of the prefix.

6 Conclusion

In this paper a set of techniques used to build a question model has been presented. They have been implemented as a question analysis module for the Polish question answering task. Several experiments using Polish questions and knowledge base have been performed to evaluate their performance in the environment of the Slavonic language. They have led to the following conclusions: firstly, the best technique to find a correct question type is to combine pattern matching with the WordNet-aided focus analysis. Secondly, it does not suffice to process the first 100 article, returned by the search engine using the default ranking procedure, as they may not contain desired information. Thirdly, the stemmer of Polish provided by the *Lucene* is not reliable enough - probably it would be best to include a full morphological analysis and tagging process in the document indexing process.

This study is part of an effort to build an open-domain corpus-based question answering system for Polish. The obvious next step is to create a sentence similarity measure to select the best answer in the source document. There exist a variety of techniques for that purpose, but their performance in case of Polish needs to be carefully examined.

Acknowledgements

Critical reading of the manuscript by Agnieszka Mykowiecka is gratefully acknowledged. Study was supported by research fellowship within "Information technologies: research and their interdisciplinary applications" agreement number POKL.04.01.01-00-051/10-00.

References

Szymon Acedański. 2010. A morphosyntactic Brill Tagger for inflectional languages. In *Proceedings of the 7th international conference on Advances in Natural Language Processing (IceTAL'10)*, pages 3–14.

Eric Brill, Susan Dumais, and Michele Banko. 2002. An analysis of the AskMSR question-answering system. In *Proceedings of the ACL-02 conference on Empirical methods in natural language processing - EMNLP '02*, volume 10, pages 257–264, Morristown, NJ, USA, July. Association for Computational Linguistics.

Hoa Trang Dang, Diane Kelly, and Jimmy Lin. 2007. Overview of the TREC 2007 Question Answering track. In *Proceedings of The Sixteenth Text REtrieval Conference, TREC 2007.*

Christiane Fellbaum. 1998. *WordNet: An Electronic Lexical Database*. The MIT Press.

Leo Galambos. 2001. Lemmatizer for Document Information Retrieval Systems in JAVA. In *Proceedings of the 28th Conference on Current Trends in Theory and Practice of Informatics (SOFSEM 2001)*, pages 243–252.

Sanda Harabagiu, Dan Moldovan, Marius Pasca, Rada Mihalcea, Mihai Surdeanu, Razvan Bunescu, Roxana Gîrju, Vasile Rus, and Paul Morarescu. 2001. The role of lexico-semantic feedback in open-domain textual question-answering. In *Proceedings of the 39th Annual Meeting on Association for Computational Linguistics - ACL '01*, pages 282–289.

Eduard Hovy, Laurie Gerber, Ulf Hermjakob, Michael Junk, and Chin-Yew Lin. 2000. Question Answering in Webclopedia. In *Proceedings of The Ninth Text REtrieval Conference (TREC 2000).*

Marek Karzewski. 1997. *Jeden z dziesięciu - pytania i odpowiedzi*. Muza SA.

Boris Katz, Jimmy Lin, Daniel Loreto, Wesley Hildebrandt, Matthew Bilotti, Sue Felshin, Aaron Fernandes, Gregory Marton, and Federico Mora. 2003. Integrating Web-based and corpus-based techniques for question answering. In *Proceedings of the Twelfth Text REtrieval Conference (TREC 2003).*

Changki Lee, Ji-Hyun Wang, Hyeon-Jin Kim, and Myung-Gil Jang. 2005. Extracting Template for Knowledge-based Question-Answering Using Conditional Random Fields. In *Proceedings of the 28th Annual International ACM SIGIR Workshop on MFIR*, pages 428–434.

Xin Li and Dan Roth. 2002. Learning Question Classifiers. In *Proceedings of the 19th International Conference on Computational Linguistics (COLING-2002)*, volume 1 of *COLING '02*.

Marek Maziarz, Maciej Piasecki, and Stanisław Szpakowicz. 2012. Approaching plWordNet 2.0. In *Proceedings of the 6th Global Wordnet Conference*.

Dan Moldovan, Sanda Harabagiu, Marius Paşca, Rada Mihalcea, Roxana Gîrju, Richard Goodrum, and Vasile Rus. 2000. The structure and performance of an open-domain question answering system. In *Proceedings of the 38th Annual Meeting on Association for Computational Linguistics - ACL '00*, pages 563–570, Morristown, NJ, USA, October. Association for Computational Linguistics.

Anselmo Peñas, Eduard H. Hovy, Pamela Forner, Álvaro Rodrigo, Richard F. E. Sutcliffe, Caroline Sporleder, Corina Forascu, Yassine Benajiba, and Petya Osenova. 2012. QA4MRE: Question Answering for Machine Reading Evaluation at CLEF 2012. In *CLEF 2012 Evaluation Labs and Workshop Online Working Notes*.

Adam Przepiórkowski. 2007. Slavonic information extraction and partial parsing. In *Proceedings of the Workshop on Balto-Slavonic Natural Language Processing Information Extraction and Enabling Technologies - ACL '07*.

Adam Przepiórkowski. 2008. *Powierzchniowe przetwarzanie języka polskiego*. Akademicka Oficyna Wydawnicza EXIT, Warszawa.

Piotr Przybyła. 2013. Question classification for Polish question answering. In *Proceedings of the 20th International Conference of Language Processing and Intelligent Information Systems (LP&IIS 2013)*.

Ines Čeh and Milan Ojsteršek. 2009. Developing a question answering system for the slovene language. *WSEAS Transactions on Information Science and Applications*, 6(9):1533–1543.

Marcin Woliński. 2006. Morfeusz — a Practical Tool for the Morphological Analysis of Polish. In Mieczysław Kłopotek, Sławomir Wierzchoń, and Krzysztof Trojanowski, editors, *Intelligent Information Processing and Web Mining*, pages 511–520.

A Comparison of Techniques to Automatically Identify Complex Words

Matthew Shardlow
School of Computer Science, University of Manchester
IT301, Kilburn Building, Manchester, M13 9PL, England
m.shardlow@cs.man.ac.uk

Abstract

Identifying complex words (CWs) is an important, yet often overlooked, task within lexical simplification (The process of automatically replacing CWs with simpler alternatives). If too many words are identified then substitutions may be made erroneously, leading to a loss of meaning. If too few words are identified then those which impede a user's understanding may be missed, resulting in a complex final text. This paper addresses the task of evaluating different methods for CW identification. A corpus of sentences with annotated CWs is mined from Simple Wikipedia edit histories, which is then used as the basis for several experiments.

Firstly, the corpus design is explained and the results of the validation experiments using human judges are reported. Experiments are carried out into the CW identification techniques of: simplifying everything, frequency thresholding and training a support vector machine. These are based upon previous approaches to the task and show that thresholding does not perform significantly differently to the more naïve technique of simplifying everything. The support vector machine achieves a slight increase in precision over the other two methods, but at the cost of a dramatic trade off in recall.

1 Introduction

Complex Word (CW) identification is an important task at the first stage of lexical simplification and errors introduced or avoided here will affect final results. This work looks at the process of automatically identifying difficult words for a lexical simplification system. Lexical simplification is the task of identifying and replacing CWs in a text to improve the overall understandability and readability. This is a difficult task which is computationally expensive and often inadequately accurate.

Lexical simplification is just one method of text simplification and is often deployed alongside other simplification methods (Carrol et al., 1998; Aluísio and Gasperin, 2010). Syntactic simplification, statistical machine translation and semantic simplification (or explanation generation) are all current methods of text simplification. Text simplification is typically deployed as an assistive technology (Devlin and Tait, 1998; Aluísio and Gasperin, 2010), although this is not always the case. It may also be used alongside other technologies such as summarisation to improve their final results.

Identifying CWs is a task which every lexical simplification system must perform, either explicitly or implicitly, before simplification can take place. CWs are difficult to define, which makes them difficult to identify. For example, take the following sentence:

> The four largest islands are Honshu, Hokkaido, Shikoku, and Kyushu, and there are approximately 3,000 smaller islands in the chain.

In the above sentence, we might identify the proper nouns (Honshu, Hokkaido, etc.) as complex (as they may be unfamiliar) or we may choose to discount them from our scheme altogether, as proper nouns are unlikely to have any valid replacements. If we discount the proper nouns then the other valid CW would be 'approximately'. At 13 characters it is more than twice the average of 5.7 characters per word and has more syllables than any other word. Further, CWs are often identified by their frequency (see Section 2.1) and here, 'approximately' exhibits a much lower frequency than the other words.

There are many reasons to evaluate the identification of CWs. This research stems primarily from the discovery that no previous comparison of current techniques exists. It is hoped that by providing this, the community will be able to identify and evaluate new techniques using the methods proposed herein. If CW identification is not performed well, then potential candidates may be missed, and simple words may be falsely identified. This is dangerous as simplification will often result in a minor change in a text's semantics. For example, the sentence:

> The United Kingdom is a *state* in northwest Europe.

May be simplified to give:

> The United Kingdom is a *country* in northwest Europe.

In this example from the corpus used in this research, the word "state" is simplified to give "country". Whilst this is a valid synonym in the given context, state and country are not necessarily semantically identical. Broadly speaking, state refers to a political entity, whereas country refers to a physical space within a set of borders. This is an acceptable change and even necessary for simplification. However, if applied blindly, then too many modifications may be made, resulting in major deviations from the text's original semantics.

The contributions of this paper are as follows:

- A report on the corpus developed and used in the evaluation phase. Section 2.2.
- The implementation of a support vector machine for the classification of CWs. Section 2.6
- A comparison of common techniques on the same corpus. Section 4.
- An analysis of the features used in the support vector machine. Section 4.

2 Experimental Design

Several systems for detecting CWs were implemented and evaluated using the CW corpus. The two main techniques that exist in the literature are simplifying everything (Devlin and Tait, 1998) and frequency based thresholding (Zeng et al., 2005). These were implemented as well as a support vector machine classifier. This section describes the design decisions made during implementation.

System	Score
SUBTLEX	0.3352
Wikipedia Baseline	0.3270
Kucera-Francis	0.3097
Random Baseline	0.0157

Table 1: The results of different experiments on the SemEval lexical simplification data. These show that SUBTLEX was the best word frequency measure for rating lexical complexity. The other entries correspond to alternative word frequency measures. The Google Web 1T data (Brants and Franz, 2006) has been shown to give a higher score, however this data was not available during the course of this research.

2.1 Lexical Complexity

All three of the implementations described in Sections 2.4, 2.5 and 2.6 require a word frequency measure as an indicator of lexical complexity. If a word occurs frequently in common language then it is more likely to be recognised (Rayner and Duffy, 1986).

The lexical simplification dataset from Task 1 at SemEval 2012 (De Belder and Moens, 2012) was used to compare several measures of word frequency as shown in Table 1. Candidate substitutions and sample sentences were provided by the task organisers, together with a gold standard ranking of the substitutes according to their simplicity. These sentences were ranked according to their frequency. Although the scores in Table 1 appear to be low, this is the kappa agreement for several categories and so should be expected. The inter-annotator agreement on the corpus was 0.488 (De Belder and Moens, 2012). The SUBTLEX dataset (Brysbaert and New, 2009) was the best available for rating word familiarity. This is a corpus of over 70,000 words collected from the subtitles of over 8,000 American English films.

2.2 CW Corpus

Simple Wikipedia edit histories were mined using techniques similar to those in Yatskar et al. (2010). This provided aligned pairs of sentences which had just one word simplified. Whereas Yatskar et al. (2010) used these pairs to learn probabilities of paraphrases, the research in this paper used them as instances of lexical simplification. The original simplifications were performed by editors trying to make documents as simple as possible. The CW is identified by comparison with the simplified sentence. Further information on the production of the corpus will be published in a future paper.

2.3 Negative Examples

The CW corpus provides a set of CWs in appropriate contexts. This is useful for evaluation as these words need to be identified. However, if only examples of CWs were available, it would be very easy for a technique to overfit — as it could just classify every single word as complex and get 100% accuracy. For example, in the case of thresholding, if only examples of CWs are available, the threshold could be set artificially high and still succeed for every case. When this is applied to genuine data it will classify every word it encounters as complex, leading to high recall but low precision.

To alleviate this effect, negative examples are needed. These are examples of simple words which do not require any further simplification. There are several methods for finding these, including: selecting words from a reference easy word list; selecting words with high frequencies according to some corpus or using the simplified words from the second sentences in the CW corpus. The chosen strategy picked a word at random from the sentence in which the CW occurs. Only one word was edited in this sentence and so the assumption may be made that none of the other words in the sentence require further simplification. Only one simple word per CW is chosen to enforce an even amount of positive and negative data. This gave a set of negative words which were reflective of the broad language which is expected when processing free text.

2.4 Simplify Everything

The first implementation involved simplifying everything, a brute force method, in which a simplification algorithm is applied to every word. This assumes that words which are already simple will not require any further simplification. A common variation is to limit the simplification to some combination of all the nouns, verbs and adjectives.

A standard baseline lexical simplification system was implemented following Devlin and Tait (1998). This algorithm generated a set of synonyms from WordNet and then used the SUBTLEX frequencies to find the most frequent synonym. If the synonym was more frequent than the original word then a substitution was made. This technique was applied to all the words. If a CW was changed, then it was considered a true positive; if a simple word was not changed, it was considered a true negative. Five trials were carried out and the average accuracy and standard deviation is reported in Figure 1 and Table 3.

2.5 Frequency Thresholding

The second technique is frequency thresholding. This relies on each word having an associated familiarity value provided by the SUBTLEX corpus. Whilst this corpus is large, it will never cover every possible word, and so words which are not encountered are considered to have a frequency of 0. This does not affect comparison as the infrequent words are likely to be the complex ones.

To distinguish between complex and simple words a threshold was implemented. This was learnt from the CW corpus by examining every possible threshold for a training set. Firstly, the training data was ordered by frequency, then the accuracy[1] of the algorithm was examined with the threshold placed in between the frequency of every adjacent pair of words in the ordered list. This was repeated by 5-fold cross validation and the mean threshold determined. The final accuracy of the algorithm was then determined on a separate set of testing data.

2.6 Support Vector Machine

Support vector machines (SVM) are statistical classifiers which use labelled training data to predict the class of unseen inputs. The training data consist of several features which the SVM uses to distinguish between classes. The SVM was chosen as it has been used elsewhere for similar tasks (Gasperin et al., 2009; Hancke et al., 2012; Jauhar and Specia, 2012). The use of many fea-

[1] The proportion of data that was correctly classified.

tures allows factors which may otherwise have been missed to be taken into account. One further advantage is that the features of an SVM can be analysed to determine their effect on the classification. This may give some indication for future feature classification schemes.

The SVM was trained using the LIBSVM package (Chang and Lin, 2011) in Matlab. the RBF kernel was selected and a grid search was performed to select values for the 2 parameters C and γ. Training and testing was performed on a held-out data-set using 5-fold cross validation.

To implement the SVM a set of features was determined for the classification scheme. Several external libraries were used to extract these as detailed below:

Frequency The SUBTLEX frequency of each word was used as previously described in Section 2.1.

CD Count Also from the SUBTLEX corpus. The number of films in which a word appeared, ranging from $0 - 8,388$.

Length The word length in number of characters was taken into account. It is often the case that longer words are more difficult to process and so may be considered 'complex'.

Syllable Count The number of syllables contained in a word is also a good estimate of its complexity. This was computed using a library from the morphadorner package[2].

Sense Count A count of the number of ways in which a word can be interpreted - showing how ambiguous a word is. This measure is taken from WordNet (Fellbaum, 1998).

Synonym Count Also taken from WordNet, this is the number of potential synonyms with which a word could be replaced. This again may give some indication of a word's degree of ambiguity.

3 Results

The results of the experiments in identifying CWs are shown in Figure 1 and the values are given in Table 3. The values presented are the mean of 5 trials and the error bars represent the standard deviation.

[2]http://morphadorner.northwestern.edu/

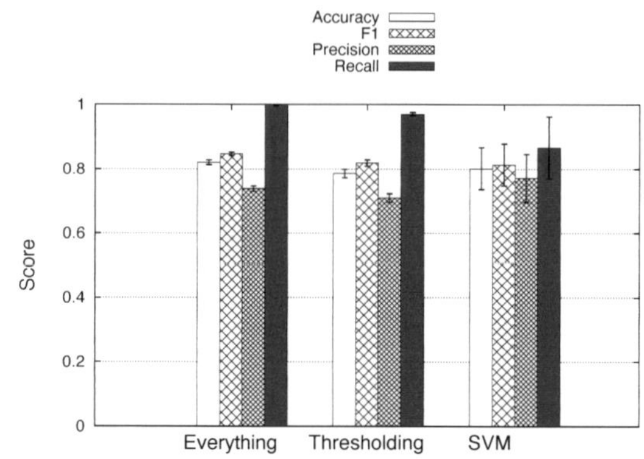

Figure 1: A bar chart with error bars showing the results of the CW identification experiments. Accuracy, F1 Score, Precision and Recall are reported for each measure.

Feature	Coefficient
Frequency	0.3973
CD Count	0.5847
Length	−0.5661
Syllables	−0.4414
Senses	−0.0859
Synonyms	−0.2882

Table 2: The correlation coefficients for each feature. These show the correlation against the language's simplicity and so a positive correlation indicates that if that feature is higher then the word will be simpler.

To analyse the features of the SVM, the correlation coefficient between each feature vector and the vector of feature labels was calculated. This is a measure which can be used to show the relation between two distributions. The adopted labelling scheme assigned CWs as 0 and simple words as 1 and so the correlation of the features is notionally against the simplicity of the words.[3] The results are reported in Table 2.

4 Discussion

It is clear from these results that there is a fairly high accuracy from all the methods. This shows that they perform well at the task in hand, reflecting the methods which have been previously applied. These methods all have a higher recall than

[3]i.e. A positive correlation indicates that if the value of that feature is higher, the word will be simpler.

System	Accuracy	F1	Precision	Recall
Simplify Everything	0.8207 ± 0.0077	0.8474 ± 0.0056	0.7375 ± 0.0084	0.9960 ± 0
Thresholding	0.7854 ± 0.0138	0.8189 ± 0.0098	0.7088 ± 0.0136	0.9697 ± 0.0056
SVM	0.8012 ± 0.0656	0.8130 ± 0.0658	0.7709 ± 0.0752	0.8665 ± 0.0961

Table 3: The results of classification experiments for the three systems.

precision, which indicates that they are good at identifying the CWs, but also that they often identify simple words as CWs. This is particularly noticeable in the 'simplify everything' method, where the recall is very high, yet the precision is comparatively low. This indicates that many of the simple words which are falsely identified as complex are also replaced with an alternate substitution, which may result in a change in sense.

A paired t-test showed the difference between the thresholding method and the 'simplify everything' method was not statistically significant ($p > 0.8$). Thresholding takes more data about the words into account and would appear to be a less naïve strategy than blindly simplifying everything. However, this data shows there is little difference between the results of the two methods. The thresholding here may be limited by the resources, and a corpus using a larger word count may yield an improved result.

Whilst the thresholding and simplify everything methods were not significantly different from each other, the SVM method was significantly different from the other two ($p < 0.001$). This can be seen in the slightly lower recall, yet higher precision attained by the SVM. This indicates that the SVM was better at distinguishing between complex and simple words, but also wrongly identified many CWs. The results for the SVM have a wide standard deviation (shown in the wide error bars in Figure 1) indicating a higher variability than the other methods. With more data for training the model, this variability may be reduced.

One important factor in the increased precision observed in the SVM is that it used many more features than the other methods, and so took more information into account. Table 2 shows that these features had varying degrees of correlation with the data label (i.e. whether the word was simple or not) and hence that they had varying degrees of effect on the classification scheme.

Frequency and CD count are moderately positively correlated as may be expected. This indicates that higher frequency words are likely to be simple. Surprisingly, CD Count has a higher correlation than frequency itself, indicating that this is a better measure of word familiarity than the frequency measure. However, further investigation is necessary to confirm this.

Word length and number of syllables are moderately negatively correlated, indicating that the longer and more polysyllabic a word is, the less simple it becomes. This is not true in every case. For example, 'finger' and 'digit' can be used in the same sense (as a noun meaning an appendage of the hand). Whilst 'finger' is more commonly used than 'digit'[4], digit is one letter shorter.

The number of senses was very weakly negatively correlated with word simplicity. This indicates that it is not a strong indicative factor in determining whether a word is simple or not. The total number of synonyms was a stronger indicator than the number of senses, but still only exhibited weak correlation.

One area that has not been explored in this study is the use of contextual features. Each target word occurs in a sentence and it may be the case that those words surrounding the target give extra information as to its complexity. It has been suggested that language is produced at an even level of complexity (Specia et al., 2012), and so simple words will occur in the presence of other simple words, whereas CWs will occur in the presence of other CWs. As well as lexical contextual information, the surrounding syntax may offer some information on word difficulty. Factors such as a very long sentence or a complex grammatical structure can make a word more difficult to understand. These could be used to modify the familiarity score in the thresholding method, or they could be used as features in the SVM classifier.

5 Related Work

This research will be used for lexical simplification. The related work in this field is also generally

[4]in the SUBTLEX corpus 'finger' has a frequency of 1870, whereas 'digit' has a frequency of 30.

used as a precursor to lexical simplification. This section will explain how these previous methods have handled the task of identifying CWs and how these fit into the research presented in this paper.

The simplest way to identify CWs in a sentence is to blindly assume that every word is complex, as described earlier in Section 2.4. This was first used in Devlin's seminal work on lexical simplification (Devlin and Tait, 1998). This method is somewhat naïve as it does not mitigate the possibility of words being simplified in error. Devlin and Tait indicate that they believe less frequent words will not be subject to meaning change. However, further work into lexical simplification has refuted this (Lal and Rüger, 2002). This method is still used, for example Thomas and Anderson (2012) simplify all nouns and verbs. This corresponds to the 'Everything' method.

Another method of identifying CWs is to use frequency based thresholding over word familiarity scores, as described in Section 2.5 and corresponding to the 'Frequency' method in this paper. This has been applied to the medical domain (Zeng et al., 2005; Elhadad, 2006) for predicting which words lay readers will find difficult. This has been correlated with word difficulty via questionnaires (Zeng et al., 2005; Zeng-Treitler et al., 2008) and via the analysis of low-level readability corpora (Elhadad, 2006). In both these cases, a familiarity score is used to determine how likely a subject is to understand a term. More recently, Bott et al. (2012) use a threshold of 1% corpus frequency, along with other checks, to ensure that simple words are not erroneously simplified.

Support vector machines are powerful statistical classifiers, as employed in the 'SVM' method of this paper. A Support Vector Machine is used to predict the familiarity of CWs in Zeng et al. (2005). It takes features of term frequency and word length and is correlated against the familiarity scores which are already obtained. This proves to have very poor performance, something which the authors attribute to a lack of suitable training data. An SVM has also been trained for the ranking of words according to their complexity (Jauhar and Specia, 2012). This was done for the SemEval lexical simplification task (Specia et al., 2012). Although this system is designed for synonym ranking, it could also be used for the CW identification task. Machine learning has also been applied to the task of determining whether an entire sentence requires simplification (Gasperin et al., 2009; Hancke et al., 2012). These approaches use a wide array of morphological features which are suited to sentence level classification.

6 Future Work

This work is intended as an initial study of methods for identifying CWs for simplification. The methods compared, whilst typical of current CW identification methods, are not an exhaustive set and variations exist. One further way of expanding this research would be to take into account word context. This could be done using thresholding (Zeng-Treitler et al., 2008) or an SVM (Gasperin et al., 2009; Jauhar and Specia, 2012).

Another way to increase the accuracy of the frequency count method may be to use a larger corpus. Whilst the corpus used in this paper performed well in the preliminary testing section, other research has shown the Google Web1T corpus (a n-gram count of over a trillion words) to be more effective (De Belder and Moens, 2012). The Web 1T data was not available during the course of this research.

The large variability in accuracy shown in the SVM method indicates that there was insufficient training data. With more data, the SVM would have more information about the classification task and would provide more consistent results.

CW identification is the first step in the process of lexical simplification. This research will be integrated in a future system which will simplify natural language for end users. It is also hoped that other lexical simplification systems will take account of this work and will use the evaluation technique proposed herein to improve their identification of CWs.

7 Conclusion

This paper has provided an insight into the challenges associated with evaluating the identification of CWs. This is a non-obvious task, which may seem intuitively easy, but in reality is quite difficult and rarely performed. It is hoped that new research in this field will evaluate the techniques used, rather than using inadequate techniques blindly and naïvely. This research has also shown that the current state of the art methods have much room for improvement. Low precision is a constant factor in all techniques and future research should aim to address this.

Acknowledgment

This work is supported by EPSRC grant EP/I028099/1. Thanks go to the anonymous reviewers for their helpful suggestions.

References

Sandra Maria Aluísio and Caroline Gasperin. 2010. Fostering digital inclusion and accessibility: the PorSimples project for simplification of Portuguese texts. In *Proceedings of the NAACL HLT 2010 Young Investigators Workshop on Computational Approaches to Languages of the Americas*, YIW-CALA '10, pages 46–53, Stroudsburg, PA, USA. Association for Computational Linguistics.

Stefan Bott, Luz Rello, Biljana Drndarevix, and Horacio Saggion. 2012. Can spanish be simpler? lexsis: Lexical simplification for spanish. In *Coling 2012: The 24th International Conference on Computational Linguistics*.

Thorsten Brants and Alex Franz. 2006. Web 1T 5-gram Version 1.

Marc Brysbaert and Boris New. 2009. Moving beyond Kucera and Francis : a critical evaluation of current word frequency norms and the introduction of a new and improved word frequency measure for American English. *Behav Res Methods*.

John Carrol, Guido Minnen, Yvonne Canning, Siobhan Devlin, and John Tait. 1998. Practical simplification of english newspaper text to assist aphasic readers. In *AAAI-98 Workshop on Integrating Artificial Intelligence and Assistive Technology*.

Chih-Chung Chang and Chih-Jen Lin. 2011. LIBSVM: A library for support vector machines. *ACM Transactions on Intelligent Systems and Technology*, 2:27:1–27:27. Software available at `http://www.csie.ntu.edu.tw/~cjlin/libsvm`.

Jan De Belder and Marie-Francine Moens. 2012. A dataset for the evaluation of lexical simplification. In *Computational Linguistics and Intelligent Text Processing*, volume 7182 of *Lecture Notes in Computer Science*, pages 426–437. Springer Berlin / Heidelberg.

Siobhan Devlin and John Tait. 1998. The use of a psycholinguistic database in the simplification of text for aphasic readers. *Linguistic Databases*, pages 161–173.

Noémie Elhadad. 2006. Comprehending technical texts: Predicting and defining unfamiliar terms. In *AMIA Annual Symposium proceedings*, volume 2006, page 239. American Medical Informatics Association.

Christiane Fellbaum. 1998. *WordNet: An Electronic Lexical Database*. Bradford Books.

Caroline Gasperin, Lucia Specia, Tiago Pereira, and Sandra M. Aluísio. 2009. Learning when to simplify sentences for natural text simplification. In *Encontro Nacional de Inteligência Artificial*.

Julia Hancke, Sowmya Vajjala, and Detmar Meurers. 2012. Readability classification for German using lexical, syntactic, and morphological features. In *Proceedings of the 24th International Conference on Computational Linguistics (COLING 2012)*, pages 1063–1080, Mumbai, India.

Sujay Kumar Jauhar and Lucia Specia. 2012. Uow-shef: Simplex – lexical simplicity ranking based on contextual and psycholinguistic features. In **SEM 2012: The First Joint Conference on Lexical and Computational Semantics – Volume 1: Proceedings of the main conference and the shared task, and Volume 2: Proceedings of the Sixth International Workshop on Semantic Evaluation (SemEval 2012)*, pages 477–481, Montréal, Canada, 7-8 June. Association for Computational Linguistics.

Partha Lal and Stefan Rüger. 2002. Extract-based summarization with simplification. In *Proceedings of the ACL*.

Keith Rayner and Susan Duffy. 1986. Lexical complexity and fixation times in reading: Effects of word frequency, verb complexity, and lexical ambiguity. *Memory & Cognition*, 14:191–201.

Lucia Specia, Sujay Kumar Jauhar, and Rada Mihalcea. 2012. Semeval-2012 task 1: English lexical simplification. In *First Joint Conference on Lexical and Computational Semantics*.

S. Rebecca Thomas and Sven Anderson. 2012. Wordnet-based lexical simplification of a document. In Jeremy Jancsary, editor, *Proceedings of KONVENS 2012*, pages 80–88. ÖGAI, September. Main track: oral presentations.

Mark Yatskar, Bo Pang, Cristian Danescu-Niculescu-Mizil, and Lillian Lee. 2010. For the sake of simplicity: Unsupervised extraction of lexical simplifications from Wikipedia. In *Proceedings of the NAACL*.

Qing Zeng, Eunjung Kim, Jon Crowell, and Tony Tse. 2005. A text corpora-based estimation of the familiarity of health terminology. *Biological and Medical Data Analysis*, pages 184–192.

Qing Zeng-Treitler, Sergey Goryachev, Tony Tse, Alla Keselman, and Aziz Boxwala. 2008. Estimating consumer familiarity with health terminology: a context-based approach. *Journal of the American Medical Informatics Association*, 15(3):349–356.

Detecting Chronic Critics Based on Sentiment Polarity and User's Behavior in Social Media

Sho Takase† **Akiko Murakami**‡ **Miki Enoki**‡ **Naoaki Okazaki**† **Kentaro Inui**†
Tohoku University† IBM Research - Tokyo‡
{takase, okazaki, inui}@ecei.tohoku.ac.jp
{akikom, enomiki}@jp.ibm.com

Abstract

There are some chronic critics who always complain about the entity in social media. We are working to automatically detect these chronic critics to prevent the spread of bad rumors about the reputation of the entity. In social media, most comments are informal, and, there are sarcastic and incomplete contexts. This means that it is difficult for current NLP technology such as opinion mining to recognize the complaints. As an alternative approach for social media, we can assume that users who share the same opinions will link to each other. Thus, we propose a method that combines opinion mining with graph analysis for the connections between users to identify the chronic critics. Our experimental results show that the proposed method outperforms analysis based only on opinion mining techniques.

1 Introduction

On a social media website, there may be millions of users and large numbers of comments. The comments in social media are related to the real world in such fields as marketing and politics. Analyzing comments in social media has been shown to be effective in predicting the behaviors of stock markets and of voters in elections (Bollen et al., 2011; Tumasjan et al., 2010; O'Connor et al., 2010). Because of their effects on the real world, some complaints may harm the reputation of a corporation or an individual and cause serious damage. Consider a comment such as "Working for *Company A* is really awful" as an example. The complaint gives viewers a negative impression of *Company A* and can increase the number of people who think the company is bad.

Some complaints are expressed by a specific user who is always criticizing a specific target entity (in this example, *Company A*). We call this user a *chronic critic* of that entity, a person who is deliberately trying to harm the reputation of the entity. That is, a chronic critic is trying to run a negative campaign against the entity. If the entity is aware of its own chronic critics, then it is able to take prompt action to stop the malicious complaints. When the complaints are false, the entity can use that defense. In contrast, if the chronic critics are justified, then the entity should address the concerns to limit the damage. Hence, to handle malicious rumors, it is important to detect the chronic critics.

However, it is generally quite difficult for a computer to detect a chronic critic's comments, since especially the comments in social media are often quite informal. In addition, there are complexities such as sarcasm and incomplete contexts. For example, if *Company A* has been involved in a widely recognized fiasco, then some chronic critics might sarcastically write "good job" or "wonderful" about *Company A*. They are using positive words, but in the context they are effectively criticizing *Company A*. Some chronic critics bash a target entity solely with sarcasm, so they damage the target with positive words. It is exceedingly difficult to directly detect these chronic critics based on their comments. In an example of an incomplete context, if one author starts an exchange with a comment such as "The new product from *Company A* is difficult to use" and another user responds with something like "Fool", we cannot easily recognize the meaning of this comment as related to "*Company A* being foolish because the product really is difficult to use" or whether "the user is the fool because the product is easy for other people to use". To find chronic critics for a given entity, we need to identify the actual target of the complaints. Take the comment "*Company B* is much worse than *Company A*" for example. This comment is probably complaining about *Company B* but not *Company A*. In contrast, most of the previous work on sentiment analysis in social media does not consider these kinds of problems (Barbosa and Feng, 2010; Davidov et al., 2010; Speriosu et al., 2011).

Switching to the behavior of each user, in social media we often see that users who have similar ideas will tend to cooperate with each other. In fact, previous work suggests that users who have the same opinions tend to create links to each other (Conover et al., 2011b; Yang et al., 2012). Because chronic critics share the purpose of attacking some target's reputation, they may also decide to cooperate. For this reason, to detect chronic critics, we believe that information about the connections among users will be effective.

In this paper, we present a method that combines opinion mining based on NLP and graph analysis of the connections among users to recognize the chronic critics. In the experiments, we demonstrate the difficulty in detecting chronic critics by analyzing only the individual comments. In addition, we investigate the effectiveness of using the connections between users, i.e., using the proposed method. For our experiments, we used Twitter, a popular social media service. In particular, we focus on Japanese comments on Twitter.

This paper is organized as follows. Section 2 reviews related work. Section 3 presents the proposed method which applies the opinion mining and graph analysis. Section 4 demonstrates the effectiveness of the proposed method and discusses the experimental results. Section 5 concludes this paper.

2 Related Work

In recent years, an interest in opinion mining in online communities has emerged (Conover et al., 2011a; O'Connor et al., 2010; Speriosu et al., 2011; Murakami and Raymond, 2010; Barbosa and Feng, 2010; Davidov et al., 2010). O'Connor et al. (2010), Barbosa and Feng (2010), Davidov et al. (2010), and Speriosu et al. (2011) proposed methods to predict a sentiment polarity (i.e., positive or negative) of a comment in social media. O'Connor et al. (2010) studied a subjectivity lexicon. Barbosa and Feng (2010) and Davidov et al. (2010) used machine learning approaches. Speriosu et al. (2011) introduced connections between words, emoticons, tags, n-grams, comments and users. These studies did not identify the target of the polarized sentiment of each comment.

Conover et al. (2011a) proposed a method that predicts the political polarity of a social media user based on the connections between users and tags. They demonstrated that label propagation on the graph representing the connections between users is effective. However, this method is not guaranteed to obtain the optimal solution. In contrast, our research uses graph analysis that converges on the optimal solution.

Murakami and Raymond (2010) proposed a method that uses the connections between users to predict each user's opinion, i.e., support or oppose a topic in online debates. They analyzed the content of the discussions to infer the connections. However, in social media, it is difficult to infer connections based on content because of such complexities as incomplete contexts. To address these problem, we analyzed the behavior of the users to predict the connections between users.

Our task is similar to spammer detection (Wang, 2010; Yang et al., 2012). Wang (2010) proposed a method using a classifier to detect spammers. They used the content in the comments and the number of linked users as features. Yang et al. (2012) analyzed spammer communities and demonstrated that spammers closely link to each other in social media. They also proposed a method that extracts spammers using the connections between users. While Wang (2010) and Yang et al. (2012) required manually annotated data for training or as seeds, we extract the seeds for the graph analysis automatically through opinion mining.

3 Proposed Method

Figure 1 presents an overview of the proposed method. The proposed method has two phases, opinion mining and graph analysis. First, we extract a few chronic critics by analyzing the opinions of many users referencing the target entity. For the opinion mining, we are initially looking for users who strongly criticize the target entity. In Figure 1, given *Company A* as a target entity, we find users "b" and "e" since they said "Working for *Company A* is really awful" and "This product from *Company A* is useless". However, we may miss the other chronic critics since they used sarcasm and incomplete contexts.

Next, we find the users who are linked to the

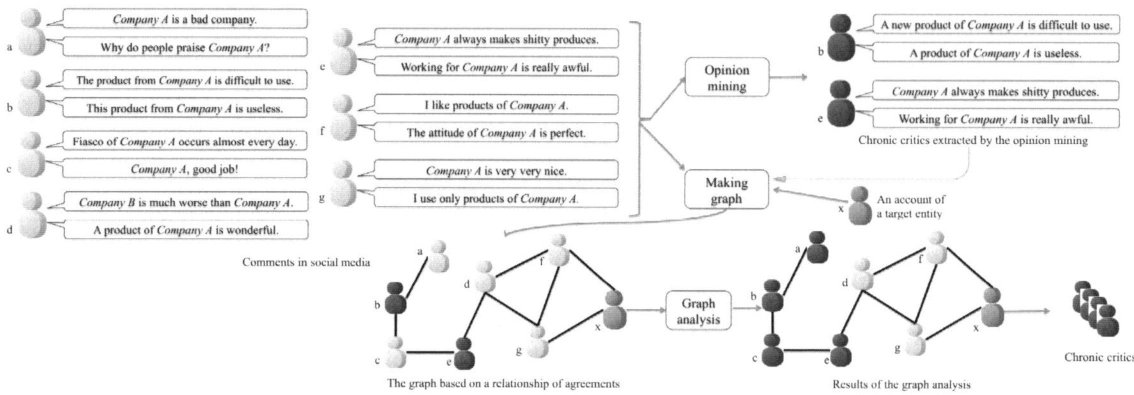

Figure 1: Overview of proposed method

chronic critics that were detected through opinion mining. We built a graph in which the users are represented by nodes and the links between the users are represented by edges.We recognize additional chronic critics based on the graph analysis. In the example of Figure 1, we find more chronic critics not recognized by the opinion mining, such as "a" and "c", because they are linked to the chronic critics "b" and "e". In this section, we explain the opinion mining and graph analysis. Since a comment in Twitter is called a *tweet*, we use the term tweet below.

3.1 Opinion Mining

As defined in Section 1, we defined a user who frequently criticizes a target entity as a chronic critic. Therefore, we classify the tweets of each user into critical or non-critical and label any users who complain about the target entity many times as chronic critics. Because we want to investigate the opinions of each user in public, we analyze public tweets, excluding the private conversations between users. In Twitter, this means we ignore a *reply* that is a response to a specific user named *username* (written in the format "@*username* response") and *QT* that is a mention in a quoted tweet from *username* (written in the format "mention RT @*username*: quoted tweet").

We assume a phrase representing negative polarity or profanity to be critical phrases. The proposed method determines whether a tweet complains about the target entity by investigating a critical phrase and the target of the phrase.

Note that a negative polarity is represented by declinable words or substantives. We used the sentiment analyzer created by Kanayama and Nasukawa (2012) to detect a phrase representing negative polarity by using declinable words. We used the lexicon collected by Higashiyama et al. (2008) to find negative polarity in substantives. For detecting profanity, we use a profane lexicon collected by Ogino et al. (2012).

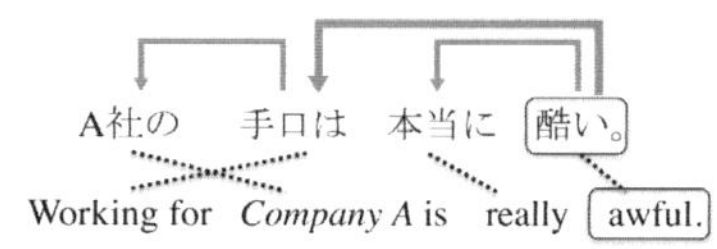

Figure 2: Example of critic tweet

The sentiment analyzer can find not only sentiment phrases but the targets of the phrases based on syntactic parsing and the case frames[1]. However, because there are many informal tweets and because most users omit the grammatical case in tweets, the sentiment analyzer often fails to capture any target. To address this problem, in addition to a target extracted by the sentiment analyzer, we obtain a target based on the dependency tree. We extract nouns in parent and child phrases within distance 2 from a critical phrase in the dependency tree.

Figure 2 shows an example of a Japanese tweet criticizing *Company A* and its English translation. The Japanese tweet is split into phrase-like units (*bunsetsu*). Each English phrase is linked to the corresponding bunsetsu by a dotted line. The dependency relationships among the bunsetsu are expressed by the arrows. In the tweet, the black-edged phrase "awful" is a critical phrase. We extract the nouns in "Working for" and "*Company A* is" as targets of the critical phrase since these

[1] A case frame is a list which represents grammatical cases of a predicate.

phrases are parents within distance 2 of the critical phrase. Therefore, we decide that the tweet is criticizing *Company A*.

Since a chronic critic frequently complains about the target entity, we can predict that most of the tweets written by a chronic critic of the target entity will be critical tweets. Therefore, we can calculate a ratio of critical tweets for all of the tweets about the target entity. We score the user u_i with equation (1).

$$score_i = \frac{n_i}{N_i} \quad (1)$$

N_i is the number of all tweets about the target entity and n_i is the number of critical tweets about the entity by that user [2]. We extract the top M users based on $score_i$ as chronic critics.

3.2 Graph Analysis

In social media, it is often very difficult to determine whether a tweet is critical since many tweets include sarcasm or incomplete contexts. The opinion mining may miss numerous complaints with sarcasm or incomplete contexts. To resolve this problem, we apply user behaviors. In social media, we assume that users having the same opinion interact with each other in order to demonstrate the correctness of their opinion. In particular, since the purpose of chronic critics is to spread the bad reputation, we assume that they want to assist each other. We supplement the opinion mining by a graph analysis using this assumption. Thus, we make a graph representing connections among the users and use label propagation on the graph based on the results of the opinion mining as the seeds.

In addition, we believe that a user will try to spread user matching opinions. This implies that a user who spreads the opinion of another of agrees with the author of that opinion. In Twitter, a user can spread an opinion as an *RT*, which is a reposting of a tweet by a *username* (written in the format "RT @*username*: tweet"). Conover et al. (2011b) demonstrated that they can make a graph representing the connections among users who support each others opinions by using RTs. Hence, an RT expresses a relationship of endorsement. We also created a graph based on this feature.

Our graph has m users ($U = \{u_1, ..., u_m\}$) as nodes, where u_i connects with u_j via an edge that has weight w_{ij} ($0 \leq w_{ij} \leq 1$) and w_{ij} corresponds to the degree to which u_i supports u_j. We calculate w_{ij} by using Equation (2).

$$w_{ij} = \frac{1}{2}\left(\frac{r_{ij}}{R_i} + \frac{r_{ji}}{R_j}\right) \quad (2)$$

r_{ij} is the total RT tweets of u_j by u_i and R_i is the number of RTs by u_i. Therefore, the more u_i and u_j RT each other, the more weight w_{ij} is close to 1. In contrast, if u_i and u_j rarely RT each other, the value of w_{ij} will approach 0. In addition, this w_{ij} definition is symmetric means (i.e., $w_{ij} = w_{ji}$).

We find more new chronic critics by label propagation on the graph. We use the chronic critics obtained by the opinion mining as seeds. It is assumed that a user who supports the target entity is not a chronic critic. Using this knowledge, we use the account of the target entity as a seed.

The label propagation assigns a confidence score $\boldsymbol{c} = (c_1, ..., c_m)$ to each node $U = u_1, ..., u_m$, where the score is a real number between -1 and 1. A score close to 1 indicates that we are very confident that the node (user) is a chronic critic. A score close to -1 indicates that we are sure that the node is not a chronic critic. In addition, the scores of seeds are fixed and cannot be changed. The scores of chronic critics obtained by the opinion mining are 1 and the score of the target entity is set to -1. To formulate the label propagation as an optimization problem, we used the loss function proposed by Zhu et al. (2003), because $w_{ij} \geq 0$ for all i, j.

$$E(\boldsymbol{c}) = \frac{1}{2}\sum_{i,j} w_{ij}(c_i - c_j)^2 \quad (3)$$

To minimize $E(\boldsymbol{c})$, c_i is close to c_j when w_{ij} is greater than 0. That is, if the users support each other, the scores of the users are close to each other. Thus, by minimizing $E(\boldsymbol{c})$, we assign the confidence scores considering the results of the opinion mining and agreement relationships among the users. We find the users that have scores greater than the threshold.

We believe that if the distance between users on the graph is large, then users slightly support each other. However, we can assign a score of 1 to each node in any subgraph that has chronic critics extracted by the opinion mining to minimize $E(\boldsymbol{c})$ if the subgraph does not include the account of the target entity, no matter how far away a node

[2] The formula (1) assigns a high score to a user if the user only produces one or two tweets about the target entity and those tweets are negative. To prevent this, we disregard the users whose the number of tweets are fewer than 5.

Table 1: Properties of the experimental datasets

Target entity	Tweets	Critics	Kappa
Company A	35,807	112	0.81
Politician A	45,378	254	1.0

is from the seeds. To avoid this problem, Yin and Tan (2011) introduced a *neutral fact*, which decreases each confidence score by considering the distance from the seeds. The neutral fact has a fixed confidence score 0 and connects with all of the nodes except the seeds. Suppose u_1 is the neutral fact, $U_l = \{u_2, ..., u_l\}$ is the set of seeds and $U_t = \{u_{l+1}, ..., u_m\}$ is the set of all nodes except seeds. To assign the weight of the edge between u_1 and other nodes considering the degrees of the nodes, we calculate the weight by as:

$$w_{1i} = \begin{cases} 0 & i = 1, ..., l \\ \mu \sum_{j>1} |w_{ij}| & i = l+1, ..., m \end{cases} \quad (4)$$

where μ is a small constant. Thus, the weight is proportional to the total weight of the edges from each node.

4 Experiments

4.1 Experimental Setting

For our experiment, we gathered tweets by using the *Twitter search API*. The twitter search API returns the tweets that contain an input query. We used the name of a target entity, words related to the entity[3], and the account name of the entity as queries. In this research, there were two target entities, *Company A* and *Politician A*. We found many critical tweets about these target entities. The entities have their own accounts in Twitter. We collected the Japanese tweets for one month. We want to extract the users who frequently express a public opinion related to a target entity. For this reason, we eliminated users whose the number of tweets except conversation (i.e., reply, QT, RT) are fewer than 5. In addition, to eliminate bots that automatically post specific tweets, we eliminated users whose conversational tweets were fewer than 2. We selected some of the remaining users for the experiment. To satisfy our definition, a chronic critic must tweet about the target entity many times. Therefore, we focused on the top 300 users based on the number of tweets as our experimental users. Table 1 shows the total numbers of tweets by the top 300 users, excluding the account of the target entity.

We created an evaluation set by manually dividing the experimental users into chronic critics and regular users. A chronic critic actively complained and tried to harm the reputation of the target entity. We also regarded a user who frequently reposted a critic's tweets and unfavorable news about the target entity as a chronic critic. For the experimental users tweeting about *Company A*, we asked two human annotators to judge whether a user was a chronic critic based on one month of tweets. The Cohen's kappa value was 0.81 which inter-annotator agreement was good. We selected the arbitrarily annotating by one of the annotators as our evaluation set. Table 1 expresses the number of chronic critics for each target entity in the evaluation set. For the experimental users tweeting about *Politician A*, we randomly extracted 50 users randomly to calculate Cohen's kappa, which is displayed in Table 1.

We evaluated the effects of combining the opinion mining with the graph analysis. We compared opinion mining (OM), graph analysis (GA), and the combination of opinion mining and graph analysis (our proposed method). GA randomly selected M users from experimental users as seeds and takes the average of the results obtained by performing label propagation three times. The number of chronic critics extracted by the opinion mining (i.e., the valuable M) was set to 30. The parameter μ, that we use to calculate the weight of the edges connected to neutral fact, was set to 0.1.

4.2 Results

Figure 3 represents the precision and recall of each method for each target entity. In OM, we varied the threshold from 0 to 0.2 in increments of 0.02 and accepted a user with a score over the threshold as a chronic critic. In GA, we varied the threshold from 0.35 to 0.8 in increments of 0.05.

In Figure 3, the results for *Company A* and *Politician A* are quite different, though there are some similar characteristics. Figure 3 shows that OM achieved high precision but it was difficult to improve the recall. In contrast, GA easily achieved high recall. The proposed method achieved high precision similar to OM and high recall. In other words, the proposed method found many

[3]We manually prepared the words that have a correlation with the entity. In this paper, we only used the name of the political party of *Politician A* as the related word.

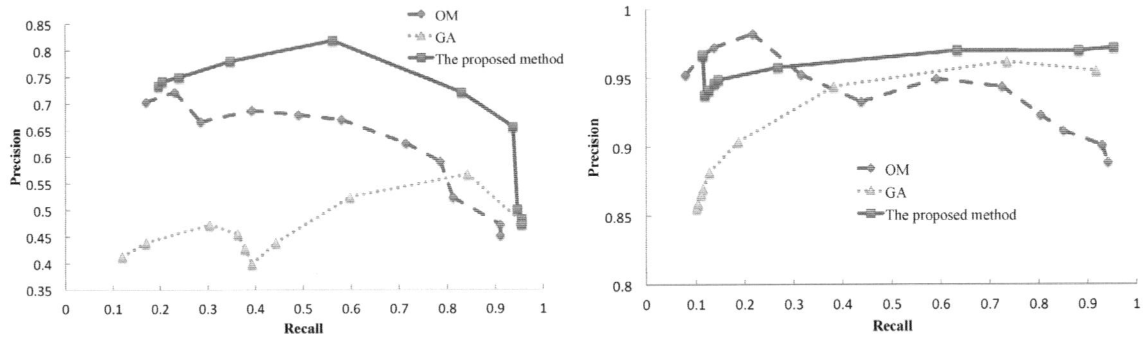

(a) *Company A* (b) *Politician A*

Figure 3: Precision and recall of each method for each target entity

Table 2: Users connected with the target entity

Target entity	Users	Non-critics
Company A	45	39
Politician A	74	35

chronic critics while retaining high precision of OM. Therefore, the combination of the opinion mining and the graph analysis improved the performance of recognizing the chronic critics.

Figure 3 shows that the recall of OM was low, which means that OM missed some of the critical tweets. In this paper, we used domain-independent lexicons to detect the critical phrases. Therefore, OM failed to find domain-dependent critic phrases such as slang words. In addition, some chronic critics do not express criticism clearly in their own tweets. To spread the bad reputation, they reference only a title and link to a webpage that criticizes the target entity such as:

> This shows the reality of *Company A*. Why do you buy products from this company? http://xxx

We believe that is often done because each tweet is limited to 140 characters. It is difficult to classify the tweet as a complaint based only on its content. However, the proposed method recognized most chronic critics that complain with these methods based on the GA.

It cannot reasonably be assumed that a user who supports the account of the target entity is a chronic critic. For this reason, in the graph analysis, we used the entity's account to recognize non-critics. We believe that using the account corrects for mistakes in selecting the seed chronic critics. Table 2 shows the number of users connected with the account. Table 2 also shows the number of non-critics among the users. As seen in Table 2, many non-critics were connected with the account. Especially for *Politician A*, most of the non-critics in the evaluation set were connected with the account. Therefore, incorporating the account into the graph analysis can correct for errors in the seeding of chronic critics. However, some chronic critics were connected with the target's account and reposted tweets from the account. We noticed that they mentioned their negative opinions about the content of such a tweet immediately after reposting that tweet. Hence, we need to analyze the contexts before and after each RT.

For *Politician A*, Table 1 shows that most of the users in the evaluation set criticized the politician. We were able to find most of the chronic critics by extracting the users linked to each other. However, for *Company A*, the precision of GA was low. This means we need high accuracy in selecting the seeds to correctly capture chronic critics. Because we used the users extracted by the opinion mining as the seeds, the proposed method outperformed OM and GA.

5 Conclusion

In this paper, we proposed a method that uses not only opinion mining but graph analysis of the connections between users to detect chronic critics. In our experiments, we found that the proposed method outperformed each technique.

In our study, we used two entities. To improve reliability, we should study more entities. We used a relationship between users that support each other. However, we suspect that the relationship includes adversaries. We hope to address these topics in the future.

Acknowledgments

This research was partly supported by JSPS KAKENHI Grant Numbers 23240018. The authors would like to acknowledge Hiroshi Kanayama and Shiho Ogino in IBM Research-Tokyo for providing their tools for our experiments.

References

Luciano Barbosa and Junlan Feng. 2010. Robust Sentiment Detection on Twitter from Biased and Noisy Data. In *Proceedings of the 23rd International Conference on Computational Linguistics*, pages 36–44.

Johan Bollen, Huina Mao, and Xiao-Jun Zeng. 2011. Twitter mood predicts the stock market. *Journal of Computational Science*, 2(1):1–8.

Michael D. Conover, Bruno Gonçalves, Jacob Ratkiewicz, Alessandro Flammini, and Filippo Menczer. 2011a. Predicting the Political Alignment of Twitter Users. In *Proceedings of the 3rd IEEE Conference on Social Computing*, pages 192–199.

Michael D. Conover, Jacob Ratkiewicz, Matthew Francisco, Bruno Gonçalves, Alessandro Flammini, and Filippo Menczer. 2011b. Political Polarization on Twitter. In *Proceeding of the 5th International AAAI Conference on Weblogs and Social Media*, pages 89–96.

Dmitry Davidov, Oren Tsur, and Ari Rappoport. 2010. Enhanced Sentiment Learning Using Twitter Hashtags and Smileys. In *Proceedings of the 23rd International Conference on Computational Linguistics*, pages 241–249.

Masahiko Higashiyama, Kentaro Inui, and Yuji Matsumoto. 2008. Learning Polarity of Nouns by Selectional Preferences of Predicates (in Japanese). In *Proceedings of the 14th Annual Meeting of The Association for Natural Language Processing*, pages 584–587.

Hiroshi Kanayama and Tetsuya Nasukawa. 2012. Unsupervised Lexicon Induction for Clause-Level Detection of Evaluations. *Natural Language Engineering*, 18(1):83–107.

Akiko Murakami and Rudy Raymond. 2010. Support or Oppose? Classifying Positions in Online Debates from Reply Activities and Opinion Expressions. In *Proceedings of the 23rd International Conference on Computational Linguistics*, pages 869–875, Beijing, China.

Brendan O'Connor, Ramnath Balasubramanyan, Bryan R. Routledge, and Noah A. Smith. 2010. From Tweets to Polls: Linking Text Sentiment to Public Opinion Time Series. In *Proceedings of the 4h International AAAI Conference on Weblogs and Social Media*, pages 122–129.

Shiho Ogino, Tetsuya Nasukawa, Hiroshi Kanayama, and Miki Enoki. 2012. Knowledge Discovery Using Swearwords (in Japanese). In *Proceedings of the 8th Annual Meeting of The Association for Natural Language Processing*, pages 58–61.

Michael Speriosu, Nikita Sudan, Sid Upadhyay, and Jason Baldridge. 2011. Twitter Polarity Classification with Label Propagation over Lexical Links and the Follower Graph. In *Proceedings of the 1st workshop on Unsupervised Learning in NLP*, pages 53–63.

Andranik Tumasjan, Timm O. Sprenger, Philipp G. Sandner, and Isabell M. Welpe. 2010. Predicting Elections with Twitter: What 140 Characters Reveal about Political Sentiment. In *Proceedings of the 4th International AAAI Conference on Weblogs and Social Media*, pages 178–185.

Alex Hai Wang. 2010. Don't Follow Me - Spam Detection in Twitter. In *Proceedings of the 5th International Conference on Security and Cryptography*, pages 142–151.

Chao Yang, Robert Harkreader, Jialong Zhang, Seungwon Shin, and Guofei Gu. 2012. Analyzing Spammers' Social Networks for Fun and Profit: A Case Study of Cyber Criminal Ecosystem on Twitter. In *Proceedings of the 21st international conference on World Wide Web*, pages 71–80.

Xiaoxin Yin and Wenzhao Tan. 2011. Semi-Supervised Truth Discovery. In *Proceedings of the 20th international conference on World Wide Web*, pages 217–226.

Xiaojin Zhu, Zoubin Ghahramani, and John Lafferty. 2003. Semi-Supervised Learning Using Gaussian Fields and Harmonic Functions. In *Proceedings of the 20th International Conference on Machine Learning*, pages 912–919.

Addressing Ambiguity in Unsupervised Part-of-Speech Induction with Substitute Vectors

Volkan Cirik
Artificial Intelligence Laboratory
Koc University, Istanbul, Turkey
vcirik@ku.edu.tr

Abstract

We study substitute vectors to solve the part-of-speech ambiguity problem in an unsupervised setting. Part-of-speech tagging is a crucial preliminary process in many natural language processing applications. Because many words in natural languages have more than one part-of-speech tag, resolving part-of-speech ambiguity is an important task. We claim that part-of-speech ambiguity can be solved using substitute vectors. A substitute vector is constructed with possible substitutes of a target word. This study is built on previous work which has proven that word substitutes are very fruitful for part-of-speech induction. Experiments show that our methodology works for words with high ambiguity.

1 Introduction

Learning syntactic categories of words (i.e. part-of-speech or POS tagging) is an important pre-processing step for many natural language processing applications because grammatical rules are not functions of individual words, instead, they are functions of word categories. Unlike supervised POS tagging systems, POS induction systems make use of unsupervised methods. They categorize the words without any help of annotated data.

POS induction is a popular topic and several studies (Christodoulopoulos et al., 2010) have been performed. Token based methods (Berg-Kirkpatrick and Klein, 2010; Goldwater and Griffiths, 2007) categorize word occurrences into syntactic groups. Type based methods (Clark, 2003; Blunsom and Cohn, 2011) on the other hand, categorize word types and yield the ambiguity problem unlike the token based methods.

Type based methods suffer from POS ambiguity because one POS tag is assigned to each word type. However, occurrences of many words may have different POS tags. Two examples below are drawn from the dataset we worked on. They illustrate a situation where two occurrences of the "offers" have different POS tags. In the first sentence "offers" is a noun, whereas, in the second sentence it is a verb.

(1) "Two rival bidders for Connaught BioSciences extended their **offers** to acquire the Toronto-based vaccine manufacturer Friday."

(2) "The company currently **offers** a word-processing package for personal computers called Legend."

In this study, we try to extend the state-of-the-art unsupervised POS tagger (Yatbaz et al., 2012) by solving the ambiguity problem it suffers because it has a type based approach. The clustering based studies (Schütze, 1995) (Mintz, 2003) represent the context of a word with a vector using neighbour words. Similarly, (Yatbaz et al., 2012) proposes to use word context. They claim that the substitutes of a word have similar syntactic categories and they are determined by the context of the word.

In addition, we suggest that the occurrences with different part-of-speech categories of a word should be seen in different contexts. In other words, if we categorize the contexts of a word type we can determine different POS tags of the word. We represent the context of a word by constructing substitute vectors using possible substitutes of the word as (Yatbaz et al., 2012) suggests.

Table 1 illustrates the substitute vector of the occurrence of "offers" in (1). There is a row for each word in the vocabulary. For instance, probability of occurring "agreement" in the position of "offers" is 80% in this context. To resolve ambiguity

Probability	Substitute Word
0.80	agreement
0.03	offer
0.01	proposal
0.01	bid
0.01	attempt
0.01	bids
.	.
.	.
.	.

Table 1: Substitute Vector for "offers" in above sentence.

of a target word, we separate occurrences of the word into different groups depending on the context information represented by substitute vectors.

We conduct two experiments. In the first experiment, for each word type we investigated, we separate all occurences into two categories using substitute vectors. In the second one we guess the number of the categories we should separate for each word type. Both experiments achieve better than (Yatbaz et al., 2012) for highly ambiguous words. The level of ambiguity can be measured with perplexity of word's gold tag distribution. For instance,the gold tag perplexity of word "offers" in the Penn Treebank Wall Street Journal corpus we worked on equals to 1.966. Accordingly, the number of different gold tags of "offers" is 2. Whereas, perplexity of "board" equals to 1.019. Although the number of different tags for "board" is equal to 2, only a small fraction of the tags of board differs from each other. We can conclude that "offers" is more ambiguous than "board".

In this paper we present a method to solve POS ambiguity for a type based POS induction approach. For the rest of the paper, we explain our algorithm and the setup of our experiments. Lastly we present the results and a conclusion.

2 Algorithm

We claim that if we categorize contexts a word type occurs in, we can address ambiguity by separating its occurrences before POS induction. In order to do that, we represent contexts of word occurrences with substitute vectors. A substitute vector is formed by the whole vocabulary of words and their corresponding probabilities of occurring in the position of the target word. To calculate these probabilities, as described in (Yatbaz et al., 2012), a 4-gram language model is built with SRILM (Stolcke, 2002) on approximately 126 million tokens of Wall Street Journal data (1987-1994) extracted from CSR-III Text (Graff et al., 1995).

We generate substitute vectors for all tokens in our dataset. We want to cluster occurrences of our target words using them. In each substitute vector, there is a row for every word in the vocabulary. As a result, the dimension of substitute vectors is equal to 49,206. Thus, in order not to suffer from the curse of dimensionality, we reduce dimensions of substitute vectors.

Before reducing the dimensions of these vectors, distance matrices are created using Jensen distance metric for each word type in step (a) of Figure 1. We should note that these matrices are created with substitute vectors of each word type, not with all of the substitute vectors.

In step (b) of Figure 1, to reduce dimensionality, the ISOMAP algorithm (Tenenbaum et al., 2000) is used. The output vectors of the ISOMAP algorithm are in 64 dimensions. We repeated our experiments for different numbers of dimensions and the best results are achieved when vectors are in 64 dimensions.

In step (c) of Figure 1, after creating vectors in lower dimension, using a modified k-means algorithm (Arthur and Vassilvitskii, 2007) 64-dimensional vectors are clustered for each word type. The number of clusters given as an input to k-means varies with experiments. We induce number of POS tags of a word type at this step.

Previous work (Yatbaz et al., 2012) demonstrates that clustering substitute vectors of all word types alone has limited success in predicting part-of-speech tag of a word. To make use of both word identity and context information of a given type, we use S-CODE co-occurrence modeling (Maron et al., 2010) as (Yatbaz et al., 2012) does.

Given a pair of categorical variables, the S-CODE model represents each of their values on a unit sphere such that frequently co-occurring values are located closely. We construct the pairs to feed S-CODE as follows.

In step (d) of Figure 1, the first part of the pair is the word identity concatenated with cluster ids we got from the previous step. The cluster ids separate word occurrences seen in different context groups. By doing that, we make sure that the occurrences

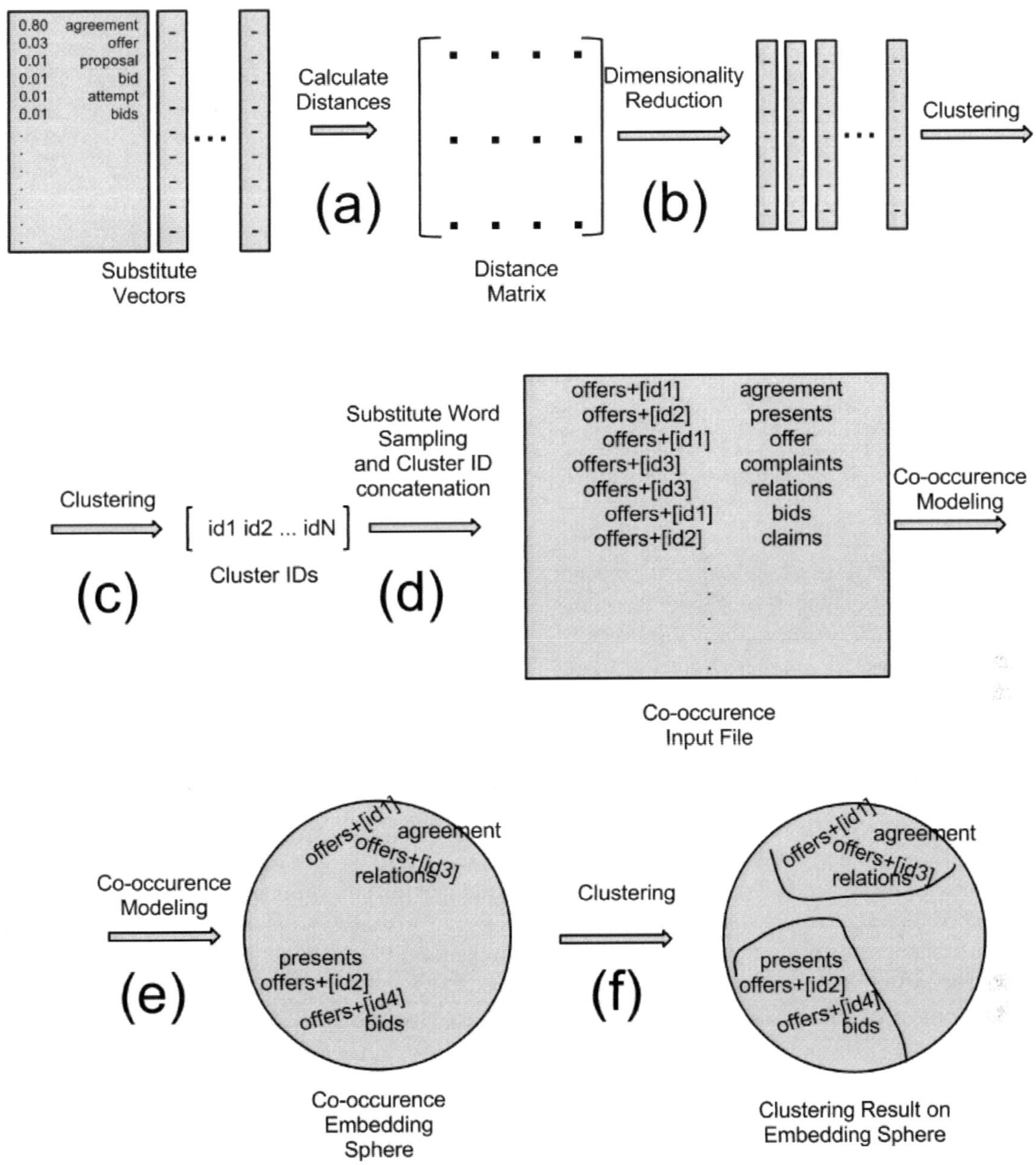

Figure 1: General Flow of The Algorithm

of a same word can be separated on the unit sphere if they are seen in different context groups.

The second part of the pair is a substitute word. For an instance of a target word, we sample a substitute word according to the target word's substitute vector probabilities. If occurrences of two different or the same word types have the same substitutes, they should be seen in the similar contexts. As a result, words occurring in the similar contexts will be close to each other on the unit sphere. Furthermore, they will have the same POS tags. We should note that the co-occurrence input file contains all word types.

In step (e) of Figure 1, on the output of the S-CODE sphere, the words occurring in the similar contexts and having the same word-identity are closely located. Thus, we observe clusters on the unit sphere. For instance, verb occurrences of "offers" are close to each other on the unit sphere. They are also close to other verbs. Furthermore, they are separated with occurrences of "offers" which are nouns.

Lastly, in step (f) of Figure 1, we run k-means clustering method on the S-CODE sphere and split word-substitute word pairs into 45 clusters because the treebank we worked on uses 45 part-of-speech tags. The output of clustering induces part-of-speech categories of words tokens.

3 Experiments

In this section, the setup of each experiment will be presented. The experiments are conducted on Penn Treebank Wall Street Journal corpus. There are 1,173,766 tokens and, 49,206 types. Out of 49,206 word types, 1183 of them are chosen as target words. They are fed to the algorithm described above. Occurrences of these target words correspond to 37.55% of the whole data. These target words are seen in the dataset more than 100 times and less than 4000 times. This subset is chosen as such because word types occurring more than 4000 times are all with low gold tag perplexity. They also increase computation time dramatically. We exclude word types occurring less than 100 times, because the clustering algorithm running on 64-dimension vectors does not work accurately. To avoid providing noisy results, the experiments are repeated 10 times. We report many-to-one scores of the experiments. The many-to-one evaluation assigns each cluster to its most frequent gold-tag. Overall result demonstrates the percentage of correctly assigned instances and standard deviation in paranthesis.

3.1 Baseline

Because we are trying to improve (Yatbaz et al., 2012), we select the experiment on Penn Treebank Wall Street Journal corpus in that work as our baseline and replicate it. In that experiment, POS induction is done by using word identities and context information represented by substitute words. Strictly one tag is assigned to each word type. As a result, this method inaccurately induces POS tags for the occurrences of word types with high gold tag perplexity. The many-to-one accuracy of this experiment is 64%.

3.2 Upperbound

In this experiment, for each word occurence, we concatenate the gold tag for the first part of the pairs in the co-occurence input file. Thus, we skipped steps (a), (b), (c). The purpose of this experiment is to set an upperbound for all experiments since we cannot cluster the word tokens any better than the gold tags. The many-to-one accuracy of this experiment is 67.2%.

3.3 Experiment 1

In the algorithm section, we mention that after dimensionality reduction step, we cluster the vectors to separate tokens of a target word seen in the similar contexts. In this experiment, we set the number of clusters for each type to 2. In other words, we assume that the number of different POS tags of each word type is equal to 2. Nevertheless, separating all the words into 2 clusters results in some inaccuracy in POS induction. That is because not all words have POS ambiguity and some have more than 2 different POS tags However, the main purpose of this experiment is to observe whether we can increase the POS induction accuracy for ambiguous types with our approach. The many-to-one accuracy of this experiment is 63.8%.

3.4 Experiment 2

In the previous experiment, we set the number of clusters for each word type to 2. However, the number of different POS tags differs for each word type. More importantly, around 41% of our target tokens belongs to unambiguous word types. Also, around 36% of our target tokens comes from word types whose gold perplexity is below 1.5. That means, the Experiment 1 splits most of our word types that should not be separated.

In this experiment, instead of splitting all types, we guess which types should be splitted. Also, we guess the number of clusters for each type. We use gap statistic (Tibshirani et al., 2001) on 64-dimensional vectors. The Gap statistic is a statistical method to guess the number of clusters formed in given data points. We expect that substitute vectors occurring in the similar context should be closely located in 64-dimensional space. Thus, gap statistic can provide us the number of groups formed by vectors in 64-dimensional space. That number is possibly equal to the number of the number of different POS tags of the word types. The many-to-one accuracy of this experiment is 63.4%.

3.5 Experiment 3

In this experiment, we set the number of clusters for each type to gold number of tags of each type. The purpose of this experiment is to observe how the accuracy of number of tags given, which is used at step (c), affects the system. The many-to-one accuracy of this experiment is 63.9%.

3.6 Overall Results

In this section we present overall results of the experiments. We present our results in 3 separated tables because the accuracy of these methods varies with the ambiguity level of word types.

In Table 2, many-to-one scores of three experiments are presented. Since we exclude some of the word types, our results correspond to 37.55% of the data. In Table 3, results for the word types whose gold tag perplexity is lower than 1.5 are presented. They correspond to 29.11% of the data. Lastly, in Table 4, we present the results for word types whose gold tag perplexity is greater than 1.5.

Experiment	Many-to-One Score
Baseline	.64 (.01)
Experiment 1	.638 (.01)
Experiment 2	.634 (.01)
Experiment 3	.639 (.02)

Table 2: Results for the target words corresponding to 37.55% of the data.

Experiment	Many-to-One Score
Baseline	.693 (.02)
Experiment 1	.682 (.01)
Experiment 2	.68 (.01)
Experiment 3	.684 (.02)

Table 3: Results for Target Words with gold tag perplexity ≤ 1.5 which corresponds to 29.11% of the data.

Experiment	Many-to-One Score
Baseline	.458 (.01)
Experiment 1	.484 (.01)
Experiment 2	.474 (.02)
Experiment 3	.483 (.02)

Table 4: Results for Target Words with gold tag perplexity ≥ 1.5 which corresponds to 8.44% of the data..

4 Conclusion

Table 2 shows that the baseline experiment is slightly better than our experiments. That is because our experiments inaccurately induce more than one tag to unambiguous types. Additionally, most of our target words have low gold tag perplexity. Table 3 supports this claim. In Table 4, we observe that our methods outscore the baseline significantly. That is because, when ambiguity increases, the baseline method inaccurately assigns one POS tag to word types. On the other hand, the gap statistic method is not fully efficient in guessing the number of clusters. It sometimes separates unambiguous types or it does not separate highly ambiguous word types. As a result, there is a slight difference between the results of our experiments.

Additionally, the results of our experiments show that, accurately guessing number of clusters plays a crucial role in this approach. Even using the gold number of different tags in Experiment 3 does not result in a significantly accurate system. That is because, the number of different tags does not reflect the perplexity of a word type.

The results show that, POS ambiguity can be addressed by using substitute vectors for word types with high ambiguity. The accuracy of this approach correlates with the level of ambiguity of word types. Thus, the detection of the level of ambiguity for word types should be the future direction of this research. We again propose that substitute vector distributions could be useful to extract perplexity information for a word type.

Acknowledgments

I would like to thank the members of the Koc University Artificial Intelligence Laboratory for their help and support. Additionally, I would like to thank two anonymous reviewers and Murat Seyhan for their comments and suggestions.

References

D. Arthur and S. Vassilvitskii. 2007. k-means++: The advantages of careful seeding. In *Proceedings of the eighteenth annual ACM-SIAM symposium on Discrete algorithms*, pages 1027–1035. Society for Industrial and Applied Mathematics.

Taylor Berg-Kirkpatrick and Dan Klein. 2010. Phylogenetic grammar induction. In *Proceedings of the 48th Annual Meeting of the Association for Computational Linguistics*, pages 1288–1297, Uppsala,

Sweden, July. Association for Computational Linguistics.

Phil Blunsom and Trevor Cohn. 2011. A hierarchical pitman-yor process hmm for unsupervised part of speech induction. In *Proceedings of the 49th Annual Meeting of the Association for Computational Linguistics: Human Language Technologies*, pages 865–874, Portland, Oregon, USA, June. Association for Computational Linguistics.

Christos Christodoulopoulos, Sharon Goldwater, and Mark Steedman. 2010. Two decades of unsupervised pos induction: how far have we come? In *Proceedings of the 2010 Conference on Empirical Methods in Natural Language Processing*, EMNLP '10, pages 575–584, Stroudsburg, PA, USA. Association for Computational Linguistics.

Alexander Clark. 2003. Combining distributional and morphological information for part of speech induction. In *Proceedings of the tenth conference on European chapter of the Association for Computational Linguistics - Volume 1*, EACL '03, pages 59–66, Stroudsburg, PA, USA. Association for Computational Linguistics.

Sharon Goldwater and Tom Griffiths. 2007. A fully bayesian approach to unsupervised part-of-speech tagging. In *Proceedings of the 45th Annual Meeting of the Association of Computational Linguistics*, pages 744–751, Prague, Czech Republic, June. Association for Computational Linguistics.

David Graff, Roni Rosenfeld, and Doug Paul. 1995. Csr-iii text. Linguistic Data Consortium, Philadelphia.

Yariv Maron, Michael Lamar, and Elie Bienenstock. 2010. Sphere embedding: An application to part-of-speech induction. In J. Lafferty, C. K. I. Williams, J. Shawe-Taylor, R.S. Zemel, and A. Culotta, editors, *Advances in Neural Information Processing Systems 23*, pages 1567–1575.

T.H. Mintz. 2003. Frequent frames as a cue for grammatical categories in child directed speech. *Cognition*, 90(1):91–117.

Hinrich Schütze. 1995. Distributional part-of-speech tagging. In *Proceedings of the seventh conference on European chapter of the Association for Computational Linguistics*, EACL '95, pages 141–148, San Francisco, CA, USA. Morgan Kaufmann Publishers Inc.

Andreas Stolcke. 2002. Srilm-an extensible language modeling toolkit. In *Proceedings International Conference on Spoken Language Processing*, pages 257–286, November.

J.B. Tenenbaum, V. Silva, and J.C. Langford. 2000. A global geometric framework for nonlinear dimensionality reduction. *Science*, 290(5500):2319.

R. Tibshirani, G. Walther, and T. Hastie. 2001. Estimating the number of data clusters via the gap statistic. *Journal of the Royal Statistical Society B*, 63:411–423.

Mehmet Ali Yatbaz, Enis Sert, and Deniz Yuret. 2012. Learning syntactic categories using paradigmatic representations of word context. In *Proceedings of the 2012 Joint Conference on Empirical Methods in Natural Language Processing and Computational Natural Language Learning*, pages 940–951, Jeju Island, Korea, July. Association for Computational Linguistics.

Psycholinguistically Motivated Computational Models on the Organization and Processing of Morphologically Complex Words

Tirthankar Dasgupta
Department of Computer Science and Engineering,
Indian Institute of Technology Kharagpur
tirtha@cse.iitkgp.ernet.in

Abstract

In this work we present psycholinguistically motivated computational models for the organization and processing of Bangla morphologically complex words in the mental lexicon. Our goal is to identify whether morphologically complex words are stored as a whole or are they organized along the morphological line. For this, we have conducted a series of psycholinguistic experiments to build up hypothesis on the possible organizational structure of the mental lexicon. Next, we develop computational models based on the collected dataset. We observed that derivationally suffixed Bangla words are in general decomposed during processing and compositionality between the stem and the suffix plays an important role in the decomposition process. We observed the same phenomena for Bangla verb sequences where experiments showed non-compositional verb sequences are in general stored as a whole in the ML and low traces of compositional verbs are found in the mental lexicon.

1 Introduction

Mental lexicon is the representation of the words in the human mind and their associations that help fast retrieval and comprehension (Aitchison, 1987). Words are known to be associated with each other in terms of, orthography, phonology, morphology and semantics. However, the precise nature of these relations is unknown.

An important issue that has been a subject of study for a long time is to identify the fundamental units in terms of which the mental lexicon is organized. That is, whether lexical representations in the mental lexicon are word based or are they organized along morphological lines. For example, whether a word such as "*unimaginable*" is stored in the mental lexicon as a whole word or do we break it up "*un-*" , "*imagine*" and "*-able*", understand the meaning of each of these constituent and then recombine the units to comprehend the whole word.

Such questions are typically answered by designing appropriate priming experiments (Marslen-Wilson et al., 1994) or other lexical decision tasks. The reaction time of the subjects for recognizing various lexical items under appropriate conditions reveals important facts about their organization in the brain. (See Sec. 2 for models of morphological organization and access and related experiments).

A clear understanding of the structure and the processing mechanism of the mental lexicon will further our knowledge of how the human brain processes language. Further, these linguistically important and interesting questions are also highly significant for computational linguistics (CL) and natural language processing (NLP) applications. Their computational significance arises from the issue of their storage in lexical resources like WordNet (Fellbaum, 1998) and raises the questions like, how to store morphologically complex words, in a lexical resource like WordNet keeping in mind the storage and access efficiency.

There is a rich literature on organization and lexical access of morphologically complex words where experiments have been conducted mainly for derivational suffixed words of English, Hebrew, Italian, French, Dutch, and few other languages (Marslen-Wilson et al., 2008; Frost et al., 1997; Grainger, et al., 1991; Drews and Zwitserlood, 1995). However, we do not know of any such investigations for Indian languages, which are morphologically richer than many of their Indo-European cousins. Moreover, Indian languages show some distinct phenomena like, compound and composite verbs for which no such investigations have been conducted yet. On the other hand, experiments indicate that mental representation and processing of morphologically complex words are not quite language independent (Taft, 2004). Therefore, the findings from experiments in one language cannot be generalized to all languages making it important to conduct similar experimentations in other languages.

This work aims to design cognitively motivated computational models that can explain the organization and processing of Bangla morphologically complex words in the mental lexicon. Presently we will concentrate on the following two aspects:

- Organization and processing of Bangla Polymorphemic words: our objective here is to determine whether the mental lexicon decomposes morphologically complex words into its constituent morphemes or does it represent the unanalyzed surface form of a word.
- Organization and processing of Bangla compound verbs (CV): compound verbs are the subject of much debate in linguistic theory. No consensus has been reached yet with respect to the issue that whether to consider them as unitary lexical units or are they syntactically assembled combinations of two independent lexical units. As linguistic arguments have so far not led to a consensus, we here use cognitive experiments to probe the brain signatures of verb-verb combinations and propose cognitive as well as computational models regarding the possible organization and processing of Bangla CVs in the mental lexicon (ML).

With respect to this, we apply the different priming and other lexical decision experiments, described in literature (Marslen-Wilson et al., 1994; Bentin, S. and Feldman, 1990) specifically for derivationally suffixed polymorphemic words and compound verbs of Bangla. Our cross-modal and masked priming experiment on Bangla derivationally suffixed words shows that morphological relatedness between lexical items triggers a significant priming effect, even when the forms are phonologically/orthographically unrelated. These observations are similar to those reported for English and indicate that derivationally suffixed words in Bangla are in general accessed through decomposition of the word into its constituent morphemes. Further, based on the experimental data we have developed a series of computational models that can be used to predict the decomposition of Bangla polymorphemic words. Our evaluation result shows that decomposition of a polymorphemic word depends on several factors like, frequency, productivity of the suffix and the compositionality between the stem and the suffix.

The organization of the paper is as follows: Sec. 2 presents related works; Sec. 3 describes experiment design and procedure; Sec. 4 presents the processing of CVs; and finally, Sec. 5 concludes the paper by presenting the future direction of the work.

2 Related Works

2.1 Representation of polymorphemic words

Over the last few decades many studies have attempted to understand the representation and processing of morphologically complex words in the brain for various languages. Most of the studies are designed to support one of the two mutually exclusive paradigms: the *full-listing* and the *morphemic* model. The *full-listing model* claims that polymorphic words are represented as a whole in the human mental lexicon (Bradley, 1980; Butterworth, 1983). On the other hand, *morphemic model* argues that morphologically complex words are decomposed and represented in terms of the smaller morphemic units. The affixes are stripped away from the root form, which in turn are used to access the mental lexicon (Taft and Forster, 1975; Taft, 1981; MacKay, 1978). Intermediate to these two paradigms is the *partial decomposition model* that argues that different types of morphological forms are processed separately. For instance, the derived morphological forms are believed to be represented as a whole, whereas the representation of the inflected forms follows the morphemic model (Caramazza et al., 1988).

Traditionally, *priming experiments* have been used to study the effects of morphology in language processing. *Priming* is a process that results in increase in speed or accuracy of response to a stimulus, called the *target*, based on the occurrence of a prior exposure of another stimulus, called the *prime* (Tulving et al., 1982). Here, subjects are exposed to a prime word for a short duration, and are subsequently shown a target word. The prime and target words may be morphologically, phonologically or semantically related. An analysis of the effect of the reaction time of subjects reveals the actual organization and representation of the lexicon at the relevant level. See Pulvermüller (2002) for a detailed account of such phenomena.

It has been argued that frequency of a word influences the speed of lexical processing and thus, can serve as a diagnostic tool to observe the nature and organization of lexical representations. (Taft, 1975) with his experiment on English inflected words, argued that lexical decision responses of polymorphemic words depends upon the base word frequency. Similar observation for surface word frequency was also observed by (Bertram et al., 2000;Bradley, 1980;Burani et al., 1987;Burani et al., 1984;Schreuder et al., 1997; Taft 1975;Taft, 2004) where it has been claimed that words having low surface frequency tends to decompose. Later, Baayen(2000) proposed the dual processing race model that proposes that a specific morphologically complex form is accessed via its parts if the frequency of that word is above a certain threshold of frequency, then the direct route will win, and the word will be accessed as a whole. If it is below that same threshold of frequency, the parsing route will win, and the word will be accessed via its parts.

2.2 Representation of Compound Verbs

A compound verb (CV) consists of a sequence of two verbs (V1 and V2) acting as a single verb and expresses a single expression of meaning. For example, in the sentence

রুটিগুলো খেলে ফেলো (/ruTigulo kheYe phela/)
"bread-plural-the eat and drop-pres. Imp"

"Eat the breads"

the verb sequence "খেলে ফেলো (eat drop)" is an example of CV. Compound verbs are a special phenomena that are abundantly found in Indo-European languages like Indian languages.

A plethora of works has been done to provide linguistic explanations on the formation of such word, yet none so far has led to any consensus. Hook (1981) considers the second verb V2 as an aspectual complex comparable to the auxiliaries. Butt (1993) argues CV formations in Hindi and Urdu are either morphological or syntactical and their formation take place at the argument structure. Bashir (1993) tried to construct a semantic analysis based on "prepared" and "unprepared mind". Similar findings have been proposed by Pandharipande (1993) that points out V1 and V2 are paired on the basis of their semantic compatibility, which is subject to syntactic constraints. Paul (2004) tried to represent Bangla CVs in terms of HPSG formalism. She proposes that the selection of a V2 by a V1 is determined at the semantic level because the two verbs will unify if and only if they are semantically compatible. Since none of the linguistic formalism could satisfactorily explain the unique phenomena of CV formation, we here for the first time drew our attention towards psycholinguistic and neurolinguistic studies to model the processing of verb-verb combinations in the ML and compare these responses with that of the existing models.

3 The Proposed Approaches

3.1 The psycholinguistic experiments

We apply two different priming experiments namely, the cross modal priming and masked priming experiment discussed in (Forster and Davis, 1984; Rastle et al., 2000;Marslen-Wilson et al., 1994; Marslen-Wilson et al., 2008) for Bangla morphologically complex words. Here, the prime is morphologically derived form of the target presented auditorily (for cross modal priming) or visually (for masked priming). The subjects were asked to make a lexical decision whether the given target is a valid word in that language. The same target word is again probed but with a different audio or visual probe called the control word. The control shows no relationship with the target. For example, baYaska (aged) and baYasa (age) is a prime-target pair, for which the corresponding control-target pair could be naYana (eye) and baYasa (age).

Similar to (Marslen-Wilson et al., 2008) the masked priming has been conducted for three different SOA (Stimulus Onset Asynchrony), 48ms, 72ms and 120ms. The SOA is measured as the amount of time between the start the first stimulus till the start of the next stimulus.

Class	Example
M+S+O+	nibAsa(residence)-nibAsi(resident)
M+S+O-	mitra(friend) - maitri (friendship)
M'+S-O+	Ama(Mango)- AmadAni (import)
M-S+O-	jantu(Animal)- bAgha (Tiger)
M-S-O+	ghaDi(watch)-ghaDiYAla (crocodile)

Table 1: Dataset for the experiment, + implies related, and - implies unrelated.

There were 500 prime-target and control-target pairs classified into five classes. Depending on the class, the prime is related to the target either in terms of morphology, semantics, orthography and/or Phonology (See Table 1).

The experiments were conducted on 24 highly educated native Bangla speakers. Nineteen of them have a graduate degree and five hold a post graduate degree. The age of the subjects varies between 22 to 35 years.

Results: The RTs with extreme values and incorrect decisions were excluded from the data. The data has been analyzed using two ways ANOVA with three factors: priming (prime and control), conditions (five classes) and prime durations (three different SOA). We observe strong priming effects ($p<0.05$) when the target word is morphologically derived and has a recognizable suffix, semantically and orthographically related with respect to the prime; no priming effects are observed when the prime and target words are orthographically related but share no morphological or semantic relationship; although not statistically significant ($p>0.07$), but weak priming is observed for prime target pairs that are only semantically related. We see no significant difference between the prime and control RTs for other classes.

We also looked at the RTs for each of the 500 target words. We observe that maximum priming occurs for words in [M+S+O+](69%), some priming is evident in [M+S+O-](51%) and [M'+S-O+](48%), but for most of the words in [M-S+O-](86%) and [M-S-O+](92%) no priming effect was observed.

3.2 Frequency Distribution Models of Morphological Processing

From the above results we saw that not all polymorphemic words tend to decompose during processing, thus we need to further investigate the processing phenomena of Bangla derived words. One notable means is to identify whether the stem or suffix frequency is involved in the processing stage of that word. For this, we apply different frequency based models to the Bangla polymorphemic words and try to evaluate their performance by comparing their predicted results with the result obtained through the priming experiment.

Model-1: Base and Surface word frequency effect- It states that the probability of decomposition of a Bangla polymorphemic word depends upon the frequency of its base word. Thus, if the stem frequency of a polymorphemic word crosses a given threshold value, then the word will decomposed into its constituent morpheme. Similar claim has been made for surface word frequency model where decomposition depends upon the frequency of the surface word itself. We have evaluated both the models with the 500 words used in the priming experiments discussed above. We have achieved an accuracy of 62% and 49% respectively for base and surface word frequency models.

Model-2: Combining the base and surface word frequency- In a pursuit towards an extended model, we combine model 1 and 2 together. We took the log frequencies of both the base and the derived words and plotted the best-fit regression curve over the given dataset.

The evaluation of this model over the same set of 500 target words returns an accuracy of 68% which is better than the base and surface word frequency models. However, the proposed model still fails to predict processing of around 32% of words. This led us to further enhance the model. For this, we analyze the role of suffixes in morphological processing.

Model-3: Degree of Affixation and Suffix Productivity: we examine whether the regression analysis between base and derived frequency of Bangla words varies between suffixes and how these variations affect morphological decomposition. With respect to this, we try to compute the degree of affixation between the suffix and the base word. For this, we perform regression analysis on sixteen different Bangla suffixes with varying degree of type and token frequencies. For each suffix, we choose 100 different derived words. We observe that those suffixes having high value of intercept are forming derived words whose base frequencies are substantially high as compared to their derived forms. Moreover we also observe that high intercept value for a given suffix indicates higher inclination towards decomposition.

Next, we try to analyze the role of suffix type/token ratio and compare them with the base/derived frequency ratio model. This has been done by regression analysis between the suffix type-token ratios with the base-surface frequency ratio.

We further tried to observe the role of suffix productivity in morphological processing. For this, we computed the three components of productivity P, P* and V as discussed in (Hay and Plag, 2004). P is the "conditioned degree of productivity" and is the probability that we are encountering a word with an affix and it is representing a new type. P* is the "hapaxed-conditioned degree of productivity". It expresses the probability that when an entirely new word is encountered it will contain the suffix. V is the "type frequency". Finally, we computed the productivity of a suffix through its P, P* and V values. We found that decomposition of Bangla polymorphemic word is directly proportional to the productivity of the suffix. Therefore, words that are composed of productive suffixes (P value ranges between 0.6 and 0.9) like "-oYAlA", "-giri", "-tba" and "-panA" are highly decomposable than low productive suffixes like "-Ani", "-lA", "-k", and "-tama". The evaluation of the proposed model returns an accuracy of 76% which comes to be 8% better than the preceding models.

Combining Model-2 and Model-3: One important observation that can be made from the above results is that, model-3 performs best in determining the true negative values. It also possesses a high recall value of (85%) but having a low precision of (50%). In other words, the model can predict those words for which decomposition will not take place. On the other hand, results of Model-2 posses a high precision of 70%. Thus, we argue that combining the above two models can better predict the decomposition of Bangla polymorphemic words. Hence, we combine the two models together and finally achieved an overall accuracy of 80% with a precision of 87% and a recall of 78%. This surpasses the performance of the other models discussed earlier. However, around 22% of the test words were wrongly classified which the model fails to justify. Thus, a more rigorous set of experiments and data analysis are required to predict access mechanisms of such Bangla polymorphemic words.

3.3 Stem-Suffix Compositionality

Compositionality refers to the fact that meaning of a complex expression is inferred from the meaning of its constituents. Therefore, the cost of retrieving a word from the secondary memory is directly proportional to the cost of retrieving the individual parts (i.e the stem and the suffix). Thus, following the work of (Milin et al., 2009) we define the compositionality of a morphologically complex word (W_e) as:

$$C(W_e)= {}_1H(W_e)+ {}_2H(e)+ {}_3H(W|e)+ {}_4H(e|W)$$

Where, H(x) is entropy of an expression x, H(W|e) is the conditional entropy between the stem W and suffix e and is the proportionality factor whose value is computed through regression analysis.

Next, we tried to compute the compositionality of the stem and suffixes in terms of relative entropy D(W||e) and Point wise mutual information (PMI). The relative entropy is the measure of the distance between the probability distribution of the stem W and the suffix e. The PMI measures the amount of information that one random variable (the stem) contains about the other (the suffix).

We have compared the above three techniques with the actual reaction time data collected through the priming and lexical decision experiment. We observed that all the three information theoretic models perform much better than the frequency based models discussed in the earlier section, for predicting the decomposability of Bangla polymorphemic words. However, we think it is still premature to claim anything concrete at this stage of our work. We believe much more rigorous experiments are needed to be performed in order to validate our proposed models. Further, the present paper does not consider factors related to age of acquisition, and word familiarity effects that plays important role in the processing of morphologically complex words. Moreover, it is also very interesting to see how stacking of multiple suffixes in a word are processed by the human brain.

4 Organization and Processing of Compound Verbs in the Mental Lexicon

Compound verbs, as discussed above, are special type of verb sequences consisting of two or more verbs acting as a single verb and express a single expression of meaning. The verb V1 is known as pole and V2 is called as vector. For example, "ওঠে পড়া" (*getting up*) is a compound verb where individual words do not entirely reflects the meaning of the whole expression. However, not all V1+V2 combinations are CVs. For example, expressions like, "নিয়ে যাও"(*take and then go*) and " ফিরে আসো" (*return back*) are the examples of verb sequences where meaning of the whole expression can be derived from the meaning of the individual component and thus, these verb sequences are not considered as CV. The key question linguists are trying to identify for a long time and debating a lot is whether to consider CVs as a single lexical units or consider them as two separate units. Since linguistic rules fails to explain the process, we for the first time tried to perform cognitive experiments to understand the organization and processing of such verb sequences in the human mind. A clear understanding about these phenomena may help us to classify or extract actual CVs from other verb sequences. In order to do so, presently we have applied three different techniques to collect user data. In the first technique, we annotated 4500 V1+V2 sequences, along with their example sentences, using a group of three linguists (the expert subjects). We asked the experts to classify the verb sequences into three classes namely, *CV*, *not a CV* and *not sure*. Each linguist has received 2000 verb pairs along with their respective example sentences. Out of this, 1500 verb sequences are unique to each of them and rest 500 are overlapping. We measure the inter annotator agreement using the Fleiss Kappa (Fleiss et al., 1981) measure (κ) where the agreement lies around 0.79. Next, out of the 500 common verb sequences that were annotated by all the three linguists, we randomly choose 300 V1+V2 pairs and presented them to 36 native Bangla speakers. We ask each subjects to give a compositionality score of each verb sequences under 1-10 point scale, 10 being highly compositional and 1 for noncompositional. We found an agreement of κ=0.69 among the subjects. We also observe a continuum of compositionality score among the verb sequences. This reflects that it is difficult to classify Bangla verb sequences discretely into the classes of *CV* and *not a CV*. We then, compare the compositionality score with that of the expert user's annotation. We found a significant correlation between the expert annotation and the compositionality score. We observe verb sequences that are annotated as CVs (like, খেয়ে ফেল)করে নে ,ওঠে পড় ,have got low compositionality score (average score ranges between 1-4) on the other hand high compositional values are in general tagged as *not a cv* (নিয়ে যা (*come and get*), ফিরে আয় (*return back*), তুলে রেখেছি (*kept*), গড়িয়ে পড়ল (*roll on floor*)). This reflects that verb sequences which are not CV shows high degree of compositionality. In other words non CV verbs can directly interpret from their constituent verbs. This leads us to the possibility that compositional verb sequences requires individual verbs to be recognized separately and thus the time to recognize such expressions must be greater than the non-compositional verbs which maps to a single expression of meaning. In order to validate such claim we perform a lexical decision experiment using 32 native Bangla speakers with 92 different verb sequences. We followed the same experimental procedure as discussed in (Taft, 2004) for English polymorphemic words. However, rather than derived words, the subjects were shown a verb sequence and asked whether they recognize them as a valid combination. The reaction time (RT) of each subject is recorded. Our preliminarily observation from the RT analysis shows that as per our claim, RT of verb sequences having high compositionality value is significantly higher than the RTs for low or non-compositional verbs. This proves our hypothesis that Bangla compound verbs that show less compositionality are stored as a hole in the mental lexicon and thus follows the full-listing model whereas compositional verb phrases are individually parsed. However, we do believe that our experiment is composed of a very small set of data and it is premature to conclude anything concrete based only on the current experimental results.

5 Future Directions

In the next phase of our work we will focus on the following aspects of Bangla morphologically complex words:

The Word Familiarity Effect: Here, our aim is to study the role of familiarity of a word during its processing. We define the familiarity of a word in terms of corpus frequency, Age of acquisition, the level of language exposure of a person, and RT of the word etc.

Role of suffix types in morphological decomposition: For native Bangla speakers which morphological suffixes are internalized and which are just learnt in school, but never internalized. We can compare the representation of Native, Sanskrit derived and foreign suffixes in Bangla words.

Computational models of organization and processing of Bangla compound verbs: presently we have performed some small set of experiments to study processing of compound verbs in the mental lexicon. In the next phase of our work we will extend the existing experiments and also apply some more techniques like, crowd sourcing and language games to collect more relevant RT and compositionality data. Finally, based on the collected data we will develop computational models that can explain the possible organizational structure and processing mechanism of morphologically complex Bangla words in the mental lexicon.

Reference

Aitchison, J. (1987). "*Words in the mind: An introduction to the mental lexicon*". Wiley-Blackwell,

Baayen R. H. (2000). *"On frequency, transparency and productivity"*. G. Booij and J. van Marle (eds), Yearbook of Morphology, pages 181-208,

Baayen R.H. (2003). *"Probabilistic approaches to morphology"*. Probabilistic linguistics, pages 229-287.

Baayen R.H., T. Dijkstra, and R. Schreuder. (1997). *"Singulars and plurals in dutch: Evidence for a parallel dual-route model"*. Journal of Memory and Language, 37(1):94-117.

Bashir, E. (1993), *"Causal Chains and Compound Verbs."* In M. K. Verma ed. (1993).

Bentin, S. & Feldman, L.B. (1990). The contribution of morphological and semantic relatedness to repetition priming at short and long lags: Evidence from Hebrew. *Quarterly Journal of Experimental Psychology, 42*, pp. 693–711.

Bradley, D. (1980). Lexical representation of derivational relation, *Juncture*, Saratoga, CA: Anma Libri, pp. 37-55.

Butt, M. (1993), *"Conscious choice and some light verbs in Urdu."* In M. K. Verma ed. (1993).

Butterworth, B. (1983). Lexical Representation, *Language Production*, Vol. 2, pp. 257-294, San Diego, CA: Academic Press.

Caramazza, A., Laudanna, A. and Romani, C. (1988). Lexical access and inflectional morphology. *Cognition, 28*, pp. 297-332.

Drews, E., and Zwitserlood, P. (1995).Morphological and orthographic similarity in visual word recognition. *Journal of Experimental Psychology:HumanPerception andPerformance*, 21, 1098–1116.

Fellbaum, C. (ed.). (1998). WordNet: An Electronic Lexical Database, MIT Press.

Forster, K.I., and Davis, C. (1984). Repetition priming and frequency attenuation in lexical access. *Journal of Experimental Psychology: Learning, Memory, and Cognition, 10*, 680–698.

Frost, R., Forster, K.I., & Deutsch, A. (1997). What can we learn from the morphology of Hebrew? A masked-priming investigation of morphological representation. *Journal of Experimental Psychology: Learning, Memory, and Cognition, 23*, 829–856.

Grainger, J., Cole, P., & Segui, J. (1991). Masked morphological priming in visual word recognition. *Journal of Memory and Language, 30*, 370–384.

Hook, P. E. (1981). *"Hindi Structures: Intermediate Level."* Michigan Papers on South and Southeast Asia, The University of Michigan Center for South and Southeast Studies, Ann Arbor, Michigan.

Joseph L Fleiss, Bruce Levin, and Myunghee Cho Paik. 1981. The measurement of interrater agreement. *Statistical methods for rates and proportions*,2:212–236.

MacKay,D.G.(1978), Derivational rules and the internal lexicon. *Journal of Verbal Learning and Verbal Behavior*, 17, pp.61-71.

Marslen-Wilson, W.D., & Tyler, L.K. (1997). Dissociating types of mental computation. *Nature, 387*, pp. 592–594.

Marslen-Wilson, W.D., & Tyler, L.K. (1998). Rules, representations, and the English past tense. *Trends in Cognitive Sciences, 2*, pp. 428–435.

Marslen-Wilson, W.D., Tyler, L.K., Waksler, R., & Older, L. (1994). Morphology and meaning in the English mental lexicon. *Psychological Review, 101*, pp. 3–33.

Marslen-Wilson,W.D. and Zhou,X.(1999). Abstractness, allomorphy, and lexical architecture. *Language and Cognitive Processes, 14*, 321–352.

Milin, P., Kuperman, V., Kosti´, A. and Harald R., H. (2009). *Paradigms bit by bit: an information-theoretic approach to the processing of paradigmatic structure in inflection and derivation*, Analogy in grammar: Form and acquisition, pp: 214—252.

Pandharipande, R. (1993). "Serial verb construction in Marathi." In M. K. Verma ed. (1993).

Paul, S. (2004). *An HPSG Account of Bangla Compound Verbs with LKB Implementation*, Ph.D. Dissertation. CALT, University of Hyderabad.

Pulvermüller, F. (2002). *The Neuroscience of Language*. Cambridge University Press.

Stolz, J.A., and Feldman, L.B. (1995). The role of orthographic and semantic transparency of the base morpheme in morphological processing. In L.B. Feldman (Ed.) *Morphological aspects of language processing*. Hillsdale, NJ: Lawrence Erlbaum Associates Inc.

Taft, M., and Forster, K.I.(1975). Lexical storage and retrieval of prefix words. *Journal of Verbal Learning and Verbal Behavior*, Vol.14, pp. 638-647.

Taft, M.(1988). A morphological decomposition model of lexical access. *Linguistics*, 26, pp. 657-667.

Taft, M. (2004). Morphological decomposition and the reverse base frequency effect. *Quarterly Journal of Experimental Psychology*, 57A, pp. 745-765

Tulving, E., Schacter D. L., and Heather A.(1982). Priming Effects in Word Fragment Completion are independent of Recognition Memory. *Journal of Experimental Psychology: Learning, Memory and Cognition,* vol.8 (4).

A New Syntactic Metric for Evaluation of Machine Translation

Melania Duma
Department of Computer Science
University of Hamburg
Vogt-Kölln-Straße 30
22527 Hamburg
duma@informatik.uni-hamburg.de

Cristina Vertan
Faculty for Language, Literature and Media
University of Hamburg
Von Melle Park 6
20146 Hamburg
cristina.vertan@uni-hamburg.de

Wolfgang Menzel
Department of Computer Science
University of Hamburg
Vogt-Kölln-Straße 30
22527 Hamburg
menzel@informatik.uni-hamburg.de

Abstract

Machine translation (MT) evaluation aims at measuring the quality of a candidate translation by comparing it with a reference translation. This comparison can be performed on multiple levels: lexical, syntactic or semantic. In this paper, we propose a new syntactic metric for MT evaluation based on the comparison of the dependency structures of the reference and the candidate translations. The dependency structures are obtained by means of a Weighted Constraints Dependency Grammar parser. Based on experiments performed on English to German translations, we show that the new metric correlates well with human judgments at the system level.

1 Introduction

Research in automatic machine translation (MT) evaluation has the goal of developing a set of computer-based methods that measure accurately the correctness of the output generated by a MT system. However, this task is a difficult one mainly because there is no unique reference output that can be used in the comparison with the candidate translation. One sentence can have several correct translations. Thus, it is difficult to decide if the deviation from an existing reference translation is a matter of style (the use of synonymous words, different syntax etc.) or a real translation error.

Most of the automatic evaluation metrics developed so far are focused on the idea of lexical matching between the tokens of one or more reference translations and the tokens of a candidate translation. However, structural similarity between a reference translation and a candidate one cannot be captured by lexical features. Therefore, research in MT evaluation experiences a gradual shift of focus from lexical metrics to structural ones, whether they are syntactic or semantic or a combination of both.

This paper introduces a new syntactic automatic MT evaluation method. At this stage of research the new metric is evaluating translations from any source language into German. Given that a set of constraint-based grammar rules are available for that language, extensions to other target languages are anytime possible. The chosen tool for providing syntactic information for German is the Weighted Constraints Dependency Grammar (WCDG) parser (Menzel and Schröder, 1998), which is preferred over other parsers because of its robustness to ungrammatical input, as it is typical for MT output. The rest of this paper is organized as follows. In Section 2 the state of the art in MT evaluation is presented, while in Section 3 the new syntactic metric is described. The experimental setup and results are presented in Section 4. The last section deals with the conclusions and future work.

2 State of the art

Automatic evaluation of MT systems relies on the existence of at least one reference[1] created by a human annotator. Using an automatic method of evaluation a score is computed, based on the similarity between the output of the MT system and the reference. This similarity can be computed at different levels: lexical, syntactic or semantic. At the lexical level, the metrics developed so far can be divided into two major categories: n-gram based and edit distance based.

[1] We will use the term reference for the reference translation and the term translation for the candidate translation.

Among the n-gram based metrics, one of the most popular methods of evaluation is BLEU (Papineni et al., 2001). It provides a score that is computed as the summed number of n-grams shared by the references and the output, divided by the total number of n-grams. Lexical metrics that use the edit distance are constructed using the Levenshtein distance applied at the word level. Among these metrics, WER (Niessen et al., 2000) is the one which is used more frequently; it calculates the minimal number of insertion, substitutions and deletions needed to transform the candidate translation into a reference.

Metrics based on lexical matching suffer from not being able to consider the variation encountered in natural language. Thus, they reward a low score to an otherwise fluent and syntactically correct candidate translation, if it does not share a certain number of words with the set of references. Because of this, major disagreements between the scores assigned by BLEU and human judgments have been reported in Koehn and Monz (2006) and Callison-Burch et al. (2006). Another disadvantage is that many of them cannot be applied at the segment level, which is often needed in order to better assess the quality of MT output and to determine which improvements should be made to the MT system. Because of these disadvantages there is an increasing need for other approaches to MT evaluation that go beyond the lexical level of the phrases compared.

In Liu and Gildea (2005), three syntactic evaluation metrics are presented. The first of these metrics, the Subtree Metric (SMT), is based on determining the number of subtrees that can be found in both the candidate translation and the reference phrase structure trees. The second metric, which is a kernel-based subtree metric, is defined as the maximum of the cosine measure between the MT output and the set of references. The third metric proposed computes the number of matching n-grams between the headword chains of the reference and the candidate translation dependency trees obtained using the parser described in (Collins, 1999).

The idea of syntactic similarity is further exploited in Owczarzak et al. (2007) which uses a Lexical Functional Grammar (LFG) parser. The similarity between the translation and the reference is computed using the precision and the recall of the dependencies that illustrate the pair of sentences. Furthermore, paraphrases are used in order to improve the correlation with human judgments. Another set of syntactic metrics has been introduced in Gimenez (2008); some of them are based on analyzing different types of linguistic information (i.e. part-of-speech or lemma).

3 A new syntactic automatic metric

In this section we introduce the new syntactic metric which is based on constraint dependency parsing. In the first subsection, the WCDG parser is presented, together with the advantages of using this parser over the other ones available, while the second subsection provides a detailed description of the new metric.

3.1 Weighted Constraint Dependency Grammar Parser

Our research was performed using a dependency parser. We decided on this type of parser because, as opposed to constituent parsers, it offers the possibility of better representing non-projective structures. Moreover, it has been shown in Kuebler and Prokic (2006) that, at least in the case of German, the results achieved by a dependency parser are more accurate than the ones obtained when parsing using constituent parsers, and this is because dependency parsers can handle better long distance relations and coordination.

The goal of constraint dependency grammars (CDG) is to create dependency structures that represent a given phrase (Schröder et al., 2000) on parallel levels of analysis. A relation between two words in a sentence is represented using an edge, which connects the regent and the dependent. Edges are annotated using labels in order to distinguish between different types of relations. A constraint is made up of a logical formula that describes properties of the tree. One property, for example, that is always enforced is that no word can have more than one regent on any level at a time. During the analysis, each of the constraints is applied to every edge or every pair of edges belonging to the constructed dependency parse tree. The main advantage of using constraint dependency grammars over dependency grammars based on generative rules is that they can deal better with free word order languages (Foth, 2004). Weighted Constraint Dependency Grammar (WCDG) (Menzel and Schröder, 1998) assigns different weights to the constraints of the grammar. Every constraint in WCDG is assigned a score which is a number between 0.0 and 1.0, while the general score of a parse is calculated as the product of all the scores of all the instances of constraints that have not been satisfied. Rules that have a score of 0 are called hard rules, meaning that they cannot be ignored, which is the case of the one regent only rule mentioned earlier. The advantage of using graded constraints, as opposed to crisp ones, stems from the fact that weights allow the parser to tolerate constraint violations, which, in turn, makes the parser robust against ungrammaticality. The parser was evaluated using different types of texts, and the results show that it has an accuracy between 80% and 90% in computing correct dependency attachments depending on the type of text (Foth et al., 2004a).

The benefit of using WCDG over other parsers is that it provides further information on a parse, like the general score of the parse and the constraints that are violated by the final result. This information can be further explored in order to perform an error analysis. Moreover, because of the fact that the candidate translations are sometimes not well-formed, parsing them represents a challenge. However, WCDG will always provide a final result, in the form of a dependency structure, even though it might have a low score due to the violated constraints.

3.2 Description of the metric

In order to define a new syntactic metric for MT evaluation, we have incorporated the WCDG parser in the process of evaluation. Because the output of the WCDG parser is a dependency tree, we have looked into techniques of measuring how similar two trees are. Our aim was to determine whether a tree similarity metric applied on the two dependency parse trees would prove to be an efficient way of capturing the similarity between the reference and the translation. Let us consider this example, in which the reference sentence is *"Die schwarze Katze springt schnell auf den roten Stuhl."*(*engl. The black cat jumps quickly on the red chair*) and the candidate translation is *"Auf den roten Stuhl schnell springt die schwarze Katze"*(*engl. On the red chair quickly jumps the red cat*). Even though the word order of the two segments is quite different, and the translation has an incorrect syntax, they roughly have the same meaning. We present in Figure 1 the dependency parse trees obtained using WCDG for the sentences considered. We can observe that the general structure of the translation is similar to that of the reference, the only difference being the reverse order between the left subtree and the right subtree. The tree similarity measure that we chose to use was the All Common Embedded Subtrees (ACET) (Lin et al., 2008) similarity. Given a tree *T*, an embedded subtree is obtained by removing one or more nodes, except for the root, from the tree *T*. The idea behind ACET is that, the more substructures two trees share, the more similar they are. Therefore, ACET is defined as the number of common embedded subtrees shared between two trees. The results reported in Lin et al. (2008) show that ACET outperforms tree edit distance (Zhang and Shasha, 1989) in terms of efficiency.

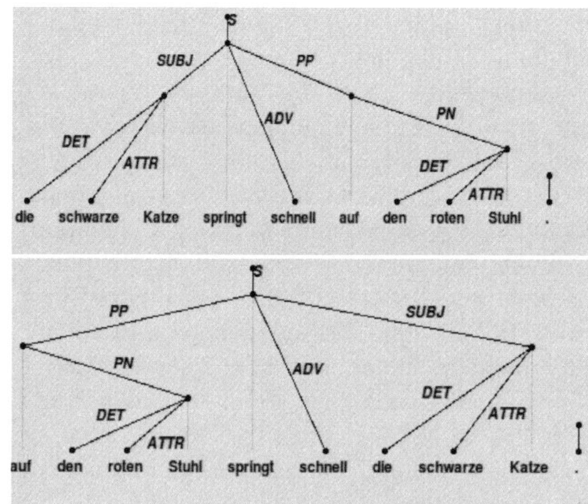

Figure 1. Example of dependency parse trees for reference and candidate translations

In our experiments, we have applied the ACET algorithm, and computed the number of common embedded subtrees between the dependency parse trees of the hypothesis and the reference. Because of the additional information provided by the parsing, pre-processing of the output of the WCDG parser was necessary in order to transform the dependency tree into a general tree. We first removed the labels assigned to every edge, but maintained the nodes and the left to right order between them.

In the following, we will refer to the new proposed metric using CESM (Common Embedded Subtree Metric). CESM was computed using the precision, the recall and the F-measure of the common embedded subtrees of the reference and the translation:

$$precision = \frac{ACET\ (tree_{ref}, tree_{hyp})}{ACET(tree_{hyp}, tree_{hyp})}$$

$$recall\ = \frac{ACET\ (tree_{ref}, tree_{hyp})}{ACET(tree_{ref}, tree_{ref})}$$

$$CESM = F_1 = \frac{2 * precision * recall}{precision + recall}$$

where $tree_{ref}$ and $tree_{hyp}$ represent the preprocessed dependency trees of the reference and the hypothesis translations.

4 Experimental setup and evaluation

In order to determine how accurate CESM is in capturing the similarity between references and translations, we evaluated it at the system level and at the segment level. The evaluation was conducted using data provided by the NAACL 2012 WMT workshop (Callison-Burch et al., 2012). The test data for the workshop consisted of 99 translated news articles in English, German, French, Spanish and Czech.

At the system level, the initial German test set provided at the workshop was filtered according to the length of segments. This was done in order to limit the time requirements of WCDG. As a result, 500 segments with a length between 50 and 80 characters were extracted from the German reference file. In the next step, we arbitrarily selected the outputs of 7 of the 15 systems that were submitted for evaluation in the English to German translation task: DFKI (Vilar, 2012), JHU (Ganitkevitch et al., 2012), KIT (Niehues et al., 2012), UK (Zeman, 2012) and three anonymized system outputs referred to as OnlineA, OnlineB, OnlineC.

After this initial step of filtering the data, the 7 systems were evaluated by calculating the CESM score for every pair of reference and translation segments corresponding to a system. The average scores obtained are depicted in Table 1. Evaluation of the metric at the system level was performed by measuring the correlation of the CESM metric with human judgments using Spearman's rank correlation coefficient ρ:

$$\rho = 1 - \frac{6 \sum d_i^2}{n(n^2 - 1)}$$

where n represents the number of MT systems considered during evaluation, and d_i^2 represents the difference between the ranks, assigned to a system, by the metric and the human judgments. The minimum value of ρ is -1, when there is no correlation between the two rankings, while the maximum value is 1, when the two rankings correlate perfectly (Callison-Burch et al., 2012). In order to compute the ρ score, the scores attributed to every system by CESM, were converted into ranks. From the different ranking strategies that were presented by the WMT12 workshop, the standard ranking order was chosen. The ρ rank correlation coefficient was calculated as being ρ = 0.92, which shows there is a strong correlation between the results of CESM and the human judgments. In order to better assess the quality of CESM, the test set was also evaluated using NIST (Doddington, 2002), which managed to obtain the same rank correlation coefficient of ρ = 0.92.

No.	System name	CESM score	NIST score
1	DFKI	0.069	4.7709
2	JHU	0.073	4.9904
3	KIT	0.090	5.1358
4	OnlineA	0.093	5.3039
5	OnlineB	0.091	5.3039
6	OnlineC	0.085	4.8022
7	UK	0.075	4.6579

Table 1. System level evaluation results

The first step in evaluating at the segment level was filtering the initial test set provided by the WMT12 workshop. For this purpose, 2500 reference and translation segments were selected with a length between 50 and 80 characters. The Kendall tau rank correlation coefficient was calculated in order to measure the correlation with human judgments, where Kendall tau (Callison-Burch et al., 2012) is defined as:

$$\tau = \frac{number\ concordant\ - number\ discordant}{number\ total\ pairs}$$

In order to compute the value of Kendall tau, we determined the number of concordant pairs and the number of discordant pairs of judgments. Similarly to the guideline followed during the WMT12 workshop (Callison-Burch et al., 2012), we penalized ties given by CESM and ignored ties assigned by the human judgments. The obtained result was a correlation of 0.058. As a term of comparison, the highest correlation for segment level reported in Callinson-Burch et al. (2012) was 0.19 obtained by TerrorCat (Fishel et al., 2012) and the lowest was BlockErrCats (Popovic, 2012) with 0.040. However, these results were obtained by evaluating on the entire test set. The rather low correlation result we obtained can be partially explained by the fact that only one judgment of a pair of reference and translation was taken into account. It will be interesting to see how the averaging of the ranks of a translation influences the correlation coefficient.

5 Conclusions and future work

In this paper, a new evaluation metric for MT was introduced, which is based on the comparison of dependency parse trees. The dependency trees were obtained using the WCDG German parser. The reason why we chose this parser was that, due to its architecture, it is able to handle ungrammatical and ambiguous input data. The experiments conducted so far show that using the data made available at the NAACL 2012 WMT workshop, CESM correlates well with the human judgments at the system level. One of the future experiments that we intend to perform is to assess metric quality on the entire evaluation set. Moreover, we plan to compare CESM with other tree-based MT metrics. Furthermore, the WMT12 workshop offers different ranking possibilities, like the ones presented in Bojar et al (2011) and in Lopez (2012). It will be determined how much are the segment level evaluation results influenced by these ranking orders.

One limitation of the proposed metric is that, at the moment it is restricted to translations from any source language to German as a target language. Because of this reason, we plan to extend the metric to other languages and see how well it performs in different settings. In further experiments we also intend to test CESM using statistical based dependency parsers, like the Malt Parser (Nivre et al., 2007) and the MST parser (McDonald et al., 2006), in order to decide whether the choice of parser influences the performance of the metric.

Another approach that we will explore for improving CESM is to compare dependency parse trees using the base form and the part-of-speech of the tokens, instead of the exact lexical match. We will try this approach in order to avoid penalizing lexical variation.

The accuracy of CESM can be further increased by the use of paraphrases, which can be obtained by using a German thesaurus or a lexical resource like GermaNet (Hamp and Feldweg, 1997). Furthermore, a technique like the one described in Owczarzak (2008) can be implemented for generating domain specific paraphrases. The results reported show that the use of this kind of paraphrases in order to produce new references has increased the BLEU score, therefore this is an approach that will be further investigated.

Acknowledgments

This work was funded by the University of Hamburg Doctoral Fellowships in accordance with the Hamburg Act for the Promotion of Young Researchers and Artists (HmbNFG), and the EAMT Project "Using Syntactic and Semantic Information in the Evaluation of Corpus-based Machine Translation".

Reference

O. Bojar, M. Ercegovčević, M Popel and O. Zaidan. 2011. *A Grain of Salt for the WMT Manual Evaluation*. Proceedings of the Sixth Workshop on Statistical Machine Translation.

C. Callison-Burch, M. Osborne and P. Koehn. 2006. *Re-evaluating the Role of Bleu in Machine Translation Research*. Proceedings of EACL-2006.

C. Callison-Burch, P. Koehn, C. Monz, M. Post, R. Soricut and L. Specia. 2012. *Findings of the 2012 Workshop on Statistical Machine Translation*. Proceedings of WMT12.

M. J. Collins. 1999. *Head-driven Statistical Models for Natural Language Parsing*. Ph.D. thesis, University of Pennsylvania.

G. Doddington. 2002. *Automatic Evaluation of Machine Translation Quality Using N-gram Co-Occurrence Statistics*. Proceedings of the 2nd International Conference on Human Language Technology.

K. Foth. 2004. *Writing weighted constraints for large de-pendency grammars*. Recent Advances in De-pendency Grammar, Workshop COLING 2004.

K. Foth, M. Daum and W. Menzel. 2004a. *A broad-coverage parser for German based on defeasible constraints*. KONVENS 2004, Beiträge zur 7, Konferenz zur Verarbeitung natürlicher Sprache, Wien.

K. Foth, M. Daum and W. Menzel. 2004b. *Interactive grammar development with WCDG*. Proc. of the 42nd Annual Meeting of the Association for Com-putational Linguistics.

K. Foth, T. By and W. Menzel. 2006. *Guiding a con-straint dependency parser with supertags*. Proceedings of the 21st Int. Conf. on Computational Linguistics.

M. Fishel, R. Sennrich, M. Popovic and O. Bojar. 2012. *TerrorCat: a translation error categorization-based MT quality metric.* Proceedings of the Seventh Workshop on Statistical Machine Translation.

J. Ganitkevitch, Y. Cao, J. Weese, M. Post and C. Callison-Burch. 2012. *Joshua 4.0: Packing, PRO, and paraphrases.* Proceedings of the Seventh Workshop on Statistical Machine Translation.

J. Gimenez. 2008. *Empirical Machine Translation and its Evaluation.* Ph. D. thesis.

B. Hamp and H. Feldweg. 1997. *GermaNet - a Lexical-Semantic Net for German.* Proc. of ACL workshop Automatic Information Extraction and Building of Lexical Semantic Resources for NLP Applications.

P. Koehn and C. Monz. 2006. *Manual and Automatic Evaluation of Machine Translation between European Languages.* NAACL 2006 Workshop on Statistical Machine Translation.

P. Koehn. 2010. *Statistical Machine Translation.* Cambridge University Press.

S. Kübler and J. Prokic. 2006. *Why is German Dependency Parsing more Reliable than Constituent Parsing?.* Proceedings of the Fifth International Work-shop on Treebanks and Linguistic Theories.

Z. Lin, H. Wang, S. McClean and C. Liu. 2008. *All Common Embedded Subtrees for Measuring Tree Similarity.* International Symposium on Computational Intelligence and Design.

D. Liu and D. Gildea. 2005. *Syntactic Features for Evaluation of Machine Translation.* ACL 2005 Workshop on Intrinsic and Extrinsic Evaluation Measures for Machine Translation and/or Summarization.

A. Lopez. 2012. *Putting human assessments of machine translation systems in order.* Proceedings of the Seventh Workshop on Statistical Machine Translation.

R. McDonald, K. Lerman and F. Pereira. 2006. *Multilingual Dependency Parsing with a Two-Stage Discriminative Parser.* Tenth Conference on Computational Natural Language Learning.

W. Menzel and I. Schröder. 1998. *Decision Procedures for Dependency Parsing Using Graded Constraints.* Workshop On Processing Of Dependency-Based Grammars.

J. Niehues, Y. Zhang, M. Mediani, T. Herrmann, E. Cho and A. Waibel. 2012. *The karlsruhe institute of technology translation systems for the WMT 2012.* Proceedings of the Seventh Workshop on Statistical Machine Translation.

S. Niessen, F. J. Och, G. Leusch and H. Ney. 2000. *An Evaluation Tool for Machine Translation: Fast Evaluation for MT Research.* Proceedings of the 2nd International Conference on Language Resources and Evaluation (LREC).

J. Nivre, J. Hall, J. Nilsson, A. Chanev, G. Eryigit, S. Kübler, S. Marinov and E. Marsi. 2007. *MaltParser: A language-independent system for data-driven dependency parsing.* Natural Language Engineering.

K. Owczarzak, J. van Genabith and A. Way. 2007. *Dependency-based automatic evaluation for machine translation.* Proceedings of SSST, NAACL-HLT 2007 / AMTA Workshop on Syntax and Structure in Statistical Translation.

K. Owczarzak. 2008. *A Novel Dependency-Based Evaluation Metric for Machine Translation,* Ph.D. thesis.

K. Papineni, S. Roukos, T. Ward and W.-J. Zhu. 2001. *Bleu: a method for automatic evaluation of machine translation.* RC22176 (Technical Report), IBM T.J. Watson Research Center.

M. Popovic. 2012. *Class error rates for evaluation of machine translation output.* Proceedings of the Seventh Workshop on Statistical Machine Translation.

I. Schröder, W. Menzel, K. Foth and M. Schulz. 2000. *Modeling dependency grammar with restricted constraints.* Traitement Automatique des Langues.

I. Schröder, H. Pop, W. Menzel and K. Foth. 2001. *Learning grammar weights using genetic algorithms.* Proceedings Euroconference Recent Advances in Natural Language Processing.

I. Schröder. 2002. *Natural Language Parsing with Graded Constraints.* Ph.D. thesis, Dept. of Computer Science, University of Hamburg.

D. Vilar. 2012. *DFKI's SMT system for WMT 2012.* Proceedings of the Seventh Workshop on Statistical Machine Translation.

D. Zeman. 2012. *Data issues of the multilingual translation matrix.* Proceedings of the Seventh Workshop on Statistical Machine Translation.

K. Zhang and D. Shasha. 1989. *Simple fast algorithms for the editing distance between trees and related problems.* SIAM Journal on Computing.

High-quality Training Data Selection using Latent Topics for Graph-based Semi-supervised Learning

Akiko Eriguchi
Ochanomizu University
2-1-1 Otsuka Bunkyo-ku Tokyo, Japan
g0920506@is.ocha.ac.jp

Ichiro Kobayashi
Ochanomizu University
2-1-1 Otsuka Bunkyo-ku Tokyo, Japan
koba@is.ocha.ac.jp

Abstract

In a multi-class document categorization using graph-based semi-supervised learning (GBSSL), it is essential to construct a proper graph expressing the relation among nodes and to use a reasonable categorization algorithm. Furthermore, it is also important to provide high-quality correct data as training data. In this context, we propose a method to construct a similarity graph by employing both surface information and latent information to express similarity between nodes and a method to select high-quality training data for GBSSL by means of the PageRank algorithm. Experimenting on Reuters-21578 corpus, we have confirmed that our proposed methods work well for raising the accuracy of a multi-class document categorization.

1 Introduction

Graph-based semi-supervised learning (GBSSL) algorithm is known as a useful and promising technique in natural language processings. It has been widely used for solving many document categorization problems (Zhu and Ghahramani, 2002; Zhu et al., 2003; Subramanya and Bilmes, 2008).

A good accuracy of GBSSL depends on success in dealing with three crucial issues: graph construction, selection of high-quality training data, and categorization algorithm. We particularly focus on the former two issues in our study.

In a graph-based categorization of documents, a graph is constructed based on a certain relation between nodes (i.e. documents). It is similarity that is often used to express the relation between nodes in a graph. We think of two types of similarity: the one is between surface information obtained by document vector (Salton and McGill, 1983) and the other is between latent information obtained by word probabilistic distribution (Latent Dirichlet Allocation (Blei et al., 2003)). Here, we propose a method. We use both surface information and latent information at the ratio of $(1-\alpha) : \alpha (0 \leq \alpha \leq 1)$ to construct a similarity graph for GBSSL, and we investigate the optimal α for raising the accuracy in GBSSL.

In selecting high-quality training data, it is important to take two aspects of data into consideration: quantity and quality. The more the training data are, the better the accuracy becomes. We do not always, however, have a large quantity of training data. In such a case, the quality of training data is generally a key for better accuracy. It is required to assess the quality of training data exactly. Now, we propose another method. We use the PageRank algorithm (Brin and Page, 1998) to select high-quality data, which have a high centrality in a similarity graph of training data (i.e. labeled data) in each category.

We apply our methods to solving the problem of a multi-class document categorization. We introduce PRBEP (precision recall break even point) as a measure which is popular in the area of information retrieval. We evaluate the results of experiments for each category and for the whole category. We confirm that the way of selecting the high-quality training data from data on a similarity graph based on both surface information and latent information is superior to that of selecting from a graph based on just surface information or latent information.

2 Related studies

Graph-based semi-supervised learning has recently been studied so much and applied to many applications (Subramanya and Bilmes, 2008; Subramanya and Bilmes, 2009; Subramanya et al., 2010; Dipanjan and Petrov, 2011; Dipanjan and Smith, 2012; Whitney and Sarkar, 2012).

Subramanya and Bilmes (2008; 2009) have proposed a soft-clustering method using GBSSL and have shown that their own method is better than the other main clustering methods of those days. Subramanya et al. (2010) have also applied their method to solve the problem of tagging and have shown that it is useful. Dipanjan and Petrov (2011) have applied a graph-based label propagation method to solve the problem of part-of-speech tagging. They have shown that their proposed method exceeds a state-of-the-art baseline of those days. Dipanjan and Smith (2012) have also applied GBSSL to construct compact natural language lexicons. To achieve compactness, they used the characteristics of a graph. Whitney and Sarkar (2012) have proposed the bootstrapping learning method in which a graph propagation algorithm is adopted.

There are two main issues in GBSSL: the one is the way of constructing a graph to propagate labels, and the other is the way of propagating labels. It is essential to construct a good graph in GBSSL (Zhu, 2005). On the one hand, graph construction is a key to success of any GBSSL. On the other hand, as for semi-supervised learning, it is quite important to select better training data (i.e. labeled data), because the effect of learning will be changed by the data we select as training data.

Considering the above mentioned, in our study, we focus on the way of selecting training data so as to be well propagated in a graph. We use the PageRank algorithm to select high-quality training data and evaluate how our proposed method influences the way of document categorization.

3 Text classification based on a graph

The details of our proposed GBSSL method in a multi-class document categorization are as follows.

3.1 Graph construction

In our study, we use a weighted undirected graph $G = (V, E)$ whose node and edge represent a document and the similarity between nodes, respectively. Similarity is regarded as weight. V and E represent nodes and edges in a graph, respectively. A graph G can be represented as an adjacency matrix, and $w_{ij} \in \boldsymbol{W}$ represents the similarity between nodes i and j. In particular, in the case of GBSSL method, the similarity between nodes are formed as $w_{ij} = sim(\boldsymbol{x}_i, \boldsymbol{x}_j)\delta(j \in K(i))$. $K(i)$ is a set of i's k-nearest neighbors, and $\delta(z)$ is 1 if z is true, otherwise 0.

3.2 Similarity in a graph

Generally speaking, when we construct a graph to represent some relation among documents, cosine similarity (sim_{cos}) of document vectors is adopted as a similarity measure based on surface information. In our study, we add the similarity (sim_{JS}) based on latent information and the similarity (sim_{cos}) based on surface information in the proportion of $\alpha : (1-\alpha)(0 \leq \alpha \leq 1)$. We define the sum of sim_{JS} and sim_{cos} as sim_{nodes} (see, Eq. (1)).

In Eq. (1), P and Q represent the latent topic distributions of documents S and T, respectively. We use Latent Dirichlet Allocation (LDA) (Blei et al., 2003) to estimate the latent topic distribution of a document, and we use a measure Jensen-Shannon divergence (D_{JS}) for the similarity between topic distributions. Incidentally, sim_{JS} in Eq (1) is expressed by Eq. (2).

$$\begin{aligned} sim_{nodes}(S,T) &\equiv \alpha * sim_{JS}(P,Q) \\ &+(1-\alpha) * sim_{cos}(tfidf(S), tfidf(T)) \quad (1) \end{aligned}$$

$$sim_{JS}(P,Q) \equiv 1 - D_{JS}(P,Q) \quad (2)$$

3.3 Selection of training data

We use the graph-based document summarization methods (Erkan and Radev, 2004; Kitajima and Kobayashi, 2012) in order to select high-quality training data. Erkan and Radev (2004) proposed a multi-document summarization method using the PageRank algorithm (Brin and Page, 1998) to extract important sentences. They showed that it is useful to extract the important sentences which have higher PageRank scores in a similarity graph of sentences. Then, Kitajima and Kobayashi (2012) have expanded the idea of Erkan and Radev's. They introduced latent information to extract important sentences. They call their own method TopicRank.

We adopt TopicRank method in our study. In order to get high-quality training data, we first construct a similarity graph of training data in each category, and then compute a TopicRank score for each training datum in every category graph. We employ the data with a high TopicRank score as training data in GBSSL.

In TopicRank method, Kitajima and Kobayashi (2012) regard a sentence as a node in a graph on surface information and latent information. The TopicRank score of each sentence is computed by Eq. (3). Each sentence is ranked by its TopicRank score. In Eq. (3), d indicates a damping factor. We, however, deal with documents, so we replace a sentence with a document (i.e. sentences) as a node in a graph. In Eq. (3), N indicates total number of documents, $adj[u]$ indicates the adjoining nodes of document u.

$$r(u) = d \sum_{v \in adj[u]} \frac{sim_{nodes}(u,v)}{\sum_{z \in adj[v]} sim_{nodes}(z,v)} r(u) + \frac{1-d}{N} \quad (3)$$

3.4 Label propagation

We use the label propagation method (Zhu et al., 2003; Zhou et al., 2004) in order to categorize documents. It is one of graph-based semi-supervised learnings. It estimates the value of label based on the assumption that the nodes linked to each other in a graph should belong to the same category. Here, $\boldsymbol{W}$ indicates an adjacency matrix. l indicates the number of training data among all n nodes in a graph. The estimation values $\boldsymbol{f}$ for n nodes are obtained as the solution (Eq. (6)) of the following objective function of an optimal problem (Eq. (4)). The first term in Eq. (4) expresses the deviation between an estimation value and a correct value of training data. The second term in Eq. (4) expresses the difference between the estimation values of the nodes which are next to another in the adjacency graph. $\lambda(>0)$ is a parameter balancing both of the terms. Eq. (4) is transformed into Eq. (5) by means of $\boldsymbol{L}$. $\boldsymbol{L}(\equiv \boldsymbol{D}-\boldsymbol{W})$ is called the Laplacian matrix. $\boldsymbol{D}$ is a diagonal matrix, each diagonal element of which is equal to the sum of elements in $\boldsymbol{W}$'s each row (or column).

$$J(\boldsymbol{f}) = \sum_{i=1}^{l} (y^{(i)} - f^{(i)})^2 + \lambda \sum_{i<j} w^{(i,j)} (f^{(i)} - f^{(j)})^2 \quad (4)$$

$$= ||\boldsymbol{y} - \boldsymbol{f}||_2^2 + \lambda \boldsymbol{f}^T \boldsymbol{L} \boldsymbol{f} \quad (5)$$

$$\boldsymbol{f} = (\boldsymbol{I} + \lambda \boldsymbol{L})^{-1} \boldsymbol{y} \quad (6)$$

4 Experiment

4.1 Experimental settings

We use Reuters-21578 corpus data set[1] collected from the Reuters newswire in 1987 as target documents for a multi-class document categorization. It consists of English news articles (classified into 135 categories). We use the "ModApte" split to get training documents (i.e. labeled data) and test documents (i.e. unlabeled data), extract documents which have only its title and text body, and apply the stemming and the stop-word removal processes to the documents. Then, following the experimental settings of Subramanya and Bilmes (2008)[2] , we use 10 most frequent categories out of the 135 potential topic categories: *earn, acq, grain, wheat, money-fx, crude, trade, interest, ship,* and *corn*. We apply the one-versus-the-rest method to give a category label to each test document. Labels are given when the estimation values of each document label exceed each of the predefined thresholds.

We prepare 11 data sets. Each data set consists of 3299 common test data and 20 training data. We use 11 kinds of categories of training data: the above mentioned 10 categories and a category (*other*) which indicates 125 categories except 10 categories. The categories of 20 training data are randomly chosen only if one of the 11 categories is chosen at least once.

Selecting high-quality training data, we use the Gibbs sampling for latent topic estimation in LDA. The number of iteration is 200. The number of latent topics in the target documents is decided by averaging 10 trials of estimation with perplexity (see, Eq. (7)). Here, N is the number of all words in the target documents. w_{mn} is the n-th word in the m-th document. θ is an occurrence probability of the latent topics for the documents. ϕ is an occurrence probability of the words for every latent topic.

$$P(\boldsymbol{w}) = exp(-\frac{1}{N} \sum_{mn} log(\sum_{z} \theta_{mz} \phi_{zw_{mn}})) \quad (7)$$

In each category, a similarity graph is constructed for the TopicRank method. The number of nodes (i.e. $|V_{category}|$) in a graph corresponds to

[1] http://www.daviddlewis.com/resources/testcollections/reuters21578/

[2] Our data sets lack any tags and information excluding a title and a text body. Therefore, we cannot directly compare with Subramanya and Bilmes' results.

the total number of training data in each category, and the number of edges is $E = (|V_{category}| \times |V_{category}|)$. So, the graph is a complete graph. The parameter α in Eq (1) is varied from 0.0 to 1.0 every 0.1. We regard the average of TopicRank scores after 5 trials as the TopicRank score of each document. The number of training data in each category is decided in each target data set. We adopt training data with a higher TopicRank score from the top up to the predefined number.

In label propagation, we construct another kind of similarity graph. The number of nodes in a graph is $|V_{l+u}| = n(= 3319)$, and the similarity between nodes is based on only surface information (in the case of $\alpha = 0$ in Eq. (1)). The parameter k in the k-nearest neighbors method is $k \in \{2, 10, 50, 100, 250, 500, 1000, 2000, n\}$, the parameter λ in the label propagation method, is $\lambda \in \{1, 0.1, 0.01, 1e-4, 1e-8\}$. Using one of the 11 data sets, we decide a pair of optimal parameters (k, λ) for each category. We categorize the remaining 10 data sets by means of the decided parameters. Then, we obtain the value of precision recall break even point (PRBEP) and the average of PRBEP in each category. The value of PRBEP is that of precision or recall at the time when the former is equal to the latter. It is often used as an index to measure the ability of information retrieval.

4.2 Result

Table 1 shows a pair of the optimal parameters (k, λ) in each category corresponding to the value of α ranging from 0.0 to 1.0 every 0.1. Figures from 1 to 10 show the experimental results in using these parameters in each category. The horizontal axis indicates the value of α and the vertical axis indicates the value of PRBEP. Each figure shows the average of PRBEP in each category after 10 trials for each α. Fig. 11 shows how the relative ratio of PRBEP changes corresponding to each α in each category, when we let the PRBEP at $\alpha = 0$ an index 100. Fig. 12 shows the macro average of PRBEP after 10 trials in the whole category corresponding to each α. Error bars indicate the standard deviations.

In all figures, the case at $\alpha = 0$ means that only surface information is used for selecting the training data. The case at $\alpha = 1$ means that only latent information is used. The other cases at $\alpha \neq 0$ or 1 mean that both latent information and surface information are mixed at the ratio of $\alpha : (1 - \alpha)$ $(0 < \alpha < 1)$.

First, we tell about Fig. 1-10. On the one hand, in Fig. 4, 5, 6, 8, 10, the PRBEPs at $\alpha \neq 0$ are greater than that at $\alpha = 0$, although the PRBEP at $\alpha = 1$ is less than that at $\alpha = 0$ in Fig. 4. On the other hand, in Fig. 2, 7, the PRBEPs at $\alpha \neq 0$ are less than that at $\alpha = 0$. In Fig. 1, 3, 9, the PRBEPs at $\alpha \neq 0$ fluctuate widely or narrowly around that at $\alpha = 0$. In addition, the PRBEPs at $\alpha = 0$ range from 7.7 to 74.3 and those at $\alpha = 1$ range from 8.0 to 72.6 in all 10 figures. It is hard to find significant correlation between PRBEP and α.

Secondly, in Fig. 11, some curves show an increasing trend and others show a decreasing trend. At best, the maximum value is three times as large as that at $\alpha = 0$. At worst, the minimum is one-fifth. Indexes at $\alpha \neq 0$ are greater than or equal to an index 100 at $\alpha = 0$ in most categories.

Finally, in Fig. 12, the local maximums are 46.2, 46.9, 45.0 respectively at $\alpha = 0.2, 0.6, 0.9$. The maximum is 46.9 at $\alpha = 0.6$. The minimum value of the macro average is 35.8 at $\alpha = 0$, though the macro average at $\alpha = 1$ is 43.4. Hence, the maximum macro average is greater than that at $\alpha = 1$ by 3.5% and still greater than that at $\alpha = 0$ by 11.1%. The macro average at $\alpha = 1$ is greater than that at $\alpha = 0$ by 7.6%. Furthermore, the macro average increases monotonically from 35.8 to 46.2 as α increases from 0.0 to 0.2. When α is more than 0.2, the macro averages fluctuate within the range from 40.3 to 46.9. It follows that the macro average values at $0.1 \leq \alpha \leq 1$ are greater than that at $\alpha = 0$. What is more important, the macro averages at $\alpha = 0.2, 0.4, 0.6, 0.7, 0.9$ are greater than that at $\alpha = 1$ and of course greater than that at $\alpha = 0$.

5 Discussion

Looking at each Fig. 1-10, each optimal α at which PRBEP is the maximum is different and not uniform in respective categories. So, we cannot simply tell a specific ratio of balancing both information (i.e. surface information and latent information) which gives the best accuracy.

From a total point of view, however, we can see a definite trend or relationship. In Fig. 11, we can see the upward tendency of PREBP in half of categories. Indexes of the PRBEP at $\alpha \geq 0.1$ are greater than or equal to 100 in most categories.

Table 1: the optimal parameters (k, λ) for each category

Category\\α	0.0	0.1	0.2	0.3	0.4	0.5	0.6	0.7	0.8	0.9	1.0
earn	(500, 1)	(50, 1)	(1000, 1)	(1000, 1)	(50, 1)	(50, 1)	(50, 1)	(50, 1)	(50, 1)	(50, 1)	(50, 1)
acq	(100, 0.01)	(100, 0.01)	(100, 0.01)	(2, 1)	(100, 0.01)	(100, 0.01)	(100, 1e-8)	(100, 1e-8)	(100, 1e-8)	(100, 1e-8)	(100, 1e-8)
money-fx	(250, 0.01)	(100, 1e-8)	(10, 1e-4)	(100, 1e-8)	(2, 0.1)	(2, 0.1)	(2, 1e-8)	(250, 1e-8)	(2, 0.1)	(2, 1e-8)	(250, 1e-8)
grain	(250, 0.1)	(2000, 1e-4)	(100, 1)	(250, 0.1)	(100, 1)	(50, 1)	(250, 1)	(50, 1)	(50, 1)	(50, 1)	(100, 1)
crude	(50, 0.1)	(2, 1)	(250, 0.01)	(50, 1e-8)	(10, 0.01)	(250, 0.01)	(250, 0.01)	(250, 1e-8)	(10, 0.01)	(250, 0.01)	(250, 0.01)
trade	(2, 1)	(10, 0.1)	(50, 0.01)	(10, 1e-8)	(10, 1e-8)	(10, 1e-8)	(50, 1e-8)	(10, 1e-8)	(10, 1e-4)	(10, 0.1)	(10, 0.1)
interest	(10, 1)	(50, 1e-8)	(50, 1e-8)	(10, 1)	(2, 0.1)	(250, 1e-8)	(250, 0.01)	(250, 0.01)	(2, 1)	(2, 0.1)	(500, 1e-8)
ship	(3318, 1)	(50, 1)	(50, 1)	(250, 0.1)	(50, 0.1)	(50, 0.1)	(50, 1e-8)	(50, 1e-8)	(100, 0.1)	(100, 0.1)	(50, 0.01)
wheat	(500, 1e-8)	(500, 1e-8)	(250, 1e-8)	(500, 1e-8)	(500, 0.01)	(1000, 0.01)	(500, 1e-8)	(250, 1e-8)	(250, 1e-8)	(250, 1e-8)	(250, 1e-8)
corn	(10, 1e-8)	(100, 1e-8)	(250, 1e-8)	(10, 1e-8)	(250, 1e-8)	(250, 1e-4)	(500, 1e-8)	(100, 1e-8)	(250, 1e-8)	(50, 0.01)	(250, 1e-4)

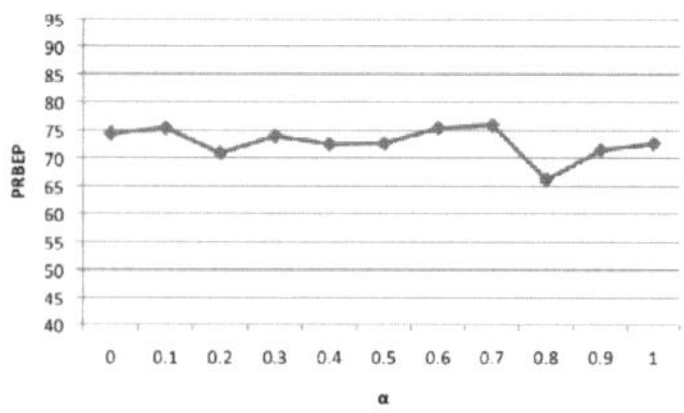

Figure 1: *earn*

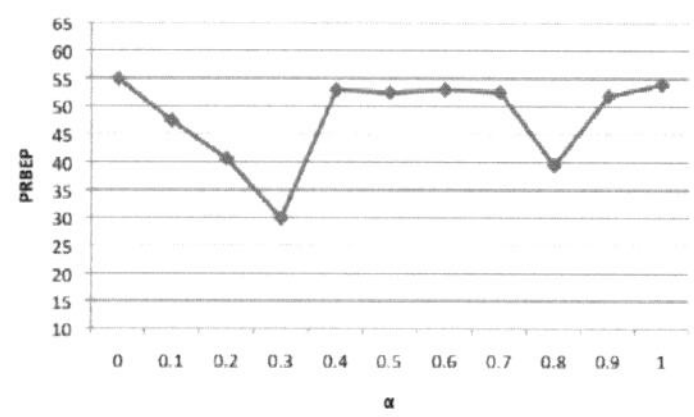

Figure 2: *acq*

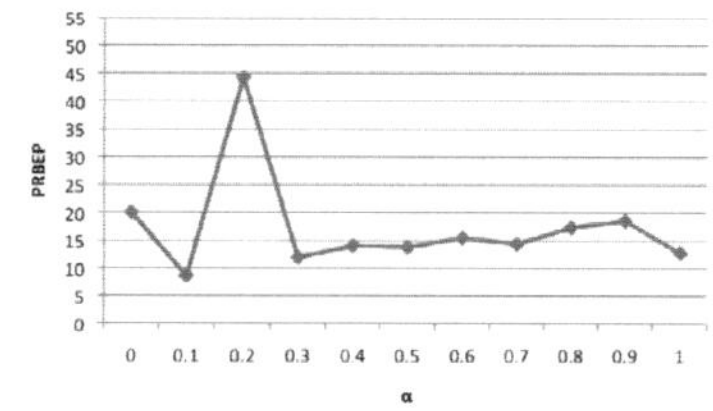

Figure 3: *money-fx*

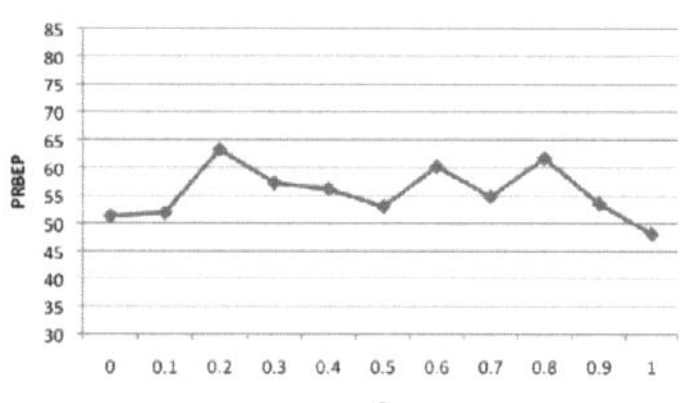

Figure 4: *grain*

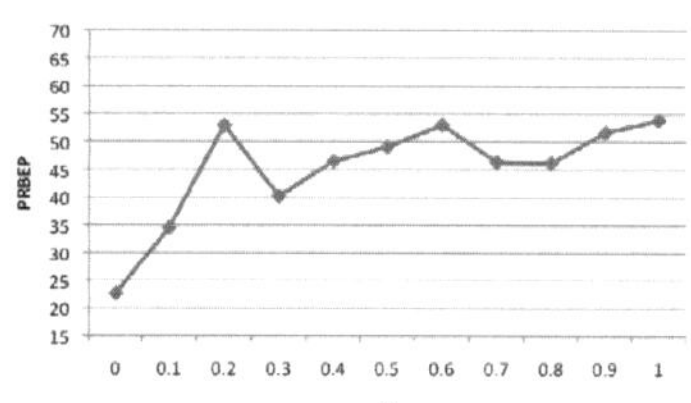

Figure 5: *crude*

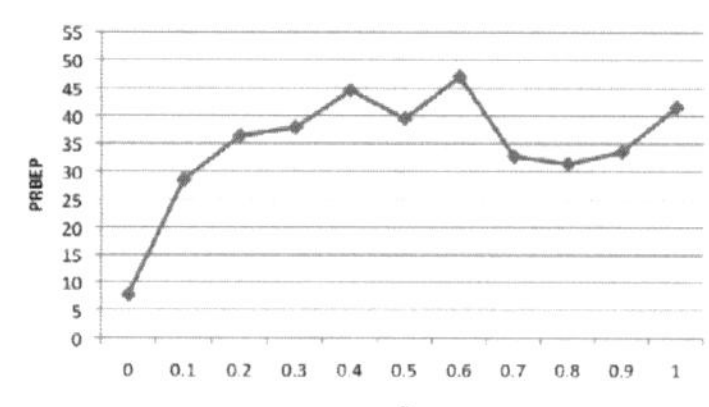

Figure 6: *trade*

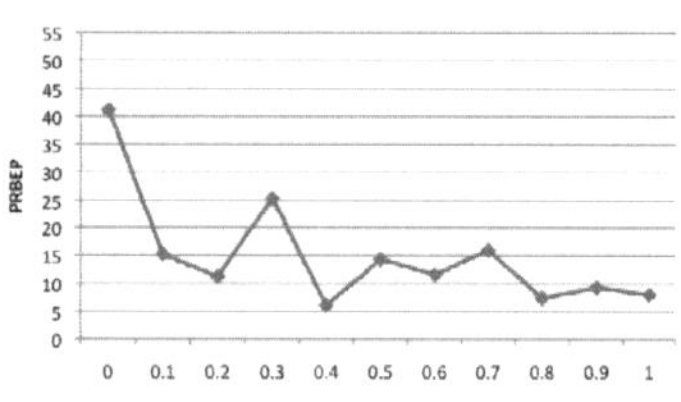

Figure 7: *interest*

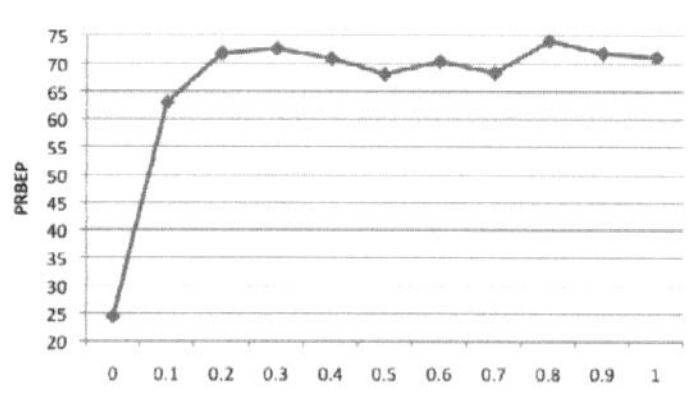

Figure 8: *ship*

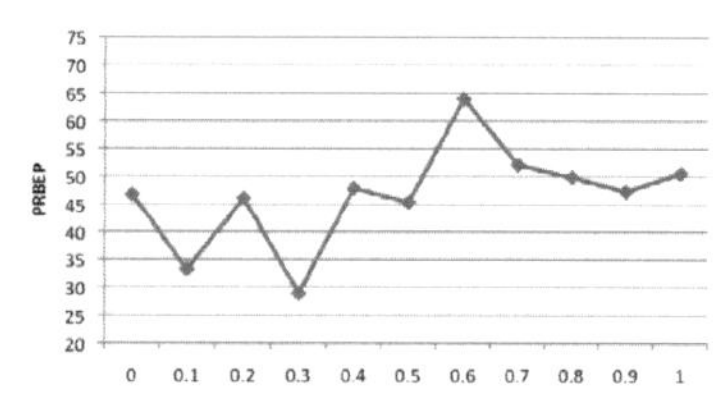

Figure 9: *wheat*

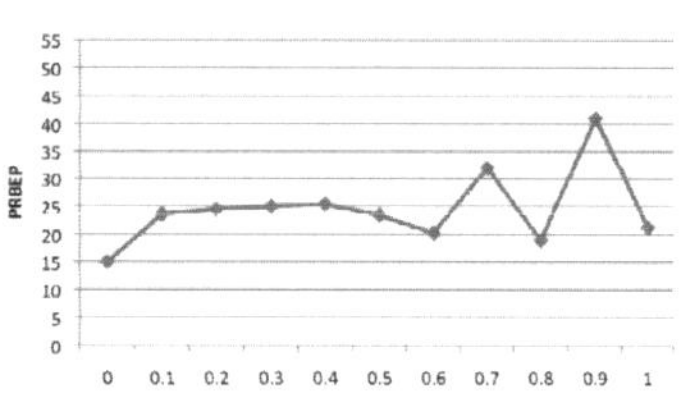

Figure 10: *corn*

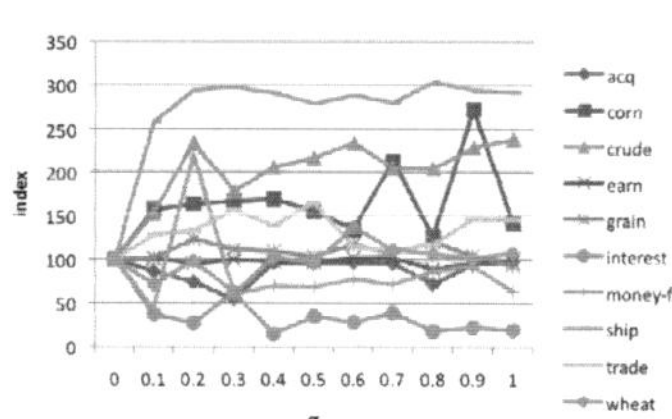

Figure 11: Relative value

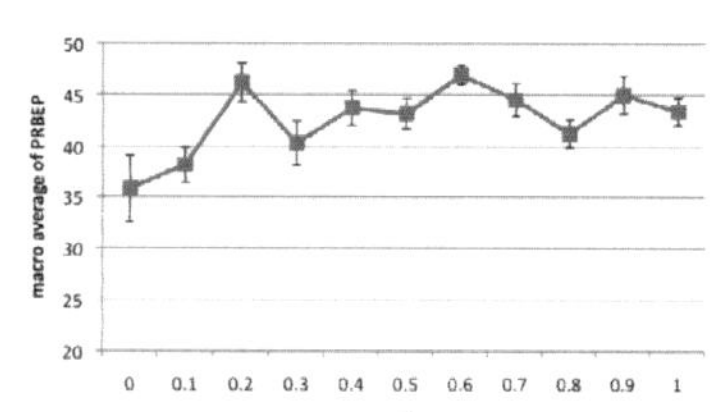

Figure 12: Macro average

The macro average of the whole category is shown in Fig. 12. Regarding the macro average at $\alpha = 0$ as a baseline, the macro average at $\alpha = 1$ is greater than that at $\alpha = 0$ by 7.6% and still more, the maximum at $\alpha = 0.6$ is greater by 11.1%. Besides, five macro averages at $0.1 \leq \alpha \leq 1$ are greater than that at $\alpha - 1$. Therefore, we can say that using latent information gives a higher accuracy than using only surface information and that using both information gives a higher accuracy than using only latent information. So, if a proper α is decided, we will get a better accuracy.

6 Conclusion

We have proposed methods to construct a similarity graph based on both surface information and latent information and to select high-quality training data for GBSSL. Through experiments, we have found that using both information gives a better accuracy than using either only surface information or only latent information. We used the PageRank algorithm in the selection of high-quality training data. In this condition, we have confirmed that our proposed methods are useful for raising the accuracy of a multi-class document categorization using GBSSL in the whole category.

Our future work is as follows. We will verify in other data corpus sets that the selection of high-quality training data with both information gives a better accuracy and that the optimal α is around 0.6. We will revise the way of setting a pair of the optimal parameters (k, λ) and use latent information in the process of label propagation.

References

David M. Blei, Andrew Y. Ng, and Michael I. Jordan. 2003. Latent dirichlet allocation. *Journal of Machine Learning Research.*

Sergey Brin and Lawrence Page. 1998. The Anatomy of a Large-scale Hypertextual Web Search Engine. *Computer Networks and ISDN Systems*, pages 107–117.

Das Dipanjan and Noah A. Smith. 2012. Graph-based lexicon expansion with sparsity-inducing penalties. In *Proceedings of the 2012 Conference of the North American Chapter of the Association for Computational Linguistics: Human Language Technologies*, NAACL HLT '12, pages 677–687.

Das Dipanjan and Slav Petrov. 2011. Unsupervised Part-of-Speech Tagging with Bilingual Graph-Based Projections. In *Proceedings of the 49th Annual Meeting of the Association for Computational Linguistics: Human Language Technologies* - Vol. 1, pages 600–609.

Güneş Erkan and Dragomir R. Radev. 2004. LexRank: Graph-based Lexical Centrality as Salience in Text Summarization. *Journal of Artificial Intelligence Research 22*, pages 457-479.

Güneş Erkan. 2006. Language Model-Based Document Clustering Using Random Walks. *Association for Computational Linguistics*, pages 479–486.

Risa Kitajima and Ichiro Kobayashi. 2012. Multiple-document Summarization baed on a Graph constructed based on Latent Information. In *Proceedings of ARG Web intelligence and interaction*, 2012-WI2-1-21.

Gerard Salton and Michael J. McGill. 1983. Introduction to Modern Information Retrieval. McGraw-Hill.

Amarnag Subramanya and Jeff Bilmes. 2008. Soft-Supervised Learning for Text Classification. In *Proceedings of the 2008 Conference on Empirical Methods in Natural Language Processing*, pages 1090–1099.

Amarnag Subramanya and Jeff Bilmes. 2009. Entropic graph regularization in non-parametric semi-supervised classification. In *Proceedings of NIPS.*

Amarnag Subramanya, Slav Petrov and Fernando Pereira. 2010. Efficient graph-based semi-supervised learning of structured tagging models. In *Proceedings of the 2010 Conference on Empirical Methods in Natural Language Processing*, pages 167–176.

Dengyong Zhou, Oliver Bousquet, Thomas Navin Lal, Jason Weston, and Bernhard Schölkopf. 2004. Learning with Local and Global Consistency. In *NIPS 16.*

Xiaojin Zhu and Zoubin Ghahramani. 2002. Learning from Labeled and Unlabeled Data with Label Propagation. Technical report, Carnegie Mellon University.

Xiaojin Zhu, Zoubin Ghahramani, and John Lafferty. 2003. Semi-Supervised Learning Using Gaussian Fields and Harmonic Functions. In *Proceedigns of the International Conference on Machine Learning (ICML).*

Xiaojin Zhu. 2005. Semi-Supervised Learning with Graphs. PhD thesis, Carnegie Mellon University.

Max Whitney and Anoop Sarkar. 2012. Bootstrapping via Graph Propagation. *The 50th Annual Meeting of the Association for Computational Linguistics.*

Simple, readable sub-sentences

Sigrid Klerke
Centre for Language Technology
University of Copenhagen
sigridklerke@gmail.com

Anders Søgaard
Centre for Language Technology
University of Copenhagen
soegaard@hum.ku.dk

Abstract

We present experiments using a new unsupervised approach to automatic text simplification, which builds on sampling and ranking via a loss function informed by readability research. The main idea is that a loss function can distinguish good simplification candidates among randomly sampled sub-sentences of the input sentence. Our approach is rated as equally grammatical and beginner reader appropriate as a supervised SMT-based baseline system by native speakers, but our setup performs more radical changes that better resembles the variation observed in human generated simplifications.

1 Introduction

As a field of research in NLP, text simplification (TS) has gained increasing attention recently, primarily for English text, but also for Brazilian Portuguese (Specia, 2010; Aluísio et al., 2008), Dutch (Daelemans et al., 2004), Spanish (Drndarevic and Saggion, 2012), Danish (Klerke and Søgaard, 2012), French (Seretan, 2012) and Swedish (Rybing and Smith, 2009; Decker, 2003). Our experiments use Danish text which is similar to English in that it has a deep orthography making it hard to map between letters and sounds. Danish has a relatively free word order and sparse morfology.

TS can help readers with below average reading skills access information and may supply relevant training material, which is crucial for developing reading skills. However, manual TS is as expensive as translation, which is a key limiting factor on the availability of easy-to-read material. One of the persistent chalenges of TS is that different interventions are called for depending on the target reader population. Automatic TS is an effective way to counter these limitations.

2 Approach

Definitions of TS typically reflect varying target reader populations and the methods studied. For our purposes we define TS to include any operation on the linguistic structure and content of a text, intended to produce new text, which

1. has semantic content similar to (a part of) the original text
2. requires less cognitive effort to decode and understand by a target reader, compared to the original text.

Operations on linguistic content may include deletion, reordering and insertion of content, paraphrasing concepts, resolving references, etc., while typography and layout are excluded as non-linguistic properties.

We cast the problem of generating a more readable sentence from an input as a problem of choosing a reasonable sub-sentence from the words present in the original. The corpus-example below illustrates how a simplified sentence can be embedded as scattered parts of a non-simplified sentence. The words in bold are the common parts which make up almost the entire human generated simplification and constitutes a suitable simplification on its own.

Original: **Der er målt** hvad der bliver betegnet som abnormt **stor**e **mængde**r af **radioaktivt materiale i hav**vand **nær** det jordskælvsramte **atomkraftværk i Japan .**

What has been termed **a**n abnormally **large amount of radioactivity has been measured in sea** water **near the nuclear power plant** that was hit by earthquakes **in Japan**

Simplified: **Der er målt** en **stor mængde radioaktivt materiale i hav**et **nær atom-kraftværk**et Fukushima **i Japan .**

A large amount of radioactivity has been measured in the **sea near the nuclear power plant** Fukushima **in Japan**

To generate candidate sub-sentences we use a random deletion procedure in combination with general dependency-based heuristics for conserving main sentence constituents, and then introduce a loss-function for choosing between candidates. Since we avoid relying on a specialized parallel corpus or a simplification grammar, which can be expensive to create, the method is especially relevant for under-resourced languages and organizations. Although we limit rewriting to deletions, the space of possible candidates grows exponentially with the length of the input sentence, prohibiting exhaustive candidate generation, which is why we chose to sample the deletions randomly. However, to increase the chance of sampling *good* candidates, we restrict the search space under the assumption that some general patterns apply, namely, that the main verb and subject should always be kept, negations should be kept and that if something is kept that originally had objects, those objects should also be kept. Another way in which we restrict the candidate space is by splitting long sentences. Some clauses are simple to identify and extract, like relative clauses, and doing so can dramatically reduce sentence length. Both simple deletions and extraction of clauses can be observed in professionally simplified text. (Medero, 2011; Klerke, 2012)

The next section positions this research in the context of related work. Section 4 presents the experimental setup including generation and evaluation. In Section 5, the results are presented and discussed and, finally, concluding remarks and future perspectives are presented in the last section.

3 Related work

Approaches for automatic TS traditionally focus on lexical substitution (De Belder and Moens, 2012; Specia et al., 2012; Yatskar et al., 2010), on identifying re-write rules at sentence level either manually (Chandrasekar et al., 1996; Carroll et al., 1999; Canning et al., 2000; Siddharthan, 2010; Siddharthan, 2011; Seretan, 2012) or automatically from parallel corpora (Woodsend and Lapata, 2011; Coster and Kauchak, 2011; Zhu et al., 2010) and possibly learning cues for when to apply such changes (Petersen and Ostendorf, 2007; Medero, 2011; Bott et al., 2012).

Chandrasekar et al. (1996) propose a structural approach, which uses syntactic cues to recover relative clauses and appositives. Sentence level syntactic re-writing has since seen a variety of manually constructed general sentence splitting rules, designed to operate both on dependencies and phrase structure trees, and typically including lexical cues (Siddharthan, 2011; Heilman and Smith, 2010; Canning et al., 2000). Similar rules have been created from direct inspection of simplification corpora (Decker, 2003; Seretan, 2012) and discovered automatically from large scale aligned corpora (Woodsend and Lapata, 2011; Zhu et al., 2010).

In our experiment we apply few basic sentence splitting rules as a pre-processing technique before using an over-generating random deletion approach.

Carroll et al. (1999) perform lexical substitution from frequency counts and eliminate anaphora by resolving and replacing the referring expressions with the entity referred to. Their system further include compound sentence splitting and rewriting of passive sentences to active ones (Canning et al., 2000). Research into lexical simplification remains an active topic. De Belder and Moens (2012; Specia et al. (2012) are both recent publications of new resources for evaluating lexical simplification in English consisting of lists of synonyms ranked by human judges. Another type of resource is graded word-lists as described in Brooke et al. (2012). Annotator agreement and comparisons so far shows that it is easy to overfit to reflect individual annotator and domain differences that are not of relevance to generalized systems.

In a minimally supervised setup, our TS approach can be modified to include lexical simplifications as part of the random generation process. This would require a broad coverage list of words and simpler synonyms, which could for instance be extracted from a parallel corpus like the DSim corpus.

For the majority of research in automatic TS the question of what constitutes cognitive load is not discussed. An exception is Siddharthan and Katsos (2012), who seek to isolate the psycholinguistically motivated notions of sentence comprehension from sentence acceptability by actually measuring the effect of TS on cognition on a small scale.

Readability research is a line of research that is more directly concerned with the nature of cognitive load in reading building on insights from psycholinguistics. One goal is to develop techniques and metrics for assessing the readability of unseen text. Such metrics are used as a tool for teachers and publishers, but existing standard metrics (like Flesch-Kincaid (Flesch, 1948) and LIX (Bjornsson, 1983)) were designed and optimized for easy manual application to human written text, requiring thehuman reader to assess that the text is congruent and coherent. More recent methods promise to be applicable to unassessed text. Language modeling in particular has shown to be a robust and informative component of systems for assessing text readability (Schwarm and Ostendorf, 2005; Vajjala and Meurers, 2012) as it is better suited to evaluate grammaticality than standard metrics. We use language modeling alongside traditional metrics for selecting good simplification candidates.

4 Experiments

4.1 Baseline Systems

We used the original input text and the human simplified text from the sentence aligned DSim corpus which consist of 48k original and manually simplified sentences of Danish news wire text (Klerke and Søgaard, 2012) as reference in the evaluations. In addition we trained a statistical machine translation (SMT) simplification system, in effect translating from normal news wire text to simplified news. To train an SMT system, a large resource of aligned parallel text and a language model of the target language are needed. We combined the 25 million words Danish Korpus 2000[1] with the entire 1.75 million words unaligned DSim corpus (Klerke and Søgaard, 2012) to build the language model[2]. Including both corpora gives better coverage and assigns lower average ppl and a simlar difference in average ppl between the two sides of a held out part of the DSim corpus compared to using only the simplified part of DSim for the language model. Following Coster and Kauchak (2011), we used the phrase-based SMT Moses (Koehn et al., 2007), with GIZA++ word-alignment (Och and Ney, 2000) and phrase tables learned from the sentence aligned portion of the DSim corpus.

[1]http://korpus.dsl.dk/korpus2000/engelsk_hovedside

[2]The LM was a 5-gram Knesser-Ney smoothed lowercase model, built using IRSTLM (Federico et al., 2008)

4.2 Experimental setup

Three system variants were set up to generate simplified output from the original news wire of the development and test partitions of the DSim corpus. The texts were dependency-parsed using Bohnet's parser (Bohnet, 2010) trained on the Danish Treebank[3] (Kromann, 2003) with default settings[4].

1. **Split** only performed simple sentence splitting.
2. **Sample** over-generated candidates by sampling the heuristically restricted space of random lexical deletions and ranking candidates with a loss function.
3. **Combined** is a combination of the two, applying the sampling procedure of Sample to the split sentences from Split.

Sentence Splitting We implemented sentence splitting to extract relative clauses, as marked by the dependency relation `rel`, coordinated clauses, `coord`, and conjuncts, `conj`, when at least a verb and a noun is left in each part of the split. Only splits resulting in sentences of more than three words were considered. Where applicable, referred entities were included in the extracted sentence by using the dependency analysis to extract the subtree of the former head of the new sentence[5]. In case of more than one possibility, the split resulting in the most balanced division of the sentence was chosen and the rules were re-applied if a new sentence was still longer than ten tokens.

Structural Heuristics To preserve nodes from later deletion we applied heuristics using simple structural cues from the dependency structures. We favored nodes headed by a subject relation, `subj`, and object relations, `*obj`, and negating modifiers (the Danish word *ikke*) under the assumption that these were most likely to be important for preserving semantics and generating well-formed candidates under the sampling procedure described below. The heuristics were applied both to trees, acting by preserving entire subtrees and applied to words, only preserving single tokens.

[3]http://ilk.uvt.nl/conll/post_task_data.html

[4]Performance of the parser on the treebank test set Labeled attachment score (LAS) $= 85.65$ and Unlabeled attachment score (UAS) $= 90.29$

[5]For a formal description see (Klerke, 2012)

This serves as a way of avoiding relying heavily on possibly faulty dependency analyses and also avoid the risk of insisting on keeping long, complex or superfluous modifiers.

Sampling Candidates for scoring were overgenerated by randomly selecting parts of a (possibly split) input sentence. Either the selected nodes with their full sub-tree or the single tokens from the flat list of tokens were eliminated, unless they were previously selected for preservation by a heuristic. Some additional interaction between heuristics and sampling happened when the deletions were performed on trees: deletion of subtrees allow non-continuous deletions when the parses are non-projective, and nodes that were otherwise selected for keeping may nevertheless be removed if they are part of a subtree of a node selected for deletion. After pruning, all nodes that used to have outgoing `obj`-relations had the first child node of these relations restored.

4.3 Scoring

We rank candidates according to a loss function incorporating both readability score (the lower, the more readable) and language model perplexity (the lower, the less perplexing) as described below. The loss function assigns values to the candidates such that the best simplification candidate receives the lowest score.

The loss function is a weighted combination of three scores: perplexity (PPL), LIX and word-class distribution (WCD). The PPL scores were obtained from a 5-gram language model of Danish[6] We used the standard readability metric for Danish, LIX (Bjornsson, 1983)[7]. Finally, the WCD measured the variation in universal pos-tag-distribution [8] compared to the observed tag-variation in the entire simplified corpus. For PPL and LIX we calculated the difference between the score of the input sentence and the candidate.

Development data was used for tuning the weights of the loss function. Because the candidate-generation is free to produce extremely short candidates, we have to deal with candidates receiving extremely low scores. Those scores never arise in the professionally simplified text, so we eliminate extreme candidates by introducing filters on all scores. The lower limit was tuned experimentally and fixed approximately two times below the average difference observed between the two parts of the aligned DSim corpus, thus limiting the reduction in PPL and LIX to 60% of the input's PPL and LIX. The upper limit was fixed at the input-level plus 20% to allow more varied candidates through the filters. The WCD-filter accepted all candidates with a tag-variance that fell below the 75-percentile observed variance in the simplified training part of the DSim corpus. The resulting loss was calculated as the sum of three weighted scores.

Below is the loss function we minimized over the filtered candidates $\mathbf{t} \in \mathcal{T}_\mathbf{s}$ for each input sentence, $\mathbf{s}$. The notation *var*() denotes the range allowed through a hard filter. Using development data we set the values of the term weights to $\alpha = 1, \beta = 6$ and $\gamma = 2$.

$$\begin{aligned} \mathbf{t}^* &= \operatorname*{argmin}_{\mathbf{t} \in \mathcal{T}_\mathbf{s}} loss(\mathbf{s}, \mathbf{t}) \\ loss(\mathbf{s}, \mathbf{t}) &= \alpha \frac{\Delta LIX(\mathbf{s}, \mathbf{t})}{\mathrm{var}(LIX(\mathbf{s}))} + \beta \frac{\Delta PPL(\mathbf{s}, \mathbf{t})}{\mathrm{var}(PPL(\mathbf{s}))} \\ &\quad + \gamma \frac{\Delta WCD(.75, \mathbf{t})}{WCD(.75)} \end{aligned}$$

If no candidates passed through the filters, the input sentence was kept.

4.4 Evaluation

Evaluation was performed by a group of proficient Danish speaking volunteers who received written instructions and responded anonymously via an online form. 240 sentences were evaluated: six versions of each of 40 test set sentences. 48 sentences were evaluated by four judges, and the remaining by one judge each. The judges were asked to rate each sentence in terms of grammaticality and in terms of perceived beginner reader appropriateness, both on a 5-point scale, with one signifying *very good* and five signifying *very bad*. The evaluators had to rate six versions of each sentence: original news wire, a human simplified version, the baseline system, a split sentence version (Split), a sampled only version (Sample), and a version combining the Split and Sample techniques (Combined). The presentation was randomized. Below are example outputs

[6] The LM was Knesser-Ney smoothed, using the same corpora as the baseline system, without punctuation and built using SRILM (Stolcke, 2002).

[7] LIX is similar to the English Flesch-Kincaid grade level in favoring short sentences with short words. The formula is LIX $=$ *average sentence length* $+$ % *long words*, with long words being of more than 6 characters. (Anderson, 1983) calculated a conversion from LIX to grade levels.

[8] suggested by(Petrov et al., 2011)

for the baseline and the other three automatic systems:

BL: **Der er hvad der bliver betegnet som abnormt store mængder radioaktivt materiale i havvand nær** frygter **atomkraftværk .**

Split: **Der er målt hvad**. Hvad **bliver betegnet som abnormt store mængder af radioaktivt materiale i havvand nær det jordskælvsramte atomkraftværk i Japan .**

Sample: **Der er målt hvad der bliver betegnet som store mængder af radioaktivt materiale i havvand japan .**

Comb.: **Der er målt hvad**. Hvad **bliver betegnet som store mængder af radioaktivt materiale det atomkraftværk i japan .**

5 Results

The ranking of the systems in terms of beginner reader appropriateness and grammaticality, are shown in Figure 1. From the test set of the DSim corpus, 15 news wire texts were arbitrarily selected for evaluation. For these texts we calculated median LIX and PPL. The results are shown in Table 1. The sentences for human evaluation were drawn arbitrarily from this collection. As expected, the filtering of candidates and the loss function force the systems Sample and Combined to choose simplifications with LIX and PPL scores close to the ones observed in the human simplified version. Split sentences only reduce LIX as a result of shorter sentences, however PPL is the highest, indicating a loss of grammaticality. Most often this was caused by tagger and parser errors. The baseline reduces PPL slightly, while LIX is unchanged. This reflects the importance of the language model in the SMT system.

In the analyses below, the rating were collapsed to three levels. For texts ranked by more than one judge, we calculated agreement as Krippendorff's α. The results are shown in Table 2. In addition to sentence-wise agreement, the system-wise evaluation agreement was calculated as all judges were evaluating the same 6 systems 8 times each. We calculated α of the most frequent score (mode) assigned by each judge to each system. As shown in Table 2 this system score agreement was only about half of the single sentence agreement, which reflect a notable instability in output quality of all computer generated systems. The same tendency is visible in both histograms in Figure 1a and 1b. While grammaticality is mostly agreed upon when the scores are collapsed into three bins ($\alpha = 0.650$), proficient speakers do not agree to the same extent on what constitutes beginner reader appropriate text ($\alpha = 0.338$). The average, mean and most frequent assigned ranks are recorded in Table 3. Significant differences at $p < 0.05$ are reported in Table 4.

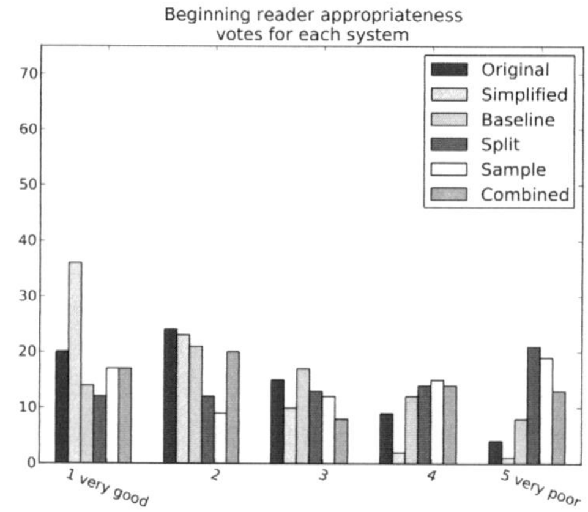

(a) Sentence – Beginner

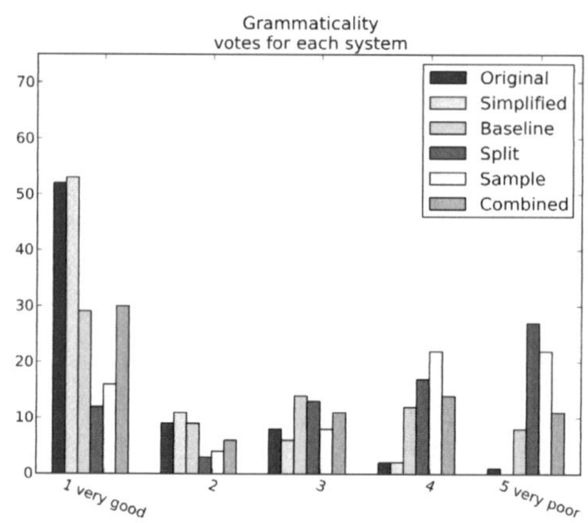

(b) Sentence – Grammar.

Figure 1: Distribution of all rankings on systems before collapsing rankings.

	Orig.	Simpl.	Base	Split	Sample	Comb.
PPL	222	174	214	234	**164**	177
LIX	45 (10)	39 (8)	45 (10)	41(9)	36 (8)	**32 (7)**

Table 1: LIX and PPL scores for reference texts and system generated output. Medians are reported, because distributions are very skewed, which makes the mean a bad estimator of central tendency. LIX grade levels in parenthesis.

Reflecting the fair agreement on grammaticality, all comparisons come out significant except the human generated versions that are judged as equally grammatical and the Combined and Baseline systems that are indistinguishable in grammaticality. Beginner reader appropriateness is significantly better in the human simplified version

	Systems	Sentences
Beginner reader	0.168	0.338
Grammaticality	0.354	0.650

Table 2: Krippendorff's α agreement for full-text and sentence evaluation. Agreement on system ranks was calculated from the most frequent score per judge per system.

compared to all other versions, and the original version is significantly better than the Sample and Split systems. The remaining observed differences are not significant due to the great variation in quality as expressed in Figure 1a.

We found that our Combined system produced sentences that were as grammatical as the baseline and also frequently judged to be appropriate for beginner readers. The main source of error affecting both Combined and Split is faulty sentence splitting as a result of errors in tagging and parsing. One way to avoid this in future development is to propagate several split variants to the final sampling and scoring. In addition, the systems Combined and Sample are prone to omitting important information that is perceived as missing when compared directly to the original, although those two systems are the ones that score the closest to the human generated simplifications. As can be expected in a system operating exclusively at sentence level, coherence across sentence boundaries remains a weak point.

Another important point is that while the baseline system performs well in the evaluation, this is likely due to its conservativeness: choosing simplifications resembling the original input very closely. This is evident both in our automatic measures (see Table 1) and from manual inspection. Our systems Sample and Combine, on the other hand, have been tuned to perform much more radical changes and in this respect more closely model the changes we see in the human simplification. Combined is thus evaluated to be at level with the baseline in grammaticality and beginner reader appropriateness, despite the fact that the baseline system is supervised.

Conclusion and perspectives

We have shown promising results for simplification of Danish sentences. We have also shown that using restricted over-generation and scoring can be a feasible way for simplifying text without relying directly on large scale parallel corpora, which for many languages do not exist. To integrate language modeling and readability metrics in scoring is a first step towards applying results from readability research to the simplification framework. Our error analysis showed that many errors come from pre-processing and thus more robust NLP-tools for Danish are needed. Future perspectives include combining supervised and unsupervised methods to exploit the radical unsupervised deletion approach and the knowledge obtainable from observable structural changes and potential lexical simplifications. We plan to focus on refining the reliability of sentence splitting in the presence of parser errors as well as on developing a loss function that incorporates more of the insights from readability research, and to apply machine learning techniques to the weighting of features. Specifically we would like to investigate the usefulness of discourse features and transition probabilities (Pitler and Nenkova, 2008) for performing and evaluating full-text simplifications.

	Sent. – Beginner			*Sent. – Grammar*		
	$\bar{x}$	$\tilde{x}$	mode	$\bar{x}$	$\tilde{x}$	mode
Human Simp.	1.44	1	1	1.29	1	1
Orig.	2.14	1	1	1.32	1	1
Base	2.58	3	1	1.88	2	1
Split	3.31	3	5	2.44	3	3
Sample	3.22	3	5	2.39	3	3
Comb.	2.72	1	1	1.93	2	1

Table 3: Human evaluation. Mean ($\bar{x}$), median ($\tilde{x}$) and most frequent (mode) of assigned ranks by beginner reader appropriateness and grammaticality as assessed by proficient Danish speakers.

	Comb.	Sample	Split	Base	Orig.
Human Simp.	b, g	b, g	b, g	b, g	b
Orig.	g	b, g	b, g	g	
Base		g	g		
Split	g				
Sample	g				

Table 4: Significant differences between systems in experiment b: Beginner reader appropriateness and g: Grammaticality. Bonferroni-corrected Mann-Whitney's U for 15 comparisons, two-tailed test. A letter indicate significant difference at corrected $p < 0.05$ level.

Acknowledgements

Thanks to Mirella Lapata and Kristian Woodsend for their feedback and comments early in the process of this work and to the Emnlp@Cph group and reviewers for their helpful comments.

References

S.M. Aluísio, Lucia Specia, T.A.S. Pardo, E.G. Maziero, H.M. Caseli, and R.P.M. Fortes. 2008. A corpus analysis of simple account texts and the proposal of simplification strategies: first steps towards text simplification systems. In *Proceedings of the 26th annual ACM international conference on Design of communication*, pages 15–22. ACM.

Jonathan Anderson. 1983. LIX and RIX: Variations on a little-known readability index. *Journal of Reading*, 26(6):490–496.

C. H. Bjornsson. 1983. Readability of Newspapers in 11 Languages. *Reading Research Quarterly*, 18(4):480–497.

B Bohnet. 2010. Very high accuracy and fast dependency parsing is not a contradiction. In *Proceedings of the 23rd International Conference on Computational Linguistics*, pages 89–97. Association for Computational Linguistics.

S. Bott, H. Saggion, and D. Figueroa. 2012. A hybrid system for spanish text simplification. In *Third Workshop on Speech and Language Processing for Assistive Technologies (SLPAT), Montreal, Canada.*

Julian Brooke, Vivian Tsang, David Jacob, Fraser Shein, and Graeme Hirst. 2012. Building Readability Lexicons with Unannotated Corpora. In *Proceedings of the First Workshop on Predicting and Improving Text Readability for target reader populations*, pages 33–39, Montr{é}al, Canada, June. Association for Computational Linguistics.

Y. Canning, J. Tait, J. Archibald, and R. Crawley. 2000. *Cohesive generation of syntactically simplified newspaper text*. Springer.

John Carroll, G. Minnen, D. Pearce, Yvonne Canning, S. Devlin, and J. Tait. 1999. Simplifying text for language-impaired readers. In *Proceedings of EACL*, volume 99, pages 269–270. Citeseer.

R. Chandrasekar, Christine Doran, and B Srinivas. 1996. Motivations and methods for text simplification. In *Proceedings of the 16th conference on Computational linguistics-Volume 2*, pages 1041–1044. Association for Computational Linguistics.

William Coster and David Kauchak. 2011. Simple English Wikipedia: a new text simplification task. In *Proceedings of the 49th Annual Meeting of the Association for Computational Linguistics: Human Language Technologies: short papers-Volume 2*, volume 2, pages 665–669. Association for Computational Linguistics.

W. Daelemans, A. Höthker, and E.T.K. Sang. 2004. Automatic sentence simplification for subtitling in dutch and english. In *Proceedings of the 4th International Conference on Language Resources and Evaluation*, pages 1045–1048.

A. Davison and R.N. Kantor. 1982. On the failure of readability formulas to define readable texts: A case study from adaptations. *Reading Research Quarterly*, pages 187–209.

J. De Belder and M.F. Moens. 2012. A dataset for the evaluation of lexical simplification. *Computational Linguistics and Intelligent Text Processing*, pages 426–437.

Anna Decker. 2003. Towards automatic grammatical simplification of Swedish text. Master's thesis, Stockholm University.

Biljana Drndarevic and Horacio Saggion. 2012. Towards Automatic Lexical Simplification in Spanish: An Empirical Study. In *Proceedings of the First Workshop on Predicting and Improving Text Readability for target reader populations*, pages 8–16, Montr{é}al, Canada, June. Association for Computational Linguistics.

M Federico, N Bertoldi, and M Cettolo. 2008. IRSTLM: an open source toolkit for handling large scale language models. In *Ninth Annual Conference of the International Speech Communication Association.*

Rudolph Flesch. 1948. A new readability yardstick. *Journal of applied psychology*, 32(3):221.

Michael Heilman and Noah A Smith. 2010. Extracting simplified statements for factual question generation. In *Proceedings of the Third Workshop on Question Generation.*

Sigrid Klerke and Anders Søgaard. 2012. DSim , a Danish Parallel Corpus for Text Simplification. In *Proceedings of Language Resources and Evaluation (LREC 2012)*, pages 4015–4018.

Sigrid Klerke. 2012. Automatic text simplification in danish. sampling a restricted space of rewrites to optimize readability using lexical substitutions and dependency analyses. Master's thesis, University of Copenhagen.

P Koehn, H Hoang, A Birch, C Callison-Burch, M Federico, N Bertoldi, B Cowan, W Shen, C Moran, R Zens, and Others. 2007. Moses: Open source toolkit for statistical machine translation. In *Proceedings of the 45th Annual Meeting of the ACL on Interactive Poster and Demonstration Sessions*, pages 177–180. Association for Computational Linguistics.

M T Kromann. 2003. The Danish Dependency Treebank and the DTAG treebank tool. In *Proceedings of the Second Workshop on Treebanks and Linguistic Theories (TLT)*, page 217.

Julie Medero. 2011. Identifying Targets for Syntactic Simplification. In *Proceedings of Speech and Language Technology in Education.*

F.J. Och and H. Ney. 2000. A comparison of alignment models for statistical machine translation. In *Proceedings of the 18th conference on Computational linguistics-Volume 2*, pages 1086–1090. Association for Computational Linguistics.

S.E. E Petersen and Mari Ostendorf. 2007. Text simplification for language learners: a corpus analysis. In *the Proceedings of the Speech and Language Technology for Education Workshop*, pages 69–72. Citeseer.

S. Petrov, D. Das, and R. McDonald. 2011. A universal part-of-speech tagset. *Arxiv preprint ArXiv:1104.2086*.

Emily Pitler and Ani Nenkova. 2008. Revisiting readability: A unified framework for predicting text quality. *Proceedings of the Conference on Empirical Methods in Natural Language Processing*.

Jonas Rybing and Christian Smith. 2009. CogFLUX Grunden till ett automatiskt textförenklingssystem för svenska. Master's thesis, Linköpings Universitet.

Sarah E Schwarm and Mari Ostendorf. 2005. Reading Level Assessment Using Support Vector Machines and Statistical Language Models. In *Proceedings of the 43rd Annual Meeting of the ACL*, pages 523–530.

V. Seretan. 2012. Acquisition of syntactic simplification rules for french. In *Proceedings of Language Resources and Evaluation (LREC 2012)*.

Advaith Siddharthan and Napoleon Katsos. 2012. Offline Sentence Processing Measures for testing Readability with Users. In *Proceedings of the First Workshop on Predicting and Improving Text Readability for target reader populations*, pages 17–24, Montr{é}al, Canada, June. Association for Computational Linguistics.

Advaith Siddharthan. 2010. Complex lexico-syntactic reformulation of sentences using typed dependency representations. *Proceedings of the 6th International Natural Language Generation Conference*.

Advaith Siddharthan. 2011. Text Simplification using Typed Dependencies: A Comparison of the Robustness of Different Generation Strategies. In *Proceedings of the 13th European Workshop on Natural Language Generation*, pages 2–11.

L. Specia, S.K. Jauhar, and R. Mihalcea. 2012. Semeval-2012 task 1: English lexical simplification. In *Proceedings of the 6th International Workshop on Semantic Evaluation (SemEval 2012)*, pages 347–355.

L. Specia. 2010. Translating from complex to simplified sentences. In *Proceedings of the 9th international conference on Computational Processing of the Portuguese Language*, pages 30–39.

Andreas Stolcke. 2002. SRILM – an extensible language modeling toolkit. In *Proceedings of the Seventh International Conference on Spoken Language Processing*.

S. Vajjala and D. Meurers. 2012. On improving the accuracy of readability classification using insights from second language acquisition. In *Proceedings of the 7th Workshop on Innovative Use of NLP for Building Educational Applications (BEA7)*, pages 163–173.

Kristian Woodsend and Mirella Lapata. 2011. Learning to Simplify Sentences with Quasi-Synchronous Grammar and Integer Programming. In *Proceedings of the 2011 Conference on Empirical Methods in Natural Language Processing (2011)*, pages 409–420.

Mark Yatskar, Bo Pang, C. Danescu-Niculescu-Mizil, and Lillian Lee. 2010. For the sake of simplicity: Unsupervised extraction of lexical simplifications from Wikipedia. In *Human Language Technologies: The 2010 Annual Conference of the North American Chapter of the Association for Computational Linguistics*, pages 365–368. Association for Computational Linguistics.

Zhemin Zhu, Delphine Bernhard, and I. Gurevych. 2010. A monolingual tree-based translation model for sentence simplification. In *Proceedings of The 23rd International Conference on Computational Linguistics*, pages 1353–1361. Association for Computational Linguistics.

Exploring Word Order Universals: a Probabilistic Graphical Model Approach

Xia Lu
Department of Linguistics
University at Buffalo
Buffalo, NY USA
xialu@buffalo.edu

Abstract

In this paper we propose a probabilistic graphical model as an innovative framework for studying typological universals. We view language as a system and linguistic features as its components whose relationships are encoded in a Directed Acyclic Graph (DAG). Taking discovery of the word order universals as a knowledge discovery task we learn the graphical representation of a word order sub-system which reveals a finer structure such as direct and indirect dependencies among word order features. Then probabilistic inference enables us to see the strength of such relationships: given the observed value of one feature (or combination of features), the probabilities of values of other features can be calculated. Our model is not restricted to using only two values of a feature. Using imputation technique and EM algorithm it can handle missing values well. Model averaging technique solves the problem of limited data. In addition the incremental and divide-and-conquer method addresses the areal and genetic effects simultaneously instead of separately as in Daumé III and Campbell (2007).

1 Introduction

Ever since Greenberg (1963) proposed 45 universals of language based on a sample of 30 languages, typologists have been pursuing this topic actively for the past half century. Since some of them do not agree with the term (or concept) of "universal" they use other terminology such as "correlation", "co-occurrence", "dependency", "interaction" and "implication" to refer to the relationships between/among linguistic feature pairs most of which concern morpheme and word order. Indeed the definition of "universals" has never been clear until recently, when most typologists agreed that such universals should be statistical universals which are "statistical tendencies" discovered from data samples by using statistical methods as used in any other science. Only those tendencies that can be extrapolated to make general conclusions about the population can be claimed to be "universals" since they reflect the global preferences of value distribution of linguistic features across genealogical hierarchy and geographical areas.

Previous statistical methods in the research of word order universals have yielded interesting results but they have to make strong assumptions and do a considerable amount of data preprocessing to make the data fit the statistical model (Greenberg, 1963; Hawkins, 1982; Dryer, 1989; Nichols, 1986; Justeson & Stephens, 1990). Recent studies using probabilistic models are much more flexible and can handle noise and uncertainty better (Daumé III & Campbell, 2007; Dunn et al., 2011). However these models still rely on strong theoretic assumptions and heavy data treatment, such as using only two values of word order pairs while discarding other values, purposefully selecting a subset of the languages to study, or selecting partial data with complete values. In this paper we introduce a novel approach of using a probabilistic graphical model to study word order universals. Using this model we can have a graphic representation of the structure of language as a complex system composed of linguistic features. Then the relationship among these features can be quantified as probabilities. Such a model does not rely on strong assumptions and has little constraint on data.

The paper is organized as follows: in Section 2 we discuss the rationale of using a probabilistic graphic model to study word order universals and introduce our two models; Section 3 is about learning structures and parameters for the two models. Section 4 discusses the quantitative analysis while Section 5 gives qualitative analysis of the results. Section 6 is about inference such as MAP query and in Section 6 we discuss the advantage of using PGM to study word order universals.

2 A new approach: probabilistic graphical modeling

2.1 Rationale for using PGM in word order study

The probabilistic graphical model is the marriage of probabilistic theory and graph theory. It combines a graphical representation with a complex distribution over a high-dimensional space. There are two major types of graphical representations of distributions. One is a Directed Acyclic Graph (DAG) which is also known as a Bayesian network with all edges having a source and a target. The other is an Undirected Acyclic Graph, which is also called a Markov network with all edges undirected. A mixture of these two types is also possible (Koller & Friedman, 2009).

There are two advantages of using this model to study word order universals. First the graphical structure can reveal much finer structure of language as a complex system. Most studies on word order correlations examine the pairwise relationship, for example, how the order of verb and object correlates with the order of noun and adjective. However linguists have also noticed other possible interactions among the word order features, like chains of overlapping implications: Prep ⊃ ((NAdj ⊃ NGen) & (NGen ⊃ NRel)) proposed by Hawkins (1983); multi-conditional implications (Daumé III, 2007); correlations among six word order pairs and three-way interactions (Justeson & Stephens, 1990); spurious word order correlations (Croft et al., 2011); chains of associations, e.g. if C predicts B and B predicts A, then C predicts A redundantly (Bickel, 2010b). These claims about the possible interactions among word order features imply complex relationships among the features. The study of word order correlations started with pairwise comparison, probably because that was what typologists could do given the limited resources of statistical methods. However when we study the properties of a language, by knowing just several word orders such as order of verb and object, noun and adpositions, etc., we are unable to say anything about the language as a whole. Here we want to introduce a new perspective of seeing language as a complex system. We assume there is a meta-language that has the universal properties of all languages in the world. We want a model that can represent this meta-language and make inferences about linguistic properties of new languages. This system is composed of multiple sub-systems such as phonology, morphology, syntax, etc. which correspond to the subfields in linguistics. In this paper we focus on the subsystem of word order only.

The other advantage of PGM is that it enables us to quantify the relationships among word order features. Justeson & Stephens (1990) mentioned the notion of "correlation strength" when they found out that N/A order appears less strongly related to basic V/S/O order and/or adposition type than is N/G order. This is the best a log-linear model can do, to indicate whether a correlation is "strong", "less strong", "weak" or "less weak". Dunn et al. (2011) used Bayes factor value to quantify the relationships between the word order pairs but they mistook the strength of evidence for an effect as the strength of the effect itself (Levy & Daumé III, 2011). A PGM model for a word order subsystem encodes a joint probabilistic distribution of all word order feature pairs. Using probability we can describe the degree of confidence about the uncertain nature of word order correlations. For example, if we set the specific value as evidence, then we can get the values of other features using an inference method. Such values can be seen as quantified strength of relationship between values of features.

2.2 Our model

In our word order universal modeling we will use DAG structure since we think the direction of influence matters when talking about the relationship among features. In Greenberg (1966a) most of the universals are unidirectional, such as "If a language has object-verb order, then it also has subject-verb order" while few are bidirectional universals. The term "directionality" does not capture the full nature of the different statuses word order features have in the complex language system. We notice in all the word order studies the order of SOV or OV was given special attention. In Dryer's study VO order is the dominant one which determines the set of word order pairs correlated with it (or not). We assume word order features have different statuses in the language system and such differences should be manifested by directionality of relationships between feature pairs. Therefore we choose DAG structure as our current model framework.

Another issue is the sampling problem. Some typologists (Dryer 1989, Croft 2003) have argued that the language samples in the WALS database (Haspelmath et al., 2005) are not independent and identically distributed (i.i.d.) because languages can share the same feature values due to either genetic or areal effect. While others (Maslova, 2010) argue that languages within a family have developed into distinct ones through the long history. We notice that even we can control the areal and genetic factors there are still many other factors that can influence the typological data distribution, such as 1) language speakers: cognitive, physiological, social, and communicative factors; 2) data collection: difficulty in identifying features; political biases (some languages are well documented); 3) random noise such as historical accidents. Here we do not make any assumption about the i.i.d property of the language samples and propose two models: one is FLAT, which assumes samples are independent and identically distributed (i.i.d.); the other is UNIV, which takes care of the possible dependencies among the samples. By comparing the predictive power of these two models we hope to find one that is closer to the real distribution.

3 Learning

To build our models we need to learn both structure and parameters for the two models. We used Murphy (2001)'s Bayesian Network Toolbox (BNT) and Leray & Francois (2004)'s BNT Structure Learning Package (BNT_SLP) for this purpose.

3.1 Data

As we mentioned earlier we will restrict our attention to the domain of word order only in this paper. In the WALS database there are 56 features belonging to the "Word Order" category. Because some of the features are redundant, we chose 15 sets of word order features which are: S_O_V[1] (order of subject, object and verb) [7[2]], S_V (order of subject and verb) [3], O_V (order of object and verb) [3], O_Obl_V (order of Object, Oblique, and Verb) [6], ADP_NP (order of adposition and noun phrase) [5], G_N (order of genitive and noun) [3], A_N (order of adjective and noun) [4], Dem_N (order of demonstrative and noun) [4], Num_N (order of numeral and noun) [4], R_N (order of relative clause and noun) [7], Deg_A (order of degree word and adjective) [3], PoQPar (position of polar question particles) [6], IntPhr (position of interrogative phrases in content questions) [3], AdSub_Cl (order of adverbial subordinator and clause) [5], Neg_V (order of negative morpheme and verb) [4]. We did some minimal treatment of data. For Neg_V which has 17 values we collapsed its values 7-17 to 6 ("Mixed"). For Dem_N and Neg_V, we treat word and suffix as the same and collapsed values 1 and 3 to 1, and values 2 and 4 to 2. After deleting those languages with no value for all 15 word order features we have 1646 data entries. This database is very sparse: in overall the percentage of missing values is 31%. For seven features more than 50% of the languages have values missing.

3.2 Learning the FLAT model

There are two big problems in learning DAG structure for the FLAT model. One is caused by large number of missing values. Because EM method for structures from incomplete data takes very long time to converge due to the large parameter space of our model, we decided to use imputation method to handle the missing data problem (Singh, 1997). The other difficulty is caused by limited data. To solve this problem we used model averaging by using bootstrap replicates (Friedman et al., 1999). We use GES (greedy search in the space of equivalent classes) algorithm in BNT_SLP to learn structure from a bootstrap dataset because it uses CPDAGs to represent Markov equivalent classes which makes graph fusion easier. The algorithm is as follows:

1) Use nearest-neighbor method to impute missing values in the original dataset D and create a complete dataset D_s.
2) Create T=200 bootstrap resamples by resampling the same number of instances as the original dataset with replacement from D_s. Then for each resample D_s^t learn the highest scoring structure G_s^t.
3) Fuse the 200 graphs into a single graph G_s using the "Intergroup Undirected Networks Integration" method (Liu et al., 2007). Then use *cpdag_to_dag.m* in BNT_SLP to change G_s into a directed graph G_s'.
4) Compute the BIC scores of G_s' using the 200 resamples and choose the highest one. If the convergence criterion (change of BIC is less than 10^{-4} compared with the previous iteration) is met, stop. Otherwise go to Step 5.
5) Learn 200 sets of parameters θ_s^t for G_s^t using the 200 resamples and take a weighted-average as the final parameters θ_s'. Also use EM algorithm and dataset D to learn parameters θ_{EM} for G_s'. Choose the parameters θ between θ_s' and θ_{EM} that gives the highest BIC score. Use MAP estimation to fill in the missing values in D and generate a complete dataset D_{s+1}. Go to Step 2.

[1] The detailed descriptions of these word order features and values can be found at http://wals.info/.

[2] The number in the square brackets indicates the number of values for that feature.

The structure for the FLAT model is shown in Figure 1.

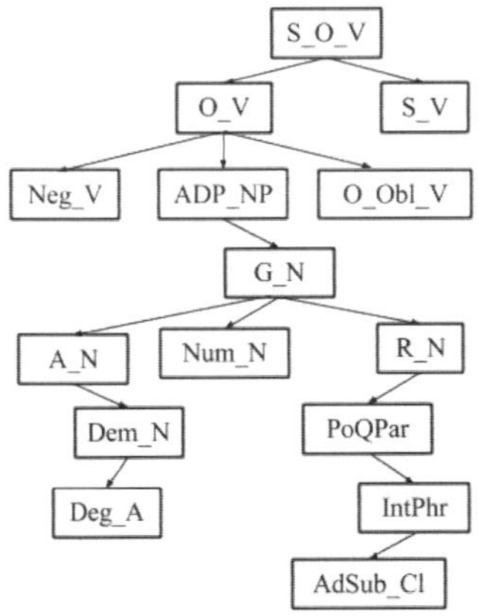

Figure 1. DAG structure of the FLAT model

3.3 Learning the UNIV model

As discussed in Section 2.2, the possible dependencies among language samples pose difficulty for statistical methods using the WALS data. Daumé III & Campbell (2007)'s hierarchical models provided a good solution to this problem; however their two models LINGHIER and DISTHIER dealt with genetic and areal influences separately and the two separate results still do not tell us what the "true universals" are.

Instead of trying to control the areal and genetic and other factors, we propose a different perspective here. As we have mentioned, the kind of universals we care about are the stable properties of language, which means they can be found across all subsets of languages. Therefore to solve the problem of dependence among the languages we take an incremental and divide-and-conquer approach. Using clustering algorithm we identified five clusters in the WALS data. In each cluster we picked *1/n* of the data and combine them to make a subset. In this way we can have *n* subsets of data which have decreased degree of dependencies among the samples. We learn a structure for each subset and fuse the *n* graphs into one single graph. The algorithm is as follows:

1) Use nearest-neighbor method to impute missing values and create *M* complete datasets D_m $(1 \leq m \leq M)$.
2) For each D_m divide the samples into *n* subsets. Then for each subset D_m^n learn the highest scoring structure G_m^n.
3) Fuse the *n* graphs into a single graph G_m using the "Intragroup Undirected Networks Integration" method (Liu et al., 2007).
4) Fuse the *M* graphs to make a single directed graph $G_M{}'$ as in Step 3 in the previous section.
5) Compute the BIC score of $G_M{}'$ using datasets D_m $(1 \leq m \leq M)$ and choose the highest score. If the convergence criterion (same as in the previous section) is met, stop. Otherwise go to Step 6.
6) Learn parameters θ_m for $G_M{}'$ using datasets D_m $(1 \leq m \leq M)$ and take a weighted-average as the final parameters $\theta_M{}'$. Also use EM algorithm and original dataset to learn parameters θ_{EM} for $G_M{}'$. Choose the parameters θ among $\theta_M{}'$ and θ_{EM} that gives the highest BIC score. Use MAP estimation to fill in the missing values in *D* and generate another *M* complete dataset. Go to Step 2.

The final structure for the UNIV model is shown in Figure 2.

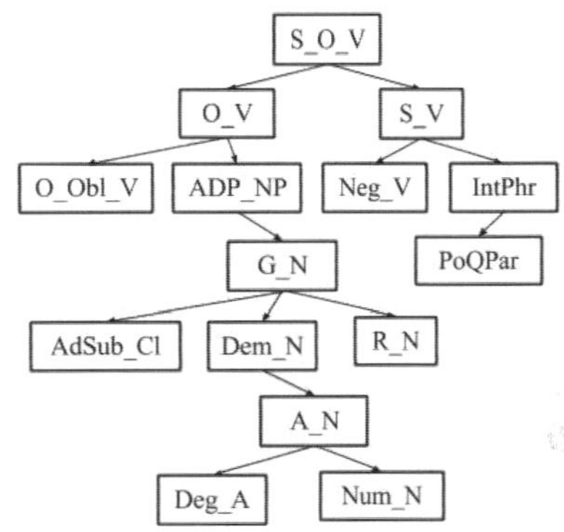

Figure 2. DAG structure of the UNIV model

The semantics of a DAG structure cannot be simply interpreted as causality (Koller & Friedman, 2009). From this graph we can see word order features are on different tiers in the hierarchy. The root S_O_V seems to "dominate" all the other features; noun modifiers and noun are in the middle tier while O_Obl_V, AdSub_Cl, Deg_A, Num_N, R, Neg_V and PoQPar are the leaf nodes which might indicate their smallest contribution to the word order properties of a language. O_V seems to be an important node since most paths start from it indicating its influence can flow to many other nodes.

We can also see there are two types of connections among the nodes: 1) direct connection: any two nodes connected with an arc directly have influence on each other. This construction induces a correlation between the two features regardless of the evidence. This type of dependency was the one most explored in the previous literatures. 2) three cases of indirect connections: a. indirect causal effect: e.g. O_V does not influence G_N directly, but via ADP_NP; b. indirect evidential effect: knowing G_N will change our belief about O_V indirectly; c. common cause: e.g. ADP_NP and O_Obl_V can influence each other without O_V being observed. Our model reveals a much finer structure of the word order sub-system by distinguishing different types of dependencies that might have been categorized simply as "correlation" in the traditional statistical methods.

4 Quantitative Analysis of Results

The word order universal results are difficult to evaluate because we do not know the correct answers. Nonetheless we did a quantitative evaluation following Daumé III and Campbell (2007)'s method. The results are shown in Figure 3.

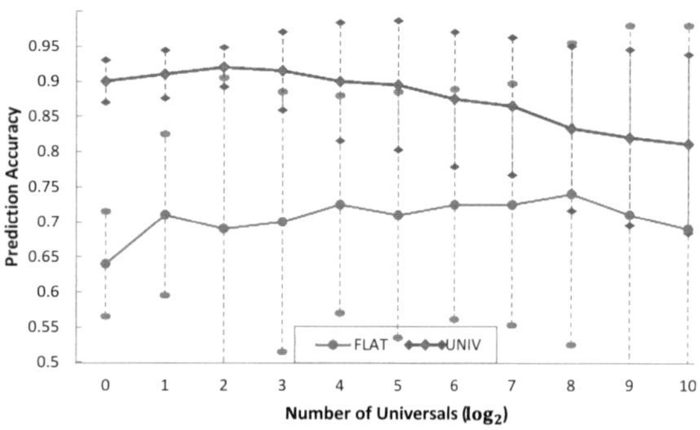

Figure 3. Results of Quantitative Evaluation

As we can see the predictive power of the UNIV model is much better than that of the FLAT model. The accuracy of our both models is lower than those of Daumé III and Campbell's. But this does not mean our models are worse considering the complexity in model learning. Instead our UNIV model shows steady accurate prediction for the top ten universals and has more stable performance compared with other models.

Using the UNIV model we can do many types of computation. Besides pairwise feature values, we can calculate the probability of any combination of word order feature values. If we want to know how value "GN" of feature "G_N" is dependent on value "POST" of feature "ADP_NP" we set POST to be evidence (probability=100%) and get the probability of having "GN". Such a probability can be taken as a measurement of dependence strength between these two values. We need more evidence for setting a threshold value to define a word order universal but for now we just use 0.5. We calculated the probabilities of all pairwise feature values in the UNIV model which can found at http://www.acsu.buffalo.edu/~xialu/univ.html.

5 Qualitative Analysis of Results

We also did qualitative evaluation through comparison with the well-known findings in word order correlation studies. We compared our results with three major works: those of Greenberg's, Dryer's, and Daumé III and Campbell's.

5.1 Evaluation: compare with Greenberg's and Dryer's work

Comparison with Greenberg's work is shown in Table 1 (in Appendix A). If the probability is above 0.5 we say it is a universal and mark it red. We think values like 0.4-0.5 can also give us some suggestive estimates therefore we mark these green. For Universal 2, 3, 4, 5, 10, 18 and 19, our results conform to Greenberg's. But for others there are discrepancies of different degrees. For example, for U12 our results show that "VSO" can predict "Initial" but not very strongly compared with "SOV" predicting "Not_Initial".

Table 2 (in Appendix A) shows our comparison with Dryer (1992)'s work. We noticed there is an asymmetry in terms of V_O's influence on other word order pairs, which was not discussed in previous work. In the correlated pairs, only ADP_NP and G_N show bidirectional correlation with O_V while PoQPar becomes a non-correlated pair. In the non-correlated pairs, Dem_N becomes a correlated pair and other pairs also show correlation of weak strength. Most of our results therefore do not confirm Dryer's findings.

5.2 Evaluation: compare with Daumé III and Campbell's work

We compared the probabilities of single value pairs of the top ten word order universals with Daumé III and Campbell's results, which are shown in the following figures.

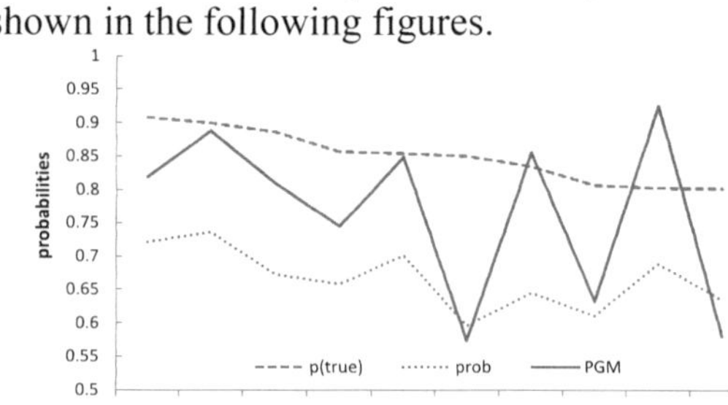

Figure 4. Compare with Daumé III and Campbell's HIER model

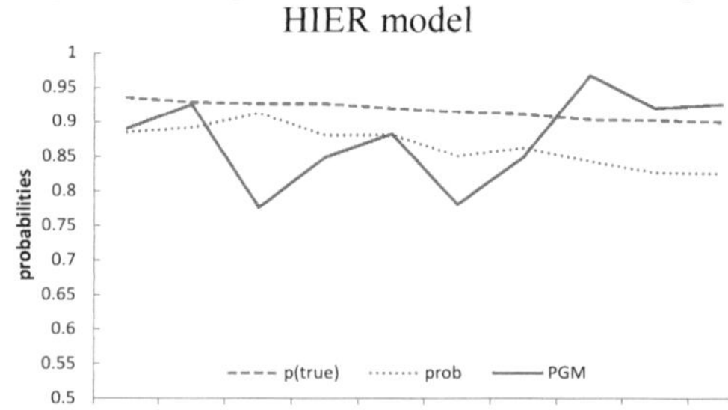

Figure 5. Compare with Daumé III and Campbell's DIST model

P(true) is the probability of having the particular implication; *prob* is the probability calculated in a different way which is not specified in Daumé III and Campbell's work. *PGM* is our model. It can be seen that our model provides moderate numbers which fall between the two probabilities in Daumé III and Campbell's results. In Figure 4 the two universals that have the biggest gaps are: 9) Prepositions ->VO and 10) Adjective-Noun->Demonstrative-Noun. In Figure 5 the three universals that have the biggest gaps are: 3) Noun-Genitive->Initial subordinator word, 6) Noun-Genitive->Prepositions and 8) OV->SV. It is hard to tell which model does a better job just by doing comparison like this. Daumé III and Campbell's model computes the probabilities of 3442 feature pairs separately. Their model with two values as nodes does not consider the more complex dependencies among more than two features. Our model provides a better solution by trying to maximize the joint probabilities of all word order feature pairs.

6 Inference

Besides discovering word order universals, our model can reveal more properties of word order sub-system through various inference queries. At present we use Samlam[3] for inference because it has an easy-to-use interface for probabilistic inference queries. Figure 6 (in Appendix B) gives an example: when we know the language is subject preceding verb and negative morpheme preceding verb, then we know the probability for this language to have postpositions is 0.5349, as well as the probabilities for the values of all other features.

The other type of query is MAP which aims to find the most likely assignments to all of the unobserved variables. For example, when we only know that language is VO, we can use MAP query to find the combination of values which has the highest probability (0.0032 as shown in Table 3 in Appendix C).

One more useful function is to calculate the likelihood of a language in terms of word order properties. If all values of 13 features of a language are known, then the probability (likelihood) of having such a language can be calculated. We calculated the likelihood of eight languages and got the results as shown in Figure 7 (in Appendix C). As we can see, English has the highest likelihood to be a language while Hakka Chinese has the lowest. German and French have similar likelihood; Portuguese and Spanish are similar but are less than German and French. In other words English is a typical language regarding word order properties while Hakka Chinese is an atypical one.

7 Discussion

Probabilistic graphic modeling provides solutions to the problems we noticed in the previous studies of word order universals. By modeling language as a complex system we shift our attention to the language itself instead of just features. Using PGM we can infer properties about a language given the known values and we can also infer the likelihood of a language given all the values. In the future if we include other domains, such as phonology, morphology and syntax, we will be able to discover more properties about language as a whole complex system.

Regarding the relationships among the features since PGM can give a finer structure we are able to see how the features are related directly or indirectly. By using probability theory we overcome the shortcomings of traditional statistical methods based on NHST. Probabilities capture our uncertainty about word order correlations. Instead of saying "A is correlated with B", we can say "A is correlated with B to a certain extent". PGM enables us to quantify our knowledge about the word order properties of languages.

Regarding the data treatment, we did very little preprocessing of data, therefore reducing the possibility of bringing in additional bias from other processes such as family construction in Dunn et al.'s experiment. In addition we did not remove most of the values so that we can make inferences based on values such as "no determinant order" and "both orders". In this way we retain the information in our data to the largest extent.

We think PGM has the potential to become a new methodology for studying word order universals. It also opens up many new possibilities for studying linguistic typology as well:

- It can include other domains to build a more complex network and to discover more typological properties of languages.
- It can be used in field work for linguists to make predictions about properties of unknown languages.

[3] SamIam is a tool for modeling and reasoning with Bayesian networks (http://reasoning.cs.ucla.edu/samiam/).

References

Bickel, B. 2010a. *Absolute and statistical universals.* In Hogan, P. C. (ed.) The Cambridge Encyclopedia of the Language Sciences, 77-79. Cambridge: Cambridge University Press.

Bickel, B. 2010b. *Capturing particulars and universals in clause linkage: a multivariate analysis.* In Bril, I. (ed.) Clause-hierarchy and clause-linking: the syntax and pragmatics interface, pp. 51 - 101. Amsterdam: Benjamins.

Croft, William. 2003. *Typology and universals.* 2nd edn. Cambridge: Cambridge University Press.

Daphne Koller and Nir Friedman. 2009. *Probabilistic Graphical Models: Principles and Techniques (Adaptive Computation and Machine Learning series).* MIT Press, Aug 31, 2009

Daumé, H., & Campbell, L. (2007). A Bayesian model for discovering typological implications. In *Annual Meeting –Association For Computational Linguistics* (Vol. 45, No. 1, p. 65).

D.M. Chickering, D. Heckerman, and C. Meek. 1997. A Bayesian approach to learning Bayesian networks with local structure. *Proceeding UAI'97 Proceedings of the Thirteenth conference on Uncertainty in artificial intelligence.*

Dryer, M. S. 1989. Large linguistic areas and language sampling. *Studies in Language 13,* 257 – 292.

Dryer, Matthew S. & Martin Haspelmath (eds.). 2011. *The world atlas of language structures online.* München: Max Planck Digital Library.

Dryer, Matthew S. 2011. The evidence for word order correlations. *Linguistic Typology 15.* 335–380.

Dunn, Michael, Simon J. Greenhill, Stephen C. Levinson & Russell D. Gray. 2011. Evolved structure of language shows lineage-specific trends in word-order universals. *Nature 473.* 79–82.

E. T. Jaynes. 2003. *Probability Theory: The Logic of Science.* Cambridge University Press, Apr 10, 2003.

Friedman, N. (1998, July). The Bayesian structural EM algorithm. In *Proceedings of the Fourteenth conference on Uncertainty in artificial intelligence* (pp. 129-138). Morgan Kaufmann Publishers Inc.

Friedman, N., Nachman, I., & Peér, D. (1999, July). Learning bayesian network structure from massive datasets: the "sparse candidate" algorithm. In *Proceedings of the Fifteenth conference on Uncertainty in artificial intelligence* (pp. 206-215). Morgan Kaufmann Publishers Inc.

Greenberg, J. H. 1963. *Some universals of grammar with particular reference to the order of meaningful elements.* In Universals of Language, J. H. Greenberg, Ed. MIT Press, Cambridge, MA, 73-113.

Greenberg, Joseph H. 1966. Synchronic and diachronic universals in phonology. *Language 42.* 508–517.

Greenberg, J. H. (1969). Some methods of dynamic comparison in linguistics. *Substance and structure of language*, 147-203.

Hawkins, John A. 1983. *Word Order Universals.* Academic Press, 1983.

Justeson, J. S., & Stephens, L. D. (1990). Explanations for word order universals: a log-linear analysis. In *Proceedings of the XIV International Congress of Linguists* (Vol. 3, pp. 2372-76).

Leray, P., & Francois, O. (2004). BNT structure learning package: Documentation and experiments.

Levy, R., & Daumé III, H. (2011). Computational methods are invaluable for typology, but the models must match the questions: Commentary on Dunn et al.(2011).Linguistic Typology.(To appear).

Liu, F., Tian, F., & Zhu, Q. (2007). Bayesian network structure ensemble learning. In *Advanced Data Mining and Applications* (pp. 454-465). Springer Berlin Heidelberg.

Maslova, Elena & Tatiana Nikitina. 2010. Language universals and stochastic regularity of language change: Evidence from cross-linguistic distributions of case marking patterns. Manuscript.

Murphy, K. (2001). The bayes net toolbox for matlab. *Computing science and statistics, 33*(2), 1024-1034.

Perkins, Revere D. 1989. Statistical techniques for determining language sample size. *Studies in Language 13.* 293–315.

Singh, M. (1997, July). Learning Bayesian networks from incomplete data. In *Proceedings of the National conference on Artificial Intelligence* (pp. 534-539). JOHN WILEY & SONS LTD.

William Croft, Tanmoy Bhattacharya, Dave Kleinschmidt, D. Eric Smith and T. Florian Jaeger. 2011. Greenbergian universals, diachrony and statistical analyses [commentary on Dunn et al., Evolved structure of language shows lineage-specific trends in word order universals*]. Linguistic Typology 15.*433-53.

Appendices

A. Comparison with others' work

Universals	Dependencies	UNIV
U2: ADP_NP<=>N_G	POST->GN PRE->NG GN->POST NG->PRE	83.59 70.29 78.45 81.91
U3: VSO->PRE	VSO->PRE	74.41
U4: SOV->POST	SOV->POST	85.28
U5: SOV&NG->NA	SOV&NG->NA	68.95
U9: PoQPar<=>ADP_NP	Initial->PRE Final->POST PRE->Initial POST->Final	41.87 49.67 15.80 31.73
U10: PoQPar<=> VSO	all values of PoQPar: VSO below 10%	below 10%
U11: IntPhr->VS	Initial->VS	24.12
U12: VSO->IntPhr	VSO->Initial SOV->Initial SOV->Not_Initial	50.54 28.52 60.41
U17: VSO->A_N	VSO->A_N	24.86
U18&19: A_N<=>Num_N<=>Dem_N	AN->NumN AN->DemN NA->NNum NA->NDem	68.86 73.74 61.74 61.00
U24: RN->POST (or AN)	RN->POST RN->AN	65.73 29.23

Table 1. Comparison with Greenberg's work

OV	UNIV	VO	UNIV
correlated pairs			
ADP_NP(POST)	90.48	ADP_NP(PRE)	82.72
G_N(GN)	79.38	G_N(NG)	61.49
R_N(RN)	19.66	R_N(NR)	75.17
PoQPar(Final)	31.89	PoQPar(Initial)	15.79
AdSub_Cl (Final)	20.90	AdSub_Cl (Initial)	49.22
IntPhr(Not_Initial)	58.74	IntPhr(Initial)	34.36
non-correlated pairs			
A_N(AN)	29.48	A_N(NA)	65.00
Dem_N(Dem_N)	52.27	Dem_N(N_Dem)	54.25
Num_N(NumN)	41.6	Num_N(NNum)	49.25
Deg_A(Deg_A)	43.48	Deg_A(A_Deg)	38.44
Neg_V(NegV)	48.06	Neg_V(VNeg)	25.13

Table 2. Comparison with Dryer's work

B. Probabilistic query example in SamIam

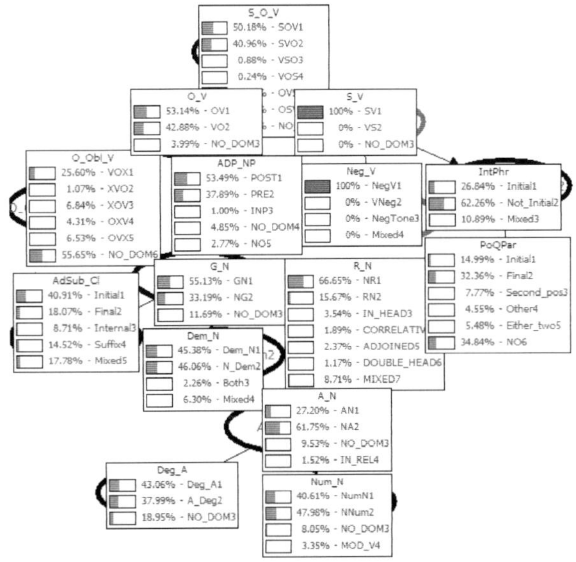

Figure 6. One query example

C. Inference examples

P(MAP,e)=0.0015052949102098631 P(MAP|e)=0.003213814742532023	
Variable	**Value**
A_N	NA
ADP_NP	PRE
AdSub_Cl	Initial
Deg_A	Deg_A
Dem_N	N_Dem
G_N	NG
IntPhr	Not_Initial
Neg_V	NegV
Num_N	NNum
O_Obl_V	VOX
PoQPar	Final
R_N	NR
S_O_V	SVO
S_V	SV

Table 3. MAP query example

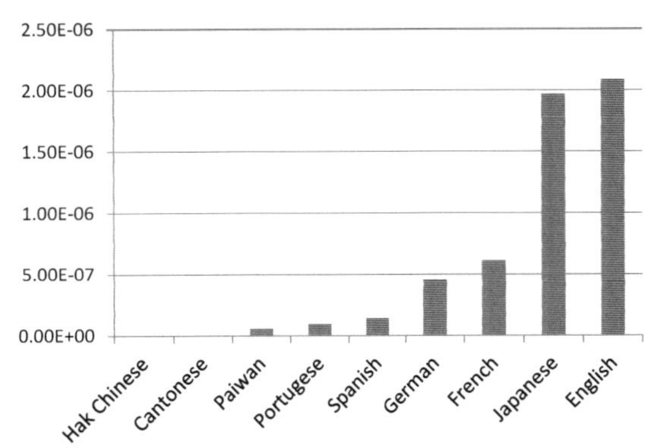

Figure 7. Likelihood of eight languages in terms of word order properties

Robust Multilingual Statistical Morphological Generation Models

Ondřej Dušek and **Filip Jurčíček**
Charles University in Prague, Faculty of Mathematics and Physics
Institute of Formal and Applied Linguistics
Malostranské náměstí 25, CZ-11800 Praha, Czech Republic
{odusek,jurcicek}@ufal.mff.cuni.cz

Abstract

We present a novel method of statistical morphological generation, i.e. the prediction of inflected word forms given lemma, part-of-speech and morphological features, aimed at robustness to unseen inputs. Our system uses a trainable classifier to predict "edit scripts" that are then used to transform lemmas into inflected word forms. Suffixes of lemmas are included as features to achieve robustness. We evaluate our system on 6 languages with a varying degree of morphological richness. The results show that the system is able to learn most morphological phenomena and generalize to unseen inputs, producing significantly better results than a dictionary-based baseline.

1 Introduction

Surface realization is an integral part of all natural language generation (NLG) systems, albeit often implemented in a very simple manner, such as filling words into ready hand-written templates. More sophisticated methods use hand-written grammars (Gatt and Reiter, 2009), possibly in combination with a statistical reranker (Langkilde and Knight, 1998). Existing NLG systems are very often applied to languages with little morphology, such as English, where a small set of hand-written rules or the direct use of word forms in the symbolic representation or templates is usually sufficient, and so the main focus of these systems lies on syntax and word order.

However, this approach poses a problem in languages with a complex morphology. Avoiding inflection, i.e. ensuring that a word lemma will keep its base form at all times, often leads to very unnatural results (see Figure 1). Some generators use a hand-made morphological dictionary

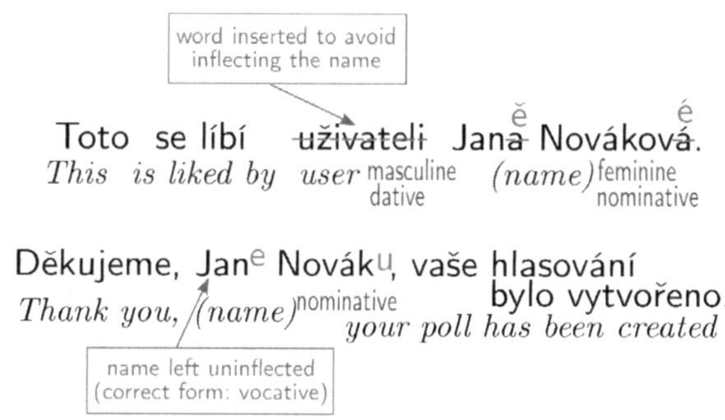

Figure 1: Unnatural language resulting from templates with no inflection.
The sentences are taken from the Czech translations of Facebook and Doodle, which use simple templates to generate personalized texts. Corrections to make the text fluent are shown in red.

for inflection (Ptáček and Žabokrtský, 2006) or a dictionary learned from automatically tagged data (Toutanova et al., 2008). That gives good results, but reaching sufficient coverage with a hand-made dictionary is a very demanding task and even using extreme amounts of automatically annotated data will not generalize beyond the word forms already encountered in the corpus. Hand-written rules can become overly complex and are not easily adaptable for a different language.

Therefore, the presented method relies on a statistical approach that learns to predict morphological inflection from annotated data. As a result, such approach is more robust, i.e. capable of generalizing to unseen inputs, and easily portable to different languages.

An attempt to implement statistical morphological generation has already been made by Bohnet et al. (2010). However, their morphology generation was only a component of a complex generation system. Therefore, no deep analysis of the capabilities of the methods has been performed. In addition, their method did not attempt to generalize beyond seen inputs. In this paper, we propose several improvements and provide a detailed evaluation of a statistical morphological inflection system, including more languages into the evaluation and focusing on robustness to unseen inputs.

The paper is structured as follows: first, we explain the problem of morphological generation (Section 2), then give an account of our system (Section 3). Section 4 provides a detailed evaluation of the performance of our system in different languages. We then compare our system to related works in Section 5. Section 6 concludes the paper.

2 The Problem of Morphological Realization

The problem of morphological surface realization is inverse to part-of-speech tagging and lemmatization (or stemming): given a lemma/stem of a word and its part-of-speech and morphological properties, the system should output the correctly inflected form of the word. An example is given in Figure 2. This does not include generating auxiliary words (such as *be* → *will be*), which are assumed to be already generated.

word + NNS	→	words
Wort + NN Neut,Pl,Dat	→	Wörtern
be + VBZ	→	is
ser + V gen=c,num=s,person=3, mood=indicative,tense=present	→	es

Figure 2: The task of morphological generation (examples for English, German, and Spanish).

While this problem can be solved by a set of rules to a great extent for languages with little morphology such as English (Minnen et al., 2001), it becomes much more complicated in languages with a complex nominal case system or multiple synthetic verbal inflection patterns, such as German or Czech. Figure 3 shows an example of ambiguity in these languages.

This research aims to create a system that is easy to train from morphologically annotated data, yet able to infer and apply more general rules and generate forms unseen in the training corpus.

3 Our Morphological Generation Setup

Similarly to Bohnet et al. (2010), our system is based on the prediction of edit scripts (diffs) between the lemma and the target word form (see Section 3.1), which are then used to derive the target word form from the lemma. This allows the

Teller *(plate)* NN	Gen,Sg,Masc Tellers	Herr *(sir)* NN	Nom,Pl,Masc Herren
Oma *(grandma)* NN	Nom,Pl,Fem Omas	Mann *(man)* NN	Nom,Pl,Masc Männer
stroj *(machine)* N	Gen=I,Cas=7,Num=S strojem	pán *(sir)* N	Gen=M,Cas=2,Num=S pána
kost *(bone)* N	Gen=F,Cas=3,Num=P kostem	kůň *(horse)* N	Gen=M,Cas=2,Num=S koně

Figure 3: Morphological ambiguity in German and Czech.
The same inflection pattern is used to express multiple morphological properties (left) and multiple patterns may express the same property (right).

system to operate even on previously unseen lemmas. The employed classifier and features are described in Sections 3.2 and 3.3. Section 3.4 then gives an overview of the whole morphological inflection process.

3.1 Lemma-Form Edit Scripts

Our system uses lemma-form edit scripts based on the Levenshtein string distance metric (Levenshtein, 1966): the dynamic programming algorithm used to compute the distance can be adapted to produce diffs on characters, i.e. a mapping from the source string (lemma) to the target string (word form) that indicates which characters were added, replaced or removed.

We use the distance from the end of the word to indicate the position of a particular change, same as Bohnet et al. (2010). We have added several enhancements to this general scenario:

- Our system treats separately changes at the beginning of the word, since they are usually independent of the word length and always occur at the beginning, such as the prefix *ge-* for past participles in German or *ne-* for negation in Czech.
- Adjacent changes in the string are joined together to produce a total lower number of more complex changes.
- If the Levenshtein edit script indicates a removal of letters from the beginning of the word, we treat the target word form as irregular, i.e. as if the whole word changed.
- In our setup, the edit scripts need not be treated as atomic, which allows to train separate classification models for word changes that are orthogonal (cf. Section 3.4).

An example of the edit scripts generated by our system is shown in Figure 4.

do	doing	>0-ing
llegar	llegó	>2-ó
Mann	Männer	>0-er,3:1-ä
jenž	jež	>2:1-
mantenir	mantindran	>0-an,2:1-d,4:1-i
sparen	gespart	>2-t,<ge
vědět	nevíme	>4-íme,<ne
be	is	*is

Figure 4: Example edit scripts generated by our system.
The changes are separated by commas. ">" denotes a change at the end of the word, "N:" denotes a change at the N-th character from the end. The number of deleted characters and their replacement follows in both cases. "<" marks additions to the beginning of a word (regardless of its length). "*" marks irregular forms where the whole word is replaced.

Our diffs are case-insensitive since we believe that letter-casing and morphology are distinct phenomena and should be treated separately. Case-insensitivity, along with merging adjacent changes and the possibility to split models, causes a decrease in the number of different edit scripts, thus simplifying the task for the classifier.

In our preliminary experiments on Czech, we also explored the possibility of using different distance metrics for the edit scripts, such as various settings of the Needleman-Wunsch algorithm (Needleman and Wunsch, 1970) or the longest common subsequence[1] post-edited with regular expressions to lower the total number of changes. However, this did not have any noticeable impact on the performance of the models.

3.2 Used Statistical Models

We use the multi-class logistic regression classifier from the LibLINEAR package[2] (Fan et al., 2008) for the prediction of edit scripts. We use L1-regularization since it yields models that are smaller in size and the resulting trained weights indicate the important features in a straightforward way. This direct influence on features (similar to keyword spotting) allows for a simple interpretation of the learned models. We examined various settings of the regularization cost and the termination criterion (See Section 4.1).

We have also experimented with support vector machines from the LibSVM package (Chang and Lin, 2011), but the logistic regression classifier proved to be better suited to this task, providing a higher edit script accuracy on the development set for German and Czech (when feature concatenation is used, cf. Section 3.3), while also requiring less CPU time and RAM to train.

3.3 Features

While the complete set of features varies across languages given their specifics, most of the features are common to all languages:

- *lemma* of the word in question,
- coarse and fine-grained *part-of-speech* tag,
- *morphological features* (e.g. case, gender, tense etc., tagset-dependent), and
- *suffixes of the lemma* of up to 4 characters.

Since morphological changes usually occur near the end of the word, they mostly depend just on that part of the word and not on e.g. prefixes or previous parts of a compound. Therefore, using suffixes allows the classifier to generalize to unknown words.

In addition, as we use a linear classifier, we have found the concatenation of various morphological features, such as number, gender, and case in nouns or tense and person in verbs, to be very beneficial. We created new features by concatenating all possible subsets of morphological features, as long as all their values were non-empty (to prevent from creating duplicate values). To avoid combinatorial explosion, we resorted to concatenating only case, number, and gender for Czech and excluding the `postype` feature from concatenation for Spanish and Catalan.

We also employ the properties of adjacent words in the sentence as features in our models for the individual languages (see Section 4). These are used mainly to model congruency (*is* vs. *are* in English, different adjectival declension after definite and indefinite article in German) or article vocalization (*l'* vs. *el* in Catalan). The congruency information could be obtained more reliably from elsewhere in a complete NLG system (e.g. features from the syntactic realizer), which would probably result in a performance gain, but lies beyond the scope of this paper.

No feature pruning was needed in our setup as our classifier was able to handle the large amount of features (100,000s, language-dependent).

[1] We used the Perl implementation of this algorithm from `https://metacpan.org/module/String::Diff`.

[2] We use it via the Python wrapper in the Scikit-Learn library (`http://scikit-learn.org`).

3.4 Overall Schema of the Predictor

After an examination of the training data, we decided to use a separate model for the changes that occur at the beginning of the word since they tend to be much simpler than and not very dependent on the changes towards the end of the word (e.g. the usages of the Czech negation prefix *ne-* or the German infinitive prefix *zu-* are quite self-contained phenomena).

The final word inflection prediction schema looks as follows:

1. Using the statistical model described in Section 3.2, predict an edit script (cf. Section 3.1) for changes at the end or in the middle of the word.[3]

2. Predict an edit script for the possible addition of a prefix using a separate model.

3. Apply the edit scripts predicted by the previous steps as rules to generate the final inflected word form.

4 Experimental Evaluation

We evaluate our morphological generation setup on all of the languages included in the CoNLL 2009 Shared Task data sets except Chinese (which, as an isolating language, lacks morphology almost altogether): English, German, Spanish, Catalan, Japanese, and Czech. We use the CoNLL 2009 data sets (Hajič et al., 2009) with gold-standard morphology annotation for all our experiments (see Table 1 for a detailed overview).

We give a discussion of the overall performance of our system in all the languages in Section 4.1. We focus on Czech in the detailed analysis of the generalization power of our system in Section 4.2 since Czech has the most complicated morphology of all these languages. In addition, the morphological annotation provided in the CoNLL 2009 Czech data set is more detailed than in the other languages, which eliminates the need for additional syntactic features (cf. Section 3.3). We also provide a detailed performance overview on English for comparison.

4.1 Overall Performance

The performance of our system in the best settings for the individual languages measured on the CoNLL 2009 evaluation test sets is shown in Table 2. We used the classifier and features described in Sections 3.2 and 3.3 (additional features for the individual languages are listed in the table). We used two models as described in Section 3.4 for all languages but English, where no changes at the beginning of the word were found in the training data set and a single model was sufficient. We performed a grid search for the best parameters of the first model[4] and used the same parameters for both models.[5]

One can see from the results in Table 2 that the system is able to predict the majority of word forms correctly and performs well even on data unseen in the training set.

When manually inspecting the errors produced by the system, we observed that in some cases the system in fact assigned a form synonymous to the one actually occurring in the test set, such as *not* instead of *n't* in English or *také* instead of *taky* (both meaning *also*) in Czech. However, most errors are caused by the selection of a more frequent rule, even if incorrect given the actual morphological features. We believe that this could possibly be mitigated by using features combining lemma suffixes and morphological categories, or features from the syntactic context.

The lower score for German is caused partly by the lack of syntactic features for the highly ambiguous adjective inflection and partly by a somewhat problematic lemmatization of punctuation (all punctuation has the lemma "_" and the part-of-speech tag only distinguishes terminal, comma-like and other characters).

4.2 Generalization Power

To measure the ability of our system to generalize to previously unseen inputs, we compare it against a baseline that uses a dictionary collected from the same data and leaves unseen forms intact. The performance of our system on unseen forms is shown in Table 2 for all languages. A comparison with the dictionary baseline for varying training data sizes in English and Czech is given in Table 3.

It is visible from Table 3 that our approach

[3]Completely irregular forms (see Section 3.1) are also predicted by this step.

[4]We always used L1-norm and primal form and modified the termination criterion *tol* and regularization strength *C*. The best values found on the development data sets for the individual languages are listed in Table 2.

[5]As the changes at the beginning of words are much simpler, changing parameters did not have a significant influence on the performance of the second model.

Language	Data set sizes			In Eval (%)		
	Train	Dev	Eval	-Punct	InflF	UnkF
English	958,167	33,368	57,676	85.93	15.14	1.80
German	648,677	32,033	31,622	87.24	45.12	8.69
Spanish	427,442	50,368	50,630	85.42	29.96	6.16
Catalan	390,302	53,015	53,355	86.75	31.89	6.28
Japanese	112,555	6,589	13,615	87.34	10.73	6.43
Czech	652,544	87,988	92,663	85.50	42.98	7.68

Table 1: The CoNLL 2009 data sets: Sizes and properties
The data set sizes give the number of words (tokens) in the individual sets. The right column shows the percentage of data in the evaluation set: *-Punct* = excluding punctuation tokens, *InflF* = only forms that differ from the lemma (i.e. have a non-empty edit script), *UnkF* = forms unseen in the training set.

Language	Additional features	Best parameters	Rule (%) accuracy	Form accuracy (%)			
				Total	-Punc	InflF	UnkF
English	W-1/LT	C=10, tol=1e-3	99.56	99.56	99.49	97.76	98.26
German	W-1/LT, MC	C=10, tol=1e-3	96.66 / 99.91	96.46	98.01	92.64	89.63
Spanish	MC	C=100, tol=1e-3	99.05 / 99.98	99.01	98.86	97.10	91.11
Catalan	W+1/C1, MC	C=10, tol=1e-3	98.91 / 99.86	98.72	98.53	96.49	94.24
Japanese	MC	C=100, tol=1e-3	99.94 / 100.0	99.94	99.93	99.59	99.54
Czech	MC	C=100, tol=1e-3	99.45 / 99.99	99.45	99.35	98.81	95.93

Table 2: The overall performance of our system in different languages.
The *additional features* include: *MC* = concatenation of morphological features (see Section 3.3), *W-1/LT* = lemma and part-of-speech tag of the previous word, *W+1/C1* = first character of the following word.
Rule (edit script) accuracy is given for the prediction of changes at the end or in the middle and at the beginning of the word, respectively.
The *form accuracy* field shows the percentage of correctly predicted (lowercased) target word forms: *Total* = on the whole evaluation set; *-Punct, InflF, UnkF* = on subsets as defined in Table 1.

maintains a significantly[6] higher accuracy when compared to the baseline for all training data sizes. It is capable of reaching high performance even with relatively small amounts of training instances. The overall performance difference becomes smaller as the training data grow; however, performance on unseen inputs and relative error reduction show a different trend: the improvement stays stable. The relative error reduction decreases slightly for English where unknown word forms are more likely to be base forms of unknown lemmas, but keeps increasing for Czech where unknown word forms are more likely to require inflection (the accuracy reached by the baseline method on unknown forms equals the percentage of base forms among the unknown forms).

Though the number of unseen word forms is declining with increasing amounts of training data, which plays in favor of the dictionary method, unseen inputs will still occur and may become very frequent for out-of-domain data. Our system is therefore beneficial – at least as a back-off for unseen forms – even if a large-coverage morphological dictionary is available.

We observed upon manual inspection that the suffix features were among the most prominent for the prediction of many edit scripts, which indicates their usefulness; e.g. `LemmaSuffix1=e` is a strong feature (along with `POS_Tag=VBD`) for the edit script `>0d` in English.

5 Related Work

Statistical morphological realizers are very rare since most NLG systems are either fully based on hand-written grammars, including morphological rules (Bateman et al., 2005; Gatt and Reiter, 2009; Lavoie and Rambow, 1997), or employ statistical methods only as a post-processing step to select the best one of several variants generated by a rule-based system (Langkilde and Knight, 1998; Langkilde-Geary, 2002) or to guide the decision among the rules during the generation process (Belz, 2008). While there are fully statistical surface realizers (Angeli et al., 2010; Mairesse et al., 2010), they operate in a phrase-based fashion on word forms with no treatment of morphology. Morphological generation in machine translation tends to use dictionaries – hand-written (Žabokrt-

[6] Significance at the 99% level has been assessed using paired bootstrap resampling (Koehn, 2004).

Train	Czech						English					
data	Unseen	Dict. acc.		Our sys. acc.		Error	Unseen	Dict acc.		Our sys. acc.		Error
part	forms	Total	UnkF	Total	UnkF	reduct.	forms	Total	UnkF	Total	UnkF	reduct.
0.1	63.94	62.00	41.54	76.92	64.43	39.27	27.77	89.18	78.73	95.02	93.14	53.91
0.5	51.38	66.78	38.65	88.73	78.83	66.08	19.96	91.34	76.33	97.89	95.56	75.64
1	45.36	69.43	36.97	92.23	83.60	74.60	14.69	92.76	73.95	98.28	95.27	76.19
5	31.11	77.29	35.56	96.63	90.36	85.17	6.82	96.21	75.73	99.05	97.13	74.96
10	24.72	80.97	33.88	97.83	92.45	88.61	4.66	97.31	77.13	99.34	97.76	75.44
20	17.35	85.69	32.47	98.72	94.28	91.02	3.10	98.09	78.52	99.46	97.57	71.65
30	14.17	87.92	31.85	98.95	94.56	91.34	2.46	98.40	79.79	99.48	97.63	67.75
50	11.06	90.34	31.62	99.20	95.25	91.69	1.76	98.69	80.53	99.54	98.04	64.81
75	9.01	91.91	31.54	99.34	95.60	91.89	1.35	98.86	82.23	99.55	98.17	60.61
100	7.68	92.88	30.38	99.45	95.93	92.21	1.12	98.94	82.53	99.56	98.26	58.85

Table 3: Comparison of our system with a dictionary baseline on different training data sizes.
All numbers are percentages. The accuracy of both methods is given for the whole evaluation set (*Total*) and for word forms unseen in the training set (*UnkF*). *Error reduct.* shows the relative error reduction of our method in comparison to the baseline on the whole evaluation set.

ský et al., 2008), learnt from data (Toutanova et al., 2008), or a combination thereof (Popel and Žabokrtský, 2009).

The only statistical morphological generator known to us is that of Bohnet et al. (2010), employed as a part of a support-vector-machines-based surface realizer from semantic structures. They apply their system to a subset of CoNLL 2009 data sets and their results (morphological accuracy of 97.8% for English, 97.49% for German and 98.48% for Spanish) seem to indicate that our system performs better for English, slightly better for Spanish and slightly worse for German, but the numbers may not be directly comparable to our results as it is unclear whether the authors use the original data set or the output of the previous steps of their system for evaluation and whether they include punctuation and/or capitalization.

Since the morphological generator of Bohnet et al. (2010) is only a part of a larger system, they do not provide a thorough analysis of the results. While their system also predicts edit scripts derived from Levenshtein distance, their edit script representation seems less efficient than ours. They report using about 1500 and 2500 different scripts for English and German, respectively, disregarding scripts occurring only once in the training data. However, our representation only yields 154 English and 1785 German[7] edit scripts with no pruning. Along with the independent models for the beginning of the word, this simplifies the task for the classifier. In addition to features used by Bohnet et al. (2010), our system includes the suffix features to generalize to unseen inputs.

[7]We get this number when counting the edit scripts as atomic; they divide into 1735 changes at the end or in the middle of the words and 18 changes at the beginning.

6 Conclusions and Further Work

We have presented a fully trainable morphological generation system aimed at robustness to previously unseen inputs, based on logistic regression and Levenshtein distance edit scripts between the lemma and the target word form. The results from the evaluation on six different languages from the CoNLL 2009 data sets indicate that the system is able to learn most morphological rules correctly and is able to cope with previously unseen input, performing significantly better than a dictionary learned from the same amount of data. The system is freely available for download at:

`http://ufal.mff.cuni.cz/~odusek/flect`

In future, we plan to integrate our generator into a semantic NLG scenario, as well as a simpler template-based system, and evaluate it on further languages. We also consider employing transformation-based learning (Brill, 1995) for prediction to make better use of the possibility of splitting the edit scripts and applying the morphological changes one-by-one.

Acknowledgments

This research was partly funded by the Ministry of Education, Youth and Sports of the Czech Republic under the grant agreement LK11221 and core research funding of Charles University in Prague. The authors would like to thank Matěj Korvas and Martin Popel for helpful comments on the draft and David Marek, Ondřej Plátek and Lukáš Žilka for discussions.

References

G. Angeli, P. Liang, and D. Klein. 2010. A simple domain-independent probabilistic approach to generation. In *Proceedings of the 2010 Conference on Empirical Methods in Natural Language Processing*, page 502–512.

J. A. Bateman, I. Kruijff-Korbayová, and G.-J. Kruijff. 2005. Multilingual resource sharing across both related and unrelated languages: An implemented, open-source framework for practical natural language generation. *Research on Language and Computation*, 3(2-3):191–219.

A. Belz. 2008. Automatic generation of weather forecast texts using comprehensive probabilistic generation-space models. *Natural Language Engineering*, 14(4):431–455.

B. Bohnet, L. Wanner, S. Mille, and A. Burga. 2010. Broad coverage multilingual deep sentence generation with a stochastic multi-level realizer. In *Proceedings of the 23rd International Conference on Computational Linguistics*, page 98–106.

E. Brill. 1995. Transformation-based error-driven learning and natural language processing: A case study in part-of-speech tagging. *Computational linguistics*, 21(4):543–565.

C. C. Chang and C. J. Lin. 2011. LIBSVM: a library for support vector machines. *ACM Transactions on Intelligent Systems and Technology (TIST)*, 2(3):27.

R. E Fan, K. W Chang, C. J Hsieh, X. R Wang, and C. J Lin. 2008. LIBLINEAR: a library for large linear classification. *The Journal of Machine Learning Research*, 9:1871–1874.

A. Gatt and E. Reiter. 2009. SimpleNLG: a realisation engine for practical applications. In *Proceedings of the 12th European Workshop on Natural Language Generation*, page 90–93.

J. Hajič, M. Ciaramita, R. Johansson, D. Kawahara, M. A Martí, L. Màrquez, A. Meyers, J. Nivre, S. Padó, J. Štěpánek, et al. 2009. The CoNLL-2009 shared task: Syntactic and semantic dependencies in multiple languages. In *Proceedings of the Thirteenth Conference on Computational Natural Language Learning: Shared Task*, page 1–18.

P. Koehn. 2004. Statistical significance tests for machine translation evaluation. In *Proceedings of EMNLP*, volume 4, page 388–395.

I. Langkilde and K. Knight. 1998. Generation that exploits corpus-based statistical knowledge. In *Proceedings of the 36th Annual Meeting of the Association for Computational Linguistics and 17th International Conference on Computational Linguistics-Volume 1*, page 704–710.

I. Langkilde-Geary. 2002. An empirical verification of coverage and correctness for a general-purpose sentence generator. In *Proceedings of the 12th International Natural Language Generation Workshop*, page 17–24.

B. Lavoie and O. Rambow. 1997. A fast and portable realizer for text generation systems. In *Proceedings of the fifth conference on Applied natural language processing*, page 265–268.

V. I. Levenshtein. 1966. Binary codes capable of correcting deletions, insertions and reversals. *Soviet Physics Doklady*, 10(8):707.

F. Mairesse, M. Gašić, F. Jurčíček, S. Keizer, B. Thomson, K. Yu, and S. Young. 2010. Phrase-based statistical language generation using graphical models and active learning. In *Proceedings of the 48th Annual Meeting of the Association for Computational Linguistics*, page 1552–1561.

G. Minnen, J. Carroll, and D. Pearce. 2001. Applied morphological processing of English. *Natural Language Engineering*, 7(3):207–223.

S. B. Needleman and C. D. Wunsch. 1970. A general method applicable to the search for similarities in the amino acid sequence of two proteins. *Journal of molecular biology*, 48(3):443–453.

M. Popel and Z. Žabokrtský. 2009. Improving English-Czech tectogrammatical MT. *The Prague Bulletin of Mathematical Linguistics*, 92(-1):115–134.

J. Ptáček and Z. Žabokrtský. 2006. Synthesis of Czech sentences from tectogrammatical trees. In *Text, Speech and Dialogue*.

K. Toutanova, H. Suzuki, and A. Ruopp. 2008. Applying morphology generation models to machine translation. In *Proc. of ACL*, volume 8.

Z. Žabokrtský, J. Ptáček, and P. Pajas. 2008. TectoMT: highly modular MT system with tectogrammatics used as transfer layer. In *Proceedings of the Third Workshop on Statistical Machine Translation*, page 167–170. Association for Computational Linguistics.

A corpus-based evaluation method for Distributional Semantic Models

Abdellah Fourtassi[1,2]
abdellah.fourtassi@gmail.com

Emmanuel Dupoux[2,3]
emmanuel.dupoux@gmail.com

[1]Institut d'Etudes Cognitives, Ecole Normale Superieure, Paris
[2]Laboratoire de Sciences Cognitives et Psycholinguistique, CNRS, Paris
[3]Ecole des Hautes Etudes en Sciences Sociales, Paris

Abstract

Evaluation methods for Distributional Semantic Models typically rely on behaviorally derived gold standards. These methods are difficult to deploy in languages with scarce linguistic/behavioral resources. We introduce a corpus-based measure that evaluates the stability of the lexical semantic similarity space using a pseudo-synonym same-different detection task and no external resources. We show that it enables to predict two behavior-based measures across a range of parameters in a Latent Semantic Analysis model.

1 Introduction

Distributional Semantic Models (DSM) can be traced back to the hypothesis proposed by Harris (1954) whereby the meaning of a word can be inferred from its context. Several implementations of Harris's hypothesis have been proposed in the last two decades (see Turney and Pantel (2010) for a review), but comparatively little has been done to develop reliable evaluation tools for these implementations. Models evaluation is however an issue of crucial importance for practical applications, i.e., when trying to optimally set the model's parameters for a given task, and for theoretical reasons, i.e., when using such models to approximate semantic knowledge.

Some evaluation techniques involve assigning probabilities to different models given the observed corpus and applying maximum likelihood estimation (Lewandowsky and Farrell, 2011). However, computational complexity may prevent the application of such techniques, besides these probabilities may not be the best predictor for the model performance on a specific task (Blei, 2012). Other commonly used methods evaluate DSMs by comparing their semantic representation to a behaviorally derived gold standard. Some standards are derived from the TOEFL synonym test (Landauer and Dumais, 1997), or the Nelson word associations norms (Nelson et al., 1998). Others use results from semantic priming experiments (Hutchison et al., 2008) or lexical substitutions errors (Andrews et al., 2009). Baroni and Lenci (2011) set up a more refined gold standard for English specifying different kinds of semantic relationship based on dictionary resources (like WordNet and ConceptNet).

These behavior-based evaluation methods are all resource intensive, requiring either linguistic expertise or human-generated data. Such methods might not always be available, especially in languages with fewer resources than English. In this situation, researchers usually select a small set of high-frequency target words and examine their nearest neighbors (the most similar to the target) using their own intuition. This is used in particular to set the model parameters. However, this rather informal method represents a "cherry picking" risk (Kievit-Kylar and Jones, 2012), besides it is only possible for languages that the researcher speaks.

Here we introduce a method that aims at providing a rapid and quantitative evaluation for DSMs using an internal gold standard and requiring no external resources. It is based on a simple same-different task which detects pseudo-synonyms randomly introduced in the corpus. We claim that this measure evaluates the intrinsic ability of the model to capture lexical semantic similarity. We validate it against two behavior-based evaluations (Free association norms and the TOEFL synonym test) on semantic representations extracted from a Wikipedia corpus using one of the most commonly used distributional semantic models : the Latent Semantic Analysis (LSA, Landauer and Dumais (1997)).

In this model, we construct a word-document matrix. Each word is represented by a row, and each document is represented by a column. Each matrix cell indicates the occurrence frequency of a given word in a given context. Singular value decomposition (a kind of matrix factorization) is used to extract a reduced representation by truncating the matrix to a certain size (which we call the semantic dimension of the model). The cosine of the angle between vectors of the resulting space is used to measure the semantic similarity between words. Two words end up with similar vectors if they co-occur multiple times in similar contexts.

2 Experiment

We constructed three successively larger corpora of 1, 2 and 4 million words by randomly selecting articles from the original "Wikicorpus" made freely available on the internet by Reese et al. (2010). Wikicorpus is itself based on articles from the collaborative encyclopedia Wikipedia. We selected the upper bound of 4 M words to be comparable with the typical corpus size used in theoretical studies on LSA (see for instance Landauer and Dumais (1997) and Griffiths et al. (2007)). For each corpus, we kept only words that occurred at least 10 times and we excluded a stop list of high frequency words with no conceptual content such as: the, of, to, and ... This left us with a vocabulary of 8 643, 14 147 and 23 130 words respectively. For the simulations, we used the free software Gensim (Řehůřek and Sojka, 2010) that provides an online Python implementation of LSA.

We first reproduced the results of Griffiths et al. (2007), from which we derived the behavior-based measure. Then, we computed our corpus-based measure with the same models.

2.1 The behavior-based measure

Following Griffiths et al. (2007), we used the free association norms collected by Nelson et al. (1998) as a gold standard to study the psychological relevance of the LSA semantic representation. The norms were constructed by asking more than 6000 participants to produce the first word that came to mind in response to a cue word. The participants were presented with 5,019 stimulus words and the responses (word associates) were ordered by the frequency with which they were named. The overlap between the words used in the norms and the vocabulary of our smallest corpus was 1093 words. We used only this restricted overlap in our experiment.

In order to evaluate the performance of LSA models in reproducing these human generated data, we used the same measure as in Griffiths et al. (2007): the median rank of the first associates of a word in the semantic space. This was done in three steps : 1) for each word cue W_c, we sorted the list of the remaining words W_i in the overlap set, based on their LSA cosine similarity with that cue: $cos(LSA(W_c), LSA(W_i))$, with highest cosine ranked first. 2) We found the ranks of the first three associates for that cue in that list. 3) We applied 1) and 2) to all words in the overlap set and we computed the median rank for each of the first three associates.

Griffiths et al. (2007) tested a set of semantic dimensions going from 100 to 700. We extended the range of dimensions by testing the following set : [2,5,10,20,30,40,50,100, 200, 300,400,500,600,700,800,1000]. We also manipulated the number of successive sentences to be taken as defining the context of a given word (document size), which we varied from 1 to 100.

In Figure 1 we show the results for the 4 M size corpus with 10 sentences long documents.

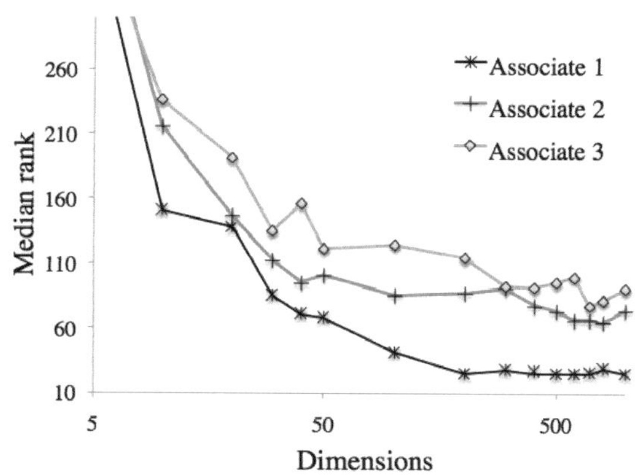

Figure 1 : The median rank of the three associates as a function of the semantic dimensions (lower is better)

For the smaller corpora we found similar results as we can see from Table 1 where the scores represent the median rank averaged over the set of dimensions ranging from 10 to 1000. As found in Griffiths et al. (2007), the median rank measure predicts the order of the first three associates in the norms.

In the rest of the article, we will need to characterize the semantic model by a single value. Instead of taking the median rank of only one of the

Size	associate 1	associate 2	associate 3
1 M	78.21	152.18	169.07
2 M	57.38	114.57	131
4 M	54.57	96.5	121.57

Table 1 : The median rank of the first three associates for different sizes

associates, we will consider a more reliable measure by averaging over the median ranks of the three associates across the overlap set. We will call this measure the Median Rank.

2.2 The Pseudo-synonym detection task

The measure we introduce in this part is based on a Same-Different Task (SDT). It is described schematically in Figure 2, and is computed as follows: for each corpus, we generate a Pseudo-Synonym-corpus (PS-corpus) where each word in the overlap set is randomly replaced by one of two lexical variants. For example, the word "Art" is replaced in the PS-corpus by "Art_1" or "Art_2". In the derived corpus, therefore, the overlap lexicon is twice as big, because each word is duplicated and each variant appears roughly with half of the frequency of the original word.

The Same-Different Task is set up as follows: a pair of words is selected at random in the derived corpus, and the task is to decide whether they are variants of one another or not, only based on their cosine distances. Using standard signal detection techniques, it is possible to use the distribution of cosine distances across the entire list of word pairs in the overlap set to compute a Receiver Operating Characteristic Curve (Fawcett, 2006), from which one derives the area under the curve. We will call this measure : SDT-ρ. It can be interpreted as the probability that given two pairs of words, of which only one is a pseudo-synonym pair, the pairs are correctly identified based on cosine distance only. A value of 0.5 represents pure chance and a value of 1 represents perfect performance.

It is worth mentioning that the idea of generating pseudo-synonyms could be seen as the opposite of the "pseudo-word" task used in evaluating word sense disambiguation models (see for instance Gale et al. (1992) and Dagan et al. (1997)). In this task, two different words w_1 and w_2 are combined to form one ambiguous pseudo-word $W_{12} = \{w_1, w_2\}$ which replaces both w_1 and w_2 in the test set.

We now have two measures evaluating the quality of a given semantic representation: The Median Rank (behavior-based) and the SDT-ρ (corpus-based). Can we use the latter to predict the former? To answer this question, we compared the performance of both measures across different semantic models, document lengths and corpus sizes.

3 Results

In Figure 3 (left), we show the results of the behavior-based Median Rank measure, obtained from the three corpora across a number of semantic dimensions. The best results are obtained with a few hundred dimensions. It is important to highlight the fact that small differences between high dimensional models do not necessarily reflect a difference in the quality of the semantic representation. In this regard, Landauer and Dumais (1997) argued that very small changes in computed cosines can in some cases alter the LSA ordering of the words and hence affect the performance score. Therefore only big differences in the Median Ranks could be explained as a real difference in the overall quality of the models. The global trend we obtained is consistent with the results in Griffiths et al. (2007) and with the findings in Landauer and Dumais (1997) where maximum performance for a different task (TOEFL synonym test) was obtained over a broad region around 300 dimensions.

Besides the effect of dimensionality, Figure 3 (left) indicates that performance gets better as we increase the corpus size.

In Figure 3 (right) we show the corresponding results for the corpus-based SDT-ρ measure. We can see that SDT-ρ shows a parallel set of results and correctly predicts both the effect of dimensionality and the effect of corpus size. Indeed, the general trend is quite similar to the one described with the Median Rank in that the best performance is obtained for a few hundred dimensions and the three curves show a better score for large corpora.

Figure 4 shows the effect of document length on the Median Rank and SDT-ρ. For both measures, we computed these scores and averaged them over the three corpora and the range of dimensions going from 100 to 1000. As we can see, SDT-ρ predicts the psychological optimal document length,

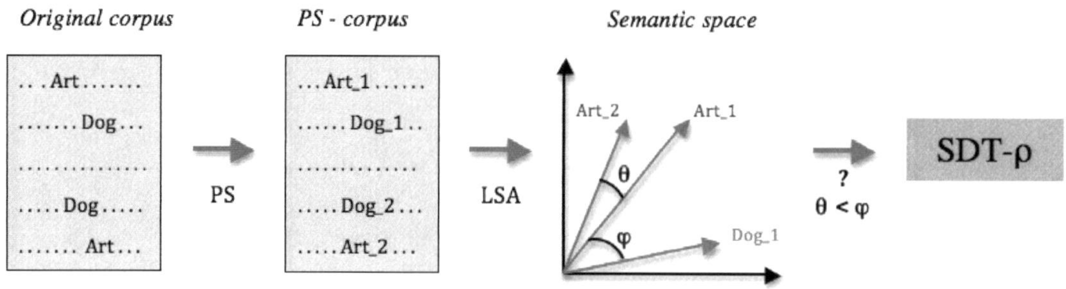

Figure 2 : Schematic description of the Same-Different Task used.

which is about 10 sentences per document. In the corpus we used, this gives on average of about 170 words/document. This value confirms the intuition of Landauer and Dumais (1997) who used a paragraph of about 150 word/document in their model.

Finally, Figure 5 (left) summarizes the entire set of results. It shows the overall correlation between SDT-ρ and the Median Rank. One point in the graph corresponds to a particular choice of semantic dimension, document length and corpus size. To measure the correlation, we use the Maximal Information Coefficient (MIC) recently introduced by Reshef et al. (2011). This measure captures a wide range of dependencies between two variables both functional and not. For functional and non-linear associations it gives a score that roughly equals the coefficient of determination (R^2) of the data relative to the regression function. For our data this correlation measure yields a score of $MIC = 0.677$ with ($p < 10^{-6}$).

In order to see how the SDT-ρ measure would correlate with another human-generated benchmark, we ran an additional experiment using the TOEFL synonym test (Landauer and Dumais, 1997) as gold standard. It contains a list of 80 questions consisting of a probe word and four answers (only one of which is defined as the correct synonym). We tested the effect of semantic dimensionality on a 6 M word sized Wikipedia corpus where documents contained respectively 2, 10 and 100 sentences for each series of runs. We kept only the questions for which the probes and the 4 answers all appeared in the corpus vocabulary. This left us with a set of 43 questions. We computed the response of the model on a probe word by selecting the answer word with which it had the smallest cosine angle. The best performance (65.1% correct) was obtained with 600 dimensions. This is similar to the result reported in Landauer and Dumais (1997) where the best performance obtained was 64.4% (compared to 64.5% produced by non-native English speakers applying to US colleges). The correlation with SDT-ρ is shown in Figure 5 (right). Here again, our corpus-based measure predicts the general trend of the behavior-based measure: higher values of SDT-ρ correspond to higher percentage of correct answers. The correlation yields a score of $MIC = 0.675$ with ($p < 10^{-6}$).

In both experiments, we used the overlap set of the gold standard with the Wikicorpus to compute the SDT-ρ measure. However, as the main idea is to apply this evaluation method to corpora for which there is no available human-generated gold standards, we computed new correlations using a SDT-ρ measure computed, this time, over a set of randomly selected words. For this purpose we used the 4M corpus with 10 sentences long documents and we varied the semantic dimensions. We used the Median Rank computed with the Free association norms as a behavior-based measure.

We tested both the effect of frequency and size: we varied the set size from 100 to 1000 words which we randomly selected from three frequency ranges : higher than 400, between 40 and 400 and between 40 and 1. We chose the limit of 400 so that we can have at least 1000 words in the first range. On the other hand, we did not consider words which occur only once because the SDT-ρ requires at least two instances of a word to generate a pseudo-synonym.

The correlation scores are shown in Table 2. Based on the MIC correlation measure, mid-

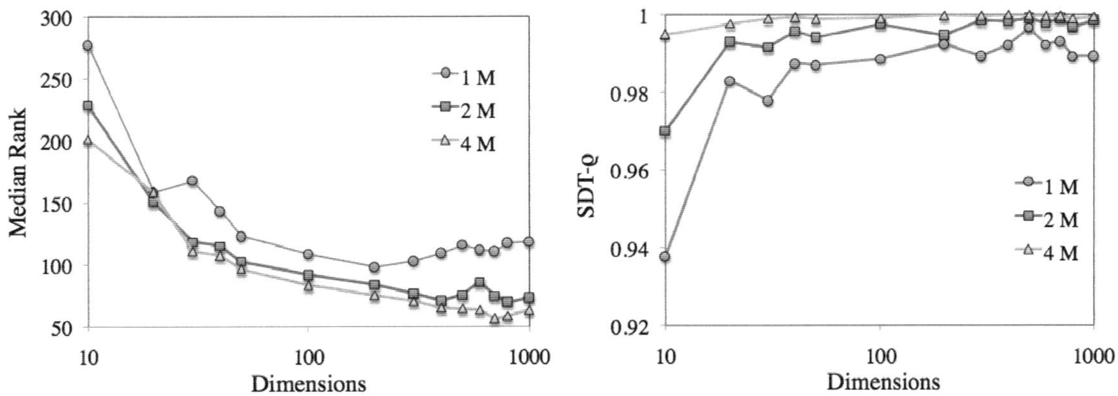

Figure 3 : The Median rank (left) and SDT-ρ (right) as a function of a number of dimensions and corpus sizes. Document size is 10 sentences.

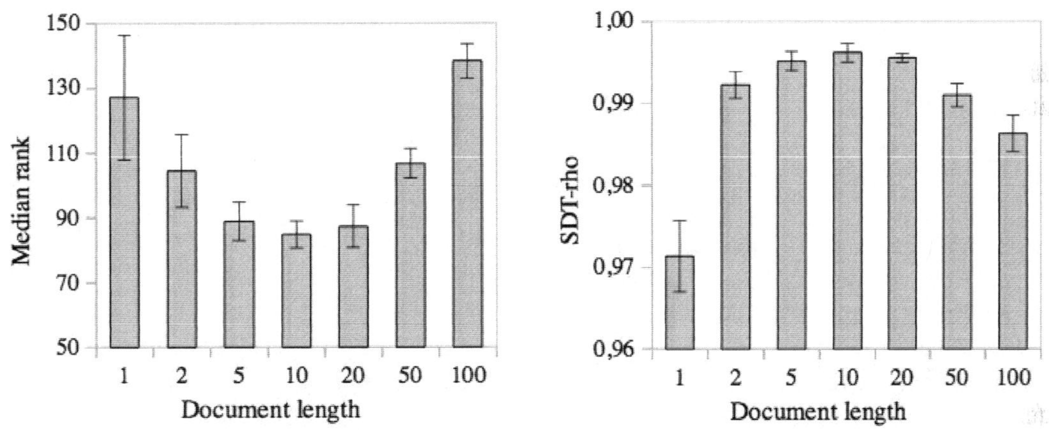

Figure 4 : The Median rank (left) and SDT-ρ (right) as a function of document length (number of sentences). Both measures are averaged over the three corpora and over the range of dimensions going from 100 to 1000.

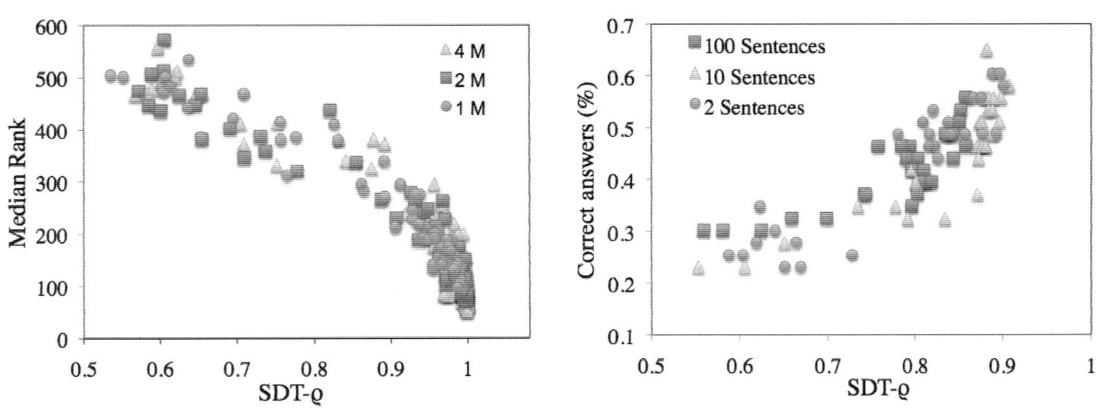

Figure 5 : Overall correlation between Median Rank and SDT-ρ (left) and between Correct answers in TOEFL synonym test and SDT-ρ (right) for all the runs. .

Freq. x	$1 < x < 40$			$40 < x < 400$			$x > 400$			**All**	**Overlap**
Size	100	500	1000	100	500	1000	100	500	1000	~ 4 M	1093
MIC	0.311	0.219	0.549^*	0.549^*	$\mathbf{0.717}^*$	$\mathbf{0.717}^*$	0.311	0.205	0.419	0.549^*	$\mathbf{0.717}^*$

$* : p < 0.05$

Table 2 : Correlation scores of the Median Rank with the SDT-ρ measure computed over randomly selected words from the corpus, the whole lexicon and the overlap with the free association norms. We test the effect of frequency and set size.

frequency words yield better scores. The correlations are as high as the one computed with the overlap even with a half size set (500 words). The overlap is itself mostly composed of mid-frequency words, but we made sure that the random test sets have no more than 10% of their words in the overlap. Mid-frequency words are known to be the best predictors of the conceptual content of a corpus, very common and very rare terms have a weaker discriminating or "resolving" power (Luhn, 1958).

4 Discussion

We found that SDT-ρ enables to predict the outcome of behavior-based evaluation methods with reasonable accuracy across a range of parameters of a LSA model. It could therefore be used as a proxy when human-generated data are not available. When faced with a new corpus and a task involving similarity between words, one could implement this rather straightforward method in order, for instance, to set the semantic model parameters.

The method could also be used to compare the performance of different distributional semantic models, because it does not depend on a particular format for semantic representation. All that is required is the existence of a semantic similarity measure between pairs of words. However, further work is needed to evaluate the robustness of this measure in models other than LSA.

It is important to keep in mind that the correlation of our measure with the behavior-based methods only indicates that SDT-ρ can be trusted, to some extent, in evaluating these semantic tasks. It does not necessarily validate its ability to assess the entire semantic structure of a distributional model. Indeed, the behavior-based methods are dependent on particular tasks (i.g., generating associates, or responding to a multiple choice synonym test) hence they represent only an indirect evaluation of a model, viewed through these specific tasks.

It is worth mentioning that Baroni and Lenci (2011) introduced a comprehensive technique that tries to assess simultaneously a variety of semantic relations like meronymy, hypernymy and coordination. Our measure does not enable us to assess these relations, but it could provide a valuable tool to explore other fine-grained features of the semantic structure. Indeed, while we introduced SDT-ρ as a global measure over a set of test words, it can also be computed word by word. Indeed, we can compute how well a given semantic model can detect that "Art_1" and "Art_2" are the same word, by comparing their semantic distance to that of random pairs of words. Such a word-specific measure could assess the semantic stability of different parts of the lexicon such as concrete vs. abstract word categories, or the distribution properties of different linguistic categories (verb, adjectives, ..). Future work is needed to assess the extent to which the SDT-ρ measure and its word-level variant provide a general framework for DSMs evaluation without external resources.

Finally, one concern that could be raised by our method is the fact that splitting words may affect the semantic structure of the model we want to assess because it may alter the lexical distribution in the corpus, resulting in unnaturally sparse statistics. There is in fact evidence that corpus attributes can have a big effect on the extracted model (Sridharan and Murphy, 2012; Lindsey et al., 2007). However, as shown by the high correlation scores, the introduced pseudo-synonyms do not seem to have a dramatic effect on the model, at least as far as the derived SDT-ρ measure and its predictive power is concerned. Moreover, we showed that in order to apply the method, we do not need to use the whole lexicon, on the contrary, a small test set of about 500 random mid-frequency words (which represents less than 2.5 % of the total vocabulary) was shown to lead to better results. However, even if the results are not directly affected in our case, future work needs to investigate the exact effect word splitting may have on the semantic model.

References

Andrews, M., G. Vigliocco, and D. Vinson (2009). Integrating experiential and distributional data to learn semantic representations. *Psychological Review 116*, 463–498.

Baroni, M. and A. Lenci (2011). How we BLESSed distributional semantic evaluation. In *Proceedings of the EMNLP 2011 Geometrical Models for Natural Language Semantics (GEMS 2011) Workshop*, East Stroudsburg PA: ACL, pp. 1–10.

Blei, D. (2012). Probabilistic topic models. *Communications of the ACM 55*(4), 77–84.

Dagan, I., L. Lee, and F. Pereira (1997). Similarity-based methods for word sense disambiguation. In *Proceedings of the 35th ACL/8th EACL*, pp. 56–63.

Fawcett, T. (2006). An introduction to ROC analysis. *Pattern Recognition Letters 27*(8), 861–874.

Gale, W., K. Church, and D. Yarowsky (1992). Work on statistical methods for word sense disambiguation. *Workings notes, AAAI Fall Symposium Series, Probabilistic Approaches to Natural Language*, 54–60.

Griffiths, T., M. Steyvers, and J. Tenenbaum (2007). Topics in semantic representation. *Psychological Review 114*, 114–244.

Harris, Z. (1954). Distributional structure. *Word 10*(23), 146–162.

Hutchison, K., D. Balota, M. Cortese, and J. Watson (2008). Predicting semantic priming at the item level. *Quarterly Journal of Experimental Psychology 61*(7), 1036–1066.

Kievit-Kylar, B. and M. N. Jones (2012). Visualizing multiple word similarity measures. *Behavior Research Methods 44*(3), 656–674.

Landauer, T. and S. Dumais (1997). A solution to plato's problem: The latent semantic analysis theory of acquisition, induction, and representation of knowledge. *Psychological Review 104*(2), 211–240.

Lewandowsky, S. and S. Farrell (2011). *Computational modeling in cognition : principles and practice*. Thousand Oaks, Calif. : Sage Publications.

Lindsey, R., V. Veksler, and A. G. andWayne Gray (2007). Be wary of what your computer reads: The effects of corpus selection on measuring semantic relatedness. In *Proceedings of the Eighth International Conference on Cognitive Modeling*, pp. 279–284.

Luhn, H. P. (1958). The automatic creation of literature abstracts. *IBM Journal of Research and Development 2*(2), 157–165.

Nelson, D., C. McEvoy, and T. Schreiber (1998). The university of south florida word association, rhyme, and word fragment norms.

Reese, S., G. Boleda, M. Cuadros, L. Padro, and G. Rigau (2010). Wikicorpus: A word-sense disambiguated multilingual wikipedia corpus. In *Proceedings of 7th Language Resources and Evaluation Conference (LREC'10)*, La Valleta, Malta.

Řehůřek, R. and P. Sojka (2010). Software framework for topic modelling with large corpora. In *Proceedings of the LREC 2010 Workshop on New Challenges for NLP Frameworks*, Valletta, Malta, pp. 45–50.

Reshef, D., Y. Reshef, H. Finucane, S. Grossman, G. McVean, P. Turnbaugh, E. Lander, M. Mitzenmacher, and P. Sabeti (2011). Detecting novel associations in large datasets. *Science 334*(6062), 1518–1524.

Sridharan, S. and B. Murphy (2012). Modeling word meaning: distributional semantics and the sorpus quality-quantity trade-off. In *Proceedings of the 3rd Workshop on Cognitive Aspects of the Lexicon*, COLING 2012, Mumbai, pp. 53–68.

Turney, P. D. and P. Pantel (2010). From frequency to meaning: Vector space models of semantics. *Journal of Artificial Intelligence Research 37*, 141–188.

Deepfix: Statistical Post-editing of Statistical Machine Translation Using Deep Syntactic Analysis

Rudolf Rosa and **David Mareček** and **Aleš Tamchyna**
Charles University in Prague, Faculty of Mathematics and Physics
Institute of Formal and Applied Linguistics
Malostranské náměstí 25, Prague
{rosa,marecek,tamchyna}@ufal.mff.cuni.cz

Abstract

Deepfix is a statistical post-editing system for improving the quality of statistical machine translation outputs. It attempts to correct errors in verb-noun valency using deep syntactic analysis and a simple probabilistic model of valency. On the English-to-Czech translation pair, we show that statistical post-editing of statistical machine translation leads to an improvement of the translation quality when helped by deep linguistic knowledge.

1 Introduction

Statistical machine translation (SMT) is the current state-of-the-art approach to machine translation – see e.g. Callison-Burch et al. (2011). However, its outputs are still typically significantly worse than human translations, containing various types of errors (Bojar, 2011b), both in lexical choices and in grammar.

As shown by many researchers, e.g. Bojar (2011a), incorporating deep linguistic knowledge directly into a translation system is often hard to do, and seldom leads to an improvement of translation output quality. It has been shown that it is often easier to correct the machine translation outputs in a second-stage post-processing, which is usually referred to as automatic post-editing.

Several types of errors can be fixed by employing rule-based post-editing (Rosa et al., 2012b), which can be seen as being orthogonal to the statistical methods employed in SMT and thus can capture different linguistic phenomena easily.

But there are still other errors that cannot be corrected with hand-written rules, as there exist many linguistic phenomena that can never be fully described manually – they need to be handled statistically by automatically analyzing large-scale text corpora. However, to the best of our knowledge,

English	Czech	
go to the doctor	jít k doktorovi	dative case
go to the centre	jít do centra	genitive case
go to a concert	jít na koncert	accusative case
go for a drink	jít na drink	accusative case
go up the hill	jít na kopec	accusative case

Table 1: Examples of valency of the verb 'to go' and 'jít'. For Czech, the morphological cases of the nouns are also indicated.

Source:	The government **spends on** the middle **schools**.
Moses:	Vláda **utrácí** střední **školy**.
Meaning:	The government **destroys** the middle **schools**.
Reference:	Vláda **utrácí za** střední **školy**.
Meaning:	The government **spends on** the middle **schools**.

Table 2: Example of a valency error in output of Moses SMT system.

there is very little successful research in statistical post-editing (SPE) of SMT (see Section 2).

In our paper, we describe a statistical approach to correcting one particular type of English-to-Czech SMT errors – errors in the verb-noun *valency*. The term *valency* stands for the way in which verbs and their arguments are used together, usually together with prepositions and morphological cases, and is described in Section 4. Several examples of the valency of the English verb 'to go' and the corresponding Czech verb 'jít' are shown in Table 1.

We conducted our experiments using a state-of-the-art SMT system Moses (Koehn et al., 2007). An example of Moses making a valency error is translating the sentence 'The government spends on the middle schools.', adapted from our development data set. As shown in Table 2, Moses translates the sentence incorrectly, making an error in the valency of the 'utrácet – škola' ('spend – school') pair. The missing preposition changes the meaning dramatically, as the verb 'utrácet' is polysemous and can mean 'to spend (esp. money)' as well as 'to kill, to destroy (esp. animals)'.

Our approach is to use deep linguistic analysis to automatically determine the structure of each sentence, and to detect and correct valency errors using a simple statistical valency model. We describe our approach in detail in Section 5.

We evaluate and discuss our experiments in Section 6. We then conclude the paper and propose areas to be researched in future in Section 7.

2 Related Work

The first reported results of automatic post-editing of machine translation outputs are (Simard et al., 2007) where the authors successfully performed statistical post-editing (SPE) of rule-based machine translation outputs. To perform the post-editing, they used a phrase-based SMT system in a monolingual setting, trained on the outputs of the rule-based system as the source and the human-provided reference translations as the target, to achieve massive translation quality improvements. The authors also compared the performance of the post-edited rule-based system to directly using the SMT system in a bilingual setting, and reported that the SMT system alone performed worse than the post-edited rule-based system. They then tried to post-edit the bilingual SMT system with another monolingual instance of the same SMT system, but concluded that no improvement in quality was observed.

The first known positive results in SPE of SMT are reported by Oflazer and El-Kahlout (2007) on English to Turkish machine translation. The authors followed a similar approach to Simard et al. (2007), training an SMT system to post-edit its own output. They use two iterations of post-editing to get an improvement of 0.47 BLEU points (Papineni et al., 2002). The authors used a rather small training set and do not discuss the scalability of their approach.

To the best of our knowledge, the best results reported so far for SPE of SMT are by Béchara et al. (2011) on French-to-English translation. The authors start by using a similar approach to Oflazer and El-Kahlout (2007), getting a statistically significant improvement of 0.65 BLEU points. They then further improve the performance of their system by adding information from the source side into the post-editing system by concatenating some of the translated words with their source words, eventually reaching an improvement of 2.29 BLEU points. However, similarly to Oflazer and El-Kahlout (2007), the training data used are very small, and it is not clear how their method scales on larger training data.

Direction	Baseline	SPE	Context SPE
en→cs	**10.85±0.47**	10.70±0.44	10.73±0.49
cs→en	**17.20±0.53**	17.11±0.52	17.18±0.54

Table 3: Results of SPE approach of Béchara et al. (2011) evaluated on English-Czech SMT.

In our previous work (Rosa et al., 2012b), we explored a related but substantially different area of *rule-based* post-editing of SMT. The resulting system, Depfix, manages to significantly improve the quality of several SMT systems outputs, using a set of hand-written rules that detect and correct grammatical errors, such as agreement violations. Depfix can be easily combined with Deepfix,[1] as it is able to correct different types of errors.

3 Evaluation of Existing SPE Approaches

First, we evaluated the utility of the approach of Béchara et al. (2011) for the English-Czech language pair. We used 1 million sentence pairs from CzEng 1.0 (Bojar et al., 2012b), a large English-Czech parallel corpus. Identically to the paper, we split the training data into 10 parts, trained 10 systems (each on nine tenths of the data) and used them to translate the remaining part. The second step was then trained on the concatenation of these translations and the target side of CzEng. We also implemented the *contextual* variant of SPE where words in the intermediate language are annotated with corresponding source words if the alignment strength is greater than a given threshold. We limited ourselves to the threshold value 0.8, for which the best results are reported in the paper. We tuned all systems on the dataset of WMT11 (Callison-Burch et al., 2011) and evaluated on the WMT12 dataset (Callison-Burch et al., 2012).

Table 3 summarizes our results. The reported confidence intervals were estimated using bootstrap resampling (Koehn, 2004). SPE did not lead to any improvements of BLEU in our experiments. In fact, SPE even slightly decreased the score (but

[1] **Dep**fix (Rosa et al., 2012b) performs rule-based post-editing on shallow-syntax **dep**endency trees, while **Deep**fix (described in this paper) is a statistical post-editing system operating on **deep**-syntax dependency trees.

the difference is statistically insignificant in all cases).

We conclude that this method does not improve English-Czech translation, possibly because our training data is too large for this method to bring any benefit. We therefore proceed with a more complex approach which relies on deep linguistic knowledge.

4 Deep Dependency Syntax, Formemes, and Valency

4.1 Tectogrammatical dependency trees

Tectogrammatical trees are deep syntactic dependency trees based on the Functional Generative Description (Sgall et al., 1986). Each node in a tectogrammatical tree corresponds to a content word, such as a noun, a full verb or an adjective; the node consists of the lemma of the content word and several other attributes. Functional words, such as prepositions or auxiliary verbs, are not directly present in the tectogrammatical tree, but are represented by attributes of the respective content nodes. See Figure 1 for an example of two tectogrammatical trees (for simplicity, most of the attributes are not shown).

In our work, we only use one of the many attributes of tectogrammatical nodes, called *formeme* (Dušek et al., 2012). A formeme is a string representation of selected morpho-syntactic features of the content word and selected auxiliary words that belong to the content word, devised to be used as a simple and efficient representation of the node.

A noun formeme, which we are most interested in, consists of three parts (examples taken from Figure 1):

1. The syntactic part-of-speech – **n** for nouns.
2. The preposition if the noun has one (empty otherwise), as in `n:`**`on`**`+X` or `n:`**`za`**`+4`.
3. A form specifier.
    - In English, it typically marks the subject or object, as in `n:`**`subj`**. In case of a noun accompanied by a preposition, the third part is always X, as in `n:on+`**`X`**.
    - In Czech, it denotes the morphological case of the noun, represented by its number (from 1 to 7 as there are seven cases in Czech), as in `n:`**`1`** and `n:za+`**`4`**.

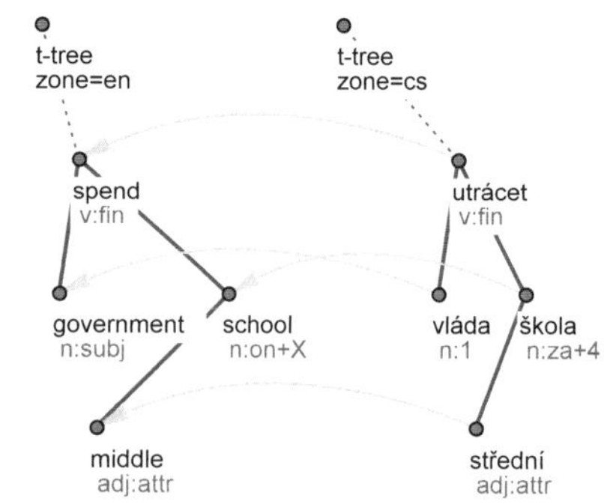

Figure 1: Tectogrammatical trees for the sentence 'The government spends on the middle schools.' – 'Vláda utrácí za střední školy.'; only lemmas and formemes of the nodes are shown.

Adjectives and nouns can also have the `adj:attr` and `n:attr` formemes, respectively, meaning that the node is in morphological agreement with its parent. This is especially important in Czech, where this means that the word bears the same morphological case as its parent node.

4.2 Valency

The notion of *valency* (Tesnière and Fourquet, 1959) is semantic, but it is closely linked to syntax. In the theory of valency, each verb has one or more *valency frames*. Each valency frame describes a meaning of the verb, together with arguments (usually nouns) that the verb must or can have, and each of the arguments has one or several fixed forms in which it must appear. These forms can typically be specified by prepositions and morphological cases to be used with the noun, and thus can be easily expressed by formemes.

For example, the verb 'to go', shown in Table 1, has a valency frame that can be expressed as `n:subj go n:to+X`, meaning that the subject goes to some place.

The valency frames of the verbs 'spend' and 'utrácet' in Figure 1 can be written as `n:subj spend n:on+X` and `n:1 utrácet n:za+4`; the subject (in Czech this is a noun in nominative case) spends on an object (in Czech, the preposition 'za' plus a noun in accusative case).

In our work, we have extended our scope also to noun-noun valency, i.e. the parent node can be either a verb or a noun, while the arguments are always nouns. Practice has proven this extension to be useful, although the majority of the corrections performed are still of the verb-noun valency type. Still, we keep the traditional notion of verb-noun valency throughout the text, especially to be able to always refer to the parent as "the verb" and to the child as "the noun".

5 Our Approach

5.1 Valency models

To be able to detect and correct valency errors, we created statistical models of verb-noun valency. We model the conditional probability of the noun argument formeme based on several features of the verb-noun pair. We decided to use the following two models:

$$P(f_n|l_v, f_{EN}) \quad (1)$$

$$P(f_n|l_v, l_n, f_{EN}) \quad (2)$$

where:

- f_n is the formeme of the Czech noun argument, which is being modelled
- l_v is the lemma of the Czech parent verb
- l_n is the lemma of the Czech noun argument
- f_{EN} is the formeme of the English noun aligned to the Czech noun argument

The input is first processed by the model (1), which performs more general fixes, in situations where the (l_v, f_{EN}) pair rather unambiguously defines the valency frame required.

Then model (2) is applied, correcting some errors of the model (1), in cases where the noun argument requires a different valency frame than is usual for the (l_v, f_{EN}) pair, and making some more fixes in cases where the correct valency frame required for the (l_v, f_{EN}) pair was too ambiguous to make a correction according to model (1), but the decision can be made once information about l_n is added.

We computed the models on the full training set of CzEng 1.0 (Bojar et al., 2012b) (roughly 15 million sentences), and smoothed the estimated probabilities with add-one smoothing.

5.2 Deepfix

We introduce a new statistical post-editing system, Deepfix, whose input is a pair of an English sentence and its Czech machine translation, and the output is the Czech sentence with verb-noun valency errors corrected.

The Deepfix pipeline consists of several steps:

1. the sentences are tokenized, tagged and lemmatized (a lemma and a morphological tag is assigned to each word)
2. corresponding English and Czech words are aligned based on their lemmas
3. deep-syntax dependency parse trees of the sentences are built, the nodes in the trees are labelled with formemes
4. improbable noun formemes are replaced with correct formemes according to the valency model
5. the words are regenerated according to the new formemes
6. the regenerating continues recursively to children of regenerated nodes if they are in morphological agreement with their parents (which is typical for adjectives)

To decide whether the formeme of the noun is incorrect, we query the valency model for all possible formemes and their probabilities. If an alternative formeme probability exceeds a fixed threshold, we assume that the original formeme is incorrect, and we use the alternative formeme instead.

For our example sentence, 'The government spends on the middle schools.' – 'Vláda utrácí za střední školy.', we query the model (2) and get the following probabilities:

- P(n:4 | utrácet, škola, n:on+X) = 0.07 (the original formeme)
- P(n:za+4 | utrácet, škola, n:on+X) = 0.89 (the most probable formeme)

The threshold for this change type is 0.86, is exceeded by the `n:za+4` formeme and thus the change is performed: 'školy' is replaced by 'za školy'.

5.3 Tuning the Thresholds

We set the thresholds differently for different types of changes. The values of the thresholds that we used are listed in Table 4 and were estimated manually. We distinguish changes where only the morphological case of the noun is changed from changes to the preposition. There are three possible types of a change to a preposition: switching one preposition to another, adding a new preposition, and removing an existing preposition. The

Correction type	Thresholds for models	
	(1)	(2)
Changing the noun case only	0.55	0.78
Changing the preposition	0.90	0.84
Adding a new preposition	–	0.86
Removing the preposition	–	–

Table 4: Deepfix thresholds

change to the preposition can also involve changing the morphological case of the noun, as each preposition typically requires a certain morphological case.

For some combinations of a change type and a model, as in case of the preposition removing, we never perform a fix because we observed that it nearly never improves the translation. E.g., if a verb-noun pair can be correct both with and without a preposition, the preposition-less variant is usually much more frequent than the prepositional variant (and thus is assigned a much higher probability by the model). However, the preposition often bears a meaning that is lost by removing it – in Czech, which is a relatively free-word-order language, the semantic roles of verb arguments are typically distinguished by prepositions, as opposed to English, where they can be determined by their relative position to the verb.

5.4 Implementation

The whole Deepfix pipeline is implemented in Treex, a modular NLP framework (Popel and Žabokrtský, 2010) written in Perl, which provides wrappers for many state-of-the-art NLP tools. For the analysis of the English sentence, we use the Morče tagger (Spoustová et al., 2007) and the MST parser (McDonald et al., 2005). The Czech sentence is analyzed by the Featurama tagger[2] and the RUR parser (Rosa et al., 2012a) – a parser adapted to parsing of SMT outputs. The word alignment is created by GIZA++ (Och and Ney, 2003); the intersection symmetrization is used.

6 Evaluation

6.1 Automatic Evaluation

We evaluated our method on three datasets: WMT10 (2489 parallel sentences), WMT11 (3003 parallel sentences), and WMT12 (3003 parallel sentences) by Callison-Burch et al. (2010; 2011; 2012). For evaluation, we used outputs of a state-of-the-art SMT system, Moses (Koehn et al., 2007), tuned for English-to-Czech translation (Bojar et al., 2012a). We used the WMT10 dataset and its Moses translation as our development data to tune the thresholds. In Table 5, we report the achieved BLEU scores (Papineni et al., 2002), NIST scores (Doddington, 2002), and PER (Tillmann et al., 1997).

The improvements in automatic scores are low but consistently positive, which suggests that Deepfix does improve the translation quality. However, the changes performed by Deepfix are so small that automatic evaluation is unable to reliably assess whether they are positive or negative – it can only be taken as an indication.

6.2 Manual Evaluation

To reliably assess the performance of Deepfix, we performed manual evaluation on the WMT12 dataset translated by the Moses system.

The dataset was evenly split into 4 parts and each of the parts was evaluated by one of two annotators (denoted "A" and "B"). For each sentence that was modified by Deepfix, the annotator decided whether the Deepfix correction had a positive ("improvement") or negative ("degradation") effect on the translation quality, or concluded that this cannot be decided ("indefinite") – either because both of the sentences are correct variants, or because both are incorrect.[3]

The results in Table 6 prove that the overall effect of Deepfix is positive: it modifies about 20% of the sentence translations (569 out of 3003 sentences), improving over a half of them while leading to a degradation in only a quarter of the cases.

We measured the inter-annotator agreement on 100 sentences which were annotated by both annotators. For 60 sentence pairs, both of the annotators were able to select which sentence is better, i.e. none of the annotators used the "indefinite" marker. The inter-annotator agreement on these 60 sentence pairs was 97%.[4]

[2] http://featurama.sourceforge.net/

[3] The evaluation was done in a blind way, i.e. the annotators did not know which sentence is before Deepfix and which is after Deepfix. They were also provided with the source English sentences and the reference human translations.

[4] If all 100 sentence pairs are taken into account, requiring that the annotators also agree on the "indefinite" marker, the inter-annotator agreement is only 65%. This suggests that deciding whether the translation quality differs significantly is much harder than deciding which translation is of a higher quality.

Dataset	BLEU score (higher is better)			NIST score (higher is better)			PER (lower is better)		
	Baseline	Deepfix	Difference	Baseline	Deepfix	Difference	Baseline	Deepfix	Difference
WMT10*	15.66	15.74	+0.08	5.442	5.470	+0.028	58.44%	58.26%	-0.18
WMT11	16.39	16.42	+0.03	5.726	5.737	+0.011	57.17%	57.09%	-0.08
WMT12	13.81	13.85	+0.04	5.263	5.283	+0.020	60.04%	59.91%	-0.13

Table 5: Automatic evaluation of Deepfix on outputs of the Moses system on WMT10, WMT11 and WMT12 datasets. *Please note that WMT10 was used as the development dataset.

Part	Annotator	Changed sentences	Improvement	Degradation	Indefinite
1	A	126	57 (45%)	35 (28%)	34 (27%)
2	B	112	62 (55%)	29 (26%)	21 (19%)
3	A	150	88 (59%)	29 (19%)	33 (22%)
4	B	181	114 (63%)	42 (23%)	25 (14%)
Total		569	321 (56%)	135 (24%)	113 (20%)

Table 6: Manual evaluation of Deepfix on outputs of Moses Translate system on WMT12 dataset.

6.3 Discussion

When a formeme change was performed, it was usually either positive or at least not harmful (substituting one correct variant for another correct variant).

However, we also observed a substantial amount of cases where the change of the formeme was incorrect. Manual inspection of a sample of these cases showed that there can be several reasons for a formeme change to be incorrect:

- incorrect analysis of the Czech sentence
- incorrect analysis of the English sentence
- the original formeme is a correct but very rare variant

The most frequent issue is the first one. This is to be expected, as the Czech sentence is often erroneous, whereas the NLP tools that we used are trained on correct sentences; in many cases, it is not even clear what a correct analysis of an incorrect sentence should be.

7 Conclusion and Future Work

On the English-Czech pair, we have shown that statistical post-editing of statistical machine translation outputs is possible, even when translating from a morphologically poor to a morphologically rich language, if it is grounded by deep linguistic knowledge. With our tool, Deepfix, we have achieved improvements on outputs of two state-of-the-art SMT systems by correcting verb-noun valency errors, using two simple probabilistic valency models computed on large-scale data. The improvements have been confirmed by manual evaluation.

We encountered many cases where the performance of Deepfix was hindered by errors of the underlying tools, especially the taggers, the parsers and the aligner. Because the use of the RUR parser (Rosa et al., 2012a), which is partially adapted to SMT outputs parsing, lead to a reduction of the number of parser errors, we find the approach of adapting the tools for this specific kind of data to be promising.

We believe that our method can be adapted to other language pairs, provided that there is a pipeline that can analyze at least the target language up to deep syntactic trees. Because we only use a small subset of information that a tectogrammatical tree provides, it is sufficient to use only simplified tectogrammatical trees. These could be created by a small set of rules from shallow-syntax dependency trees, which can be obtained for many languages using already existing parsers.

Acknowledgments

This research has been supported by the 7th FP project of the EC No. 257528 and the project 7E11042 of the Ministry of Education, Youth and Sports of the Czech Republic.

Data and some tools used as a prerequisite for the research described herein have been provided by the LINDAT/CLARIN Large Infrastructural project, No. LM2010013 of the Ministry of Education, Youth and Sports of the Czech Republic.

We would like to thank two anonymous reviewers for many useful comments on the manuscript of this paper.

References

Hanna Béchara, Yanjun Ma, and Josef van Genabith. 2011. Statistical post-editing for a statistical MT system. *MT Summit XIII*, pages 308–315.

Ondřej Bojar, Bushra Jawaid, and Amir Kamran. 2012a. Probes in a taxonomy of factored phrase-based models. In *Proceedings of the Seventh Workshop on Statistical Machine Translation*, pages 253–260, Montréal, Canada. Association for Computational Linguistics.

Ondřej Bojar, Zdeněk Žabokrtský, Ondřej Dušek, Petra Galuščáková, Martin Majliš, David Mareček, Jiří Maršík, Michal Novák, Martin Popel, and Aleš Tamchyna. 2012b. The joy of parallelism with CzEng 1.0. In *Proceedings of the 8th International Conference on Language Resources and Evaluation (LREC 2012)*, pages 3921–3928, İstanbul, Turkey. European Language Resources Association.

Ondřej Bojar. 2011a. Rich morphology and what can we expect from hybrid approaches to MT. Invited talk at International Workshop on Using Linguistic Information for Hybrid Machine Translation (LIHMT-2011), November.

Ondřej Bojar. 2011b. Analyzing error types in English-Czech machine translation. *Prague Bulletin of Mathematical Linguistics*, 95:63–76, March.

Chris Callison-Burch, Philipp Koehn, Christof Monz, Kay Peterson, Mark Przybocki, and Omar Zaidan. 2010. Findings of the 2010 joint workshop on statistical machine translation and metrics for machine translation. In *Proceedings of the Joint Fifth Workshop on Statistical Machine Translation and MetricsMATR*, pages 17–53, Uppsala, Sweden, July. Association for Computational Linguistics.

Chris Callison-Burch, Philipp Koehn, Christof Monz, and Omar Zaidan. 2011. Findings of the 2011 workshop on statistical machine translation. In *Proceedings of the Sixth Workshop on Statistical Machine Translation*, pages 22–64, Edinburgh, Scotland, July. Association for Computational Linguistics.

Chris Callison-Burch, Philipp Koehn, Christof Monz, Matt Post, Radu Soricut, and Lucia Specia. 2012. Findings of the 2012 workshop on statistical machine translation. In *Proceedings of the Seventh Workshop on Statistical Machine Translation*, pages 10–51, Montréal, Canada, June. Association for Computational Linguistics.

George Doddington. 2002. Automatic evaluation of machine translation quality using n-gram co-occurrence statistics. In *Proceedings of the second international conference on Human Language Technology Research*, pages 138–145. Morgan Kaufmann Publishers Inc.

Ondřej Dušek, Zdeněk Žabokrtský, Martin Popel, Martin Majliš, Michal Novák, and David Mareček. 2012. Formemes in English-Czech deep syntactic MT. In *Proceedings of the Seventh Workshop on Statistical Machine Translation*, pages 267–274, Montréal, Canada. Association for Computational Linguistics.

Philipp Koehn, Hieu Hoang, Alexandra Birch, Chris Callison-Burch, Marcello Federico, Nicola Bertoldi, Brooke Cowan, Wade Shen, Christine Moran, Richard Zens, Chris Dyer, Ondřej Bojar, Alexandra Constantin, and Evan Herbst. 2007. Moses: Open source toolkit for statistical machine translation. In *ACL 2007, Proceedings of the 45th Annual Meeting of the Association for Computational Linguistics Companion Volume Proceedings of the Demo and Poster Sessions*, pages 177–180, Prague, Czech Republic, June. Association for Computational Linguistics.

Philipp Koehn. 2004. Statistical significance tests for machine translation evaluation. In *Proc. of EMNLP*, Barcelona, Spain.

Ryan McDonald, Koby Crammer, and Fernando Pereira. 2005. Online large-margin training of dependency parsers. In *Proceedings of the 43rd Annual Meeting on Association for Computational Linguistics*, pages 91–98. Association for Computational Linguistics.

Franz Josef Och and Hermann Ney. 2003. A systematic comparison of various statistical alignment models. *Computational Linguistics*, 29(1):19–51.

Kemal Oflazer and Ilknur Durgar El-Kahlout. 2007. Exploring different representational units in English-to-Turkish statistical machine translation. In *Proceedings of the Second Workshop on Statistical Machine Translation*, pages 25–32. Association for Computational Linguistics.

Kishore Papineni, Salim Roukos, Todd Ward, and Wei-Jing Zhu. 2002. BLEU: a method for automatic evaluation of machine translation. In *ACL 2002, Proceedings of the 40th Annual Meeting of the Association for Computational Linguistics*, pages 311–318, Philadelphia, Pennsylvania.

Martin Popel and Zdeněk Žabokrtský. 2010. TectoMT: modular NLP framework. In *Proceedings of the 7th international conference on Advances in natural language processing*, IceTAL'10, pages 293–304, Berlin, Heidelberg. Springer-Verlag.

Rudolf Rosa, Ondřej Dušek, David Mareček, and Martin Popel. 2012a. Using parallel features in parsing of machine-translated sentences for correction of grammatical errors. In *Proceedings of Sixth Workshop on Syntax, Semantics and Structure in Statistical Translation (SSST-6), ACL*, pages 39–48, Jeju, Korea. ACL.

Rudolf Rosa, David Mareček, and Ondřej Dušek. 2012b. DEPFIX: A system for automatic correction of Czech MT outputs. In *Proceedings of the Seventh Workshop on Statistical Machine Translation*, pages 362–368, Montréal, Canada. Association for Computational Linguistics.

Petr Sgall, Eva Hajičová, and Jarmila Panevová. 1986. *The meaning of the sentence in its semantic and pragmatic aspects*. Springer.

Michel Simard, Cyril Goutte, and Pierre Isabelle. 2007. Statistical phrase-based post-editing. In *Human Language Technologies 2007: The Conference of the North American Chapter of the Association for Computational Linguistics; Proceedings of the Main Conference*, pages 508–515, Rochester, New York, April. Association for Computational Linguistics.

Drahomíra Spoustová, Jan Hajič, Jan Votrubec, Pavel Krbec, and Pavel Květoň. 2007. The best of two worlds: Cooperation of statistical and rule-based taggers for Czech. In *Proceedings of the Workshop on Balto-Slavonic Natural Language Processing 2007*, pages 67–74, Praha, Czechia. Univerzita Karlova v Praze, Association for Computational Linguistics.

Lucien Tesnière and Jean Fourquet. 1959. *Eléments de syntaxe structurale*. Éditions Klincksieck, Paris.

Christoph Tillmann, Stephan Vogel, Hermann Ney, Alex Zubiaga, and Hassan Sawaf. 1997. Accelerated dp based search for statistical translation. In *European Conf. on Speech Communication and Technology*, pages 2667–2670.

Author Index

Association for Computational Linguistics
209 N. Eighth Street
Stroudsburg, Pennsylvania 18360

CURRAN ASSOCIATES INC
proceedings.com